comfort and joy

Andrew Kuyvenhoven

Comfort and Joy

A Study of

the Heidelberg

Catechism

GRAND RAPIDS, MICHIGAN

Cover design: Frank Gutbrod

Library of Congress Cataloging-in-Publication data

Kuyvenhoven, Andrew.
Comfort and joy: a study of the Heidelberg catechism/Andrew Kuyvenhoven.
p. cm.
ISBN 978-0-930265-57-1
1. Heidelberger Katechismus. I. Title. II. Title: Comfort and joy.
BX9428.K86 1988
238'.42—dc19

88-39763
CIP

10 9 8 7 6

To the Christian Reformed churches of Lethbridge, Alberta, First Church of Hamilton, the congregations of Wallaceburg and of Clarkson (Mississauga) in Ontario, thankfully dedicated.

***Q** What must you know to live and die in the joy of this comfort?*

***A** Three things:*
first, how great my sin and misery are;
second, how I am set free from all my sins and misery;
third, how I am to thank God for such deliverance.

Contents

Preface ... 11

1. I Belong to Jesus / Lord's Day 1 ... 13
2. The Knowledge of Misery / Lord's Day 2 ... 17
3. The Extent of Our Misery / Lord's Day 3 ... 23
4. The Righteousness of God / Lord's Day 4 ... 31
5. The Mediator / Lord's Day 5 & 6 ... 35
6. True Faith / Lord's Day 7 ... 41
7. The Bible Tells Me So / Lord's Day 7 (cont.) ... 45
8. God in Three Persons / Lord's Day 8 ... 53
9. The Creator Is My Father / Lord's Day 9 ... 59
10. My Father's Hands / Lord's Day 10 ... 65
11. Jesus Saves / Lord's Day 11 ... 71
12. The Messiah and His People / Lord's Day 12 ... 77
13. Our Brother and Our Lord / Lord's Day 13 ... 83
14. He Stooped to Conquer / Lord's Day 14 ... 89
15. Man of Sorrows / Lord's Day 15 ... 95
16. The Last Enemy / Lord's Day 16 ... 101
17. He Lives! / Lord's Day 17 ... 111
18. Uniting Heaven and Earth / Lord's Day 18 ... 115
19. Christ's Kingdom / Lord's Day 19 ... 123
20. I Believe in the Holy Spirit / Lord's Day 20 ... 131
21. The Holy Catholic Church / Lord's Day 21 ... 137
22. This Is the Life / Lord's Day 22 ... 145
23. Right with God / Lord's Day 23 ... 153
24. Works Without Wages / Lord's Day 24 ... 159
25. The Means of Grace / Lord's Day 25 ... 165
26. Baptism / Lord's Day 26 & 27 ... 171
27. The Lord's Supper / Lord's Day 28, 29 & 30 ... 179
28. The Keys of the Kingdom / Lord's Day 31 ... 187
29. Saved to Serve / Lord's Day 32 ... 191
30. Conversion / Lord's Day 33 ... 195
31. The Ten Words / Lord's Day 34 ... 201
32. How to Worship God / Lord's Day 35 ... 207
33. Our Use of His Name / Lord's Day 36 & 37 ... 213
34. Celebrating Sabbath / Lord's Day 38 ... 219
35. Authority and Obedience / Lord's Day 39 ... 227
36. Love Your Neighbor / Lord's Day 40 ... 233
37. God, Sex, Marriage / Lord's Day 41 ... 239

38. God and Goods / Lord's Day 42. 245
39. Taming the Tongue / Lord's Day 43 251
40. My Heart's Desire / Lord's Day 44. 257
41. Teach Us to Pray / Lord's Day 45 265
42. The Address of Our Prayers / Lord's Day 46. 273
43. Praying for God's Glory / Lord's Day 47 277
44. Your Kingdom Come! / Lord's Day 48 283
45. Prayer and Obedience / Lord's Day 49 289
46. Our Daily Bread / Lord's Day 50 295
47. Forgiveness: Prayer and Practice / Lord's Day 51 301
48. Faith Under Fire / Lord's Day 52 307
49. From Prayer to Praise / Lord's Day 52 (cont.) 313

Preface

For generations Reformed churches have accepted the truth of God as packaged in the Heidelberg Catechism. Understanding the gospel through the framework of sin, salvation, and service has enriched and unified these churches.

Because this catechism is so basic to the Reformed faith, I have preached on it and taught it often—especially in the four Canadian churches to whom I dedicate this book. This study is based mainly on my sermon notes and was first published in installments in THE BANNER (January 1985-April 1988), the weekly magazine of the Christian Reformed Church.

What I know I have learned from others. But some of it I made my own so long ago that I have forgotten from whom I learned it. Now that this wisdom is printed over my name, I may fail to give credit to whom it is due.

Throughout the years I have benefitted from many Dutch commentaries and printed sermons on the catechism, but also from the books of Karl Barth (German) and Herman Hoeksema (English) who preached and wrote the good news along the lines of this confession. I have made careful and personal Bible study of every topic treated in the catechism.

The Heidelberg Catechism is the best confessional and teachable summary of the will of God for the life of the church. I pray that churches in North America who have inherited this confession may not lose sight of that fact. Currently many of these churches tend to neglect the catechism, ignoring it in their pulpits and classrooms. I will praise God if this book helps to reverse that trend.

The Heidelberg Catechism is not beyond criticism. I have not hesitated to state what I thought should be omitted or to indicate where the doctrine could be improved. But for more than 425 years this document has taught people how to live in the comfort and joy of the Christian gospel. It is still a great teacher. AK

Andrew Kuyvenhoven
Summer 1988

Lord's Day 1

I BELONG TO JESUS

Q What is your only comfort in life and in death?

A That I am not my own, but belong—body and soul, in life and in death—to my faithful Savior Jesus Christ.

He has fully paid for all my sins with his precious blood, and has set me free from the tyranny of the devil. He also watches over me in such a way that not a hair can fall from my head without the will of my Father in heaven: in fact, all things must work together for my salvation.

Because I belong to him, Christ, by his Holy Spirit, assures me of eternal life and makes me wholeheartedly willing and ready from now on to live for him.

—Q & A 1

What Is Comfort?

Comfort is a good thing that takes care of a bad situation. It does not always take away the bad situation, but the good thing makes us strong enough to endure the evil. We are comforted or fortified by the good to endure the bad.

All people need comfort in ordinary troubles of human existence. Thousands of years ago a man named Lamech called his son "Noah," which means "comfort." "He named him Noah and said, 'He will comfort us in the labor and painful toil of our hands'" (Gen. 5:29). Another man, Isaac, was still weeping over the death of his mother when God gave him a lovely wife, Rebekah. "And Isaac was *comforted* after his mother's death" (Gen. 24:67). All of us need these stretches of sunshine in a dreary world. That's why, ever since Lamech, millions of fathers have said to their sons, "You are my right hand." And millions of husbands have told their Rebekahs, "You are my sunshine."

To have its comforting effect, the good thing must enter our consciousness so fully that the awareness of the good defeats the pain of evil. When your little boy wakes up at night with a nightmare (he is in the land of man-eaters and tigers, and he screams with fright), it is usually enough for you to say: "Okay Johnnie, be quiet now; Dad and Mom are going to sleep too." When he hears you talking to him, and when the awareness that you are there and that he is in his bed has fully entered his consciousness, he is all right. He is comforted.

Comfort is a good thing that takes care of a bad situation. Sometimes it acts as a tear-dryer. Sometimes it is a shot in the arm. Comfort is the strength to keep going. Comfort is survival power.

Christian Comfort.

The *good thing* that we have heard in the gospel and spelled out in our confession is simply this: We belong to Jesus. That's the confession of the church. The whole Christian church, in Heidelberg and Holland, in Japan and Jamaica, in China and Chile, has only one comfort: We belong to Jesus. That's the flag on our ship and the confession in our books: We are the property of Jesus Christ. This one fact makes all the difference to us. And it makes us different.

The first question and answer of the Heidelberg Catechism lead us straight to the heart of the matter: I am the property of Jesus Christ. All of me: "body and soul."

And for all times: "in life and in death." How did that happen? By purchase and deliverance: "He has fully paid . . . with his precious blood and has set me free from the tyranny of the devil." How does it last? By his protection: "Not a hair can fall from my head without the will of my Father." How do I know it? "Christ, by his Holy Spirit, assures me of eternal life." How do I show it? By my readiness to live for him.

This is the one and only Christian comfort that is explained in the Heidelberg Catechism. We are going to have fifty-one more "Lord's Days" in which the doctrine (or "teaching") of comfort is explained. But in this first chapter we must look at the whole truth in a nutshell. You and I must ask ourselves if we belong to Christ. We must confess with Paul and with the church: "Whether we live or die, we belong to the Lord" (Rom. 14:8). "You are not your own; you were bought at a price" (1 Cor. 6:19-20). "[God] has rescued us from the dominion of darkness and brought us into the kingdom of the Son he loves" (Col. 1:13).

If this comfort, this knowledge of belonging to Christ, has fully entered our consciousness, we can endure all pain, fight every battle, and be confident of the outcome. "Thank you, Lord, for comforting me; you are mine and I am yours."

Reformed and Universal.

The people who confessed this in the time of the Reformation were being persecuted for their faith. They feared for their lives. But, they said, even if we get killed, we belong to Jesus, body and soul, in life and in death. They confessed their comfort in the face of all threats.

They also confessed their faith against the background of the religion they had so recently rejected. That was a religion of works and not faith. A religion of works creates a life of uncertainty. You never know if you have done enough. You are always afraid that something is lacking. You go from church to cathedral and from pillar to post. You contemplate the lives of saints, you burn candles and pay money, you search and seek . . .

Against the religion of uncertainty they confessed the rediscovered gospel of assurance: "He has fully paid for all my sins, he has made me his own, and nothing can separate me from his love." The confession of the Reformers came from hearts fortified by the majestic peace of the gospel of grace.

Yet the confession of this comfort is much more than a historical document. It is *the* Christian answer to life's deepest questions and death's darkest riddles. For here and for now it is the only comfort available. Without this comfort, life is senseless and death is hopeless. We need to say with great emphasis that this is the one and only comfort for all people.

When we read, preach, or study the Heidelberg Catechism together, we might become victims of a very cozy and familiar feeling. We should be warned that we are not talking about our "one-and-only-Heidelberg-Catechism-comfort," as if we had something here that would make us a unique and specially favored people. We are not gloating over ancient words, as sects do when they honor their leaders and heroes. Studying the catechism is not an exercise in filial piety for sons and daughters of the Reformation. It is infinitely more serious.

We are confessing, before God and in the presence of each other, that there is only one Way and Savior and that to know him is the only comfort. While we say this, we are acutely aware that we share this planet with more than four billion people who need the comfort of the Lord's Day 1 as badly as we do. Thus we are duty-bound to work and pay and pray until all people know the goodness of the Lord. "O God, let *all* men praise Thee, let *all* nations sing!"

Not every tribe on earth needs to travel to Heidelberg to get the doctrine of comfort. But everyone will have to go to Bethlehem, to Golgotha, and to the open tomb in the garden of Joseph. When they have learned and believed this gospel of salvation, they must also formulate their comfort, and they must phrase their testimony. Their confession of faith cannot be essentially different from ours. Once they have been delivered from the tyranny of the devil, they will confess who their owner is, how he protects them, and how he assures them of eternal life.

All Christians agree with Lord's Day 1 of the Heidelberg Catechism; otherwise they would lack the comfort revealed in the Bible.

Last Remedy or Daily Vitamin?

Generations have memorized Lord's Day 1 about the Christian's only comfort. We make it a rule in church school that young people should know and understand this answer by the time they are fourteen years old.

Often we quote this confession to dying Christians. These words revive the faith lodged deep in their souls. Frequently, dying persons who cannot react to anything else will react to this confession. Their only comfort is also their ultimate comfort.

Another passage with similar power is Romans 8:31-39. In fact, much of the first answer of the catechism is based on Romans 8. "If God is for us, who can be against us? . . . Who shall separate us from the love of Christ? . . . I am convinced that neither death nor life . . . neither height nor depth, nor anything else in all creation, will be able to separate us from the love of God that is in Christ Jesus our Lord."

All of us agree, I suppose, that it is entirely appropriate to quote Lord's Day 1 at a deathbed and to read Romans 8 at the funeral of our beloved. But should you save these confessions for those occasions? People who reach for these confessions as an ultimate medicine, a last cheer-me-up when everything else has failed, may discover that the remedy does not have the desired effect. To die is gain only when to live is Christ (Phil. 1:21). Christian comfort will show its power for the dying when it is used as a daily vitamin for the living.

We may and we must live this very day as comforted or fortified people. Lord's Day 1 and Romans 8 are not our bomb shelters in which we will hide in the last hour. Rather they are descriptions of the power by which we live today.

"I am the property of Christ because he has bought me." That's the confession and conviction with which I begin every living day. From this stance of faith I hurl my challenges at whatever and whoever threatens me: "Who shall condemn? Who shall separate me from his love? Who is against us and who can harm us if he is for us?"

Comfort makes us strong. When the knowledge of God as Father, Christ as Savior, and the Spirit as his pledge has deeply entered my consciousness, I have what it takes to live as a Christian and to die in the Lord.

The Enjoyment of Comfort.

In order that you and I may live as Christians and die in the Lord, we must know three things: "how great my sin and misery are; how I am set free from all my sins and misery; how I am to thank God for such a deliverance."

The question is not, How do you get this comfort? but, How do you enjoy it? We are not asking how you become a Christian but how you live out of the riches of Christian comfort. And, as some of you know, getting possessions is not so hard, but enjoying a treasure is an art. All of you know about Jesus Christ, the Savior. But if you wish to "live and die in the *joy* of this comfort," you must increase in the knowledge of sin and salvation and service. You cannot enjoy God's comfort if you don't apply yourself to this art.

***Q** What must you know to live and die in the joy of this comfort?*

***A** Three things: first, how great my sin and misery are; second, how I am set free of all my sins and misery; third, how I am to thank God for such deliverance.*

—Q & A 2

By "knowledge" we don't mean lessons from books, in which you might be interested. Yes, books are used to convey that knowledge, especially God's book. We mean the kind of knowledge that is both simple and profound. It's a Spirit-taught knowledge of misery, deliverance, and gratitude—not one of which can be missed.

You know, of course, that these "three things" are not three stations on the road to happiness. You never leave the one behind you when you reach the next one. Certainly, your sins are forgiven when you have found your Savior. But that does not mean that you have done with the knowledge of sin. How can you love him unless you know what he did for you? And how can you know the depth of sin unless you look at Golgotha? And as for the third part of comfort, you know that a person who has no Christian gratitude is not yet a Christian; an unconverted Christian is an unbeliever. So there are always three parts to the full enjoyment of the gospel.

Long ago, when Billy Graham was a young man, he wrote a book called *Peace with God*. The book has three parts: The Problem, The Solution, The Results. We recognize that this was an effort of Billy Graham to present the true gospel of sin, salvation, and service.

Much longer ago, when Ursinus was twenty-eight years old and Olevianus was twenty-six, they wrote the Heidelberg Catechism. This catechism, or instruction in the Christian faith, had to be a true exposition of the gospel. Therefore it was divided into three parts: how great my sin and misery are; how I am set free from all my sins and misery; how I am to thank God for such a deliverance.

The only part of the Bible that comes close to a systematic gospel presentation is the epistle to the Romans. It is divided into three parts: sin, salvation, and service.

True faith has knowledge of sin, grace, and gratitude. If people have a superficial faith, they have a superficial knowledge of sin, of salvation, and of gratitude. Anyone who is growing in faith is growing in the knowledge of guilt, grace, and gratitude. And those of us who have deep faith have a deep knowledge of sin, a warm knowledge of our Savior, and a profound sense of gratitude.

Lord's Day 2

THE KNOWLEDGE OF MISERY

Q *How do you come to know your misery?*

A *The law of God tells me.*

—Q & A 3

Diagnosis.

The trouble with most people is that they don't know the trouble we are in. Therefore their proposed solutions make no sense. One cannot prescribe a cure before one has diagnosed the illness.

When we have car problems, we go to the auto mechanic. We look at the expert and we describe the car's symptoms: "When I try to start it, it turns over, sputters, and dies." Then we expect the mechanic to say what's wrong and what should be done about it. We go through the same routine at the doctor's office. We describe the symptoms, expect a diagnosis, and hope for a prescription that will beat the disease and restore our health. When the diagnosis is correct, there is hope for a cure for the car and for ourselves. But without the right assessment of our problem, our troubles multiply.

Everybody agrees that humanity is in trouble. The list of our maladies is as long as our five thousand years of recorded history. But how do we come to know *what* is wrong? "How do you come to know your misery?" Who is qualified to give the right diagnosis?

It sounds unbelievable, but most people appear to skip the diagnosis. Noble sons and daughters of humanity throw themselves headlong into the battle against misery. They insist that every human being has a right to clean socks and indoor plumbing. But they cannot move us one inch closer to the solution of the problem, because they don't have a clue *what* the problem is.

Our problems are so deep that nobody can plumb the depth of the pit. Of course, we can *describe* our misery. Non-Christian writers, film-makers, artists, and philosophers are able to give us haunting pictures of the awesome truth of human bondage. But nobody knows *what* our misery is unless God has told him or her. Only those who know God learn to know themselves. When we know the law of God, we can diagnose the human predicament.

"How do you come to know your misery?"

"The law of God tells me."

Law-Environment.

In our world everything must go according to the will of the Maker. That's what keeps the planets in their courses. That's what makes trees grow and plants bloom. That's also the reason those houseplants died: your wife had said, "Don't forget to give them water while I am away." And you forgot. When she came back, the geranium was drooping and the begonia was nearly dead. For the life-rule of the plant is that it must have so much light, so much water, so much soil. Break the rule and you break the plant.

One will rules all that lives on earth—the will of the sovereign God. If we would live according to the rules of the Maker, we would be completely happy and perfectly adjusted to the environment in which he has placed us.

And what are these rules? Most of us know many of them. We must eat and drink. We have to work and we have to rest. These rules are part of the Creator's will for us. But he has also decreed that we should be in continuous contact with the source of our lives. You and I must love him with all that we are and all of the time. He intended us to live a life directed to God and connected with our neighbors. "This is my will for you," he says. "Live according to my will and you will really live! Love me with your whole heart, with your soul, with your strength, and with the mind I gave you; and love your neighbor. Be as concerned about him or her as you are about yourself. Do this and you will live."

However, I don't do that. And *that's* my misery. Now I am as alienated from my true environment as a fish that's out of the water. To the fish God says: "You must live in the water. That's your environment. That's your life." And when a fish comes on dry ground, it is absolutely miserable and is going to die. To us God says, "You must love, because that's my will for your life." And when we don't, we become absolutely miserable. We are going to die.

Jesus' Law.

The catechism says that Jesus teaches us this double rule of love as a summary of God's law.

Summary may mean the gathering together of the main points. The word *summary* may convey the notion that, when Christ gave us this abridgment, he omitted many other, less essential laws of God.

However, the love-commandment is not merely a *shorter* law; it is *the* law of God. All rules must be understood in the light of this one, and we have not kept any of God's commandments unless we have obeyed his law of love. It is a summary because it is the *sum total* of God's requirements: the law and the prophets.

"*Christ* teaches us this . . . summary," says the catechism. In Matthew 22 he does indeed. A Jewish rabbi asks him, "Teacher, what is the great commandment in the law?" Then Jesus gives the answer that is quoted in the catechism. In Mark 12 a Jewish teacher asks: "Which commandment is the first of all?" To which Jesus gives essentially the same answer, but the wording is quite different from Matthew's record. However, in Luke 10 a "lawyer," an expert in the law of Moses, asks Jesus, "Teacher, what shall I do to inherit eternal life?" Jesus counters, "What is written in your law?" And the man answers with the same words that Jesus speaks in Matthew and Mark. So that man knew the summary that Christ taught us.

We may conclude, *first*, that the commandments to love God above all

***Q** What does God's law require of us?*

***A** Christ teaches us this in summary in Matthew 22—Love the Lord your God with all your heart and with all your soul and with all your mind and with all your strength. This is the first and greatest commandment. And the second is like it: Love your neighbor as yourself. All the Law and the Prophets hang on these two commandments.*

—Q & A 4

and to love our neighbors as ourselves were already embodied in the law of Moses. The double commandment is a combination of Deuteronomy 6:5 and Leviticus 19:18b. *Second,* some Jewish teachers had correctly recognized that the combination of these two commandments constituted the heart of God's law as revealed in the Old Testament. Jesus sided with those who had this insight. *Third,* the law of love was concealed in the Old Testament but revealed in the New. True, there never was another will of God for human beings. God required of Adam what he demands of you and me: that we love God above all and our neighbors as ourselves. But our Lord Jesus made the love-commandment the centerpiece of his teaching. In fact, his whole ministry was designed to teach us that *love* is God's law, which everyone has broken, as well as God's gift that enables all of Jesus' followers to lead a new life. Therefore the love-commandment may be called a law we learned from Jesus Christ (Gal. 6:2).

Q *Can you live up to all this perfectly?*

A *No. I have a natural tendency to hate God and my neighbor.*

—Q & A 5

Sin Is Missing the Mark.

The Christian word for the cause of human misery is *sin.* You know what it is when you know God's law. Sin is lawlessness (1 John 3:4).

The Bible has many words for sin: *transgression, trespass, unrighteousness, iniquity,* and so on. These different names can be reduced to two kinds of sin. The one kind is fairly well known. The other kind you know when you are a Christian.

The first kind is transgression or trespass. You commit such a sin when you step over the line, when you wander into territory that's off limits, when you break the rules and do what you are not supposed to do.

The other kind of sin the Bible calls "missing the mark." It is easy to understand what is meant by this figure of speech, especially now that bows and arrows are back in the store. Here is the target. The small center circle on the target is the bull's eye. Shoot! Way off to the left. Another arrow. Over to the right. You shoot again, and miss the mark once more.

This arrow is your new day, fresh and unused. But when the arrow is spent, it has not reached the target. This one is your marriage, and it must reach God's goal. But it fails to hit the bull's eye. This arrow is your life. What if it misses God's target?

To sin is to fail in reaching the goal. All sin, all miss the target, all fall short of the glory of God (Rom. 3:23).

Years ago Art Linkletter used to entertain adults by writing and talking about children. Once he interviewed little children, and he asked them what person they love most. "My teacher," one of them said. "My mom," said another. Then he asked a little boy, "Whom do you love most?" and the little boy said, "The Lord Jesus." Immediately Art zeroed in, "Why do you love him so much?" "Because he died for my sins." "Is that so? . . . Did you do many sins?" "Yep." "What sins did you do?" "I don't know." "Come on, just mention one." "Sometimes I steal from the cookie jar."

And that's what most grownups still understand by *sin.* It's stealing from the cookie jar. The cookie jar is different for a six-year-old than it is for a sixteen-year-old, and when people are forty-six years old they may get their fingers in yet another jar, but it is the same old concept. It's appealing because it tastes so nice and it is forbidden by the rules of ordinary citizens. That's why it is called a sin. And all "mature adults" smile.

The Christian understanding of sin goes deeper. Sin is our inability to love God and to love our neighbors. Sin is not merely that we do bad things and think dirty thoughts and make mistakes and are not perfect; sin is lack of love. The misery of humankind is not that we still have starvation on a grand scale, not that a few are rich at the expense of many, not that we have accidents that break off lives, and not that old age makes wrecks of strong men and lovely women. All these are certainly part of the misery of humanity. But our misery is that we don't love God above all and our neighbor as ourselves. That has always been our misery, that is still our misery, and that will be the last misery of hell when God has taken away the last warmth of his love.

We are floundering people on a whirling globe. By nature none of us can reach our destiny. We are straying arrows and rudderless ships. We simply don't have it in us to love God above all and our neighbors as ourselves. We are estranged from our true environment. As a matter of fact, by nature we hate God and our neighbors.

Love, Indifference, or Hatred.

"I have a natural tendency to hate God and my neighbor."

Many of us are hesitant to use the strong word *hatred.* We'll admit that human nature is indifferent to God and that everybody is at heart an egotist. But to say that our natural disposition is one of *hatred* toward God and neighbor seems to be an unduly harsh judgment.

We'll have occasion to return to the question of the extent of human wickedness. For now we should consider two things. First, those of us who doubt that human beings really hate God and their neighbors base their protest on their own experience. Most of us have known ourselves and our neighbors in fairly civilized circumstances and in the context of a tolerant democracy. We ought to thank God for those circumstances and pray that the Lord will continue to retain this gracious preservation of civility. Chances are, however, that we too will one day be led through a crisis in which we come to see what is in a human heart, including our own. Some day our hearts will admit that the Bible is correct.

And that is our second point. Our confession that the inclination of the human heart is hatred instead of love is not a Calvinistic hobby of our teachers or a hangover from barbaric times; it is the biblical *interpretation* of the human condition. You and I may think that those who ignore God while they play in his world, with hands full of goodies, are merely cool and indifferent. We may think that the person who lives for here and now is just too careless to be religious. But the Bible interprets the "mind that is set on the flesh" as a case of "hostility," of "enmity." Such a person hates God! He does not and cannot submit to God's law (Rom. 8:7). The person who thinks he or she does not need the Creator to live life or to teach philosophy is, by biblical standards, not merely politely indifferent but a "fool" who hates the One who sustains his or her breathing (Ps. 14:1, etc.). And when biblical light falls over the gossip circles in taverns and beauty salons, these people are spitting out the poison of vipers (Rom. 3:13-14) and spreading a fire that was lit in hell (James 3:6).

To Redirect the Arrows.

There was at least one Man in this world whose life was so goal-directed that he reached God's target, crying out, "Finished! It is finished!" Jesus loved his Father with his heart and soul and mind and with every ounce of his strength. His was a successful life. This arrow hit the bull's eye.

We have said earlier that the law of love is as old as creation, yet the sum of it was revealed to us by Jesus Christ. It is an old commandment, because it is the law of God for humanity; yet it is new, because it came to us through the word and work of Jesus. Even the apostle John seems to stutter when he writes about this love-commandment that is old yet new. "I am writing you no new commandment, but an old commandment . . . . Yet I am writing you a new commandment, which is true in him and in you, because the darkness is passing away and the true light is already shining. He who . . . hates his brother is still in darkness. Whoever loves his brother lives in the light . . ." (1 John 2:7-10).

Hatred is darkness in which misdirected people wander. Love is light that came into the world with Jesus and stays in the world by his Spirit.

You know how the geese fly south: each goose does not take off and try to get there on its own power. They fly in formation, sure of their goal. They fly in the form of a V for victory, determined and bound for their target.

None of us can take off and reach the goal. But Christ gathers us, loves us, and teaches us how to obey the love-commandment. Now we go in the direction we could not and would not go. "Follow me."

If we agree with God's diagnosis, we know that there is only one solution: Jesus. It does not help us to know the law, because we cannot do the law. But it does help us to know Jesus. He alone can deflect the course of the arrow and change the direction of our lives.

God, who requires love, has given love. That love was flesh and blood in Jesus Christ. And since Christ is still living, those who look to him will now receive the same quality of love by the Holy Spirit (Rom. 5:5).

Lord's Day 3

THE EXTENT OF OUR MISERY

***Q** Did God create people so wicked and perverse?*

***A** No. God created them good and in his own image, that is, in true righteousness and holiness, so that they might truly know God their creator, love him with all their heart, and live with him in eternal happiness for his praise and glory.*

—Q & A 6

It's Good for You.

When I was a child, my mother sometimes served food that I did not like. But in those days we were made to eat whatever was served. "It's good for you," my parents said.

You must be careful not to pick and choose when you study your Bible. You must accept what God has prepared. All Scripture is inspired and profitable. If you choose according to your liking, you will never be "thoroughly equipped for every good work" (2 Tim. 3:16-17).

Since ministers can be as choosy as children, it is wise that the church prescribes at least some of the menu for a year's preaching. Otherwise some congregations would never hear a sermon on total depravity. And other congregations might hear it every week.

The message on the corruption of humanity must not be understood as the bad news that comes along with the good news. Rather, the knowledge of this truth will increase the enjoyment of our only comfort. It is given to us because it is good for us.

Spotless Origin.

We have already answered the question *how* we know what's wrong with us. Now we wish to know how the trouble *started* and what the *extent* of the misery is.

The trouble did not start with God. "God is light; in him there is no darkness at all" (1 John 1:5). Anyone who, in reckless anger or in theological argument, would want to make God responsible for our mess has transgressed the limits and has become a fool.

The Bible reveals our spotless origin especially in Genesis 1 and 2. What the Bible reveals clearly is retained dimly in the collective memory of humankind. Ancient philosophers used to say that the unreality of our ideals is a recollection of our golden dawn of goodness. Lost paradise has stamped us with a vague but indelible mark. The human race still hums some haunting tunes, but the words of the song have been forgotten. We need a visitor from the beyond before we can sing again.

Our origin lies in God. He is the Father of all people. The rumor about our great Father is still strong among the tribes in the jungles and on the tundras. But the whisper about God also persists in universities and laboratories.

Some thoughtful observers of our present world have said that for the last twenty years or so people have not so much been looking for God or a god; they have been fascinated by the questions: Who am I? and How can I be happy?

But it doesn't really matter which question you start with—Who am I? or Who is God? Sooner or later it becomes clear that there is one revelation that answers both questions. Even pagans can reach the conclusion that if there is a God, we did not make him but he made us. "We are his offspring" (Acts 17:28). And if we, the offspring, could live in harmony with our origin, would we not find the happiness for which we thirst?

Therefore, the story of creation in the first chapters of the Bible is more than ancient history. It is a liberating word the whole world needs to hear: Our origin is in God and God is good. Originally, you were good.

Images of God.

"Then God said, 'Let us make man in our image, in our likeness. . . .' So God created man in his own image . . . male and female he created them" (Gen. 1:26-27).

We are the images of God. Not "image-bearers," as many teachers say, but we are images—we look like God. Just as you can say of a son that he is the "spitting image" of his father—because you see the father's features in the child—so we were made to show the traits of God.

You must be careful, however, that you don't handle this delicate truth with a crude imagination. That's what the Mormons have done. They claim that God is a big Man. They have to believe that because Joseph Smith, their prophet, saw God with his own eyes. When Joseph was fifteen years old, he saw two persons, the Father and the Son. And now the Mormons are living with this picture of God. Later they defended the picture with an appeal to Genesis 5:3, Adam "had a son in his own likeness, in his own image; and he named him Seth." So Adam was in the image of God just as Seth was in the image of Adam. Seth and Adam had two arms, two legs, two eyes, and one nose. And now we know what God looks like. But that's a crude way of reasoning.

The only picture we may ever have of God is the picture given to us by Jesus. For "no one has ever seen God"—not even Joseph Smith—but "the only Son . . . has made him known" (John 1:18). We were made in God's image. But we may not make God in our image. People were shaped by God, but woe to the people who shape their god.

Governor Under God.

The word "image" says something about the *role* God gave us in his creation and about the *relationship* in which he placed us with himself.

"Let us make man in our image, in our likeness, and let them rule over" everything (Gen. 1:26). Since a human being is made in God's image, he or she has God-like powers over sea and earth. Just as God rules over all things, people included, so people must rule over all things that God has placed under them.

The same teaching you can find in Psalm 8, which is Genesis 1 in poetry:

> You made him a little lower than the heavenly beings
> and crowned him with glory and honor.

You made him ruler over the works of your hands;
  you put everything under his feet.

We are the governors of the earth and the sea. God has placed all mineral deposits and all other resources in our care.

This "image" is the dignity we must defend in human society. It involves a deep respect for human beings. We must honor as human beings even those who behave dishonorably. It is because they are God's images that people's blood may not be shed (Gen. 9:6) and their names may not be cursed (James 3:9-10).

Moreover, governors may not be governed by what God has placed under them. Human beings may not be on the leash of their pet; human beings may not be ruled by money or machines or whatever God has given them to use. Whenever human beings are enslaved by what God has placed in their service, they, kings and queens, become beggars.

Relationship.

"Image of God" not only describes our *role* in creation; it also spells out our *relationship* to the Creator. In exercise of our high office, we are called to reflect all the virtues of our Father. We can govern God's world only while we are governed by God's Word.

This second aspect, the relation of the image to the Maker, is not fully stated in Genesis 1 and 2. The New Testament makes this clearer when it speaks of the remaking of God's likeness in people by the Spirit of God. The new nature of reborn people is "created to be like God in true righteousness and holiness" (Eph. 4:24). This is one of the many texts in the New Testament that shows that Christ does not make us a new race of beings but restores us to the original design. Only the true children of God are the true stewards in creation. Our role in creation can be restored when our relationship to God has been restored. We are God-like rulers of all that God has placed in our care when we ourselves are bound to him as children to their father, as mirrors of his own righteousness and holiness.

The Cracked Mirror.

All people are still images of God. The mark of their Maker cannot be erased. But it is also true that all people who are born today look so little like their Father that all of them must be born anew. The image is broken and the mirror is cracked.

The world itself shows royal glory. We have the power of obtaining, retaining, and applying insight. We have dominion over the earth and the sea, and we can fly in the sky. We can cultivate the earth and harvest the sea. We have science, technology, film, TV, and we can explore the far-flung planets.

Don't speak evil of human accomplishments and abilities. And don't pin your hopes on them. Admire these things because they are good: they are the glories of God in man. At the same time, these things are no good because they cannot really profit us. For whatever we have received from God, we have used against him. The governors have become rebels. The sacred trust of God's power we have attempted to use for our own glory. Therefore "that which was good to us has become death to us."

We can still do many things, but we can never repair what has been broken. God, be merciful!

A Question Mark.

We lost our purity by the fall of Adam and Eve in Paradise (Gen.3). This is the biblical explanation of the origin of our misery. The misery did not start when someone claimed the right to private property, or when people began to build cities and use tools; the origin of evil is not in science, sex, or money, but it began when our first parents disobeyed God.

This is as far as the Bible goes in explaining the origin of evil in humanity. We are inclined to push the curtain back even more. Before sin erupted in the heart of Eve, evil dwelt in the serpent. And "ancient serpent" is one of several names for the devil (Rev. 20:2), who is the cosmic mastermind of all evil. Where did he come from? If all visible and invisible reality has been brought into existence by the creative power of the good God, how, when, and where did evil arise?

***Q** Then where does this corrupt human nature come from?*

***A** From the fall and disobedience of our first parents, Adam and Eve, in Paradise. This fall has so poisoned our nature that we are born sinners—corrupt from conception on.*

—Q & A 7

We may press the search for the origin of evil as far back as we can, but the Bible won't allow us to blame God or to use the devil as an excuse. The origin of sin is not explained to us. In this matter we have to live with a question mark. And it is not the only question with which Christians have to live.

True knowledge of evil involves much more than intellectually solving the riddle of wickedness. True knowledge of evil occurs when a sinner personally confesses his or her guilt before God.

Original Sin.

Adam and Eve sinned as "our first parents." Their sin was a representative act.

The idea of representation is firmly embedded in the Bible. And it is not unknown to us. We know how the acts of parents affect the whole family, for better or for worse. We know how the representatives of countries can make agreements to which all of us are bound. From the Old Testament, we remember leaders and kings who brought judgment to many or by whose godliness the whole nation was blessed.

"One trespass was condemnation for all men," says the Bible. "Through the disobedience of the one man the many were made sinners" (Rom. 5:18-19). The act of one decided the lot of many. "Sin entered the world through one man, and death through sin, and in this way death came to all men, because all sinned—" (Rom. 5:12). Paul does not say that all men die because all people commit sins. But he says that all sinned when Adam sinned. We were represented by our first father and mother. In them we sinned; with them we die.

Something in us objects to the teaching because it makes us part of the herd. We would much rather be called "unique personalities." We are both, of course. We are cut from one cloth, yet each is unique. And at this point we ought to admit our corporate guilt. Not only would we make fools of ourselves by trying to deny our oneness with humanity, but, more importantly, we may not forget *why* the New Testament discusses our fall in Adam. Paul talks about Adam because he wants to clarify the representative acts of Jesus! He writes Romans 5 to assure us that the lot of the many was decided in the deeds of One. The position of Adam helps us to understand the position of Jesus. Both are representative heads of humanity.

Meanwhile, you and I must confess that we are born as sinners. "Original sin," we call it. Our actual sins do not make us sinners, but we have by nature a sinful condition that is the root and hotbed of all our actual sins.

This is an important teaching with many practical implications: Does a person sin *because* he or she is a sinner, or do we *become* sinners when we commit sins?

If you don't have any understanding of original sin, you go along with the majority of people, who call drunkards, murderers, and drug pushers sinners because they commit crimes; who say that people become sinners when they sin. But if you are a Christian, informed by God's revelation, you say that people commit crimes because they are sinners. You don't divide the town into good guys and bad guys, and you don't say that the good guys go straight and the bad guys are sinners until they are straightened out. No, people sin because they are sinners. Therefore we are careful even when we talk about Jack the Ripper and Mary the adulterer. We say, "There, but for the grace of God, I go." That does not mean that we have lost our sense of proportion. We know very well that robbing a bank is worse that dreaming about bank robbery. But the thought of adultery is already a punishable sin in the sight of God, and love of money can send us to hell even if we never rob a bank. Actual sins are the full-grown weeds and thistles of the original sin with which we are born.

"Inherited Pollution."

Our nature has been "poisoned" since the disobedience of our first parents, says the catechism. It intentionally calls Adam and Eve our "parents," thereby teaching that, just as black parents get black children and white parents get white children, so sinful parents get sinful children, whether they are yellow, red, black, or white. None of us can escape this poison, for all of us have parents. That's the teaching.

The technical term for the poison is "inherited pollution." The standard expression is that we are all "conceived and born in sin."

We should have a closer look at this teaching because it has led to some unbiblical notions. People began to ask themselves how this "poison" from our first parents was transmitted to following generations. Very early in church history some teachers said that the poison was passed on by the sexual act. Since everybody, after Adam and Eve, comes into the world as a result of sexual intercourse between his or her father and mother, and since the church for very many years considered sexual desire a sin, sex was blamed for the perpetuation of sin. Even today some churches consider sexual play between husband and wife impure; only when it is aimed at the birth of a child is it justified. And Pierre Berton (Canadian author and TV personality) tells us in his book *The Comfortable Pew* that he quit the (Anglican) church when he found out that it taught that sex is sin. And how did Mr. Berton find that out? By reading the form of baptism, which says that we are "conceived and born in sin."

If even intelligent people so misunderstand the biblical teaching that we are sinners by birth, maybe we should drop the expression "conceived and born in sin."

The expression comes from Psalm 51:3-5 which reads in context:

For I know my transgressions,
    and my sin is always before me.
Against you, you only, have I sinned,
    and done that which is evil in your sight,
so that you are proved right when you speak
    and justified when you judge.
Surely I was sinful at birth,
    sinful from the time my mother conceived me.

You know that in Psalm 51 David confesses his sin with Bathsheba and implores God for forgiveness. In the lines quoted, he confesses that his whole selfhood is rooted in sin. His dalliance with Bathsheba was not merely a bad mistake, an isolated error, but a corruption for which he takes full responsibility. Overwhelmed by a sense of sin, he cries for cleansing ("Cleanse me with hyssop, and I will be clean"), for forgiveness ("Hide your face from my sins, and blot out all my iniquity"), and for a new heart ("Create in me a pure heart, O God").

David's thoughts don't go from his mother's marriage bed to his sin with Bathsheba, as if to say that you cannot expect anything else. Rather, he thinks with horror not only of his sinful act but also of his sinful self, his very existence. And he realizes, long before Jesus told the same thing to Nicodemus, that a man needs a new heart if he is to live before the face of God.

The Bible has no theory on "inherited pollution" and no teaching that says how the poison is transmitted. But it teaches that sin is not only an act that we commit, not only a human failure that makes us inadequate, not only a condition of spiritual impotence, but also a power that enslaves us—a power from which no one but God can rescue us. That power rules us from birth. None of us is born free. We are born in prison.

Total Depravity.

Sin is worse than we are inclined to think, and salvation is bigger than any church can tell.

The Bible teaches that, by nature, people are "totally depraved." This is again a technical term, and it might be helpful to say, first, what it does *not* mean. We don't mean to say that people are as bad as they can possibly be. Most of the time, most of them are not. Neither do we mean that ordinary decent people cannot perform acts of kindness, helpfulness, courtesy, and so on. Many people do, and we thank God for the milk of human kindness and the paint of civilized surroundings.

***Q** But are we so corrupt that we are totally unable to do any good and inclined toward all evil?*

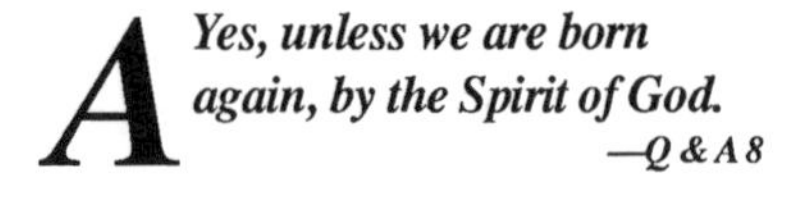

***A** Yes, unless we are born again, by the Spirit of God.*
—Q & A 8

By total depravity we mean that sin has affected every part of every human being. The mind is not free, as the rationalists claim. The will is not free, as the Arminians seem to think. If there is such a thing as the "seat of sin," the corruption must not be located in the head, or in the subconscious drives, or in the sexual organs, or in the will, but in the *heart*. The heart is where you are *you* and I am *I*. It is the center of a person. The heart is the place whence the springs of life flow (Prov. 4:23). From this center all thoughts, plans, deeds, and words proceed, and here they are defiled before they are shaped, performed, or spoken (Matt. 15:18-20). This well is "deceitful above all things and beyond cure" (Jer. 17:9).

The only solution to total depravity is total renewal. No person can do anything that is really acceptable to God unless he or she has a new heart.

Unless One Is Born Anew.

"Are we so corrupt that we are totally unable to do any good and inclined toward all evil?"

If you say no to this question, you may be one of those who has never seen his or her life in the light of God's Word. But if you say yes, if you admit that you are totally unable to do any good in God's sight and that you have a permanent tendency toward evil, we would have to ask you if you know Jesus Christ as your Savior and Lord. When you say that you are totally depraved, you are testifying to the power of sin. God wants us to testify to the power of his Spirit.

Total depravity is the state from which Christians are delivered by the power of Christ. You he made *alive*, when "you were dead in your transgressions and sins" (Eph. 2:1). "Through Christ Jesus the law of the Spirit of life set me *free* from the law of sin and death" (Rom. 8:2).

We are totally depraved, yes, unless we are revived. We are dead in Adam, yes, unless we are raised in Christ. And now that we are "in Christ," dare we say that we are able to do good and that we are no longer inclined toward evil? Of course we *must* be able to say that! We must say it with Paul and with all New Testament Christians. And yet Christians in the Reformed tradition tend to hesitate.

Our hesitation stems from two sources; one is bad, and one is legitimate.

The bad source of our hesitation is neither in the Bible nor in our confessions but in our upbringing. Somehow many of us came to believe that it is a truly Christian thing to call ourselves "totally depraved." But it is not. It shows a deep respect for the power of sin, but it does not show enough faith in the power of the Savior.

In this respect even the simplest people in the "I-am-born-again" movement should put us to shame. They testify to the power of the new life, and they know that becoming a Christian is indeed a transition from death to life.

Second, it seems to me that there is a legitimate hesitation to write off our depraved nature as a thing of the past. This hesitation arises from a biblical kind of "fear and trembling." It will be discussed when we speak of "conversion" (Lord's Day 33). For now, let me give an example:

We are thankful for those among us who devote themselves to the rehabilitation of alcoholics and drug addicts. People who are seriously involved in this kind of work never speak of a "cured alcoholic" but always of an alcoholic who has quit drinking. In these circles knowledgeable people have a profound suspicion of overconfidence. The former victims of the old demons have broken the bondage of their habits. They are free but never safe. They may sense that, at every moment, they are at the edge of the crater. And therefore many live their restored lives with all sorts of crutches: they seek the shelter of certain places and the company of buddies, but they avoid other places and people. I know one cured alcoholic who is always in the company of his teapot. These people know the joy of freedom, but they cannot and may not forget the power of the demon.

You and I will speak of the liberating power of Jesus. He paid the debt, and he set me free from the inability to do good. He broke my inclination to all evil, and he gave me a desire to live for him. But when I think of the old power of sin, I am not looking back along a horizontal line to an ever dimmer past. That would be true if the sin were merely a bad habit from which the saved person was delivered in chapter nine of his or her biography. When I look for the old enemy, I look deep inside at the levels of my own existence. My "old nature" is not a twenty-year-old photograph but a hated and familiar enemy, beaten a hundred times over, yet clinging to my heart with slimy tentacles until God does his last surgery on me.

We will speak of the liberating power of Jesus: "I have been crucified with Christ and I no longer live, but Christ lives in me. The life I live in the body, I live by faith in the Son of God who loved me and gave himself for me" (Gal. 2:20).

Hallelujah! We are no longer totally depraved. But while saying our hallelujah, we lean heavily on Jesus because the edge of the crater is close.

Lord's Day 4

THE RIGHTEOUSNESS OF GOD

The Protests of Our Flesh.

This is the third and last Lord's Day in which we confess the truth about the misery of humanity. Perhaps it is the most difficult one. We must now admit that God is righteous in his verdict, in his punishment, and in his ultimate wrath.

Our flesh speaks the questions in the catechism with a show of logic, with irritation, and in self-defense. In the answers the Word of God comes to silence the protests of our hearts.

What we try to do in these questions and answers must happen in everyone's life. God's Word must bring us to surrender. We must become still and admit that God is sovereign and that God is righteous.

The three questions follow:

a. Isn't it unfair that God would ask of us what we cannot give to him?

b. Even if we are guilty, should not God suspend the sentence, seeing that "everybody is doing it"?

c. So God is righteous; but he is also merciful, isn't he?

The three questions are true to life. The three answers are true to the Bible.

***Q** But doesn't God do us an injustice by requiring in his law what we are unable to do?*

***A** No, God created humans with the ability to keep the law. They, however, tempted by the devil, in reckless disobedience, robbed themselves and their descendants of these gifts.*

—Q & A 9

Is it Fair?

Is it fair that God demands of us what we are unable to do? Who would ask a million of a penniless beggar?

This question is asked by countless people in tones ranging from arrogant mockery to honest despair. Perhaps the question arises in every human heart sooner or later.

It is fruitless to argue the question with an appeal to a human sense of justice and a common sense for fair play. We should first determine *who* is entitled to answer the question. Obviously, it cannot be settled by an opinion poll or a panel discussion. The answer will have to come from the other side—from God.

To God's ear it is a silly question. To him we sound like a drunk driver who says to the police officer: "I couldn't help driving in the wrong lane, 'cause I'm drunk."

God holds us accountable for the "reckless disobedience" by which we prevented ourselves from walking in the way of his commandments. Even the temptation by the devil is mentioned in the Bible and in the catechism not as an excuse but as an accusation: You belonged to me, but you listened to him!

Still, we bristle in self-defense: That temptation happened to Adam and Eve. It happened millennia ago. Why should we be doomed for what none of us remembers?

Here again, it's a matter of perspective. We protest like individualists. But the Bible says that the very fact that we are able to think of ourselves as unrelated, disunited individuals presents evidence of our sinful perspective. God's revelation views the human race not as a pile of gravel but as a giant tree. We are not pebbles thrown together but twigs and branches on a tree, all organically united.

We form a corporate unity. In many respects you and I have never doubted it. The national debts, the astronomical amounts of money that our nations owe to bankers and other creditors in the world, are your and my debts. Yet when the debts were incurred, some of us were not yet born and none of us were asked. Similarly, the debt of the human race is yours and mine.

God Is Righteous.

We have become unrighteous. We have forsaken God and denied the relationship we had to him from the beginning. What does God do now? Does he cut us off? Does he act as if the relationship never existed? No, God remains righteous, and he will judge all people in righteousness (Ps. 98:9).

By the "righteousness of God," the Bible means that God has not shifted position but has remained true to himself and to the relationship he has with us. Righteousness is his unwavering covenant faithfulness.

God never surrenders the claim he has on us. Even when people give up on him, God does not give up on them. He pursues everyone with his original covenant claim: "My son—or daughter—give me your heart and let your eyes keep to my ways" (Prov. 23:26).

People can degenerate so much that they prefer to live like swine. Some have openly chosen for a "different life-style," and they don't mind admitting that they are going to the dogs. But God keeps addressing us as the people he created: "My son, my daughter, give me your heart." He does so because he is righteous. God is righteous in his judgment when he declares us guilty. And he forgives because he is righteous: "If we confess our sins, he is faithful and *righteous* to forgive our sins" (1 John 1:9).

The longer we think about it, the more we will praise our God for his unfailing righteousness.

Crime and Punishment.

If the situation is so desperate that all of us are guilty before God, must all of us be punished?

In our society it is impossible to maintain a legal code that is transgressed by everybody. You cannot send the whole town to jail. When a certain illegal behavior has become commonly accepted behavior, the illegal practice is "decriminalized."

***Q** Will God permit such disobedience and rebellion to go unpunished?*

***A** Certainly not. He is terribly angry about the sin we are born with as well as the sins we personally commit. As a just judge he punishes them now and in eternity. He has declared: "Cursed be everyone who does not continue to do everything written in the Book of the Law."*

—Q & A 10

However, if the whole town breaks the law of God, God will punish the whole town. God would not be God if he could change his code. "Not the smallest letter, not the least stroke of a pen, will by any means disappear from the Law until everything is accomplished" (Matt. 5:18).

God does not always punish immediately. We are now living in the time of God's forbearance or long-suffering. This period began just after the flood, with the covenant of Noah. After God had flushed the wickedness of the world away, he vowed that he would henceforth withhold his judgment, "because of man, even though every inclination of his heart is evil from childhood" (Gen. 8:21). Today we are living under the threat of God's judgment and under the rainbow of God's long-suffering. Let no one show contempt for God's kindness; it is supposed to lead us to repentance (Rom. 2:4). And don't fall asleep while the kindness endures: even if God allows people to eat and drink and marry, let the church tell the nation that the great day of wrath is coming; it will be the coming of the Son of man (Matt. 24:38-39).

God does not bring his punishment upon us as a tyrant, arbitrarily, but he teaches us the relationship between sin and punishment. As a mother says to the child, "When you touch the fire, you will be burned," so God says, "When you eat of it you will surely die" (Gen. 2:17), and, "The wages of sin is death" (Rom. 6:23).

Therefore, in the Bible death is not so much a punishment administered by God as it is the bitter fruit of our own evil works. Death is the paycheck for a life wrongly spent. Death is the separation from God caused by the knife-cuts of sin. Love heals. Love is the seed of life, which is communion with God and human beings. But sin separates, and death *is* separation. Eternal death is eternal separation. The total absence of love and life is hell.

However, hell is not only the climax of our wickedness, the dreary darkness of our doing; it is also the "supreme penalty" (Answer 11) administered by a righteous God.

This is a deep riddle. People have thought up theories to escape the harsh teaching of hell. Some have said that we will get a second chance (but see Hebrews 9:27), or that we will have an ultimate universal pardon (but see Matthew 25:46), or that, in the end, only believers will have a continued, conscious existence, while the wicked will be annihilated (but see John 5:28-29).

Eternal punishment is a dark truth. God forbid that we would ever discuss it with relish. For us it is impossible to see how an eternal punishment can contribute to the glory of God. But someday, when the last issues of life and death have become clear, we will confess that God is righteous in all his ways.

There are two things in God that are very much beyond the reach of human beings: God's love and God's wrath. But on Golgotha we come close to both in the body of One.

***Q** But isn't God also merciful?*

***A** God is certainly merciful, but he is also just. His justice demands that sin, committed against his supreme majesty, be punished with the supreme penalty—eternal punishment of body and soul.*

—Q & A 11

Isn't God Merciful?

The last of the three excuses attempts to play off God's justice against God's mercy. Polytheists (pagans who believe in many gods) do that: they call on one god for protection against another. But our God is one (Deut. 6:4), and in the heart of our

Father-Judge are no such contradictions.

"God is certainly merciful, but he is also just." God is the only one who maintains justice to all eternity. He never shifts position. He claims us as his offspring and he never alters his claim. There must be a wedding feast between heaven and earth, even if the Bridegroom has to be a lamb.

The Revelation of Righteousness.

All we have been trying to do thus far in our Heidelberg Catechism is an imitation of what the apostle Paul does in his Epistle to the Romans. Throughout his introduction he argues that Gentiles are sinners and that Jews are no better. He says that God is righteous and that nobody will escape his well-deserved punishment in body and soul. He maintains that the law-word of the Lord is unalterable, and that, by its universal application, "every mouth may be silenced and the whole world held accountable" (Rom. 3:19) for wicked deeds to the everlasting God.

Then he says: "But now a righteousness from God . . . has been made known" (Rom. 3:21). It has now come out into the open, on the scene of this earth, in the light of day. God is righteous, and he has shown it because he has now punished all sin in the death of Jesus. Now you can see God's justice: He poured out his wrath on Jesus. And by the same divine righteousness, God forgives everyone who believes in Jesus.

Why did Paul write the first part of Romans, and why do we confess Lord's Days 2, 3, and 4? It's not because he and we enjoy telling all people what great sinners they are. That would be cheap and unloving. What Paul was doing and what the Christian church is doing is this: We want to nail shut all doors that lead nowhere. We want to take all excuses out of our hearts and remove all false confidence from our souls. We don't want to rely on good intentions or warm feelings, on churchgoing or water-sprinkling. We can't go through these doors—they lead nowhere. God has shut them and no man shall open them. We do all this because we want ourselves and our neighbors and the world to get out of all dead-end streets and find the door, the only door. This door God has opened and no one shall shut. Here the righteousness of God has been revealed. This door is Jesus.

You and I have to do with a righteous God. He always punishes sin, temporally, eternally, in body and soul. Now our sins are either punished in Jesus—then it is all over—or we have to bear our own punishment.

Lord's Day 5 and 6

THE MEDIATOR

***Q** According to God's righteous judgment we deserve punishment both in this world and forever after: how then can we escape this punishment and return to God's favor?*

***A** God requires that his justice be satisfied. Therefore the claims of his justice must be paid in full, either by ourselves or by another.*

—Q & A 12

***Q** Can we pay this debt ourselves?*

***A** Certainly not. Actually, we increase our guilt every day.*

—Q & A 13

***Q** Can another creature—any at all—pay this debt for us?*

***A** No. To begin with, God will not punish another creature for what a human is guilty of. Besides, no mere creature can bear the weight of God's eternal anger against sin and release others from it.*

—Q & A 14

Back to School.

In Lord's Day 5 and 6 the catechism seems to be treating us as if we were back in school. Listen to these questions and answers:

Q. Can we escape punishment and get back to the favor of God?

A. Not so fast; satisfaction must be rendered.

Q. Can we do that ourselves?

A. No, we make it worse.

Q. Maybe another creature can do it?

A. No, that would not be fair and that would not be possible.

Q. What kind of mediator do we need, then?

A. A true and righteous one who is also God.

Q. Why must he be true God?

A. Because it takes the power of God to save us.

Q. Who is he?

A. Jesus.

We call this a school-like or scholastic kind of teaching. You don't find it very often in the catechism.

The Bible does not teach the doctrine of the Mediator this way. The Bible presents Jesus. The voice from heaven says: "This is my Son, whom I love. Listen to him!" (Mark 9:7). Afterwards, when we get to know him better, we also learn that he is exactly the One we need. But the catechism starts at the other end; first it makes up a list of requirements and finally it asks: "Now, children, who is the one who meets all the requirements?" Then all of us are supposed to say: "Jesus Christ."

No matter the method, the truth is crystal clear: Jesus Christ is the only Mediator who saves us by taking our place, and he rescues us with the power of God. Or, in different and more difficult words: The Mediator whom God has given us is unique, vicarious, and sufficient.

No Other Mediator.

There is only one God and there is only one Mediator between God and man (1 Tim. 2:5). Jesus Christ is the Way (John 14:6). A way or a road is the means by which you get from one place to another. We teach that there is no way to God other than Jesus.

This is an intolerant teaching. It gives no saving credit to other religions, and it declares all human efforts hopeless.

Every day we meet people who expect to be "saved" by their works. They don't worry about their final destiny, they say, because they have always been good and honest. They are especially fond of their honesty. "I'm not saying that I am a Holy Joe, but I am not a hypocrite." In fact, their "honesty" was why they never joined the church—"that bunch of hypocrites."

We must tell them that their self-reliance is a way of death and that they need a mediator. Honestly!

Thousands of people seek their salvation in a religious life. "Lord, I was a member in good and regular standing. Churchgoing was my second nature. I saw them go on the Sabbath, those secular people, touring and fishing and living for their own pleasure. My heart hated their ways, and I determined to stick to the oldtime religion." But he will answer: "Don't knock on that door; that road leads nowhere."

Hundreds of thousands believe that rites and ceremonies are roads to the everlasting God. They sprinkle water, they dip and immerse, they burn candles, and they say litanies. Or they chant verses until their minds are numb. They call on saints and holy people, make pilgrimages, sing songs, pay money. But the Lord says that there is only one Mediator between God and man.

According to the Scriptures, Christians are bound to acknowledge only one Mediator, by whom all people must come to God. That does not mean that we are disrespectful of all who would seek access to God elsewhere. It means that the Christian religion is a missionary religion. If Christian faith does not show its urge to bring all men to the Mediator, it has become untrue to its very character. As soon as it outgrows its "narrow" view that Jesus is the only way, the Christian church loses its missionary zeal; in fact, it ceases to be Christian.

***Q** What kind of mediator and deliverer should we look for then?*

***A** One who is truly human and truly righteous, yet more powerful than all creatures, that is, one who is also true God.*

—Q & A 15

***Q** Why then must he be truly human and truly righteous?*

***A** God's justice demands that human nature, which has sinned, must pay for its sin; but a sinner could never pay for others.*

—Q & A 16

***Q** Why must he also be true God?*

***A** So that, by the power of his divinity, he might bear the weight of God's anger in his humanity and earn for us and restore to us righteousness and life.*

—Q & A 17

***Q** And who is this mediator—true God and at the same time truly human and truly righteous?*

***A** Our Lord Jesus Christ, who was given us to set us completely free and to make us right with God.*

—Q & A 18

Vicarious Atonement.

All people need Jesus Christ as the Mediator because he gave his life as a *ransom* (1 Tim. 2:6). He took the punishment for our sins. He died because the wrath of God against our sins was poured out on him. Nobody can bear the punishment of God and live. But Jesus died in our place. Now God is satisfied, and we can live.

We call this teaching the "vicarious atonement of Jesus." All Christians who hold to the gospel will confess this vital truth. The word *atonement* you know from the Old Testament. When a person had broken the covenant, he or she had to make atonement for sin. Usually atonement involved the sacrifice of an animal. When the sacrifice went up in smoke, that person knew that God's demands had been met and that God's punishment no longer needed to be feared. This person was now *reconciled* to God.

Jesus' self-sacrifice atoned for our sins. He died, not for his own sins, but "in our place." That's what we mean by *vicarious*. If you are Roman Catholic, Anglican, or Episcopalian, you know that the *vicar* is that man who rules the church "in the place of" Christ. And everyone knows that the *vice* consul can take the place of the consul, and the *vice* president may have to take the place of the president.

Jesus died on the cross *vicariously*. He caught all the wrath of God in his body. "God made him who had no sin to be sin for us [vicariously], so that we might become the righteousness of God" (2 Cor. 5:21).

Penalties and Thieves.

This teaching, that Jesus paid the debt of our sins by giving himself over to the wrath of God, meets with much resistance. Our hearts oppose it because it utterly humiliates us that we can be saved by nothing but the blood of Jesus.

There is also a rational objection to this teaching. It does not seem morally right for God to deal with Jesus as if he were a sinner. We know that we can transfer money debts to each other. If I stole two thousand dollars and had no money to pay it back, you might step in as my friend, and pay two thousand dollars on my behalf. But I would still be the thief, even if you paid my penalty. And so it seems wrong for Jesus to take our guilt. We must not take this objection lightly. The people who make this objection are especially aggravated by those Christians who forever speak of the death of Christ as a money payment: God presents the invoice to me, I cannot pay, Jesus pays on my account, God writes on it, "Paid in full," and I go free. That is, indeed, a very simplistic way of presenting the gospel. Certainly, Christ's death on Golgotha means much more than this example of debt transfer brings out.

The moral earnestness of liberals who say that you cannot transfer moral guilt may not cause us to lose the teaching of the vicarious atonement. Fundamentalists may have an irritatingly simple way of explaining the death of Jesus with their money example, but if you follow the "thoughtful liberals," you are left with a Christ who is an inspiring example and a stimulus to self-giving love, but no Mediator.

The picture of Christ as a benevolent millionaire who pays our debts does not really do justice to the work of Jesus. Scripturally we must think of Christ as the Head of the covenant. He is an Adam-figure who represents his people when he hangs on the cross and when he rises from the grave on Sunday morning as the first fruit of the new harvest. He could take our place—undergoing what we should have suffered and giving us claim to what he earned—because in his death we died, and in his resurrection *we* began to live for God (Rom. 6:1-14). And today our relationship to him is much more than saying "thank you" for the paid invoice. He and we form an organic unit. We are part of "his body." We have been "incorporated in Christ Jesus."

I am not saying that there is a way in which we can understand that Jesus died for our sins. Good news must be believed. But we will try to think about Christ and his work along biblical lines: he was given to us as the Mediator of a new and better covenant. "In him" we paid the penalty; through him we have peace with God.

Cur Deus Homo? (Why Must God Be Man?)

The job of a mediator is to serve as intermediary, or middle-person, in order to bring two conflicting parties together. Later we will discuss this *work* of the Mediator—what he *did* to bring God and man together. For the moment we want to confess that he is the only *person* who could effectively mediate between God and man because he *is* God and he *is* man.

Why must he be truly human? Why must he also be true God? We should not pretend that we have a compelling logical argument by which we can "prove" that our Mediator had to be God and man in one person. The Bible presents him that way. God gave him to us. And we accept him in faith and with adoration.

The Bible does speak of a "necessity" according to which the one who makes us holy should have the same human nature as the people he came to make holy (Heb. 2:11). It was by a man that we fell victim to death, and it is by a human being that we rise from death (1 Cor. 15:21). But when we say that he *had to be* God and man in one person, we don't mean that we have discovered a law of logic to which even God is subject. Rather we recognize that according to God's will for our salvation, this Jesus had to be our Mediator. It could be no one else, and our salvation could happen in no other way.

This holy *must* lies in the wisdom of God. Immediately after the fall of humanity, God spoke these words: "The man has now become like one of us, knowing good and evil. He must not be allowed to reach out his hand and take also from the tree of life and eat, and live forever" (Gen. 3:22). These words are a sort of divine irony. God seems to be quoting the devil (Gen. 3:5) with a compassionate mockery that a father uses sometimes when his little son has gotten himself into trouble because he overestimated himself.

But God was utterly serious when he had angels say that the Savior was born in the city of David: "This will be a sign to you: You will find a baby . . ." (Luke 2:12).

Here is a divine necessity, not conceived in any human heart. God says: you wanted to be like one of us, now I *must* become like one of you. It is the *must* of God's salvation plan. The same necessity compelled God, "for whom and through whom everything exists," to lead Jesus through the school of suffering as the only possible way to bring "many sons to glory" (Heb. 2:10). This divine logic is the will to which Jesus submits his life: he *must* be in his Father's house (Luke 2:49), the Son of man *must* suffer many things (Luke 9:22), and the Father cannot take away the cup of suffering (Luke 22:42). And when all the misery is over and the glory is revealed, Jesus asks if we agree with the logic of God's plan of salvation: "Did not the Christ *have to* suffer these things and then enter into his glory?" (Luke

24:46). Yes, looking back, after the Scriptures have been opened to us, we can say "amen" to God's logic for this Mediator.

All-Sufficient Mediator.

He is truly man and truly God. This is not only a lesson in the school of religious education but a pillar in the house of faith. The man Christ Jesus saved us from God's wrath by receiving God's holy anger in his own body, shielding us. He stood there and was despised, he hung there and suffered, but he did not cease to believe in God and to love us. I glory in the fact that he was a man, for now there is a way from earth to heaven. It was a human being who was buried so that the fear of death would be taken out of dying (Heb. 2:9). And it was a man who arose from the grave so that all of us human beings would see light at the end of the tunnel.

As our Mediator he bore "the weight of God's anger in his humanity." That's when he suffered what we should have suffered, as a thief for the thieves and condemned for the damned. By those stripes we are healed. But the Mediator did not only "bear the weight of God's anger" by this action; he performed a perfect obedience so that he might "earn for us and restore to us righteousness and life." The penalty has been paid for us because he suffered our anguish. And righteousness has been restored to us because in him we fulfilled all that God commands. He paid what we could not pay, and he earned what we could never have attained.

Thus he is our perfect and all-sufficient Mediator. Nothing and nobody else are needed or wanted to unite us with God. He is the bridge from earth to heaven, for he is a true human being. He is the bridge from heaven to earth because he is truly God.

He is the mystery of the ages, hidden in God's counsel, revealed in the fullness of time. This Mediator is neither invented nor understood by us. He was "*given* us to set us completely free and to make us right with God."

This Mediator is God's only open door. All people must enter here.

Lord's Day 7

TRUE FAITH

***Q** Are all saved through Christ just as all were lost through Adam?*

***A** No. Only those are saved who by true faith are grafted into Christ and accept all his blessings.*

—Q & A 20

The Painful Question.

We must now answer the question whether or not all people are going to be saved. The catechism says, "No, they are not."

We give this negative answer with pain in our hearts. For all people are our brothers and sisters. All of us received life through one blood, and we fell from favor by one deed. It is therefore natural that we desire all people to be saved by one blood and through one great deed. But *not* all people are going to be saved by Christ, although all were lost in Adam.

You are a bad person and an even poorer Christian if you do not know the desire that all people be saved. God himself has that desire. In the Old Testament he said through one of his prophets: "Turn to me and be saved, all you ends of the earth" (Isa. 45:22). And in our era God has ambassadors going to every country saying: "We implore you on Christ's behalf: Be reconciled to God" (2 Cor. 5:20). In fact, one of the few known reasons why the Lord has not yet come in final judgment is his desire that no one should perish, but all should repent (2 Pet. 3:9). God desires the salvation of all people (1 Tim. 2:4), and so do we.

Moreover, we have often experienced the unity of the human race in touching ways. Whenever there's a big fire, a flood, a tornado, or some other catastrophe, many human hearts respond with compassion to the victims. A crying child can still move selfish human beings to sympathetic deeds. Charity begins with Christians, I hope, but human kindness is certainly not limited to them and sometimes hard to find among them. And, therefore, if you can say of my unbelieving but otherwise exemplary neighbor that he is headed for eternal punishment—if you and I can say that without pain in our hearts and without participating in the mission of the church, we are bad human beings and even poorer Christians.

Nevertheless, wishing for the salvation of all people may lead us to teach universal salvation. We would be underestimating the power of sin, and we would make ourselves laughable by climbing on the throne of God.

We must always remind ourselves that we don't know what misery is (not lack of health or wealth or education, but *real* misery) unless we are taught by God. Neither do we know justice, fairness, or love unless God is our Instructor.

Therefore we must be careful when we are asked this painful question. We must not answer with a hateful heart or sympathetic feelings. We must sit at the feet of the Master. Let him say it with infinite wisdom, supreme love, and incorruptible justice: No, not all people are saved in Christ as they are condemned in Adam. In order to be saved, a person must believe in Jesus.

The Necessity of Faith.

"Only those are saved who by true faith are grafted into Christ and accept all his blessings."

That's a masterful and biblical answer. The catechism could have said: "Only those are saved who are elect since the foundation of the world." Or "Only those whose names have been written in the Book of the Lamb." Such statements would not have been wrong, because election is the ground of our salvation. But they would have been wrong answers to this question. The message of the Bible is not that you will be lost if you are not elect, but that you cannot be saved unless you believe!

Many Christians appear to know the doctrines (teachings) of the Bible yet are causing confusion because they say the right thing at the wrong time. We must not only know the teachings of the Bible; we must also know what answers belong to what questions.

With this answer we come to the Great Divide. Here is the crack that runs through humanity, a fissure that will one day turn out to be a chasm no one will cross (Luke 16:26). Two will be in one bed, and one will be accepted and the other will be rejected. Two will cooperate in the drive for crippled children; one will be accepted and the other will be rejected. And the reason for the separation will be in the person's relationship to Christ.

This is the only division in humanity that's worth pointing out. Most other divisions are due to sin and circumstance, and none are insurmountable for those who believe. But this one has to do with Jesus Christ and our relationship to him. We should quit getting worked up about other divisions by learning to get excited about this division. Christ is the God-given Divider. He is the "rock of salvation" or the "stumbling stone" (1 Pet. 2:8). A person is either "for" and "with" him or "against" him (Matt. 12:30). Ground is never neutral where his cross has been planted. By faith in Christ a person is saved, but "how shall we escape if we ignore [not reject, but neglect] such a great salvation?" (Heb. 2:3).

New questions are being raised every day. The church, too, faces new "problems" every year. We cannot deny the validity of many questions that disturb us today, even though they were never raised by our parents. But one question is basic to all questions: What do you think of Jesus? By the answer to that question all people will be judged. If you have not yet raised and answered that question in all your coffee-talk, neighborhood-talk, family-talk, and church-talk, your conversations have been unspeakably superficial.

A Branch on the Vine.

Saving faith is "receiving" Jesus Christ by "believing in his name" (John 1:12). That is a very personal act. No one can do it for someone else.

Everyone must personally "accept" Jesus Christ, although none of us can have a "personal" Savior. I must personally accept him as the One who saves *me*. But I can't have a "personal" Savior anymore than I can have a "Christian Reformed" or a "Baptist" Savior. All of us must be saved by the Christ who is the Head of his own people and the Vine who feeds all the branches. We may not have an individualistic notion of the Savior and of salvation, for individualism is exactly one of the sins from which we need to be saved.

By a true faith we are "grafted" or transplanted into Christ. That picture tells us, first of all, that Christians are alive. Just as in horticulture branches are taken from one tree and live only because they feed on another, so we are alive and producing fruit because we are by faith united to Christ. Through him we get life, that is, the Spirit, and by that power we produce the fruit that pleases God (John 15:5, Rom. 11:17).

The picture of being "grafted into Christ" not only indicates how we are living but also shows that we are organically united. We are the branches on the new tree, and the tree is Christ. Together we constitute the new human race, the people of God in Christ. They who accept Jesus Christ find that he places them in a community of those whom he has accepted. You cannot have the One (Jesus) without the other (community).

When we speak of saving faith, we must stress the personal, but not at the expense of the communal; we must stress the active, but not at the expense of the passive. Exercising faith is a human activity. But the catechism says more about what we undergo than what we do. By true faith we are *grafted*—which is done *to* us rather than *by* us. And we *accept* all Christ's blessings. Accepting puts us again at the receiving end. It's more passive than active.

True faith finds it easier to speak of God's doings than of ours.

***Q** What is true faith?*

***A** True faith is not only a knowledge and conviction that everything God reveals in his Word is true; it is also a deep-rooted assurance, created in me by the Holy Spirit through the gospel, that, out of sheer grace earned for us by Christ, not only others, but I too, have had my sins forgiven, have been made forever right with God, and have been granted salvation.*

—Q & A 21

The Nature of Faith.

Faith is the instrument—and the only one at that—by which we receive God's goodness into our lives.

If you were a stranger to electricity, and you were wondering how a lamp is lit, I would point to the wires. It is not the wiring that makes the light burn, but the wiring is the instrument that conveys the current first into the house and then to the bulb. Similarly, faith is the instrument—and the only one—by which God's goodness enters our lives.

Yet "faith" is much more than the instrument by which we receive God's grace. Even Paul, who uses the word "faith" frequently as the opposite of "works"—as the only way of salvation, as the only instrument of receiving God's grace—can also say: "everything that does not come from faith is sin" (Rom. 14:23). Then he speaks of faith as the whole-life response to God.

The letter to the Hebrews describes faith as a certainty based on the Word of God; a believer is someone whose whole life is governed by these unseen realities (Heb. 11).

James says that we have no faith unless it leads us to be upright and unprejudiced in social relations (James 2, 4). Also in the gospels we find that faith and obedience are two sides of one act.

Therefore it is extremely difficult, if not impossible, to define faith. The catechism attempts a description: Faith means that we acknowledge the truth of the Bible and that we are assured that its good news is for us.

Indeed, these are two indispensable components of faith—knowledge and trust—and we can never have one without the other. If we don't know, we cannot trust. And if we don't trust, it is because we don't know how reliable he is.

I have often asked classes of church school students: "Should we believe in the Bible or should we believe in God?" They are always stunned by that question, at least for a few moments. Rightly so, because it is an unfair question. Our faith rests in God himself; it is a personal relationship to our heavenly Father. But apart from the Bible, God is unknown to us. Faith swears by the truth of the Bible.

The catechism is an early Reformation document. Therefore it takes position against a view of faith that reduces ordinary believers to "faithful sons and daughters of the church." Instead of an implicit faith that agrees with whatever the clergy teaches, the Reformers emphasized personal knowledge of God's Word, the ultimate truth, and personal assurance of salvation, created in us by the Holy Spirit through the gospel. We maintain this concept of faith. The church is often plagued and never blessed by children and grandchildren of believers who stay with the organization as if their membership were the premium to be paid for eternal life insurance. They have no personal Bible knowledge, and they lack the joyful assurance that "not only others, but I too, have had my sins forgiven, have been made forever right with God, and have been granted salvation."

Although we maintain the validity of this description of faith, we should also agree that faith, in the biblical sense of the word, is much broader and deeper than a personal assurance of salvation. In order to do justice to the biblical idea of faith, we would also have to study the Old Testament and learn what faith is against the background of its opposite: unbelief or idolatry. We should study the life of Abraham, who is a biblical model of what it means to live with God and to make a whole-life response to God's promises. Abraham is the father of all who have faith. All believers in the Old and the New Testament periods have a similar way of responding to the words and the promises of God (Rom. 4, Heb. 11:8-12, James 2:20-24).

Faith is the only right response of human life to the words and works of God. Faith is openness to his grace and truth. Only when we live by faith can we function as truly human beings. And from God's side there is nothing more grieving and exasperating than human unbelief.

All of this must also get its due when we discuss Christian living. For the moment we focus on faith as the means by which we embrace the Mediator: a conviction that God's Word is true and an assurance that Jesus Christ is my Savior.

Lord's Day 7

THE BIBLE TELLS ME SO

***Q** How do you come to know this [that Jesus Christ is mediator]?*

***A** The holy gospel tells me. God himself began to reveal the gospel already in Paradise; later, he proclaimed it by the holy patriarchs and prophets, and portrayed it by the sacrifices and other ceremonies of the law; finally, he fulfilled it through his own dear Son.*

—Q & A 19

***Q** What then must a Christian believe?*

***A** Everything God promises us in the gospel. That gospel is summarized for us in the articles of our Christian faith—a creed beyond doubt, and confessed throughout the world.*

—Q & A 22

The Content of Faith.

These questions and answers concern the content of faith: *What* must a Christian believe?

Lord's Day 7 of our confession does not speak of "true faith" in the sense of a "sincere" faith. That is also important. But many Muslims are sincere, and many Jehovah's Witnesses impress us with their sincere devotion to an untrue faith. The question that counts with God is not *if* you believe but *what* you believe.

Back to God Hour radio preacher Rev. Peter Eldersveld used to tell this story:

In 1939 an Iowa judge came face to face with the confusion that confounds church members about the fundamentals of the Christian faith. A medical doctor had died, willing $75,000 of his estate "to persons who believe in the fundamental principles of the Christian religion and in the Bible and who are endeavoring to promulgate the same." Ten of his nephews and nieces went to court to break the will.

Witnesses testified on both sides of the case. Many of them were Protestant and Roman Catholic clergymen. One of the late doctor's friends testified that the definition of the faith as given in the Apostles' Creed was the intention of the will. But that did not dissipate the confusion. Many ministers and a Roman Catholic chaplain testified that theologians are in complete disagreement over Christianity's fundamental principles.

And the poor judge was in the middle of all this. He gave himself several weeks to make up his mind, but finally he was compelled to say that on the basis of the evidence there is no clear-cut answer to the question. What is the Christian faith? So the will was broken and Christianity lost $75,000, which was quite a sum in 1939.

The real tragedy, however, was that by that official legal verdict our civilization reached the point where nobody can legally say what constitutes the Christian faith. We just don't know.

If a person wants to find God today, he or she is confronted by a bewildering choice of sects, cults, groups, movements, and churches that contradict each other. Therefore, churches still holding to the historic Christian faith currently have a solemn duty. They must spell out the fundamentals and their unity in the fundamentals as road signs for their religiously confused contemporaries. Love for God and compassion for our rootless society should compel us to articulate the basics of the Christian faith—and to do so together.

Q *What are these articles?*

A ***I believe in God, the Father almighty, creator of heaven and earth. I believe in Jesus Christ, his only Son, our Lord, who was conceived by the Holy Spirit and born of the virgin Mary. He suffered under Pontius Pilate, was crucified, died, and was buried; he descended to hell. The third day he rose again from the dead. He ascended to heaven and is seated at the right hand of God the Father almighty. From there he will come to judge the living and the dead. I believe in the Holy Spirit, the holy catholic church, the communion of saints, the forgiveness of sins, the resurrection of the body, and the life everlasting. Amen.***

—Q & A 23

The Fundamentals.

It is not arrogant for us to say that we know the truth. God himself has revealed and preserved the truth. His Word is truth.

A Christian must believe "everything God promises us in the gospel." By "the gospel" our confession means the Scriptures, as is clear when one compares catechism answer 22 with answer 19.

There is still one universal confession of faith. All Christians subscribe to it; all Christian churches honor it. We call it the *Apostolicum*, or the Apostles' Creed. The church has had this creed in its current form since A.D. 400. As a simple statement of faith, it says in twelve articles what the apostolic Christian church has always and everywhere believed and taught.

The Reformed faith was never intended to be a special refinement of Christianity but a restatement of the historic Christian faith. We do not want to be more, and we dare not be less, than truly apostolic and catholic in our confession. Therefore, when the catechism sets forth what a Christian believes, it explains the twelve articles of the Apostles' Creed (Lord's Day 8-22). These are the fundamentals of the Christian faith.

It may happen to you, as it happened to me, that while you are visiting with friends who are of a different religious persuasion, the talk shifts to the "basics of the Christian faith." Then, if you aren't on your guard, the drift of the conversation may lead you to agree that the essence of our faith is in the love commandment, or that respect for all that lives is at the basis of all that we believe, or you might settle for some other moral precept or religious feeling. In such a conversation you might even say good and profound things. However, these are not the fundamentals of the Christian faith.

"I believe in God, the Father, Creator. I believe in his Son, the Savior, and in the Spirit Sanctifier." Our faith rests in God. Our hope is built on what he did, is doing, and will do. We cannot truthfully talk about the basics of the Christian faith by reaching deeply into the human soul or by quoting moral precepts to which even noble humanists can give their assent. The fundamentals of the Christian faith lie in God and his work. In other words, faith focuses on the Bible as God's word-revelation.

The Bible Is Good News.

The catechism refers to the Bible as the "gospel."

"How do you come to know Jesus as the mediator?"
"The holy *gospel* tells me."
"What then must a Christian believe?"
"Everything God promises us in the *gospel*."

There are people today who want to drive a wedge between the Bible and the gospel. They would probably like to find support in the catechism, as if it were saying that what matters to our faith is not the whole Bible but only the gospel. Such an appeal to the catechism would be unfair. The next line in answer 19 ("God himself began to reveal the gospel already in Paradise") shows that the authors are thinking of the whole Bible when they speak of the gospel. It is foolish and sinful to lift the gospel *out of* the Bible as if it were the nut to be eaten and the rest a shell to be thrown away.

Yet we need to take hold of the truth that the Bible is essentially gospel, "good news," because it presents Jesus Christ. When you pick up the Book, you must be ready to meet the Savior. And unless you meet God's Savior, your preoccupation with the Book is worthless (John 5:39).

Every Bible is a "good news" Bible because the Bible is the holy gospel. Therefore an uneducated person who reads the Bible as God's gospel has a better understanding of the Book than a scholar who searches the Greek and Hebrew texts but fails to find Jesus Christ. Gospel-believing scholars, however, are a blessing to the church because they can exhibit God's treasures from Genesis to Revelation.

History of Redemption.

God "began to reveal" the gospel in Paradise, he "proclaimed" it by patriarchs and prophets, he "portrayed" it by sacrifices and ceremonies, and he "fulfilled" it through his Son. The subject of all these do-words, these active verbs, is God himself. God began to reveal, God proclaimed, God portrayed, and God fulfilled.

We can see the beginning only because the end has come: Since the resurrection of Jesus and the outpouring of the Holy Spirit, followers of Jesus have learned to read the Scriptures with new insight. Suddenly, throughout the books of the Old Testament, we find concealed references to God's salvation in Christ Jesus. Already in Paradise God began to speak about Satan's crushing defeat (Gen. 3:15), now accomplished by Christ. God proclaimed to Abraham that all the families of the earth would eventually share in Abraham's blessing (Gen. 12:3, Gal. 3:8). And God portrayed the atoning work of Christ when he had Aaron sprinkle blood on the mercy seat (Lev. 16:15, Heb. 9:12).

The Bible is therefore first and foremost a history of God's redemption in and through Jesus. That's how God himself explains his own words and deeds. After his resurrection, Jesus Christ interpreted the Scriptures to his disciples (Luke 24:27). More than that, he "opened their minds to understand" the Scriptures (Luke 24:45).

Christ has to do this twofold work for all of his church members. He must open the *Scriptures* to us so that we see that they are the history of God's work of redemption fulfilled in Jesus Christ. And Christ must open our *hearts* and *minds* so that we understand the Scriptures. God uses Bible teachers and church magazines and books to open the Scriptures, and he uses his Spirit to give us true insight into the Scriptures. A "prayer for illumination" is therefore much more than a liturgical fringe. Without God's illumination, Bible study does not dispel darkness. The desired illumination is nothing mystical or spiritualistic. We don't ask that the little words become little windows to God. But the illumination we crave is the confrontation with Jesus through the Bible.

Unless God opens the Bible to us, we cannot see Jesus. And unless we see Jesus, the Bible remains a closed book.

Knowledge in the Last Days.

Since the Bible is a *history* of revelation, not every part has the same clarity. At first God's purposes and God himself were veiled and hardly known. Later they became unveiled, revealed, and more fully known by those who believed.

We are living in the last days. This is the time between the ascension of the Lord and his return. In these last days we know God better and more intimately than we have in all previous revelation history.

Not only are we of the New Covenant communally richer in spiritual possessions than the people of the Old Covenant, but we are also richer than the prophets, priests, and other members of the Old Covenant who received special gifts. God's prophets of the Old Covenant could never fully comprehend what they themselves were saying because they were actually serving *us*, speaking God's Word about Christ and the last days (1 Pet. 1:10-11; Acts 1:17, 25, 30).

Jesus said that John the Baptist was the greatest of the Old Testament prophets. This does not mean that John got an "A" for his work and Isaiah a "B+" for his. Greatness is measured by our closeness to Christ himself. And because John was last in the long row of prophets—the only one who could say, "Behold, the Lamb of God!"—he is the greatest of all those who pointed forward to Christ. Jesus immediately added that the least in the kingdom was greater than John. Again, this does not mean that the least among us has more courage and greater faith than John the Baptist. It means that those who know the secret of the Messiah-who-had-to-die know more than John the Baptist. We are closer to the heart of God because we know the mystery of the cross and the glory of the resurrection. The least among us who has experiential knowledge of the gospel of salvation knows more than the prophets of Israel and the angels in heaven (Matt. 11:11-15, 1 Pet. 1:10-12).

Read the Bible Backward.

When we who are redeemed by Christ and led by the Spirit turn to a passage in the Old Testament, we must not forget that we are reading the Word of God, and we must remember what place this passage has in the history of revelation. We must, of course, read it to understand what it says. I have many books that help me *understand* what the text says without helping me much in *hearing* what God says to me as a member of the church after Pentecost. And yet that is the purpose of our Bible reading.

When we read the book of Isaiah or hear a sermon based on the book of Isaiah, we should hear the Word of the Lord not merely as Judah heard it. It should be a new interpretation of Isaiah, such as what Philip was able to give to the Ethiopian, when he "began with that very passage of Scripture and told him the good news about Jesus" (Acts 8:35). We come to the passage with the full light, the revelation of Jesus. We must know not only the historical circumstances leading up to the text but also the history of salvation that explains the text. Then, if we are good listeners, we hear not only what Isaiah said to Judah but what the Spirit says to the churches today. Isaiah will never conflict with what the Spirit says to us. But we should understand more of the speech of the Spirit than Judah, or even Isaiah, was able to hear.

That's "reading the Bible backward." We read the Old Testament from the perspective of knowing Jesus Christ and of using the hearing aids of the church after Pentecost.

The same holds for the reading of the Psalms. Some churches insist that, at least in the official worship, the church of Christ may sing nothing but the Psalms of David. Even if these churches keep their dignity longer than the congregations that prefer the latest song from a youth rally, the question should be asked whether churches that sing only Psalms are sufficiently assured of the riches, newness, and freedom of the New Covenant.

Since our Savior died with the Psalms on his lips, and since the apostles used Psalm 2 in their prayer meeting (Acts 4:25-31), the Psalms must be read with new insight. All the old concepts about enemies and battles and victory and defeat have been developed and explained in salvation history. Zion, the temple, and Jerusalem have been relocated. The poor and helpless and even law and sin have gotten a more profound meaning for us. The wisdom of Israel's king and the glories of his kingdom are grander for us than they ever were for the most ardent admirer of Solomon. And we have deeper insight into the suffering of the righteous than had Asaph.

It is the Spirit of Christ and the Scriptures of the New Covenant that teach us this new interpretation. The Spirit enables us to sing the songs of Zion in the church of Christ. But he also directs us to "sing a new song"—a brand-new song—unto the Lord.

The Whole Bible Is God's Word.

When our confessions were written, nearly everyone believed in the authority of the Bible and the inspiration of the Scriptures. Today we have to say a few things that go beyond our confessions.

When we argue that we are now living on a higher plane of revelation, someone will ask: "Doesn't that mean the Old Testament—and maybe some of the New—has become *outdated*?"

The word *outdated* may be used for schoolbooks but not for the Bible. In the Bible the old is never abolished when the new comes. The new is concealed in the old and the old fulfilled in the new. Just as childhood and adolescence are not abolished in adulthood but brought to maturity, so newness in God's plan brings the old to fruition.

All of the Bible comes from God. And God did not send his Son into the world to abolish the law but to fulfill the law and the prophets (Matt. 5:17).

Most of us have a meager idea of what fulfillment is. We think of predictions that are *fulfilled* when that which was foretold has become reality. We consider a promise *fulfilled* when God has made good on his word.

But now think of a glass of water that is being filled until it is entirely full. In many instances this image will be most helpful. In Matthew 5, Jesus shows what is meant by fulfillment, by the *filling up* and the *filling out* of the commandments of God. God will not and cannot retract or abolish what he commanded. All of it must be "full-filled." Blessed is the person who continues teaching the "full-fill-ment" of the law of God. But woe to the teacher who considers a commandment outdated (Matt. 5:19).

The Bible in its entirety, the Old and the New Testaments in all their history, prophecy, wisdom literature, and other poetry must be made full. The church may never disregard and must always study the old Scriptures. We need to be fully equipped to do the work to which New Testament Christians have been called, and the only place for this equipping is the academy of the Spirit. The Spirit of God wrote the Bible and lives in the church. Therefore we must tirelessly study and apply these Scriptures; otherwise we cannot do the good works for which he has appointed us (2 Tim. 3:16-17).

Fullness in the Future.

We are in a time of adulthood compared with those who lived in Old Testament times. But compared to the future we are still children, speaking and acting in immaturity, knowing in part and prophesying with an impaired vision. When we see face to face, however, and when the last Word has been "full-filled," we shall love as we ought, and we shall fully understand (1 Cor. 13:11-12). Then the progressive revelation will reach its climax. God will remove his last veil.

Interpretation and the Word.

Bible interpretation is frequently regarded with suspicion in the church. The fear is understandable. Leading interpreters have often tried to be as original as novelists. Many ordinary church members feel that when these interpreters finish "explaining" a text, it ends up meaning something opposite of what the words say at face value.

In spite of sinful theologians, however, and with the help of dedicated theologians, the church must get on with its work. Our work is to know and to do the will of the Lord. And that requires Bible interpretation. Don't let anyone fool you by saying that we need no methods or standard of interpretation. Be a bit more suspicious of those who say that they just read what it says and receive the Word as it comes. All of us would like to do that, I hope. But nobody can read without interpreting what he or she reads. If you read without interpreting, you cannot retain what you have read. If you want to make the truth that comes through words your very own, you must interpret them. The order is this: reading, interpretation, appropriation (that is, making it your own). And you cannot get to appropriation without interpretation.

We must always encourage Bible study and Bible interpretation because misinterpreters often threaten church members more than do those who *deny* the truth of the Bible. The majority of sects and cults insist that they believe every word in the Bible. But it is their Bible interpretation that makes them a snare to the church and a disgrace to Christ.

The Word Is Everlasting.

What God said from Mount Sinai is everlastingly valid. But it did not settle all questions for all time so that the Holy Spirit could retire after writing the Bible. Today you and I must ask seriously how "the just requirement of the law" is to be "fulfilled in us, who walk not according to the flesh but according to the Spirit" (Rom. 8:4, RSV). Interpretation is not a threat to orthodoxy but a requirement of a church that wants to be faithful. It is part of the self-activity to which our Lord calls us. People whose minds have been "transformed" by the Holy Spirit may not be "conformed" to the present world. According to the new principle, now active in them, they must "prove," that is, *determine by interpretation and conversation,* "what God's will is—his good, pleasing, and perfect will" (Rom. 12:2).

Everyone who speaks a message from a biblical text must determine what God says in that text to the church. That is a matter of interpretation, but it is *not* a matter of subjectivism. The Bible warns us that we may not interpret the Word according to our private likes and dislikes. The rightful Interpreter of the Scriptures is he who gave them to us: the Holy Spirit (2 Pet. 1:20-21). He breathed the Scriptures and gave the life of God to the church of God. Hence, Bible interpretation is a *corporate* responsibility because the Spirit and the Bible belong to the *corpus*, or body. We may have our individual insights, but our Bible interpretation may not be individualistic. Those who speak, write, and broadcast the message from the Bible must do so as members of the body of Christ, with due respect for the church's confession and history.

The Heidelberg Catechism makes this connection between the Bible and the church's confession when it states that a Christian must believe everything God promises in the gospel, which gospel is summarized for us in the articles of our Christian faith as "a creed beyond doubt, and confessed throughout the world."

Lord's Day 8

GOD IN THREE PERSONS

***Q** How are these articles [the Apostles' Creed] divided?*

***A** Into three parts: God the Father and our creation; God the Son and our deliverance; God the Holy Spirit and our sanctification.*

—Q & A 24

***Q** Since there is but one God, why do you speak of three: Father, Son, and Holy Spirit?*

***A** Because that is how God has revealed himself in his Word: these three distinct persons are one, true, eternal God.*

—Q & A 25

Such Knowledge Is Too Wonderful for Me.

We confess that we believe in God, and we must now try to say who he is. This is difficult but not impossible. It is possible for us to say who God is—not because we are so smart but because he has graciously revealed himself.

It is possible to say who God is, but it is not possible to say it adequately. Every talk or book about God should be introduced and closed by Psalm 139:6: "Such knowledge is too wonderful for me, too lofty for me to attain." The church confesses to believe in one God: Father, Son, and Holy Spirit. This is the heart of the whole Christian confession. I want to describe—with some confidence and at considerable risk—how this knowledge of God is a dogma the church confesses, a life we live, and a song we begin to sing.

The Dogma of Trinity.

Our confession concerning God was formulated at the beginning of the church. The formula says that God is one being who exists in three persons—the Father, Son, and Holy Spirit. This formula we teach to our children in church school as if it were holy mathematics. The students have trouble remembering the formula. Often they will say that God is one in essence but consists of three persons. Then the teachers try to correct: "God does not *consist of* three persons, but he *exists in* three persons; there aren't three parts that make up God; each person is God, and there is only one God. He exists in three persons."

The teachers use all the familiar examples: when two people marry, their lives are enriched, and they become a unity. When they receive a child, they become a kind of tri-unity, one unit with three distinct persons.

Or, the teachers say, look at a triangle, at "three-angles." Sometimes one of the three corners is in the foreground (God the Father, our Creator), but the other angles are always connected and involved. When the second angle is in view (God the Son, our Redeemer), the others are still there. And when the focus is on the third (God the Spirit, our Sanctifier), we may not forget that he is still part of the triangle. For God is three in one.

Then, in a moment of frustration or honesty, the teachers admit that all the examples fail to equal what the Bible has to say on this topic. But (the teachers insist) church and students may never forget that all things are from God, through God, and unto God (Rom. 11:36); yet there are not three gods but only one true God.

So Mary puts up her hand and says, "Must we make it so hard? Can't we just believe in God?" And her teacher says, "What about the Lord Jesus?" "Well, he is God," she says. "That's what I was trying to say all along," sighs the teacher.

Johnnie makes it even more difficult: "Is all of that in the Bible?" he asks. And the answer is "Yes, but not in the same words as in the catechism."

Personally, I have always been happy teaching church school, but I have always had misgivings about teaching the Trinity to young people. The doctrine of the Trinity is a formula that is supposed to answer a question about God which every serious student must eventually ask. Teaching the formula to those who have never asked the question, however, may do more harm than good.

The church has accepted the trinitarian formulation of the Council of Nicea (A.D. 325), but we should not really fight about the formula. Water was here long before it was called H_2O. Even so, the formula of Nicea is one of the best formulas to describe the everlasting God. But we should not want to stick to the formula as if salvation depended on it. We do, however, want to stick to the truth expressed by this formulation because this truth is indeed a matter of life or death for the church of Jesus Christ. As far as the formula is concerned, Calvin says that he would not mind if it were "buried in oblivion," as long as everyone held to this faith: that "the Father, Son, Holy Spirit are the one God; and that nevertheless the Son is not the Father, nor the Spirit the Son, but that they are distinguished from each other by some peculiar property" (*Institutes*, I, xiii, 5).

Testify to the Truth.

The formula of A.D. 325 was necessary because Arius was teaching that Christ was a created being, substantially different from the Father. Today the Jehovah's Witnesses say the same thing. If you quote Jesus' own saying "I and the Father are one" (John 10:30), they will say that there is indeed some sort of unity between God and Christ, the kind of unity that exists between an architect and a builder. And the Spirit is not God, they say. He is not "somebody"—just as my own spirit is not somebody but a power within me—so calling him God's Spirit is just a way of speaking of God's power.

The church must declare war on the teachings of the Jchovah's Witnesses.

This was the same battle the Council of Nicea faced. Arius was opposed by Athanasius. And the faith of Athanasius won. He did not win because he was more clever with texts but because he saw this: if Jesus Christ is not God, then I cannot be sure of my salvation.

Jesus' enemies understood him better than the Jehovah's Witnesses do. When Christ said to the paralyzed man, "Take heart, son; your sins are forgiven," some of the Jews fumed because only God can forgive sins. "This fellow is blaspheming," they said (Matt. 9:2-3). It is an understandable anger. If you don't believe in Jesus but you are committed to the confession "Jehovah is one" (Deut. 6:4), the claims of Christ are insufferably arrogant. "You, a mere man, claim to be God," said the Jews (John 10:33). For that reason Jesus' enemies wanted to stone him, and for that reason they later crucified him (John 19:17).

The dogma that God the Lord is one Lord is basic to all that the Bible teaches us about God: he says, "You shall have no other gods before me" (Ex. 20:3). When people bow before a creature, the Bible says, "No!"

You remember Paul and Barnabas. When they arrived in Lystra, the people there thought they were gods and came with oxen and garlands to make sacrifices to them. Such behavior arouses the ire of every Jew and Christian. Therefore Paul and Barnabas "tore their clothes and rushed out into the crowd, shouting, 'men why are you doing this? We too are only men, human like you. We are bringing good news, telling you to turn from these worthless things to the living God . . .'" (Acts 14:14-15). The worship of a creature next to or in the place of the only God is irreconcilable with biblical faith.

In the last chapter of the Bible it happened again: John was so overcome with his vision of heavenly things that he bowed—not for a man but for an angel. Then the angel said, "Do not do it! I am a fellow servant with you. . . . Worship God" (Rev. 22:9)—God and God alone. That's the refrain throughout the Bible. Jehovah is one. And yet, in the same book a hymn is sung by man and angels to God *and* to Christ: "You are worthy, our Lord and God . . ." (4:11), "worthy is the Lamb who was slain . . ." (5:12). They sing, "To him who sits upon the throne and to the Lamb be praise and honor and glory and power for ever and ever!" And to this paean of praise the whole cosmos says a rousing "Amen!" (5:13-14). Such adoration is a model for the true worship of God.

The awareness of the mystery of the Trinity started after Easter, when the man who could not believe finally had to fall to his knees and confess: "My Lord and my God!" (John 20:28). Mind you, Thomas was a Jew. Every day he recited, "The LORD our God, the LORD is one" (Deut. 6:4). But now he was confronted with the mystery of Jesus, and he confessed the faith that is beyond comprehension. Ever since Easter the church has confessed that he who is from the Jewish race according to the flesh is also "God over all, forever praised!" (Rom. 9:5, cf. 1:3-4).

If Jesus were not God, how could the Bible not only permit, but command, the worship of the Son? And if Jesus were a different creature, neither God nor man but a different substance (according to Arius and the Jehovah's Witnesses), all who worship him would commit idolatry, by biblical standards.

As for the Holy Spirit, because he is both Gift and Giver, the Bible speaks of him as a blessed power as well as a holy person. Yet he is not "something" but a somebody. For Jesus does not merely say that he will send comfort but "another Comforter" (or Counselor, or Advocate, or Paraclete; John 14:16). He is a person and he is God. Therefore Peter could say that Ananias and Sapphira had lied "to the Holy Spirit" and could explain by adding "You have not lied to men but to God" (Acts 5:3-4).

The church must confess the triune God, for all of the church has been baptized into the *one* "name of the Father and of the Son and of the Holy Spirit" (Matt. 28:19). He is the one and only God, who exists in three persons.

The Trinity in Our Lives.

In Article IX of the Belgic Confession we confess that we know the persons of the triune God "from the testimonies of Holy Scripture as well as from the effects of the persons, especially from those we feel within ourselves." We do not mean that our feelings constitute a second source for our knowledge of God, but we are saying that we experience in our lives the work of the triune God we know from the Bible. "The effects of the [divine] persons . . . we feel in ourselves." Once we fall into the good hands of God, we ourselves are the territory of his operations.

For how do we come to the Father? Through the Son. And how shall we approach the Son? By the Spirit. And how do we go to the Spirit? We don't go to the Spirit; he comes to us. Whenever the Word hits our ears, the Spirit of God knocks at the door of our inner selves. And when he has broken our resistance, the whole landscape of our lives becomes the field of operation of the triune God.

According to the general teaching of the Bible, the Father is above us, the Son is for us, and the Spirit is in us. We are creatures of the Father, we are restored by the work of the Son, and by the operation of the Spirit we become an offering of praise. Once we have been taken up into the magnetic field of God's operation, however, it is no longer possible for us to distinguish between the work of the Father, Son, and Spirit. In his operations God is always one.

In our ordinary Christian living we do not relate to three holy persons but to the one and only God in his threefold fullness. We must try to be "theologically correct" when speaking of God's work in us and for us and with us, but the Bible itself does not always maintain these distinctions. It says that the Spirit of God lives in us and that Christ dwells in us (Rom. 8:10-11). Jesus said that if we love him and live by the Word of our heavenly Father, Father and Son will make their home in our lives (John 14:23)—an awe-inspiring promise.

He who is above me and for me and in me is the same, for God is one. The unity of God-in-three-persons must be confessed in a creed, but the proof of the confession is in daily living.

We all know that, if we hate our neighbor but say we love God, we are liars (1 John 4:20). We cannot claim, through the Son, to have God as Father without having the love of God's Spirit within, for God is one. It is precisely because God is triune that a Christian cannot say to a needy brother or sister, "Go and be happy" (1 John 3:17, James 2:16). These are the very practical implications of the dogma of the Trinity. Or, in the words of the Belgic Confession, we know that God is triune not only from what we read in the Bible but by God's works that we feel in our lives.

All of us who have been Christians for some time know that God is above us and for us only when he is in us. It is only when we love and abide in love that we know God. Unless we have the Holy Spirit, we do not have the Father and the Son. And by the same token we can participate in the forgiveness of sins only when we forgive those who have sinned against us. For God is one.

He Is Our Song.

The deepest difference between believers and unbelievers is that believers know God and unbelievers don't. All other differences are the result of this fact.

And what is the highest thing we can do with this knowledge? We might be inclined to answer that our neighbors ought to be the beneficiaries of our knowledge of God. And it is undoubtedly true that God has appointed the people who bear his name to be the light of the world. But we and our neighbors have been created for one purpose: to praise God. All of us come to our goal when we can offer praise to the one true God. All talk about God, all sermons on God, and all books about God miss the point unless they help us to praise him.

The greatest moments in our lives are those in which we spontaneously come to the hymn of praise: "Praise to the Lord, O let all that is in me adore him!" When gratitude and love for God well up in our beings and we reach for God as our supreme joy, we walk on mountains of happiness. Perhaps you, too, have experienced that. Maybe it was in a worship service that you sang a song with so much inner strength and freedom that the walls of the building seemed to be in your way. The doxology always demands room. And the hymn of the free always requests everyone to join in. In Psalm 98, for example, Zion sings a song of salvation that reverberates throughout creation: it is supported by harps and trumpets; the sea resounds the praises; the rivers clap their hands; the mountains sing together. And now the church has been appointed as the cosmic choir director. We know the Lord, and we teach all nations to sing the praises of his name.

In such moments of praise we begin to understand that we were created for God. But we do not always know that. Our lives are lived on different levels, and too frequently we sit in the basement. God is often a problem for us. And when we come to him, it's nearly always as beggars: "Give me, bless me, help me, I, I, me, me. . . ." This is a real and seemingly unavoidable level of Christian living, while we live most of the time somewhere between the despair of the cellar and the joy of the mountaintop. But real living is praising God.

The meaning of life is found in God. Therefore you are not yet alive when you merely exist. And your greatest hour is not payday or graduation but when you start praising God. Then you are truly human, free, and great. In the doxology you climb the stairway to heaven and suddenly you find it easy to let go of everything: bread and butter, paycheck and furniture, money and misery—yes, even sickness and sin. You leave it all when you can say, "My God, oh, let all that is in me adore Thee!"

This is the hour in which you have grasped the truth that of him and through him and unto him are all things, even your troubles. It is the moment in which you bring it all to him. For once, you do not *ask*, but you *give* to God; and while you give, you know that he is the source of all your gifts.

You don't have to understand everything in order to come to the goal of living. People don't have to become theologians or artists in order to praise. Praise is the right of existence of the unintelligent, the weak, and the so-called burdens of society. This is why babies are important and why the old must be honored, even when their minds wander and their bodies are frail. They live for the glory of God. God can prepare praise out of their lives.

We must now begin to voice the doxology to God while on our way, you at your bedside and I at mine. "My God, how wonderful Thou art." Say it after the Lord's Supper or at the baptismal font or at sunset. Sing it at the baby's crib and in church school. Hum it with the organ on the wedding day and at the funeral service. "My God, oh, let all that is in me adore Thee!" For he is God. He can bless people with sorrow, and he can punish with prosperity. He can convert unrighteousness into justice and turn evil to our profit. He alone can do that because he is God. To him we bring glory today and tomorrow, next week and next year, and forever.

Lord's Day 9

THE CREATOR IS MY FATHER

***Q** What do you believe when you say: "I believe in God, the Father almighty, creator of heaven and earth"?*

***A** That the eternal Father of our Lord Jesus Christ, who out of nothing created heaven and earth and everything in them, who still upholds and rules them by his eternal counsel and providence, is my God and Father because of Christ his Son.*

I trust him so much that I do not doubt he will provide whatever I need for body and soul, and he will turn to my good whatever adversity he sends me in this sad world.

He is able to do this because he is almighty God; he desires to do this because he is a faithful Father.

—Q & A 26

We Are So Small.

Imagine that we could reduce the earth to the size of a little marble and place it on a table. Then we could place another marble, half the size of the first, two feet away from "earth." The second marble would be the moon. Three hundred feet away from the earth-marble we could set a ball the size of a volleyball: the sun. The sun is our nearest star. If we wanted to include the next star, we would have to place it in China because, although the sun is 93 million miles away from the earth, the distance to the next star is 300,000 times farther. Nine planets circle the sun, and planet Earth is not the biggest. But in the depth of space are countless other stars and planets, somehow kept together in whirling masses we call galaxies.

Only in the last few decades, since we have invented space probes and giant telescopes, have we begun to realize how unimaginably vast the universe is and how planet Earth is but a pinprick in space.

We Are So Vulnerable.

We have also discovered how vulnerable life is on this planet. Our little marble has an outside crust, and sometimes the crust cracks—just a slight movement—the earth quakes, and proud buildings crumble. Around our little marble is a blanket of air, the atmosphere. If that blanket were pulled away for an hour or so, everything on Earth would be burnt to a crisp by unfiltered heat from the sun. There are other threats to our existence, threats for which we bear direct responsibility: we can make the atmosphere of the world so foul that we inflict an incurable sickness on the life of our planet. Or we can press the buttons for our nuclear missiles and destroy ourselves.

On this tiny marble, with its many millions of tiny people, we make our confession of faith: "I believe in God, the Father almighty, creator of heaven and earth." These small persons on this tiny earth, this speck in the universe, claim that God is their Father!

Isaiah 40.

The Creator is our Father.

"Surely the nations are like a drop in a bucket"; (and who pays attention to a drop from a pail full of water?) "they are regarded as dust on the scales"; (you don't notice a speck of dust on a weighing scale); "he weighs the islands as though they were fine dust. Lebanon is not sufficient for altar fires, nor its animals enough for burnt offerings. Before him all the nations are as nothing; they are regarded by him as worthless and less than nothing" (Isa. 40:15-17).

How puny is a human being. Isaiah said it before the astronomers knew it.

But how unimaginably great is God!

"To whom, then, will you compare God?" (40:18). "To whom will you compare me? Or who is my equal?" says the Holy One.

"Lift your eyes and look to the heavens": (by all means, use your biggest telescopes; train your 100-inch reflecting telescopes on the far away lights) "Who created all these? He who brings out the starry host one by one, and calls them each by name. Because of his great power and mighty strength, not one of them is missing" (40:26).

Did you know that there are more stars in space than people on earth? And God knows every star.

If God is so great and we are so small, we might be inclined to think that we should not get too familiar with him. If Algonquin or Yellowstone Park is not sufficient as a sacrifice, surely we cannot have every John and Jane and Tony in Toronto and Chicago address him as "Father." And it takes some boldness to tell little Richard, when he gets his sandwich, that he should first close his eyes and say to him who keeps the galaxies together, "Lord, bless this food for Jesus' sake, Amen."

It is remarkable, though, that the reasoning in Isaiah 40 is exactly opposed to our inclination. Scripture does not say, "Because God is so great that nations are dust on the weighing scale, he cannot be bothered with Mom's headache and Rickie's sandwich." It says, "Because God is so great, how could you possibly say that he does not know you?"

"Why do you say, O Jacob, and complain, O Israel, 'My way is hidden from the LORD; my cause is disregarded by my God'? Do you not know? Have you not heard? The LORD is the everlasting God, the Creator of the ends of the earth. He will not grow tired or weary, and his understanding no one can fathom. He gives strength to the weary . . . " (40:27-29). Isaiah doesn't say, "How do you dare call him Father?" but, "How do you dare say that he does not see you? You are dealing with God the Father, Almighty, Maker of heaven and earth!"

God, Father, Almighty, Creator.

"I believe in God, the Father almighty, creator of heaven and earth." These words can be read in different ways. Ursinus said that God is called Father in distinction from the Son and that *Almighty* describes God as "creator of heaven and earth." It seems to be more correct, however, to read the confession as saying, "I believe in God, who is Father, who is almighty, and who is creator of heaven and earth."

God is Father, and there has never been a time when he was not (yet) Father. Therefore his title, *Father*, is not taken from human relationships and then applied symbolically to God. Fatherhood is original with God and is reflected in our fathers. The name *father* did not go up from us but came to us from above. God is the Father of all fatherhood, as the hard-to-translate phrase of Ephesians 3:15 has it. He is Father in the broadest and absolute sense: in him is life, and from him comes all that has life. God is the Originator, Beginning, "Father of spirits" (Heb. 12:9), "Father of lights" (James 1:17), "fountain of all good" (Belgic Confession, Art. I).

As creatures we call God *Father*, meaning the "triune being who is root, well, and origin of existence." We may see within the being of God a distinction between the Father and the Son. We speak of the "eternal Father of our Lord Jesus Christ." This is called the doctrine of eternal generation, and by it we mean that there was never a time when the Father was not yet Father or when the Son was not yet Son. Within God's being is an everlasting father-son relationship.

He is the Almighty. Hereby the Apostles' Creed does not mean one of God's many qualities, for he is also invisible, indivisible, all-knowing, and everywhere present. When confessing faith in God Almighty, the church says that before him we stand in awe. Knowing him, we are not surprised by miraculous deeds, but we expect miracles because he is God Almighty.

This God, who is eternally life and everlastingly Father, "created heaven and earth and everything in them" and he did so "out of nothing." "Heaven and earth" means reality as seen from the creature's side. "All that is in them" refers to all visible and invisible creatures. And God created "out of nothing" precisely because he is the Almighty.

Creation Versus Evolution.

The debate about creation or evolution concerns a matter that is much bigger than the question of the origin of the world. In fact, Christians must be careful that they don't allow themselves to be drawn into a debate with so narrow a focus. It isn't merely a matter of placing one "theory" over against another "theory" and then demanding equal time. Too often Christians have gone into such debates fearful of things they don't have to fear and asserting as truth matters that God has not revealed to us in Scripture. God has not revealed to us the age of the earth. And no Christian needs to be afraid of old bones, ancient dinosaur trails, or fossilized remains of "another age."

Evolutionism is much more than a theory about the origins of Earth and man. Evolutionism is a powerful assumption about reality, including humanity. It shows its godless character especially when it explains religion, freedom, or even human destiny. When the evolution-faith deals with these topics, it is much easier for Christians to combat.

Similarly, creationism is not merely a theory, to be taught in alternative day schools, about the origin of the universe. Creationism is a creed, an article of faith: "By faith we understand that the universe was formed at God's command" (Heb. 11:3). Of course such faith can also inform the geologist and the genetic anthropologist. But it does not promise to answer every geological question, though it rules out certain answers—theories, if you will. Our doctrine of creation does answer the basic religious questions. These questions cannot be answered by the evolutionist and are bound to embarrass him or her. The basic questions are: Who am I? Where do I come from? What is my destiny?

Everyone will admit that it makes a big difference whether we are created by God or happen to be here as a result of a chemical accident. If we "happen" to be here, we had better try to keep ourselves pleasantly occupied.

We should not ask many questions, for there cannot be answers. And some day or some night we will "happen" to die. But if we were created, then there is One, infinitely greater than we are, who made us for a purpose. For creation means purpose and destiny. Then the world has a Father, and we always exist in the presence of the Other, the One who encompasses our lives from the mysterious beginning to the even more mysterious end. We have been created, the universe is ruled by the counsel of God, and all of us have been set on a journey of which God himself is also the goal.

Fatherhood in Christ.

If people carefully scan the book of God's creation, they have at least some understanding that this world was fathered by God. "For since the creation of the world God's invisible qualities—his eternal power and divine nature—have been clearly seen, being understood from what has been made, so that men are without excuse" (Rom. 1:20). People are inclined to "suppress" this truth (1:18), with disastrous results. And, yet, even when they are open to God's revelation through starry heavens, dewdrops, and the inner voice of our creatureliness, none can find God as Father but through Jesus Christ.

Earlier we saw that the Bible does speak of God as eternal Father, beginning and origin of all good. But the Bible also teaches emphatically that we can experience the Father-child relationship only through Jesus. Therefore each of us confesses in the catechism: "The eternal Father of our Lord Jesus Christ is my God and Father because of Christ his Son." Although we live in God's own creation, in the Father's house, so to speak, we have become so alienated from God that we cannot love him as Father until we have experienced his saving love in the Son.

Yet when we know the Maker and Maintainer of the universe as our "Abba," we receive no special insight into the history of our planet. We don't even understand our personal weal and woe. But we have faith in our Father: "I trust him so much that I do not doubt he will provide whatever I need for body and soul, and he will turn to my good whatever adversity he sends me in this sad world."

Evil to Good.

Yes, you read that correctly: "He will turn to my good whatever adversity [evil] *he* [God] sends me in this sad world" (or "vale of tears"; in German, *jammerthal*). God will turn to my good whatever evil he first sends upon me. But should that not read that God will turn to my good whatever evil the devil sends my way? No, the catechism is right. The devil has much to do with it, and we should mention sin when we talk about "adversity" and the "vale of tears." But we are now confessing faith in God Almighty, the Sovereign who created heaven and earth and who rules them and upholds them without interruption. Because God reigns, he sends adversity. But we believe that, when it pleases him to deal with us harshly, he has a further plan for our profit.

Perhaps you say that you don't see that and that you find it hard to accept. But you cannot see a faraway star either. Only when the sky is very dark can you see a tiny speck of light. Yet that star is hundreds of times bigger than the whole earth. We have the unshakable guarantee that everything will be all right with you and me and all who love the Lord (Rom. 8:28).

And we don't have to give up on planet Earth. The earth is going to be all right. It's going to be free (8:21).

Therefore we are of good courage. We continue our work as a church in the world. We are not afraid to get deeply involved "in this sad world," this "valley of tears." As long as our faith has the right focus, we show an unworldly optimism. And when one of us faces a seemingly impossible obstacle, all of us recite our creed:

"I trust him so much that I do not doubt he will provide whatever I need for body and soul. . . . He is able to do this because he is almighty God; he desires to do this because he is a faithful Father."

In every valley and on every mountain we will sing the song together:

"This is my Father's world:
Why should my heart be sad?
The Lord is King, let the heavens ring!
God reigns; let the earth be glad."

Lord's Day 10

MY FATHER'S HANDS

***Q** What do you understand by the providence of God?*

***A** Providence is the almighty and ever present power of God by which he upholds, as with his hand, heaven and earth and all creatures, and so rules them that leaf and blade, rain and drought, fruitful and lean years, food and drink, health and sickness, prosperity and poverty—all things, in fact, come to us not by chance but from his fatherly hand.*

—Q & A 27

***Q** How does the knowledge of God's creation and providence help us?*

***A** We can be patient when things go against us, thankful when things go well, and for the future we can have good confidence in our faithful God and Father that nothing will separate us from his love. All creatures are so completely in his hand that without his will they can neither move nor be moved.*

—Q & A 28

Hands.

Three times Lord's Day 10 refers to the hand of God: God "upholds, as with his *hand*, heaven and earth and all creatures." Nothing happens to us by chance, but all things come "from his fatherly *hand*." And we confess that all things are so completely in God's *hand* that they cannot move or be moved without his will.

During my youth in the Netherlands everybody read the books of Anne De Vries on Bartje. In the first of these books Bartje stands at the deathbed of his father, who worked for a farmer in Drenthe. His father had many children and few pennies. A young horse has crushed Bartje's father's skull. Bartje's father is dead. As the boy looks at his dad here on the bed, he cannot take his eyes off his father's hands. To Bartje, his father's whole being was in those hands. Otherwise his father really was not so important. "His words were not many. His eyes were somber. But those hands, his whole life was engraved in those hands." Those hands once spanked Bartje, but they also carried him. Those hands saved him from drowning in the canal. Those hands worked—for him and for the others. They were shaped from holding a shovel. But those hands are now at rest. And while Bartje is trying to pray, he feels ashamed for having cursed the hands that spanked him.

God's people have always been fascinated by their Father's hands in creation (Ps. 19:1), providence (104:28), and salvation (118:15-16). God's children sing "All I have needed thy *hand* hath provided," "By his own *hand* he leadeth me," and "I am weak, but you are mighty; hold me with your powerful *hand*." When we die, we will say, as Jesus taught us, "Father, into your *hands* I commit my spirit" (Luke 23:46).

To confess God's providence is to contemplate the hands of our Father, who is in heaven.

Upheld by His Hand.

By the providence of God we mean that God upholds and rules everything. God personally maintains and governs the cosmos and all that is in it.

Some people like to speak of an ongoing creation. The thought is in Psalm 104. In this psalm the earth is a great garden protected (v. 9) and tended by an almighty God. Thanks to God's restless and powerful activity, trees can grow, cattle have grass, goats can climb, badgers can hide, and people can make a living (vv. 14, 24) and enjoy happy times (v. 15). Springtime is actually an act of creation: "When you send your Spirit, they are created, and you renew the face of the earth" (v. 30).

Speaking with the psalms, that is, speaking poetically, we may declare an ongoing creative activity of God. Although plants, animals, and people procreate, it is really God who creates new life on earth.

In Psalm 139 the poet says that God knows him so well because God was the one who "knit [him] together in [his] mother's womb" (v. 13). While speaking of God's activity in forming the embryo, the poet uses a remarkable but not altogether clear allusion to the creation of the first person, as if to underline that God's creation continues in human procreation: "My frame was not hidden from you when I was made in the secret place. When I was woven together in the depths of the earth, your eyes saw my unformed body" (vv. 15-16). This connection between the development of the embryo in the mother's womb and the original creation by God would explain the religious shudder of fear and joy that sensitive people experience before and during the birth of a baby.

This biblical and religious thinking and feeling form a sharp contrast with the prevailing mood of our culture. Most people seem to have a materialistic or secular understanding of life. *Secular* means the same as the more old-fashioned word *worldly. Secular* stands opposed to *sacred.* Secularism is a line of thinking and a set of values determined by the world, apart from God. Secularism is the tragedy of the Western world, but it is usually presented as our "liberation."

So when it comes to procreating, secular people talk freely about "making a baby" if family conditions are favorable and about "getting into trouble" if they are not. That's why some medical clinics, when a pregnancy test is positive, ask the standard question, "Are you going to abort, or do you want to keep it?" A generation that can be so cold at the springs of life itself has already lost its religious awareness in the ordinary, everyday routine of sunrise and sunset, "leaf and blade, rain and drought, fruitful and lean years, food and drink, health and sickness, prosperity and poverty"—all the things in which, according to our confession, we are supposed to see our Father's hand.

Two Old Enemies.

It is customary for Reformed preachers, when they are holding forth on the providence of God as we confess it in Lord's Day 10 of the Heidelberg Catechism, to combat deism and pantheism. I will adhere to that custom because these ancient foes are still around in new clothes.

Deism says that God is the first cause of everything but that, now that everyone is here, we live by natural laws and the light of reason. There is a god, but he does not *do* anything. He certainly does not uphold everything "as with his hand." The classic example is a clock: it is wound up "in the beginning," but it runs according to its built-in mechanism.

Countless people who have never even heard of this theory live as deists. They say that they believe in God, but their everyday living is Godless. They don't believe that God has anything to do with ordinary things like sickness and sunset. Perhaps God was the generator, they say, but it is our job to run the machine.

According to the biblical view, however, the world is like a big palace full of servants. All things move by the command of the King. He calls the stars, he sends ice, he feeds the fish, he keeps an eye on the sparrows, he establishes the mountains, and he keeps the names of his children right in front of him. No servant moves unless God commands. If he did not uphold the cosmos and issue commands, there would be no spring, summer, fall, or winter, no gravity, no muscles, no sound, and no light. At every moment the world and you and I are dependent on "the almighty and ever present power of God."

Pantheism is in some respects the opposite of deism. With deists God is so far away that he is out of sight, but with pantheists God is so close that he cannot be distinguished from his own work. Pantheists say that God is the lifestream of the universe. He is in you and in me and in all that lives. He is not a personal God above and beyond creation but is himself a part of creation. He is its hidden fire, nature's eternal soul, the ocean from which all of life derives and into which all rivers flow.

During the past twenty years many people in our society have rebelled against the rule of dollars and machines. So they have immersed themselves in "nature." Their creeds are popular forms of Eastern religions. They engage in some transcendental meditation and organic gardening. And they are mostly very sympathetic people.

Nature.

We should be on guard, though, whenever the word *nature* is used. Many who have no knowledge of God will begin to talk about nature as soon as they feel religious. They will even speak of "Mother Nature"—and not always jokingly. But the word *nature* does not come from a biblical environment. The Bible uses *creation* or *the earth* where we tend to speak of nature. It is wise to keep the word *creation* in one's vocabulary. When we call the environment "creation," no one will be inclined to attach independent existence to it. But we are far less likely to think of God when we say "nature," "laws of nature," or "freaks of nature." Imperceptibly the word *nature* takes a shape of its own. We want to spell it with a capital letter. *Nature* becomes a god or goddess. Or it remains a vague word that hides the religious embarrassment of secular orphans in a scientific age.

God is personal. For the deist and for the pantheist God is not a personal Father. For the deist he is an unmoved mover, and for the pantheist he is a warm blanket or a wild force.

We believe in a personal God who is our Father. We don't believe in nature; God is above nature. When we talk about the principles and rules that operate in our environment, we speak of "natural laws." We do not mean, of course, that nature has made certain laws. Nature is no lawgiver; God is. God is the sovereign who commands the Earth to rotate and the geese to migrate. And our King is no tyrant who gives arbitrary commands according to the whims of the moment. The almighty God is a faithful Father. His faithfulness characterizes his rule. And the reliability of God's reign makes science possible.

Thoroughly Religious.

We confess that God is in complete control of everything. "All things . . . come to us not by chance but from his fatherly hand" (Answer 27). "All creatures are so completely in his hand that without his will they can neither move nor be moved" (Answer 28). If God is God, he is in complete control. Therefore there is absolutely nothing that takes place outside of his government. Both Augustine and Calvin concluded that, if there is anything at all that can happen outside of God's providence, "the whole world revolves at random." They were right.

This teaching can be abused by those who lack piety and ambition.

In a Roman Catholic country the village priest would customarily ride through the fields on a donkey in springtime, when the farmers were seeding the soil. He would pronounce the blessings of God on the acreage, while the workers kneeled next to their tools. Once he came to the field of a notoriously lazy farmer. The field had not been plowed or fertilized. The priest made his donkey run as fast as it could, and he did not pray or bless until he came to the neighboring field. When the lazy farmer came to complain, the wise priest said, "God will bless only those fields that have manure on them."

We have no problem with this arrangement of God's. God uses "secondary causes." He makes rain fall and plants grow, but he has also ordained the conditions that are favorable to rainfall, plant growth, human health, and so on. And he has assigned certain responsibilities to us in these processes.

This teaching of God's all-embracing government is especially difficult for young Christians who have recently left the superstitious world of animism and who do not have an eye for secondary causes.

In Africa, where people are coming to Christ faster than people in Western Europe are forsaking him, changes in attitudes and lifestyles threaten to destroy all that many tribes have held sacred. They must adjust in twenty years to what we adjusted to in a few hundred years. Only a little while ago these people were thoroughly religious. Sowing a field was, first of all, a matter of religion. Bringing in a crop, building a house, conducting a funeral were ordinary activities that simply could not be done without pacifying the world of the spirits. Then came Westerners, the worldwise Westerners. They came with trucks and farm machinery and fertilizer. They showed that, in order to be successful, people should take matters into their own hands: "Give fertilizer to your fields and birth-control pills to your women."

However, with the stream of tractors, combines, and road machinery, missionaries arrived with Bibles and even with the Heidelberg Catechism—faithful missionaries, some from our own church, some sent specifically to teach farmers how to grow better crops. Through us God has sent hundreds of workers to Africa to tell the people that herbs and grain, "leaf and blade, rain and drought, fruitful and lean years, food and drink, health and sickness, prosperity and poverty—all things, in fact, come to us not by chance but from [God's] fatherly hand."

"What a confusion," someone might say.

But you and I must not doubt for a moment that, in the midst of the "future shocks" that hit all peoples, the government of this world remains in the strong hands of our heavenly Father. It is true that many Africans, while trying to escape the religious bondage of the past, are becoming victims of an even greater darkness: plain secularity, or this worldliness. Yet God is gathering his church in Africa as never before. On any Sunday, while we are preaching and hearing catechism sermons in our churches, more Christians are worshiping in churches established through the missionary work of the Christian Reformed Church than in the Christian Reformed Church itself. And I was moved to the core when I heard them say: "We have received the Spirit, not again unto fear [the fear of false gods with cruel claws] but the Spirit of adoption, by whom we cry, 'Abba, Father.'"

Don't worry that young Christians will misunderstand Lord Day's 10. They don't depend on us; they, too, are in our Father's hands.

It's Not Always "God's Will."

The Christian teaching that there is no chance or fortune but that all things come to us from God's hand also proves to be confusing to immature Christians.

A man was killed on the freeway because he missed a turn. He was driving at seventy miles per hour. He missed his turn because his senses were dulled by the alcohol he consumed before getting into the car. When his wife heard the news, she was first stunned, then she sobbed, and next she said, "It must have been God's will." It would have been a bad moment to say it, but you and I would have had the whole Bible on our side if we had said to the widow, "No, that was not God's will; drunk driving is *against* God's will."

How Many "Wills"?

Suppose your Christian friend has lost a loved one through death and someone was clearly at fault: he should not have drunk, or she should not have let the children out of her sight, or they should have covered that pit, or today everybody knows what nicotine does to your lungs, or .... I'm sure you can fill in your own example. What are you going to say to your Christian friend?

Anyone who finds it easy to know what to say is probably wrong. There is blame: disobedience, stupidity, willful sin, negligence. But there is also the obligation of *love*, to hide some things under a cloak of kindness. When kindness becomes an excuse, though, to say that wrong is right, we have lost integrity and credibility and are no longer servants of that which is good.

Somewhere in your conversation Lord's Day 10 will have to be applied or denied. This terrible thing happened in a world that is governed by the God and Father of our Lord Jesus Christ, by him who is also *our* Father. Perhaps we may have to say that it did not happen in accordance with God's will, but we cannot deny that it happened in a world where God rules. In that sense it remains "within God's will."

Lord's Day 11

JESUS SAVES

Q *Why is the Son of God called "Jesus," meaning "savior"?*

A *Because he saves us from our sins. Salvation cannot be found in anyone else; it is futile to look for any salvation elsewhere.*

—Q & A 29

Learning About the Son.

When the catechism explains to us what Christians need to know, it instructs us in the Apostles' Creed. It says we must know of God the Father and our creation, God the Son and our salvation, God the Spirit and our sanctification.

We have already thought about the work of God the Father—how he created and maintains the whole world and how he governs our lives. Now we are going to learn about the Son and our salvation. The catechism first considers the names and titles of the Son and then discusses his works. The names we must learn are *Jesus, Christ, only begotten Son,* and *Lord.* His works began with his coming from heaven to be born as a baby and will continue until his second coming as the Judge of the world.

Know His Name.

The child who was born in Bethlehem had to have a name. But Joseph did not have to find one, and Mary did not have to think of one. The angel had commanded, "You are to give him the name Jesus, because he will save his people from their sins" (Matt. 1:21). And an angel must be obeyed because he is a messenger of the Lord.

So the child's name became Jesus.

All of us have names. Names serve as handles. By means of our names we can call, indicate, "handle" each other. And all of us know that the name of the Son of God who took on human nature is *Jesus.* He became like us: he even had a name—and it was an ordinary name for a person in his place among his people. *Jesus,* or *Jehoshua,* was rather common. Literally the name says, "Jehovah saves."

Having names and giving names may be an ordinary business among us, but in the Bible and in the religious language of Christians this matter of *the* Name becomes very important. Christians are baptized in the Name, they pray every day that their Father's Name be hallowed, they are told by their Master to confess his Name, and they know that there is no other Name by which we can be saved than the Name of Jesus.

God's name or Christ's name means God or Christ as they have revealed themselves—and as we now know them.

Let's say that there is a young woman named Mary Jones. She is just another person with an ordinary name. But she is not just an ordinary person to John Brown, who is in love with her. He calls her "darling" and "sweetheart" and many other names. Finally the day or the night comes when they reveal what they are to each other. And he calls her "wife" and she whispers "husband." These names say who Mary Jones is to John Brown and who John Brown is to Mary Jones.

Imagine the day Joseph and Mary came to present their firstborn son: in the temple are more parents with babies; men are standing in small circles talking; women are standing and showing babies to each other. "And what is his name?" "His name is Jesus." "What a nice baby and a nice name."

Then an old man comes straight to Mary. His eyes are shining and his voice is trembling. And Mary hands over the baby because the man has the face and appearance of a prophet. He holds the baby and looks to heaven. Hear how he chants:

> Now may thy servant, Lord, according to thy word,
> depart in exultation.
> My rest shall be serene,
> for lo, mine eyes have seen
> thy wonderful salvation.

This is the first man to know the Name—"Call his name Jesus, for he will save his people from their sins."

There are still many people who call on the name of Jesus when they hurt their finger or when they talk about the World Series or the playoffs for the Stanley Cup. "Jesus," they say. At work they drop his name, and when they tell a joke they mention him.

It is bad that they "cuss." But it is worse that they are ignorant. They don't know him. In their lives there has never been a day—or a night—when the veils were lifted and the revelation took place. There has not (yet!) come a moment for them when they knew his name. They don't know yet who he is for them.

When a person comes to know Jesus, the cussing is over and the confession begins. And confession is a mutual affair—not only in marriage but in every covenant. When John knows her as his wife, Mary knows him as her husband. And when you confess the name of your Savior on earth, Jesus will confess your name before his Father in heaven. For in the Bible covenants hold for both parties, and they are made to last forever.

Saved from What?

What does it mean that Jesus "saves" us? From what does he save, and where are we after he has saved us?

In the basic sense, Jesus saves us from *death* to give us *life*. That's the ordinary sense in which we use the words *save* and *lifesaver*, for example. Think of a person drowning or in a burning house: a hero or a lover jumps into the water or dashes through the flames and pulls that drowning or burning person away from certain death. That's salvation. Or think of a child playing on railroad tracks. The train is coming, but the child does not hear it and does not move. You jump and grab the child and then carry him home and give him to his mother. That's an act of salvation from death to life.

The best-known Bible text says that God so loved the world that he sent Jesus so that "whoever believes in him shall not perish but have eternal life"

(John 3:16). To perish means to drown, to burn, to go to hell. And the everlasting opposite of pain and death and separation is eternal life.

In the basic sense, salvation is always from sin to goodness, from death to life.

All-inclusive Salvation.

We should admit that, when Jesus came into the world, people did not think he came to save them from *sin*. The Jewish people were looking for a savior from misery—all misery and especially the misery of Roman occupation. In Israel's history saviors were people, like the judges and the kings, who broke the yokes of tyrants. God sent those deliverers for just that purpose.

Now look at a well-known story in Luke 5 and see how Jesus introduced himself as the Savior. Friends of a polio patient, a paralyzed man, carried the poor fellow to Jesus, and when they could not get through the door of the house, they let him down through the roof, bed and all. "When Jesus saw their faith . . ."(v. 20). What kind of faith? It could not have been the kind of faith that acknowledges Jesus as Lord and Savior, the kind that makes you a Christian. No, it could not, because the "secret" of the Messiah had not yet been revealed; that is, God had not yet revealed that Jesus had to die for our sins and rise from death to inherit the kingdom. But it *was* faith in the sense that the man and his friends expected help from no one but Jesus. They had to get to Jesus, through the door or through the roof, because only Jesus could help. Note that the passage says he saw *their* faith. That must have included the men who carried the bed as well as the sufferer on the bed.

"Friend, your sins are forgiven" (v. 20). When Jesus said that, he surprised everybody and angered the theologians. "Who is this fellow who speaks blasphemy? Who can forgive sins but God alone?" (v. 21).

We must admit that the Pharisees of those days did have an insight that many contemporary church people have lost: sins are omissions and transgressions that render us guilty before God! It is *God's* prerogative to condemn and to forgive. The Pharisees were quite right when they accused Jesus of doing what only God can do.

And Jesus replied, "Which is easier: to say, 'Your sins are forgiven,' or to say, 'Get up and walk'?" (v. 23). He means to say that both are beyond human power: only God can forgive sins, and only God can make a lame man walk.

"But that [they might] know that the Son of Man has authority on earth to forgive sins," Jesus said to the paralyzed man, "I tell you, get up, take your mat and go home" (v. 24).

Note carefully how he said that: the one thing that everybody must know is that the Son of man has authority on earth to forgive sins. *Son of man* is a title for the Messiah. Jesus always used this name for himself. In the book of Daniel it is the Son of man who gets the everlasting kingdom from the One who sits upon the throne (Dan. 7:13-14). So Jesus put enormous emphasis on this title. The people in the crowded house had to recognize the divine power given to him. He made the paralyzed man walk *in order that* we should know he has the authority to forgive sins.

Priorities in the Kingdom.

Certainly, the Jews were right in expecting a savior like the judges and the kings. Once deliverance is accomplished, *all* misery will be flushed away. We too can expect redemption in the Son of man, whom God has clothed with authority. He saves the businessman, and he will save the business. Jesus brings a salvation into this world that leaves no room for poverty, injustice, sickness, and death; all of it must disappear. All sufferers in all hospitals will some day hear: "Take up your bed and go home." But there is an order in the coming of the kingdom of God and in the dismantling of the kingdom of this world.

First, Christ goes to the *cause* of our curse and the *heart* of our misery: "Friend, your sins are forgiven." But Jesus also makes the blind see and the lame leap. These are evidences of the presence of God's kingdom. He does not say, however, by healing the cripples and cleansing the lepers, that now this kind of suffering is past. No, the *order* of the coming of the kingdom of God must still be observed. A first enemy and a last enemy must be destroyed. The last one is death (1 Cor. 15:26). Death is the final item on God's agenda for the dismantling of the kingdom of evil.

There is also a priority in the revelation of the kingdom of God. Its first fruit is the forgiveness of sin; its last is the new creation. The order is first the cross and then the crown. That does not mean that God cannot show flashes of glory today. Sometimes—and for his own reasons—God raises the sick and overthrows the unrighteous as if to assure us that suffering and injustice will not remain forever.

Our first need—and God's first gift—is the forgiveness of sin. Therefore, when we confess that Jesus saves, we know that his salvation covers all of life and all of the globe. But what is first must come first.

Jesus Alone.

Many things, many people, and many ideologies promise salvation. But Jesus is the only Savior authorized by God to bring the kingdom. He has saved us from sin, and he will give us the eternal kingdom.

The Jesus of the Scriptures is the Savior we need because he alone can say, with the voice of God, "Your sins are forgiven."

Perhaps he is not the Savior people like. He certainly is not the Savior we want. But it is God's truth that he is the Savior we need.

Hunger is hard, and millions pray to be delivered from it. Poverty is a shame, and multitudes are looking for a way out. Sickness is painful and debilitating, and patients and all who love them cry for a saving medicine. Death is heartrending, and we are willing to spend all that we have in order to keep living. Oppression by tyrants is intolerable for people who are meant to be free. All the enslaved look for a savior. But to live and die in sin is the worst of all! Becoming aware of this reality is the first sign of salvation.

Even if you don't understand it, please try to believe it: all trouble starts here. We have no hope and no future as long as we have no peace with God. But there is now no reason for anyone to remain in sin, because God has sent the Savior. He is exactly the One we need, because he begins at the roots. First he deals with sin, and at last he makes us ready to inherit a new world.

Sometimes we get irritated by churches and preachers who play but one string with their bows: Jesus saves; he died for our sins. Yet such a gospel and such company are a thousand times better than that of those who merely reflect on the history of religions and who offer the latest fixes for human salvation.

We must have our priorities in the right order: do not say that our first needs are for jobs, bread, and health. All of us need first a Savior. All of us need Jesus, or we have nothing.

***Q** Do those who look for their salvation and security in saints, in themselves, or elsewhere really believe in the only savior Jesus?*

***A** No. Although they boast of being his, by their deeds they deny the only savior and deliverer, Jesus. Either Jesus is not a perfect savior, or those who in true faith accept this savior have in him all they need for their salvation.*

—Q & A 30

All-sufficient Savior.

When the Heidelberg Catechism has us say that those who seek salvation and security in saints or in their own works actually deny the sufficiency of God's appointed Savior, it obviously is speaking about Roman Catholics.

The catechism often refers to the sins and shortcomings of the Roman Catholic Church because it was written in 1563. Throughout the catechism we are told not only what the Bible teaches and what we ought to believe but also what the Roman Catholic Church has done with that biblical truth. For us who live near the close of the twentieth century, this denouncing of Roman Catholics can be annoying or embarrassing. And we wonder whether we look arrogant and whether we sound as if we know things better than anybody else.

The Heidelberg Catechism is not alone in contrasting truth with error. The Scriptures set gospel truth against false teachings and prophets throughout. Yet the Bible also teaches *how* to speak of false teachers and teachings. For us it's hard to guess what was taught by those immoral teachers whom Paul said lived "as enemies of the cross of Christ." "Their god is their stomach," he said, "and their glory is their shame" (Phil. 3:18,19). Paul does not tell us *what* these false teachers said, but for us it's important to note *how* Paul said it. He said it repeatedly, and he said it "with tears."

We have no right to teach each other about the sins of the Roman Catholics if we do not "tearfully" speak with them about the great evil of seeking salvation and security in saints and good works rather than in the all-sufficient Mediator God has given.

Lord's Day 12

THE MESSIAH AND HIS PEOPLE

Q ***Why is he called "Christ," meaning "anointed"?***

A ***Because he has been ordained by God the Father and has been anointed with the Holy Spirit to be our chief prophet and teacher who perfectly reveals to us the secret counsel and will of God for our deliverance; our only high priest who has set us free by the one sacrifice of his body, and who continually pleads our cause with the Father; and our eternal king who governs us by his Word and Spirit, and who guards us and keeps us in the freedom he has won for us.***

—Q & A 31

His Office: Messiah

Many people think that *Christ* is Jesus' nickname or that it is his last name. But church people know better. *Jesus* is the personal name of the Savior, and *Christ* is his official name.

When I say "George Washington, the President," *George Washington* is his personal name, and *the President* is his official name. *President* describes the office he holds, the job that has been assigned to him. Similarly *Christ* describes the office Jesus holds and the task assigned to him. *Christ* is the Greek word for the Hebrew word *Messiah.* The English term is *Anointed One.*

Actually one has to be a Jew—or very familiar with the Old Testament, the Jewish Bible—to really appreciate the word *Messiah.* During the past twenty-five years or so, a large number of Jews have been converted to Christ. But they don't call themselves Christians. They call themselves Messianic Jews. They mean to say, "We are what we have always been: Jewish people. But we have found the Messiah, and his name is Jesus! We are Messianic Jews." Or, "We are Jews for Jesus."

Early Christians Were Jews.

Any Jew who is aware of his or her heritage looks for the Messiah. The Messiah is the Son of David, appointed by God and anointed by the Holy Spirit to restore Israel. Israel's national purpose was to produce the Messiah.

Not only the Jews but many other nations knew that it was the Jews' privilege to bring forth the king who would usher in a new era. The wise men from the east looked for his star (Matt. 2), and a Samaritan woman shared the expectation: "I know that Messiah . . . is coming. When he comes, he will explain everything to us" (John 4:25). The king would be a prophet through whom God would explain his will with finality—and even a loose-living Samaritan woman had heard the rumor about him.

The church of Christ consists of people who confess that Jesus is the promised Messiah. About halfway through his official earthly ministry, Jesus asked, "Who do you say I am?" And Simon Peter answered, "You are the

Messiah" (Matt. 16:16, Mark 8:29, Luke 9:20). But since our New Testament is in Greek, the word *Messiah* is given as *Christ.* John sometimes uses the word *Messiah* in Greek letters and then gives the Greek name, *Christ,* right after it. Thus Andrew reports to his brother Simon: "'We have found the Messiah' (that is, the Christ)" (John 1:41).

The deepest question that everyone must answer is, Who is Jesus? And the true confession is this: Jesus is the Christ, or Messiah, or God's Anointed. And God will not hold guiltless those who deny it. "Who is the liar? It is the man who denies that Jesus is the Christ. Such a man is the antichrist—he denies the Father and the Son" (1 John 2:22).

Appointed and Anointed.

His name is Christ, says the catechism, "Because he has been ordained by God the Father and has been anointed with the Holy Spirit" to be our prophet, priest, and king.

Christ's calling began (and who knows the beginning?) with ordination by the Father. That means he was appointed for his office in the council of God. We don't quite understand that, but the Bible says that "he was chosen before the creation of the world" (1 Pet. 1:21). And "in him we were also chosen" (Eph. 1:11). Christ and all Christians are ordained by the Father and anointed by the Spirit to perform an assignment. The Father calls us, and the Spirit gives us power to obey the call. The Father gives the job; the Spirit qualifies us to do the job.

What began in the halls of the triune God became a historical event at the baptism of Jesus: then and there he was appointed and anointed.

John the Baptizer did not know what to make of it. He was administering the baptism of repentance for the remission of sins. Therefore he declined to baptize Jesus. One does not wash those who are clean. But Jesus said that he and John had to obey the will of God. So Jesus stepped into the Jordan. He stood in a place of sinners. He went into the water where John was washing the dirt of the world away. He thus showed that he was accepting the assignment God had given him. He took the first step on the way that would lead to the cross. Then heaven reaffirmed his ordination: "You are my Son, whom I love; with you I am well pleased" (Luke 3:22).

At the Jordan the Spirit descended on Jesus. This was the anointing. Jesus then became what he was called to be: the Messiah. In the Old Testament, kings and priests were anointed with oil, and the oil was a symbol of the Holy Spirit. When Samuel, sitting in the house of Jesse, saw the shepherd boy come in, the Lord said: "'Rise and anoint him; he is the one.' So Samuel took the horn of oil and anointed him in the presence of his brothers, and from that day on the Spirit of the Lord came upon David in power" (1 Sam. 16:12-13).

When Jesus was anointed, no oil was used, but the Spirit himself appeared in the form of a dove.

We need the same Spirit, and we receive the same Spirit. No one—not even Jesus—can do a work for God without being appointed by the Father and anointed by the Spirit.

Threefold Office.

During the Old Covenant, God related to his people through three offices: prophet, priest, and king. A prophet is someone who speaks for God to the people. A priest brings the people to God through sacrifice and prayer. A king rules over the people on behalf of God.

In the New Covenant, all these offices are climaxed and fulfilled in Jesus. The Messiah makes God known to us, leads us to the Father, and rules over us forever.

Chief Prophet and Teacher.

The catechism says that Jesus "perfectly reveals to us the secret counsel and will of God for our deliverance."

When the relationship to God was set by the terms of the Sinai covenant, no one could know God's revelation except Moses.

When Moses' end approached, he said to the people, "God will raise up for you a prophet like me from among your own brothers. You must listen to him" (Deut. 18:15).

Peter said that Jesus, "the Christ," was the prophet announced by Moses. And he added, "Anyone who does not listen to him will be completely cut off from among his people" (Acts 3:23).

In the Old Testament, Moses is the prophet through whom God gave the law, and Elijah is the thundering voice that calls a straying people back to God's Word. But when Jesus is on the mount of transfiguration—tasting heavenly glory at the portals of his final suffering—Moses and Elijah greet him as the chief Prophet. And heaven confirms his office: "This is my Son, whom I love . . . . Listen to him!" (Matt. 17:5)

Unless we listen to Jesus, we will remain ignorant. He is the eternal Word who became flesh. He communicates to us the final revelation of God.

King and Priest.

The office of king is the most natural connection with the Messiah. That's what most Israelites thought of when the messianic hope flared in their hearts. They longed for the appearance of the Son of David, the King who would right what was wrong, who would defeat the tyrants to set up an everlasting kingdom. When Jesus said that the kingdom of God was about to be revealed, people started to wonder if Jesus could be the Messiah. But his suffering and death seemed to end those hopes. "We had hoped that he was the one who was going to redeem Israel," said Cleopas and his friend (Luke 24:21). Whoever says "I had hoped" admits disappointment.

The mystery of Messiah Jesus is that he had to give his life as an offering in order to reign as Lord. Our Messiah became a king by accepting the role of the lamb. He is King because he was willing to be Priest. And his journey from cross to crown has patterned the lifestyle of all who follow him.

In Revelation 5:5-6 the whole mystery of the King-Priest is summed up in one picture. When John sheds tears because the plan and purpose of history remain hidden—the scroll is sealed in the hand of God—an elder says that there is a hero who will execute the plan, to whom it is given to hold the helm of history and to steer the course of the world. So John is prepared to see "The Lion of the tribe of Judah, the Root of David," the great and mighty one. "Then I saw a Lamb, looking as if it had been slain," says John.

This Lamb who is a Lion, who reveals to us the heart of God, is the only true Messiah, ordained by God and filled with his Spirit.

Devalued Christians.

This is one of the most important answers in the catechism. Sometimes the catechism bears the marks of the thought patterns and controversies in which its authors were caught. Some questions and answers ought to be reformulated, updated, and improved. But Answer 32 is a confession to which the church must return. It's a truth from which we have strayed.

> ***Q** But why are you called a Christian?*
>
> ***A** Because by faith I am a member of Christ and so I share in his anointing. I am anointed to confess his name, to present myself to him as a living sacrifice of thanks, to strive with a good conscience against sin and the devil in this life, and afterward to reign with Christ over all creation for all eternity.*
>
> *—Q & A 32*

You know what devaluation is: when the dollar is no longer a dollar but seventy-five cents or so, we speak of a devalued dollar.

In religion, devaluation began long before it hit the economy. The catechism rightly says that a Christian is someone who belongs to Christ by faith and shares in what Christ has; the Christian has the Spirit of Christ. That's the golden standard for being Christian. But in a period of devaluation someone whose father or grandmother was active in church and who has not explicitly broken with the institution is also called a Christian. Christianity has devalued to "churchianity." It would be comical if it weren't so serious. Go around the block and ask people for "their religion." Only some fanatics will deny that they belong to a church. Most people whose parents live or lived in North America will mention a church. People still know the name of the church they are not attending.

In periods of religious devaluation the discovery of Christianity's true and ordinary value is always startling. Thus Watchman Nee startled people with his discovery that "ordinary" Christians have died to sin and are now alive with Christ. C. S. Lewis called his rich rediscovery of the Christian faith "mere" Christianity, and Lewis Smedes calls the golden standard for ethical behavior "mere" morality. In the same way we should reread Question and Answer 32 of the catechism and apply the golden standard to our devalued Christian environment and to our own understanding of what it means to be a Christian. This confession describes an ordinary Christian: one who by faith received Christ, shares in Christ's Spirit, and has been called and anointed to do a job, a threefold job: prophet, priest, and king.

The Definition.

The catechism is not interested in a historical description of the name *Christian.* It gives a theological, confessional definition.

Historically the name was probably first used by non-Christians as a nickname for the new group: "The disciples were first called Christians at Antioch" (Acts 11:26). But when Agrippa asked Paul, "Do you think that in such a short time you can persuade me to be a Christian?" (Acts 26:28), it was his understanding that a Christian is someone who accepts Jesus as the promised Messiah. And when Peter wrote, "if you suffer as a Christian, do not be ashamed, but praise God that you bear that name" (1 Pet. 4:16), the word *Christian* already had the rich idea of sharing in all that belongs to Christ, a concept that's worked out in the catechism.

Anointing Follows Faith.

"By faith I am a member of Christ and so I share in his anointing," says the catechism. It is not true that I must first prove I am anointed or Spirit-endowed in order to qualify for membership in Christ. That would destroy grace. No, Christianity starts with faith: humble and confident acceptance of Jesus as the Christ. Merely believe that what he claims about himself (what the Bible tells about him) is really true. Confess it and confess him. Rely on that Word and rely completely on him. Then you are incorporated in him, forgiven by his blood, renewed by his Spirit.

Nobody can have a share in Christ's blood without sharing in his Spirit. No one can have forgiveness without renewal. "And if anyone does not have the Spirit of Christ, he does not belong to Christ" (Rom. 8:9).

Neopentecostalism has rightly emphasized that without the anointing of the Spirit we are at best what they call "carnal Christians." The catechism said it before they said it. One should not be too dogmatic, however, about the "second blessing" and teach that the way in which the Samaritan believers were incorporated into the life of Christ and his church is now the rule for all of us (Acts 8). Rather, where the gospel is received, the Spirit enters. The Bible is "dogmatic" on that point. On the other hand, none of us should be averse to, and all of us should eagerly be reaching for, the second third, and fourth blessing. For being a Christian is a growing experience, and the fullness of the Spirit is a promise for all who obey the command to be filled.

For All Christians.

Ideally church-membership and Christ-membership are the same thing. As I said earlier, "churchianity" tends to replace Christianity. But where the true church is gathered, the living Lord is himself at work. And what he says in his Word he confirms by the sacraments: we are forgiven by the blood and renewed by the Spirit. He was killed on the cross but rose to a new life. We were dead and buried in the old man but made alive in the new man. Christians always have the two sides and never have the one without the other: we are members of Christ by faith alone and are therefore participants in the anointing.

This double blessing holds for all Christians. The catechism rightly quotes Acts 2:17 to remind us that the Spirit anoints, without discrimination, old and young, slave and free (that is, without social prejudice), and men as well as women (that is, without sexist bias). Scripture says to the whole congregation: "You have an anointing from the Holy One, and all of you know the truth" (1 John 2:20). In these last days, the Spirit of Christ has made each of us an office holder. All Christians are appointed and anointed for a prophetic, priestly, and royal task.

General and Special Offices.

The office of all believers is the *general* office. The church also recognizes three or four *special* offices as gifts of Christ for the upbuilding of its members. Today we recognize four of them: minister or teaching elder, presbyter or ruling elder, deacon, and evangelist. But the classic trio is preacher, elder, and deacon, in which we have been taught to see Christ as prophet (the preacher), Christ as ruler (the elder), and Christ as priest (the deacon).

The special offices are necessary in the church for good order and growth. But the general office—the office of all believers—is much more important. As a matter of fact, the special offices exist only to stimulate all members in exercising the general office. And if the special offices (preacher, elder, deacon) do not manage to cause the growth of the church members, they fail to fulfill the function Christ assigned to them (Eph. 4:11-14).

Whenever in church history all members stand in awe of a special office, a perversion of values and an invasion of worldliness occur. This was the antibiblical situation that necessitated the Reformation of the sixteenth century. But the worrisome thing is that the special office always tends to exalt itself at the expense of the office of all believers.

This Is Your Life.

Christians are people who have a job to do and a mission to accomplish. We have a job, and we have a Job. We aren't merely clerks, computer whizzes, factory workers, teachers, students, homemakers, lab technicians, carpenters, and whatnot, but we are all officebearers. We belong to Christ; therefore we have been appointed and anointed for prophetic, priestly, and royal tasks. We have been empowered to render a particular service.

"The life that I now live in the flesh" is the fulfillment of my office, and my "retirement" is my promotion to glory—to reign forever, to sing forever, and to give without reservation.

Life is not eating, drinking, mating, growing old, seeing the doctor, paying the bills, keeping going until we are finally let down into a hole, six by three feet. Jesus saved us from this kind of slow death; Christ appointed us to another style: life is the fulfillment of the calling. The nobility of living is holding office. And it is this office that lends dignity to whatever job we are doing. God's officebearers can hold any jobs, as long as they fulfill their offices!

Three Aspects of the Office.

The catechism declares, "I am anointed to confess his name." Every church member has been anointed to confess Christ's name in the world. All of us must live prophetically. We are the people of the Word, and our lives are graciously used to spell out the message.

I am appointed and anointed "to present myself to him as a living sacrifice of thanks." Everyone in the congregation is a thank offering. Everyone's life is a flame that burns for God. In a world where everyone grabs when the grabbing is good, we are a priestly race because we have been saved to serve.

And we are not being ruled by the spirits of our age, but we are equipped by the Spirit to do our part in the great war. There is war and we must fight. In our culture our peers are shooting for early retirement, winter cruises, and windfall profits. But if we get any "breaks," it will be in order to fight better. The people of the Messiah hunger and thirst for righteousness. They fight against sin and evil "with a good conscience," says the catechism. That means they fight without making secret alliances with the enemy.

We did not appoint ourselves to this great task; God ordained us to live this life. We may despair of the kind of life to which God has appointed us. But God makes no mistakes. Besides, he also anoints, or qualifies, us to be what he has called us to be and to do what he requires us to do. And since he who has called us is faithful and never far away, we will at last share in his glory just as we are now bearing the cross.

Lord's Day 13

OUR BROTHER AND OUR LORD

***Q** Why is he called God's "only [begotten] Son" when we also are God's children?*

***A** Because Christ alone is the eternal, natural Son of God. We, however, are adopted children of God—adopted by grace through Christ.*

—Q & A 33

Three Circles.

The children of God come in two kinds, says the catechism. But there is only one of the first kind: Jesus is the "eternal" and "natural" Son of God. The other children are God's sons and daughters by adoption.

Actually, the Bible is more generous than the catechism in using the phrase "children of God." Paul said that pagan poets are right in singing that all of us are God's offspring (Acts 17:28). And perhaps you remember those beautiful lines from the book of Job that say God laid the earth's foundations "when the morning stars sang together and all the sons of God shouted for joy" (Job 38:7, RSV). By *sons of God* the book of Job means "angels" (cf. 1:6, 2:1).

Creator God has parented the whole cosmos. Therefore everything and everybody in heaven and on earth have been "named" after him (Eph. 3:15). But among people we see three circles. The widest circle includes all people. In the original, creaturely sense, all people are God's children. But they have become so estranged from their Father that the Bible also calls them children of disobedience and objects of wrath. Although they can never shake their most original connection to God, all people resemble their Father so poorly that only when they are "born again" may they properly be called God's children. Thus, within the widest circle that embraces all human beings there is a smaller circle of those who have been adopted as God's children. And finally there is the one original Child of God: Jesus.

The Only Begotten Son.

The strange-sounding term *only begotten* first of all indicates how precious this child is to his or her parent. In the original Greek the term is used, for instance, for the widow of Nain's only son, who was being carried to his grave when the Lord stopped the funeral procession (Luke 7:11-17). The word means "only," "beloved," "favorite." That's why the best-known Bible text, John 3:16, carries such a load of pain and compassion: "God so loved the world that he gave his one and only son. . . ."

But the term *only begotten* not only says something about the unique love relationship of the Son and the Father; it also hints at the unique birth relationship between them.

Begotten comes from *beget*, which means "to become the father of." To beget means to get something of the same kind as yourself. A man begets children, a beaver begets beavers, and a bird begets eggs that become little birds. Humans make cradles, beavers build dams, and birds make nests. But what they *make* does not have the nature of the maker (only the mark of the maker). What they have *begotten* shares their being (C. S. Lewis).

We confess through the catechism that Christ "is the eternal, natural Son of God." It's impossible for us to think that through. For us there is a time when we are not yet fathers or mothers and then a time when we get a son or daughter. But of God the Father we confess that there was never a time when he was not yet Father, and of God the Son we say that there was never a time when he was not. In the being of God is an eternal father-son relationship. God is not stillness and lonesomeness. God is always movement and relationship, for God is love.

Adopted by God.

"We, however, are adopted children of God—adopted by grace through Christ."

In a family, strangers do not have the same rights as children. Only my brothers and sisters have the right, with me, to call my parents father and mother. Once a stranger has been adopted, however, she or he receives all the rights of the children—even rights of inheritance.

Becoming a child of God is something that happens *to* us; it's not something we do. God does the adopting, and he does it "by grace through Christ."

I can still remember the first line in my high school French reader: *Je suis un enfant trouvé*—"I am a foundling," a child who was found. That comes from the time when desperately poor peasants or unwed mothers would put newborn children on rich and benevolent people's doorsteps, hoping the children would be adopted. Such children would be sure of a future only if the rich took pity on them. Today these scenes are repeated in Third World countries.

Sometimes I think of these lines from the catechism when I see parents bringing their child to be baptized. In that ceremony the parents are really laying the baby on the doorstep of God's dwelling, trusting that he will give it his name. And I think that the first thing that child should confess, as soon as she is able, is something like that line in my French reader: *Je suis un enfant trouvé*—I am a foundling, but God gave me his name.

An Active Role.

Though being adopted into God's family is as passive as being laid at his feet and being lifted up by his arms, we must not think we can be part of God's family while our will is neutral. "To all who received him [the eternal Son, or Word], to those who believed in his name, he [Christ] gave the right to become children of God—children born not of natural descent, nor of human decision or a husband's will, but born of God" (John 1:12-13).

We do not *assume* the right of children. The Bible says clearly that the right is *given* to us. That gift must be *received.* And "receiving him" is explained by the words *believing in his name*. A person must yield his or her life to Jesus Christ. One should completely trust the claims of the Word of God and very practically obey Christ. That's what it means to "receive" him, or to "believe in his name."

Thus we must not only tell our baptized children that they are adopted by the heavenly Father but also ask them to "receive" Jesus and to "believe in his name."

Amazement.

Our adoption into God's family transfers us from rags to riches. Some of the splendor of being God's children must be experienced in the present life, though most of it will be revealed later, in the great reunion.

I used to think of our adoption as a purely legal matter; now I know that it is more. It is not only a *declaration*—like justification—but through it we receive something of God's substance in us. We all agree that *the* Son shares fully in the life of the Father. We should also agree that *all* children share a measure of this life. It is in us right now, wonderfully fresh, full of light and hope.

As soon as I write or say this, I'm afraid that I am stating too much. But I have learned also that this fear-of-overstatement is part of being God's adopted child. I can hardly believe that I am the rich person the Bible says I am. "The Spirit himself testifies with our spirit that we are God's children" (Rom. 8:16). Good thing he does: it is a new and amazing reality. The first letter of John shows the same kind of amazement, bordering on this feeling that our adoption is too good to be true: "How great is the love the Father has lavished on us, that we should be called children of God!" And because John feels the resistance and the toning down in his own heart and in the hearts of his hearers, he exclaims, "And that is what we are!" (3:1).

Estrangement.

The reality of our adoption amazes us about ourselves and estranges us from our unbelieving neighbors. By *estranges* we do not mean that we run away from them or isolate ourselves from them; rather, we go to them with a new kind of concern. For we now learn to love with the kind of love that is in God, that was revealed in Jesus, and that is poured into our hearts by the Spirit. Spiritual separation does not mean physical isolation.

When we are consciously living as children of the holy God, we notice ever more clearly how little we have in common with those who belong to the old and passing world.

"He who does what is sinful is of the devil. . . . No one who is born of God will continue to sin, because God's seed remains in him; he cannot go on sinning, because he has been born of God. This is how we know who the children of God are and who the children of the devil are: Anyone who does not do what is right is not a child of God; neither is anyone who does not love his brother" (1 John 3:8-10).

Coming Reunion.

If our present life as God's children is so amazing that we have to be convinced of it by the Word and the Spirit and by the communion of saints, then the future life, when we move into our Father's living room, is almost too much to contemplate.

"Dear friends, now we are children of God, and what we will be has not yet been made known. But we know that when he appears, we shall be like him, for we shall see him as he is." Contemplating that future, however, does not move us to speculation but (again) to clean and righteous living:

"Everyone who has this hope in him purifies himself, just as he is pure" (1 John 3:2, 3). The more we estrange ourselves from sin, the closer we get to our real home. We must all behave as worthy members of the family into which we have been adopted, keeping our eyes on our eldest Brother.

Our "Lord."

In teaching us about God the Son and our deliverance, the catechism explains first his name, Jesus, which means "Savior," and then his titles: Christ (and why we are Christians), only Son (and that we are God's children), and Lord (and that we are his servants).

When we confessed Christ as "eternal, natural Son of God," we thought of him in light of his origin—what he was from the beginning. But when we think of him as our "Lord," we think of a title he acquired after he had lived and died on earth. After he had humbled himself and after he had become "obedient to death—even death on a cross . . . God exalted him to the highest place and gave him the name that is above every name." That's the position he holds until every knee will bow "and every tongue confess that Jesus Christ is Lord" (Phil. 2:8-11).

Q ***Why do you call him "our Lord"?***

A ***Because—not with gold and silver, but with his precious blood—he has set us free from sin and from the tyranny of the devil, and has bought us, body and soul, to be his very own.***

—Q & A 34

Lordship.

This is what got the early Christians into trouble: confessing Jesus as Lord. And it will get *you* into trouble.

The early Christians got into trouble with their fellow Jews because they gave to Jesus honor that was due to Jehovah alone. For the same reason we offend the so-called Jehovah's Witnesses. But Jesus deserves that honor. He must be distinguished from the Father, but he cannot be separated from him.

The early Christians also got into trouble with the Romans, because the Roman emperors demanded absolute allegiance and the Christians' ultimate loyalty was to Jesus. They believed that even the emperor would someday bow to Christ. So they refused to bow to Caesar. They could not afford to sacrifice to the emperor. They preferred to die rather than deny Jesus as Lord. This basic Christian confession may still get us into trouble with our peer groups, with current public opinion, with the governing spirit in most areas of life, and, sometimes, with our governments.

It is always better to obey the Lord than to try to please any other person or power.

Lords and Servants.

When we confess Jesus as oldest Brother, we join his family. When we confess him as Lord, we are enlisted in his army. Both are realities of biblical Christianity. But we must not exaggerate the distance between Brother and Master. This Master has been a slave. And all who serve our Lord must serve him in the Spirit in which he served.

This means, very practically, that we must think of our lives as service. "The Son of Man did not come to be served, but to serve" (Matt. 20:28). We live, work, and have our aspirations under the same motto.

In washing his disciples' feet, Christ summarized his mission as in a parable: "Do you understand what I have done for you? . . . You call me 'Teacher' and 'Lord,' and rightly so, for that is what I am. Now that I, your Lord and Teacher, have washed your feet, you also should wash one another's feet" (John 13:12-14). We acknowledge Jesus as Lord when we serve each other. We are true followers of him who laid down his life for us when we "lay down our lives for our brothers" (1 John 3:16).

Powerful King.

Some evangelical Christians say that since his resurrection and ascension Jesus has become Lord but has not yet become King. That's a frivolous distinction they introduce only because they have to cling to a theory that Jesus must sit on a throne in earthly Jerusalem before he is the powerful King announced in the Scriptures of the Old Testament. In other words, Jesus would have to come back once again. Then he would be the kind of earthly Messiah that he said he wasn't when he first came to his people.

As a matter of fact, Jesus is now exactly the kind of powerful King, David's Son and David's Lord (Psalm 110:1), whom the Scriptures said he would be. But he rules his messianic kingdom by no worldly means; nor does the expansion of his kingdom depend on people and their armies.

The Bible portrays Christ as Lord: both as a king in the line of David and as a master who has paid for and now possesses us as his slaves. The catechism concentrates on the latter, reminding us throughout that Christ paid with his blood to make us completely (body and soul) his own. And that picture assures us that, because our Lord first paid so dearly and now is so powerful, he is not likely to let us go again.

Lord's Day 14

HE STOOPED TO CONQUER

***Q** What does it mean that he "was conceived by the Holy Spirit and born of the virgin Mary"?*

***A** That the eternal Son of God, who is and remains true and eternal God, took to himself, through the working of the Holy Spirit, from the flesh and blood of the virgin Mary, a truly human nature so that he might become David's true descendant, like his brothers in every way except for sin.*

—Q & A 35

The Fundamentals.

Today the name *fundamentalists* is used for those who literally and uncritically accept the authority of their holy book(s) and who fanatically assert this truth—at the cost of their lives, if necessary.

Historically the name comes from the publication, between 1910 and 1912, of *The Fundamentals,* a series of studies on the fundamentals of the Christian faith. The first chapter of the first study was on the virgin birth.

Most of us who hold to the Christian faith as expressed in the Protestant confessions resent being called fundamentalists. But by the grace of God we have always adhered to the fundamental doctrines of the once-for-all-delivered faith, and we hope to continue doing so. Thus we confess with the church of all ages that the eternal Son of God became a human being when he was conceived by the Holy Spirit in the womb of the virgin Mary. This is called "the virgin birth." It's an offense to rationalists and naturalists.

Condescension.

We don't believe that the teaching that God "overshadowed" a young woman named Mary (Luke 1:35) introduces a pagan myth about gods having intercourse with mortals. Rather, we believe that the Holy Spirit's miracle in Mary's womb and the birth of the holy Child climax a history of condescension by Almighty God.

The whole history of salvation is a story of God's coming (*condescend* means "to come down") and seeking us. We didn't climb to him; he descended to us. Immediately after the first sin shattered the relationship between God and our first parents, God came to look for them. "Where are you?" he cried (Gen. 3:9). God visited with Abraham. In the shape of a human traveler the Creator of the world stopped to have lunch with Abraham: they had meat and curds and milk (Gen. 18). God had a special meeting place, a "tent of meeting," while his people traveled through the wilderness. In this tent "the Lord would speak to Moses face to face, as a man speaks with his friend" (Ex. 33:11). God had a permanent address in

Jerusalem when Israel was established in the land, although he remained invisible to human eyes. And finally he met us in the flesh.

In the beginning the devil fired the pride of humanity by saying: "You will be like God" (Gen. 3:5). But in the fullness of time, God became like us. The road of redemption runs from heaven to earth and not from earth to heaven.

And throughout the history of salvation God used humanly unlikely or impossible births to make his point that we are saved by his grace and by his divine power. Abraham and Sarah got the child of the promise only after every human possibility was exhausted. When they were both too old and all other roads (such as adoption) had failed, God did his miracle through the seed of Abraham and the womb of Sarah. And so the story of the new dispensation begins with the birth of John the Baptizer from a woman who was too old to have a child and with the birth of the Son of God from a woman who was still a virgin.

Act of Humiliation.

We confess that "the eternal Son of God . . . took to himself . . . a truly human nature" by being born. We acknowledge that he himself performed an act of love. He was always Son and always God; now he "took to himself . . . a human nature," first that of a fetus, then of an infant, next of a child, then of a teenager. Finally he grew to be a mature man. The Bible teaches not only that the Father "sent" the Son and that God "gave" the Son but also that the Son laid down his glory, "emptied" himself, and became what he was not: a human being and servant (Phil. 2:6-8). It was an act of his own will. He desired to fulfill God's righteous demands: "I have come to do your will, O God" (Heb. 10:7); "Though he was rich, yet for your sakes he became poor" (2 Cor. 8:9). When we share the glory that the Son had before he came to our rescue (John 17:24), we will know what he in love relinquished.

Although we will never fathom the *incarnation* (the eternal Son taking on human *carnis*, "flesh"), we should try to formulate our faith carefully. What happened was not really "God becoming man," for he did not cease being God. It is better and more careful to say, with the catechism, "that the eternal Son of God, who is and remains true and eternal God, took to himself, through the working of the Holy Spirit, from the flesh and blood of the virgin Mary, a truly human nature."

Christ's birth was the first step of his humiliation. It took as much love to lie in the manger as it did to hang on the cross.

He could have refused giving up the glory and going to the squalor. In a scriptural hymn the early Christians used to recite with wonder how Christ, "being in very nature God, did not consider equality with God something to be grasped . . ." (Phil. 2:6-11). The sons and daughters of Adam and Eve blush while saying it. For, being human, we reached and grasped for that which belonged to God. *He* took on the "nature of a servant," but *we* were not satisfied with that role. By our sin *we* marred our divine likeness, but *he* chose to be "made in human likeness." *He* "became obedient to death" because *we* had incurred death by disobedience. Christ assumed our role in order to change our hopeless course. And now our "attitude should be the same as that of Christ Jesus" (v. 5).

Invasion.

When the eternal Son of God took on human life, something entirely new occurred. God identified with us in a totally new and loving way. God's nature and human nature wedded in one person. And the human race experienced a new beginning.

It is therefore altogether fitting that we count the years of human history to and from the birth of Jesus Christ: in the Christian tradition we place a date with either *B.C.*, meaning "Before [the birth of] Christ," or *A.D.*, meaning *"Anno Domini,"* "in the year of the [reign of our] Lord."

Human and Divine.

A young woman in Nazareth was the first to receive the miraculous work of God for our salvation. Mary's faith is exemplary. She offered herself as God's humble helper: "I am the Lord's servant . . . . May it be to me as you have said" (Luke 1:38).

God used Mary—that is, our own "flesh and blood"—for the conception and birth of a new human being, like all others and unlike all others. He was like all others because he grew in the womb of a woman and was born by the usual painful delivery. And he was unlike all others because he did not have an earthly father.

We cannot help asking ourselves why this way—the way of the virgin birth—was necessary for God's union with the human race in the person of Jesus. It is because that birth emphasizes our Savior's *unity* with the human race and his *difference* from the sinful human race. This entrance, by conception in and birth through the virgin Mary, guarantees the true humanity of Jesus. The fatherhood of the Spirit of God, in an immediate act of interference, makes Jesus holy, set apart, sinless, and guarantees his divinity.

When the church thinks about the mystery of our Savior's birth, it is tempted to draw unwarranted conclusions. At times the church has said that the virgin birth shows that the sexual intercourse by which we are conceived pollutes us with sin. But sexuality and sexual intercourse are part of the good creation.

Mary.

The church has fallen for the temptation to make the mother of Jesus the source of his sinlessness and holiness. Instead of maintaining that Christ's holiness and "immaculateness" begin with the miracle God wrought in Jesus' conception, the miracle is pushed back to Mary. In church folklore Mary becomes the sinless one, the symbol of purity since her birth, forever virginal, who did not die but ascended to heaven, where she reigns as queen.

This well-intentioned fantasy about Mary has done indescribable harm to the church of Christ. It will not yield to logical or biblical arguments. Pious fantasy is not bothered by logic such as this: if the inheritance of sin was stopped with Mary's own birth, what must we believe concerning Mary's parents? The Bible does not venerate Mary. However, once tradition has declared her virgin-forever, she and Joseph are denied sexual union (obviously implied in Matt. 1:25), and her sons and daughters (13:55-56) are spiritualized. The beautiful greeting by the angel, "Hail," or *"Ave"* (Latin), or "Hello," or "Greetings!" has become a litany, endlessly repeated. And "full of grace" and "highly favored" are used as if Mary dispenses grace and favor rather than, as the angel (Luke 1:28) and Elizabeth (v. 42) said, received God's grace in great measure.

Praise with Mary.

As a reaction to this blatant superstition of the Roman Catholics, Protestants are often too skimpy in praising Mary. After all, no person was richer, no woman more blessed. But her son Jesus, who loved and cared for her even when he hung on the cross (John 19:26), has always discouraged people from shouting, "Blessed is the mother who gave you birth and nursed you" (Luke 11:27). Jesus reserved his beatitudes (blessings) for "those who hear the word of God and obey it" (v. 28). The Scriptures do not invite us to praise *Mary* but to praise God *with* Mary: "My soul praises the Lord and my spirit rejoices in God my Savior" (Luke 1:46-47).

She is an encouragement to all who are meek and humble and a confirmation that, while rulers and their thrones will topple, the humble will be exalted.

Although she suffered deeply when the sword pierced her soul (Luke 2:35), Mary was twice blessed by the Holy Spirit: he fathered her firstborn Son, and he descended on her a second time when she and her other sons were part of the congregation that experienced the first Pentecost (Acts 1:14).

That's where the Scriptures place her: in the congregation of Jesus Christ, encouraging us to praise God with her.

David's True Descendant.

The sentence in the Heidelberg Catechism that says the eternal Son of God became David's true descendant by being born of Mary seems to imply that Mary was of the tribe of Judah and a descendant of David. The Bible does not say that. But the Bible emphatically states that Joseph was a son of David. Since Joseph was not the natural (but the legal) father of Jesus, we might wonder how Jesus could really be called David's son. That might bother us, but it would not have troubled anybody in Israel. In the world in which the Bible was written, Jesus was regarded as a descendant of David because Joseph was a son of David. To Israelites, the legal tie between father and son was as real as the tie of the flesh. Even children born to a widow by another father, according to the rules of levirate marriage, were the children and heirs of her deceased husband.

Genealogies.

Those long lists of names and "begats" that we skip in devotional Bible readings are very important to the history of salvation. They are the cords of God's covenant faithfulness, the bridges over which the promises are carried to us. Matthew starts with a genealogy from Abraham (the great promise) to David (the golden age) to the exile (the low point) to Christ (the climax), reporting fourteen generations between each of these milestones (1:17).

Luke's genealogy carries the origin of Jesus back to Adam. Between these two genealogies are many discrepancies. One possible explanation is that Matthew gives the ancestors of Joseph and that Luke gives those of Mary. In that case both Joseph and Mary would be descendants of David.

Most of us wish that the evangelists had told us some stories about Jesus' youth in Nazareth. But they give us genealogies. For those who have ears to hear, though, the message is rich: the curse of Adam has now been halted. The promise to Abraham has been realized. And the kingdom of the Son of David has been inaugurated. In the birth of this Baby the human race has received a new beginning.

Q How does the holy conception and birth of Christ benefit you?

A He is our mediator, and with his innocence and perfect holiness he removes from God's sight my sin—mine since I was conceived.

—Q & A 36

Restoration.

Salvation requires a new beginning. It requires the virgin birth of a sinless human being who becomes a fetus, an infant, a child, an adolescent, an adult, as our "Mediator." The birth, life, death, and resurrection of that Child have given new life and new hope to the human race. Some babies are unwanted. People destroy them before they are born. This horror degrades human beings—the only species that annihilates its offspring before delivery. All who respect life because they sense the mysterious Source of life, tremble with sadness and rage at reports of arrogant, desperate abortions.

I trust that those who are reading this prize the birth of a baby. Among us a new life brings rejoicing. God gave us the awesome power to procreate children: handsome children, smart children, but no children that can save us and the human race. Our children are all special, but they are also all sinners. We and our children need to be saved. Whenever a new human being is born, its whole existence lies in the shadow of the inescapable forces of sin and law and death.

But thanks be to God for the one Baby who sanctifies all stages of human life. There is no condemnation but new hope for those who are in Christ Jesus—those who are conceived, who grow as fetuses, are born as infants, live as children, and grow to adolescence and maturity, all of it "in Christ Jesus." It's the only way to live.

Lord's Day 15

MAN OF SORROWS

***Q** What do you understand by the word "suffered"?*

***A** That during his whole life on earth, but especially at the end, Christ sustained in body and soul the anger of God against the sin of the whole human race.*

This he did in order that, by his suffering as the only atoning sacrifice, he might set us free, body and soul, from eternal condemnation, and gain for us God's grace, righteousness, and eternal life.

—Q & A 37

Three Questions.

The church confesses: we believe in Christ, who "suffered under Pontius Pilate; [and] was crucified." About this confession the catechism asks three questions: what is the meaning of his suffering, why do you have Pontius Pilate in your creed, and is it important that he died on a cross rather than in bed?

The Meaning of Suffering.

Suffering is the present world's greatest problem. It has all sorts of medical, social, moral, and religious implications, and it challenges every philosopher. When the believing community begins to speak about suffering, however, it speaks of the suffering of only One—Jesus. That may seem disappointing. Yet in concentrating on the suffering of Jesus we don't turn our back on the world's suffering. On the contrary, in Christ's suffering we find our only clue to all suffering and our only hope of getting us beyond the valley of tears.

We must invite the whole world to listen to our confession. Many say that they cannot believe in a good God who would allow suffering and pain in the lives of nice people. Very many unbelievers say this after doing very little thinking about the subject; few have said it after wrestling hard with the problem. All should at least be mildly interested to hear that, at zero hour, when God came into our world to do something about our misery, he came as the Man of Sorrows!

Beyond Measure.

Although the Son of God identified with our sorrows and so revealed the compassion of God, his suffering is beyond any pain we have ever encountered. Yet, looking at him without the insight of faith and comparing him with other sufferers, one would say that other people suffered more than he did. We hear much about the manger and stable, but countless children have been born that did not receive the care he got. Besides, babies don't usually care what their cribs look like. It is true that the threat of death hung over him from the start, but from what we know, he had a good home, Joseph's carpenter shop, and a relatively quiet and happy life for about thirty years in a small village. At the end of his life he suffered cruel insults, humiliation, and pain, but many people have suffered more pain for much longer.

Why, then, do we speak so much of his unique and bottomless sorrow? Because his suffering is incomparably qualified by *who he is* and by *what he suffered.* He is the Son of God, and he suffered the wrath of God that should kill us.

The Wrath of God.

"Christ sustained in body and soul the anger of God against the sin of the whole human race." Some of his suffering we understand, and much of it we will share. But there are dimensions we shall never know because he was the Son of God and he bore God's wrath.

Every time has its errors and omissions. One of ours is that we are insufficiently aware of God's holy anger. We are accustomed to sin. Sin seldom shocks us. And most people seem to assume that it is God's business to overlook sin. They find it easier to believe that God forgives sin than that he punishes it.

If we want to get to know sin, we should look closely at Jesus and his cross. Look at his suffering and recite 2 Corinthians 5:21: "God made him who had no sin to be sin for us, so that in him we might become the righteousness of God." God deals with his son as he deals with sin. Amazing.

Sermons on God's Wrath?

Ministers are unfair to their listeners and to the Bible if they don't make clear what God thinks of sin. In earlier, less prosperous days, when we had less control over our environment, people tended to accept pain and inconvenience as God's way of chastising us and reminding us that his wrath rests on our present existence. Today we face such matters not as punishments to be borne but as challenges to be met. We demand funds to supply housing and to beat cancer. Sometimes this self-assured *homo sapiens* talk does bother us.

But let's not overreact. Preoccupation with the anger of God, in previous generations, did much harm to people's image of God—and to people themselves, for people take on the image of the God they know. Watch out for the mentality that suspects good things and expects scarcity, pain, and disaster as the trouble we have coming from an angry God.

At the same time, we ought to know whence comes our help. The promise to wipe away all tears is a point written in God's throne speech, the final item on *his* agenda. He'll do it at his time and with his resources. No Rockefeller Foundation or medical discovery can accomplish it. As for today's idea of God, it needs biblical correction. While most people cannot believe that God punishes sin and are inclined to believe that forgiveness is a matter of course, the Bible teaches that punishment is the natural consequence of transgression and that forgiveness is a miracle, a divine surprise.

Sin and punishment are real, but justification in Jesus Christ is just as real. If we have seen Jesus, who was made sin for us, bearing the wrath of God, we should also be convinced (and our sermons, essays, and church school lessons should say it clearly) that God's anger is stilled and that we are forgiven. Our gain is "God's grace, righteousness, and eternal life."

Continued Suffering.

God did not remove suffering from the world or from our lives after he poured his wrath out on Jesus. Suffering will last as long as the cosmos groans. We experience different kinds of suffering. Some of it is self-inflicted. Students suffer after flunking a test for which they did not study. All of us suffer consequences of mistakes and sins—sins of omission and sins of commission. That's a simple reality, and we should remember it when we feel pity, especially for ourselves. When judging this kind of suffering, Christians ought to be tough on themselves and easy on others.

Another kind of suffering belongs to the warp and woof of our natural environment, the texture of life. Death and being torn asunder belong to our present existence. Although we taste our sin and God's anger in these events, as people in Christ we see another dimension. Such sufferings have become God's tools to mold us for his future, because he loves us in Christ.

And "suffering with Christ" is a big item on God's agenda for all who are included in Jesus' death and resurrection. This is the crossbearing to which he calls us. Through it, we identify with his life (Spirit) just as he identified with us in his death. It's the unmatched adventure, the pain and glory of the Way: "I want to know Christ and the power of his resurrection and the fellowship of sharing in his sufferings, becoming like him in his death, and so, somehow, to attain to the resurrection from the dead" (Phil. 3:10-11).

***Q** Why did he suffer "under Pontius Pilate" as judge?*

***A** So that he, though innocent, might be condemned by a civil judge, and so free us from the severe judgment of God that was to fall on us.*

—Q & A 38

History.

In the Apostles' Creed the church recites that Jesus Christ was crucified "under Pontius Pilate." We use the name of the Roman governor in the creed not to blame him for the deed but to date the event.

Christianity is a historical religion. It stands or falls with the truth of certain events: there was a man named Jesus, he lived in Palestine, and he was condemned to death by Pontius Pilate, a Roman governor of Judea. Today we would date the event by a year. But in earlier times people indicated a date by the rule of a governor. The Roman historian P. Cornelius Tacitus dated the event in the same way: "The founder of the Christians was Christ, who during the reign of the emperor Tiberius was executed by the procurator Pontius Pilate" (*Annales,* XIV, 22).

The Judge, God's Deacon.

The creed includes Pontius Pilate just to date a historical event, but the catechism finds the deeper reason why God allowed his Son to be innocently condemned before an earthly judge. And it wants believers to spell it out: Jesus was innocently condemned by the civil judge so that, when we appear before the heavenly Judge, we may go free!

In Jesus' trial, the greatest drama of all time, every player has a role assigned by God. And Pontius Pilate, though he bears full responsibility for his deeds, is serving the purpose of God.

Pilate was a Roman judge, an administrator of one of the best and fairest legal systems the world has ever seen. Every judge is a servant of God, regardless of the judge's perceptions. We may say to every judge what Jesus said to Pilate: "You would have no power . . . if it were not given to you from above" (John 19:11). The power to take away freedom, honor, even life, from a person bearing God's image belongs to God alone, but he has entrusted it to certain people. These people, with their God-like powers, remain responsible to their Commissioner: God "gives judgment among the gods" (the judges), and he says, "How long will you defend the unjust and show partiality to the wicked?" God does not tolerate injustice. He thunders, "Defend the cause of the weak and fatherless; maintain the rights of the poor and oppressed. Rescue the weak and needy; deliver them from the hand of the wicked" (Ps. 82:1, 2, 3-4).

Roman judges came close to God's ideal. Their personification of Justice, Lady Justitia, blindfolded and bearing the scales, is a picture still honored in lands that prize justice without partiality. And Pontius Pilate was no exception: he saw clearly that Jesus was innocent. "I find no basis for a charge against him," he reported (John 19:6). The record states: "Pilate tried to set Jesus free, but the Jews kept shouting, 'If you let this man go, you are no friend of Caesar'" (v. 12). Then Pilate became afraid. And any judge who acts from fear or seeks favor destroys justice.

"Finally Pilate handed him over to them to be crucified" (v. 16).

Judgment Day.

A great miscarriage of justice took place on this Friday almost two thousand years ago. The Jewish leaders, heirs of the promises of David's great son, denied their nobility and shouted, "We have no king but Caesar" (v. 15). They abandoned their Messianic hopes. The leaders of the chosen people talked like the Gentiles.

And when the Jewish people were allowed to vote between Barabbas and Jesus, they chose Barabbas, a criminal and a murderer. They rejected the One who had lovingly healed their sick and had comforted those who suffered.

The Roman governor became corrupt on this Friday. The famous imperial order of peace and justice, the *Pax Romana,* was betrayed by a cowardly judge who sent an innocent man to the cross.

But those who believe the Scriptures and who confess what the catechism teaches admit that a higher will ruled what happened on the Stone Pavement (the *Gabbatha* in Aramaic) on this Friday, the day on which the Passover was being prepared (v. 13). Actually, when Pilate "handed him over . . . to be crucified," the Judge of heaven and earth was pronouncing a verdict. On this day, the Messiah became a lamb, and God prepared the passover. For one man it *was* a good Friday. That man was Barabbas. They yanked him from his dungeon and placed him on the Pavement in the rays of the rising sun. And while his eyes were still blinking, they told him that he was a free man; not he, but Jesus, would be killed.

It is a sinful arrogance to write the name of Barabbas—or to write *my* name—on the same ballot with the name of Jesus. It is beyond the rules of justice to ask for a vote between a murderer and the One who *is* goodness and love. But that is exactly what happened. The Innocent was killed, and the sinner was set free.

Therefore this day has been observed by generations of forgiven sinners as GOOD Friday. With Barabbas, we are overwhelmed by the light of a new day and a new freedom. Our prison is open, but Jesus goes to the place of execution.

Q Is it significant that he was "crucified" instead of dying some other way?

A Yes. This death convinces me that he shouldered the curse which lay on me, since death by crucifixion was accursed by God.

—Q & A 39

Crucified.

Jesus did not die in bed after an illness; he was killed on a cross. The Romans used crucifixion to execute low-class criminals, such as slaves and foreigners. They would not crucify a Roman citizen. The Jews performed capital punishment by stoning. Sometimes they would hang the dead body on a tree, or they would expose it, impaled on a pole. Deuteronomy 21:22-23 speaks of such a situation: "If a man guilty of a capital offense is put to death and his body is hung on a tree, you must not leave his body on the tree overnight. Be sure to bury him that same day, because anyone who is hung on a tree is under God's curse. You must not desecrate the land the Lord your God is giving you as an inheritance." The New Testament says that this curse of God also rested on Jesus when he hung on the tree. "Christ redeemed us from the curse of the law by becoming a curse for us, for it is written: 'Cursed is everyone who is hung on a tree'" (Gal. 3:13).

To Bless and to Curse.

We use the words *bless* and *curse* lightly: nice things are blessings, and bad words are curses. In the Bible, however, *bless* and *curse* are much weightier words. The ultimate authority to bless and to curse belongs to God.

For example, God blessed Abraham and passed that blessing on to Jacob but not to Esau. In another instance, when Balaam tried to curse Israel, the blessed nation, he found that one cannot curse those whom God has blessed (Num. 22-24). When and where God blesses, prosperity, wholeness, and happiness result, as in this picture of the blessed land:

> You care for the land and water it;
> you enrich it abundantly.
> The streams of God are filled with water
> to provide the people with grain,
> for so you have ordained it.
> You drench its furrows
> and level its ridges;
> you soften it with showers
> and bless its crops.
> You crown the year with your bounty,
> and your carts overflow with abundance.
> (Ps. 65:9-11)

When God looks favorably on people, families, or countries, he blesses them. But when God turns away his face, his smile, his countenance, he curses them. The desert and the badland are the places from which God has turned away in anger.

God told the priests in Israel, "This is how you are to bless the Israelites. Say to them: 'The Lord bless you and keep you; the Lord make his face shine upon you and be gracious to you; the Lord turn his face toward you and give you peace.' So they [the priests] will put my name on the Israelites, and I will bless them" (Num. 6:22-27).

In that day the curse was on the scapegoat that carried the guilt of God's people to a solitary place in the desert. Everyone who had come near the goat or who had touched it had to be ritually cleansed (Lev. 16). On the Day of Atonement God's people were blessed with grace and peace, *shalom.* But the goat was not allowed to return; the curse was to be removed forever: "As far as the east is from the west, so far has he removed our transgressions from us" (Ps. 103:12).

The Curse on Golgotha.

"Cursed is everyone who is hung on a tree." The curse of God rested on Jesus when he hung suspended on the wooden cross on Golgotha. He was unclean. He bore the burden of the curse of God. It was not only Pilate who sent him to the the place of execution. It was not merely the Jews who cried "Away with him; crucify him." It was God who said "Away with him." For it is God who has the ultimate authority to curse and to bless. This was the day on which the curse was removed from the nations, and the blessing once given to Abraham came to the Gentiles. Christ removed our curse "by becoming a curse for us, for it is written: 'Cursed is everyone who is hung on a tree.'"

Praise the Lord, O my soul, and count your blessings, if you can.

Lord's Day 16

THE LAST ENEMY

***Q** Why did Christ have to go all the way to death?*

***A** Because God's justice and truth demand it: only the death of God's Son could pay for our sin.*

—*Q & A 40*

Discussing Death.

Almost thirty years ago people suddenly discovered that they feared talking about death. As the anthropologist George Gorer said in an oft-quoted article, in the 1950s death held the same position that sex had in the Victorian age: it was a topic one did not talk about if one had good taste. Things have changed a bit. Now high school classes organize field trips to funeral parlors, and colleges offer courses in geriatrics. First Dr. Elizabeth Kübler-Ross broke the taboo with popular books on death and dying; today we have many authorities on the "grieving process."

Our society cannot keep still about death for very long. We probably try harder than any other culture to deny the approach of death. Yet death remains our constant companion. And the death rate is one out of one.

Human society always tries to come to terms with the brevity of life and the nearness of death. For 2,000 years the major role of philosophy was to prepare people for death. Elaborate rites and customs concerning death and burial serve countless tribes and nations with occasions for weeping, honoring, and remembering. People concerned about the mental health of our own society have been warning us for some time that we, too, need honesty about death and outlets for grief.

Christian Speech About Death.

In the Christian community we are not—or we should not be—afraid of discussing death. When we do talk about it, we use our own Christian vocabulary, we often mention the death of Jesus, and we mean much more by *death* than the termination of physical existence. In the Apostles' Creed we confess that Christ was *dead* and *buried* and that he *descended into hell.* Our catechism, or instruction in Christian comfort, takes up every one of these words and shows the whole church the benefits that come to us from these extreme humiliations of the Savior. The catechism first asks why it was necessary that Christ go all the way to death. Was it really necessary for him to go that far?

The question is not merely theoretical, certainly not for Jesus. He was gripped by the terror of death and its connection with sin when he saw the weeping for his friend Lazarus. It brought tears to his own eyes (John 11:35). And twenty-four hours before his death he prayed in agony, "Please, Father, if possible, let there be another way." He sweat blood beneath the olive trees in Gethsemane (Luke 22:44). But he could not be permitted to avoid death.

We often say that the example of our Lord gives us the freedom to weep and the right to hate death. True, but we may not forget that Christ faced death as punishment and that we don't.

No Other Way.

Death was the only way for Christ, says our book of comfort, because God is true and God is just. We might add, and God is love. The only other way would have been death for us who had sinned rather than the curse for him who bore our sin.

Earlier the catechism instructed us in the righteousness and truth of God (Lord's Days 4 and 5). But now that we come to the creed's line about death, burial, and descent into hell, we must again remember that there could not be another way. The Father is the Judge. He loves justice, and anyone who seeks righteousness is his child. It is unthinkable that the loving Father forgets fairness. And he is truthful. What he has said is unalterably established. "When you eat of it [the fruit of the forbidden tree] you will surely die" (Gen. 2:17). The word was not forgotten but fulfilled, and the second Adam had to die. Christ had to go "all the way to death" because "only the death of God's Son could pay for our sin." *(Q & A 41 will be discussed after Q & A 43.)*

Death Is Unavoidable.

***Q** Since Christ has died for us, why do we still have to die?*

***A** Our death does not pay the debt of our sins. Rather, it puts an end to our sinning and is our entrance into eternal life.*

—Q & A 42

The catechism dwells for a long time on the death of our Savior. Too long, we'd almost think. But if we are patient enough, this little book will teach us how the key to our living and dying is in the death of Jesus Christ.

First it shows that there is a great benefit in the death of Jesus for our dying.

The question why we have to die is not strange for those who take seriously that (a) death is a punishment for sin and (b) Jesus bore our punishment when he died for us. If these great facts stand, why must we still die, and why aren't we lifted up in God's chariot, like the old prophet Elijah?

Strictly speaking, the catechism does not answer its own question. It says that you cannot really call this death dying. We merely pass on. This death isn't a payment for sin: it's just a door to eternal living.

The teacher from Heidelberg is saying that there's nothing to be afraid of. Death is frightening when it is a punishment from God. But once that "sting" has been removed, it's really harmless, like a wasp without a stinger (1 Cor. 15:56).

Death Is a Door.

The catechism makes it almost too nice: death, it says, is God's final remedy for his children. "It puts an end to our sinning." The Spirit of Christ is teaching us every day not to sin but to love and to obey. Yet we do not get beyond the taint of sin until the day God pulls us to himself through the door of death. And then it's all over.

Death "puts an end to our sinning and is our entrance into eternal life."

It's not the only entrance, of course. Those who live on earth when the Lord descends will have an ascension (1 Thess. 4:17). They will be changed without going through the dark door. In one eye-blinking moment they will put on incorruption (1 Cor. 15:52).

The best thing we can say about death is that it is a dark door through which the Lord pulls us to himself. It is the last medicine in our process of sanctification. But the best thing the catechism can say about death as a door does not yet make death a friendly thing. It is still an enemy of God and therefore of us. It is the last enemy to be defeated. Not the worst enemy; that's sin. But death is the last one on God's list for the elimination of enemies (1 Cor. 15:26). Death has been conquered, death has been disarmed, but it has not yet been destroyed. And this could have been the answer the catechism fails to give when it asks, "Why do we still have to die?" The answer lies in God's inscrutable decision to keep his enemy death around until the end. Meanwhile God uses death as a way to bring his children home.

***Q** What further advantage do we receive from Christ's sacrifice and death on the cross?*

***A** Through Christ's death our old selves are crucified, put to death, and buried with him, so that the evil desires of the flesh may no longer rule us, but that instead we may dedicate ourselves as an offering of gratitude to him.*

—Q & A 43

Were You There?

We must not only confess what the benefit of Christ's death is for our dying (Q & A 42), but we must also say what his death means for our living (Q & A 43). Most people are sooner inclined to say that Jesus took the fear out of dying than to confess that he puts us to death while we are living. We don't mind "dying in the Lord," when the time comes, but we would like to continue having our own life as long as we're here.

However, dying is gain only for those whose living is Christ (cf. Phil. 1:21). Because Jesus died for me, dying is easy; but once I have said this, I should add, "I no longer live, but Christ lives in me" (Gal. 2:20).

So the question is, Were you included in the death of Christ? Were you there when our Lord was crucified?

A Representative Death.

The Bible never talks about the death and resurrection of Jesus as something that happened merely to an individual such as the death and resurrection of Lazarus. The death of Christ is a death *for* others and *of* others. He died for us, that is, in our place, as a payment for our sins, and we died with him, that is, he was our representative, our covenant head. In 2 Corinthians 5:14 the two thoughts occur in one sentence: "We are convinced that one died for all, and therefore all died."

In his Adam-role (Rom. 5:14, 1 Cor. 15:22) Jesus represented us. What he did, we did. In him we paid for our sins. Through him we overcame death, and by his Spirit we now live a different kind of life than those who live "according to the flesh," that is, according to the old sinful Adam. As far as we are concerned, the old has passed away, and because we are in Christ, all things have become new (2 Cor. 5:17).

When Did You Die?

One may give three different answers to the question "When did you die?" The first is "I died on Golgotha when Jesus died." When the Bible says that "we died with Christ" (Rom. 6:8), it does mean that we died, really died, historically died, on Calvary in and with the person of Jesus Christ, because we were most definitely included in him. However, if this is the only answer you can give to the question "When did you die?" you are probably going to teach a universal atonement and an incomplete, incorrect gospel.

The second answer one might give to this question is "In my baptism." This answer is also correct. We died to sin by being baptized into the death of Jesus (Rom. 6:2-4). Our baptism was not only a sign of Jesus' death for us, but it also sealed or guaranteed to us that we died with Christ (and entered with him into a new life by his Spirit).

However, if the second answer is the only answer you give to the question "When did you die?" you will probably be called a sacramentalist, because you put too much trust in the magic of your baptism.

A third possible and truthful answer to the question "When did you die?" could be "When I was converted" or "When I was born again." (Today evangelical Christians talk about the birth from above as the moment of conversion. We would rather think of the new birth as a secret work of God's Spirit and of conversion as the conscious break with sin and the personal acceptance of Christ.)

It is true that, *when we were converted*, we "crucified the sinful nature with its passions and desires" (Gal. 5:24). And unless one is converted, one does not know what death and the pain of dying are all about. But if you seek the certainty of your death (and life) merely in your conversion, you are going to be a subjectivist who does not have his or her anchor in solid ground.

We, Too, Died.

We died with Christ on Golgotha. His death is guaranteed as ours when we are baptized. And we personally taste this death (and the new life!) only when we are converted.

Christ made us his own when he died on Golgotha. This is the objective, historical ground of our salvation. God came to us and assured us, in our baptism, that we participate in Christ's death and resurrection. But the reality of Jesus' death and of his life can be experienced only if we consciously believe his Word and walk in his way.

Q ***Why was he "buried"?***

A ***His burial testifies that he really died.***

—Q & A 41

Comfort Around the Grave.

Most teachers in the church have pointed out that this answer is incomplete. The grave was not needed as proof that Jesus had died. That testimony had already been given while he hung on the cross, when the soldier pierced his side with a spear (John 19:34).

Yet the burial is a part of the gospel by which we must be saved, says Paul: "that Christ died for our sins according to the Scriptures, *that he was buried*, that he was raised on the third day . . ." (1 Cor. 15:3-4). But it is not easy to say what the saving significance is of Jesus' burial.

Beginning with Ursinus, one of the authors of the catechism, some people have taught that the burial of Jesus has forever "sanctified" the grave, a word that is preserved in one of the liturgical forms used in the Christian Reformed Church. It's a strong expression. It's not very clear, and it seems to say too much. Undoubtedly the fact that Jesus was buried greatly comforts Christians who stand around a grave. We say to each other, "Don't forget, they buried him, too, in the garden of Joseph of Arimathea." That gives us comfort and hope. But the grave is hardly "sanctified" or "hallowed" because Jesus has been in a tomb.

Burial Is Honorable.

To be buried, in the biblical record, is not the worst thing that can happen to a person. Dead persons are honored by a decent burial. But leaving a body unburied was a dishonor ("as for Jezebel, dogs will devour her . . . and no one will bury her" [2 Kings 9:10]). One might therefore ask whether Jesus' burial was still a part of his humiliation. Superficially it does not seem that way: his body was no longer in the power of his enemies but of rich friends (John 19:39) and loving relatives. The tomb, we are told, had never been used, as if we are to take pride in that fact. This burial seems to have recognized that Jesus was special: he was laid in a tomb "in which no one had yet been laid" (Luke 23:53); earlier he had mounted a colt that "no one [had] ever ridden" (19:30).

Thus, according to the general teaching of Scripture, a burial is an honorable ending, and Jesus' burial was rich and special.

All Luster Lost.

Yet putting a person in the ground is a last humiliation for a being who was made "a little lower than the heavenly beings and crowned . . . with glory and honor" (Ps. 8:5).

Death and burial remain ignoble and painful. We must bow, give up, give in to an enemy. We lose a fight; by all appearances we suffer defeat. Our lifeless bodies are surrendered to decay. And although this process is not painful to the departed, it hurts badly for those who attend the funeral.

When a person is buried, we witness a dethronement of God's image. We were created to rule and to have the earth "under our feet." But in the end we lose all luster. We return to dust. Jesus submitted to the human being's final humiliation: he was buried. People surrendered him to the womb of the earth. They placed spices on him to ward off the odors of decay. Then God interfered. The Holy One cannot be at home in Hades (Ps. 16:10). And because this Holy One has made us holy, Hades cannot devour us either.

Praise the Savior for submitting to the ultimate humiliation: he, too, was buried.

***Q** Why does the creed add, "He descended into hell"?*

***A** To assure me in times of personal crisis and temptation that Christ my Lord, by suffering unspeakable anguish, pain, and terror of soul, especially on the cross but also earlier, has delivered me from the anguish and torment of hell.*

—Q & A 44

Meaning of the Creed.

The catechism's interpretation is not faithful to the original meaning of the Apostles' Creed.

I remember asking my teacher in catechism class about the "descent into hell," just as many catechumens have done before and have done since. "If it means," I said, "that Jesus suffered the torments of hell during the God-forsaken three hours on the cross, then we should move the words in the Apostles' Creed. We should say that he 'was crucified, descended into hell, was dead and buried.' And we should not say that he 'was . . . dead, and buried; he descended into hell' because then the Roman Catholics, who say that Jesus' soul went to get the Old Testament saints out of hell (Limbus Patrum) while his body was in the grave, would be right."

But my dominie, who was also my catechist, said that in this instance the Apostles' Creed does not follow a chronological order. In the creed death, burial, and descent into hell are not in order of time but of intensity, he said. The degree of humiliation is increased with every step. And Jesus suffered the deepest forsakenness in the descent into hell, which actually took place while he hung on the cross. My dominie went on to say that we, not the Roman Catholics (or the Lutherans), had it right: just remember, he said, Jesus did not go to hell, but hell came to Jesus during the three hours of darkness while he hung on the cross.

In those days I had an implicit faith (as Roman Catholics call it), and I accepted my dominies's teaching. Much later I saw that he had been overly zealous. The Apostles' Creed has the descent into hell at the end because it meant a descent into *Hades*, which isn't the place of torture but the place where dead people go.

Hades and Gehenna.

Actually, I think that my teacher knew all about Hades and Gehenna, but he probably figured he'd confuse the whole class if he were to try to explain all that. When I myself was teaching catechism, I was often tempted to be just as absolute and simple about the truth. If one wants to teach well, one must keep the lesson simple. Complexity leads to confusion.

Hence you may forget what follows if you will but remember the catechism's teaching that you will not go to hell because hell has gone to Jesus. That's worth remembering.

Hades in Greek and *Sheol* in Hebrew are general words for the grave or the shadowy domain where the souls of dead people go—without distinction between people who go to heaven and people who go to hell. If your mother has died, she has gone to Sheol (Hades). And when Jesus died, he descended into Hades (Sheol). These words aren't saying anything about bliss or punishment. They're merely saying "death, grave." Thus Jacob said that he did not want to be comforted—"In mourning will I go down to Sheol, to my son"—when he thought Joseph was dead (Gen. 37:35). And David was not teaching that infants go to heaven when they die, as at least one preacher concluded from 2 Samuel 12:23. He was merely asserting that we will all die and that the dead do not return to the living when he said of his little son, "I will go to him, but he will not return to me." He thought of his baby son as being in Sheol.

The Bible also mentions a place of eternal punishment for the wicked. That place is named *Gehenna*, after the dump near Jerusalem. And this is a topic about which the catechism has something important to say. But first a few more things about *Hades* as the kingdom of death.

Where Did Jesus Go?

Jesus was dead from Friday afternoon until Sunday morning. Did his soul go to Hades, and did he bring a message to the other souls or spirits who were there?

Some people hold firm ideas about this "intermediate state" and seem to know exactly what happened in the shadows of Sheol. Roman Catholic doctrines have divided Hades into a number of waiting rooms, claiming that the church holds the timetable of passage. Roman Catholics claim also to have the means to speed up the process. But Martin Luther gave a spine-tingling sermon about Christ hitting these doors of Hades with his empty cross, crying "Victory, victory!" I think he told a beautiful truth in this parable.

The text in 1 Peter about Jesus-in-the-Spirit, who "went and preached to the Spirits in prison" (3:19-20) is certainly not clear enough to serve as the foundation of *any* church doctrine.

We *can* say one thing with certainty about where Jesus was between his death and resurrection: he was with his Father. "Father, into your hand I commit my spirit" (Luke 23:46). His last breath formed his last prayer, and it was certainly answered. And the spirits of departing believers are also with God or with Jesus the moment they die. That's an insight we did not get until the new age dawned—after the death and resurrection of Christ. David talked about going to Hades and finding his infant son. But Stephen, the disciple of Jesus, spoke of going to Jesus when he died: "Lord Jesus, receive my spirit" (Acts 7:59).

Victory over Hades.

Even if we did not follow the interpretation of the Heidelberg Catechism but understood the descent into Hades as Christ's entering the kingdom of death, this article of the creed would hold lasting comfort. For we are all going to die, and no matter how sophisticated or learned we are or act, none of us has ever looked behind the dark curtain that has taken countless loved ones beyond our touch and view. Unless Jesus returns with a bang, we'll die with a weak whimper, and we have no idea what will happen next, on the other side of the wall.

When fright attacks us with a sickening blow to the pit of our stomach, Jesus does to us what he once did to John, who wrote in Revelation, "He placed his right hand on me [what an infinitely gentle gesture] and said: 'Do not be afraid. I am the first and the last. I am the Living One; I was dead, and behold I am alive for ever and ever! And I hold the keys of death and Hades' " (Rev. 1:17-18).

"You must not worry about going into that place," he says. "I was there, and I came back. And I have the key. That place is in my power; that's why I have the key. I am alive, and you are mine. And I won't let you out of my sight, not even in Hades." We must not pretend to have a blueprint of the beyond. But we must exhibit great trust when it's our turn to fall through the trap door. Death has no final say-so over us. The last power we'll meet is not death but Christ. We know that, when we begin to fall toward the pit of Hades, we'll drop into the arms of Jesus.

The Approach of the Catechism.

When we read the catechism's article about the descent into hell, we might want to think of hell as Gehenna, the place of punishment, rather than as an ill-defined Hades. That's what Calvin did, and that's what our catechism teaches. This understanding is more sophisticated than Jacob's or David's idea of Hades. Yet it's a confession that is true to the Scriptures.

The Bible conceives of death as much more than the end of our physical, earthly existence. *Death is separation*, and *life is communion*. Sin is the cause of all separation, just as love is the cause of communion. The catechism sees Jesus as walking the way of separation, the way of Adam, until the bitterest hour, when he was forsaken by God. And then he experienced hell in our place and on our behalf.

Death in Three Phases.

We believe that Adam died as soon as he sinned. No creature can be separated from God and continue to live. He died a *spiritual* death. He lost God as his Father. And if God in his mercy had not come to look for our first parents ("Adam, where are you?" cf. Gen. 3:9), death would have run its full and bitter course.

All people who do not have God as their Father are spiritually dead. They are "dead in [their] transgressions and sins" (Eph. 2:1), "separate from Christ . . . without hope and without God in the world" (v. 12).

In spiritual death a person is separated from God. In *physical* death the soul or the life is separated from the body. In physical death two things that God joined together (Gen. 2:7) are wrenched apart, *and* a person is removed from his or her place under the sun. Ties with other people are cut, and pain is experienced. But the greatest pain comes to those who suffer *eternal* death. This is the removal of all ties, a separation from God and man; this is *hell.*

Although he did not fall beyond the reach of God's love, and therefore was not totally forsaken, Adam began to die when the tie with God was cut. In Genesis 3 the tie with God is broken, and the marriage partners blame each other. In Genesis 4 brother kills brother. When the first separation is suffered, the other breach of communion must follow. Humanity sets its feet on the road away from God. Hell is the end.

The Last Adam.

God gave us Jesus, which was the most loving thing he ever did for us. Jesus lived in constant communion with his heavenly Father. He did that already when he was 12 years old (Luke 2:41-49). And when he grew up, his most fulfilling activity was to do the work of his God (John 4:34). He was a real Son of God.

Yet this Jesus came to bear the full consequences of human separation. He was cast into hell. They nailed him to a cross suspended between heaven and earth. And there "God made him who had no sin to be sin for us" (2 Cor. 5:21).

Jesus in Hell.

He was forsaken by people. His disciples were scattered when their shepherd was struck (Matt. 26:31). He assigned his own mother to the care of another (John 19:26-27). His clothes were stolen, and one soldier got his undergarment with a lucky throw of the dice (vv. 23-24). He lost his friends, his relatives, and his dignity.

Then the sunlight was taken from him (Luke 23:44). He himself had pictured the heavenly Father as one who makes his sun to shine on the evil and the good without distinction (Matt. 5:45). But now even the favors of God's "common grace" were being withheld. Christ's eye could not see the people anymore, and finally he could not find his Father anymore. "My God, my God!" At that point he experienced the full terror of separation. He had said that the Father stands at the road when the son comes home (Luke 15:20). He had said that the good Father always answers when his children ask for bread or an egg or the Spirit (Luke 11:9-13). But then Jesus sought and could not find; he called, and he received no answer. It was dark, and God was distant. "My God, my God, why have you forsaken me?" (Matt. 27:46).

Hell is where God has stopped calling, "Adam, where are you?" and where the second Adam cried, "My God, where are you?"

Now Is the Day of Salvation.

Today it is not hell on earth because God is still calling: by the sunshine, the Word, and the Spirit of Jesus. "Today, if you hear his voice, do not harden your hearts" (Ps. 95:7-8, Heb. 4:7). Enter into holy *communion* with the Lord. It's communion now, or it will be hell later.

> Yet I am always with you;
> you hold me by my right hand.
> You guide me with your counsel,
> and afterward you will take me into glory.
> (Ps. 73:23-24)

Lord's Day 17

HE LIVES!

***Q** How does Christ's resurrection benefit us?*

***A** First, by his resurrection he has overcome death, so that he might make us share in the righteousness he won for us by his death.*

Second, by his power we too are already now resurrected to a new life.

Third, Christ's resurrection is a guarantee of our glorious resurrection.

—Q & A 45

The Benefits.

The catechism discusses not the *problem* of the resurrection but the *benefits.* "How does Christ's resurrection *benefit* us?" is the one and only question on the topic. The answer enumerates three benefits: we share in Christ's righteousness, we have begun the new life, and we shall share his glory.

"Count your blessings," says the song. When we start counting blessings, not only children but also mature Christians are inclined to think of health and wealth, the exam we passed, and the car we bought. But such "blessings" are only peanuts compared to the ones our catechism counts: Jesus lives; therefore the past is forgiven, the present is meaningful, and the future is certain!

He Gives What He Earned.

Christ lives "so that he might make us share in the righteousness he won for us by his death." By dying he earned our righteousness; but, says 1 Corinthians: "If Christ has not been raised, your faith is futile; you are still in your sins" (15:17). Therefore the full confession is "He was delivered over to death for our sins and was raised to life for our justification" (Rom. 4:25). That is to say, our transgressions made it necessary that he be delivered up, but when he arose, our justification became as plain as daylight.

The whole misery and mystery of the death of Jesus Christ became plain with the resurrection. Then the disciples saw that the trial and execution were not a miscarriage of justice and a horrible mistake. Jesus was not an idealistic martyr and an inspirational figure but a Savior. His crucifixion was planned by God, and his death had a purpose. By raising him up, God was saying that he accepted and approved Jesus' work.

This is the first blessing to be counted and never forgotten: his resurrection means that the debt has been paid and that our righteousness has been obtained. Now we must remember that our righteousness is *in Jesus Christ.* You and I must seek our righteousness outside of ourselves and in Christ Jesus. We lose many worries once we have learned this act of faith: seeing ourselves "in Christ," forgiven and justified. Then we can live without the anxieties of forever digging in our own souls for something that encourages us to stand before God. Our righteousness is *in Christ.* And on resurrection morning God said what he said at creation: it is good, it is very good.

[*Our*] work faileth,
Christ's availeth;
He is all our righteousness.

The Second Benefit.

"By his power we too are already now resurrected to a new life."

In Lord's Day 16 we confess that by Christ's death on the cross "our old selves are crucified, put to death, and buried with him." Here, speaking of Christ's resurrection, we confess that we "are already now resurrected to a new life."

First we need to say as carefully as possible what our confession teaches at this point. Do we say that we *have been* resurrected or that we *are being* resurrected by Christ's power? Perhaps you don't feel that there's much difference between the two readings. But Reformed teachers such as A. Kuyper and H. Veldkamp used to stress that we are in the process of being raised to a new life but have not yet risen. They emphasized that our resurrection is a process, not an accomplished event. And until ten years ago our English catechism read, "We also are raised up by his power to a new life." That can be read as an ongoing action: "We . . . are [being] raised up by his power." But our new translation, accepted in 1975, says, "By his power we *too are already now resurrected* to a new life." The *already now* has support in the German and Latin versions of the catechism, but both the German and Latin have the idea of "becoming" rather than the notion that resurrection is an accomplished fact.

Well, what does the Bible say? Are we slowly rising, or are we already resurrected?

Romans 6.

The fifth chapter of Romans deals with the certainty of our righteousness in Christ. That certainty lies in the significance of Jesus as the second Adam and in his death for all who are in him. Through his death we have paid the debt, and by his obedience we have obtained righteousness. Just as Adam's sin meant the fall of us all, so Christ's righteousness is reckoned as our righteousness when we believe in him.

But Romans 5 does not say whether we ourselves change when we receive God's bountiful forgiveness. Therefore Romans 6 begins with a question that Paul's opponents might have asked: may we now go on sinning under cover of this Christ-given righteousness? No, says Paul (6:2); that's an impossible thought for those who know Christ. Justification by faith is not obtained by accepting a theory but by accepting Christ. And the congregation's relationship to Jesus Christ is made clear in baptism as the incorporation—the em-"body"-ment—in Christ Jesus (6:3-4). Everyone who is in Christ participates in Christ's death, burial, and resurrection. We join not only in his death but also in his life. Therefore the baptized congregation must consider itself "dead to sin but alive to God in Christ Jesus" (6:11).

In Romans 6 Paul teaches that "we too are already now resurrected to a new life," as the newest translation of the catechism puts it (with more truth than elegance).

Union with Christ.

The Bible takes Christ's representative role very seriously. Whatever happened to him happened to those who are "in" him. Thus the New Testament teaches not only that we died with him and were raised with him but also that we were exalted in his ascension and are seated with him at God's right hand (Eph. 2:6) and that when Christ is revealed in glory *our* glory will be seen (Col. 3:4).

We must take our union with Christ with equal seriousness. What he has, we have, because we are in him. Because he is alive, we cannot remain in the bondage of sin and death.

Victory.

God's Word says that we can be victorious over sin. We are weak and sinful in ourselves. But in Christ we can obey God.

This victory begins not with a feat of strength but with faith. We may begin every new day in this faith: we are "dead to sin" (sin has no hold on us anymore) and "alive to God in Christ Jesus." And every day the Spirit of the risen Lord continues his blessed work in us, converting our old desires into new ones: making us "wholeheartedly willing and ready from now on to live for him" (Lord's Day 1, A. 1).

The Bible teaches us to *confess* the victory and then also to *fight* for it: "Do not let sin reign in your mortal body. . . . Offer yourselves to God, as those who have been brought from death to life" (Rom. 6:12-13). Our victory in Christ is an announcement to be believed and a command to be obeyed.

The confession of our victory in Christ and the effort to win the war always go together. Only when we believe the gospel of the resurrection can we obey the command to live the new life. And we have believed the good news of our broken bondage only when we have obeyed the command to live as new people.

The Third Benefit.

Finally, here is the third benefit of the resurrection: "Christ's resurrection is a guarantee of our glorious resurrection."

Christ's resurrection assures us of our righteousness in him—we have begun our new life by his power, but we also receive the pledge that we will be like him: he "will transform our lowly bodies so that they will be like his glorious body" (Phil. 3:21).

Vanity.

The present life and the present world are subject to sin. We recognize sin in works of unrighteousness and immorality. Less frequently do we stop to think of sin as vanity. When we say that life is vanity, we mean that we cannot answer the question regarding the meaning of our existence. As a matter of fact, in our culture people try to avoid even the question.

The topic of vanity is a haunting refrain in the book of Ecclesiastes. *Vanity* means emptiness, fluff, a fistful of wind, a pocketful of nothing. It means to pay the mortgage for all of your working days and then to die. It means working hard and running fast and getting nowhere. Vanity is a political speech that means exactly nothing. Vanity is the hope that tomorrow will be different, that there is gold at the end of the rainbow; vanity is wisdom and folly, hard work and laziness, laughter, seriousness, and everything, because everything leads nowhere.

It's very remarkable that the idea of vanity occurs once again in 1 Corinthians 15, the chapter about the resurrection. Verse 14 says that faith and going to church and making a sermon are nothing but vanity, wind, and noise if Jesus did not rise from his grave. Here the apostle Paul hangs the meaning of everything on one nail: the resurrection. And in the last verse of the chapter—after he has told us the mystery that everything must be changed and that the corruptible must put on incorruption—he makes that most cheerful exhortation: "Therefore, my dear brothers, stand firm. Let nothing move you. Always give yourselves fully to the work of the Lord, because you know that your labor in the Lord is *not in vain.*"

Inconsistency?

Instead of being irritated by wild worldliness, alcoholism, carousing, and whatnot, we should be surprised that not all unbelievers get stoned every day. "If the dead are not raised, 'Let us eat and drink [get drunk and drugged], for tomorrow we die'" (1 Cor. 15:32). Actually it is a happy inconsistency that the world is not worse than it is. But we are delivered from vanity; we have experienced a new beginning, and we have a glorious future ahead of us. We must now live consistently by faith.

Lord's Day 18

UNITING HEAVEN AND EARTH

***Q** What do you mean by saying: "he ascended into heaven"?*

***A** That Christ, while his disciples watched, was lifted up from the earth into heaven and will be there for our good until he comes again to judge the living and the dead.*

—Q & A 46

Forty Days.

After Jesus had risen from the dead on that famous Sunday morning, his relationship to his disciples was never again what it had been. He "appeared" to his disciples "over a period of forty days" (Acts 1:3), but he also *dis*appeared again. He did not live with them anymore. He showed himself to prove that he was alive. And on the fortieth day "he ascended into heaven," our creed says. The apostles saw him go up into the sky "while he was blessing them" (Luke 24:51), "and a cloud hid him from their sight" (Acts 1:9).

What Is Heaven?

The ancient Christian confession that Jesus went from earth to heaven while the disciples saw him go up into the sky gives us few difficulties as long as we think that heaven is "just beyond the blue." In the space age we still have to use spatial terms when we talk about heaven and earth—how else are we going to say it?—but we know that the terms are very inadequate.

Heaven, in biblical language, is, *first,* what you see when you look up into the sky. It's the vault over the earth. At night the stars show themselves as "the host of heaven." Heaven is the third, or upper, story of the world as God created it. We live on earth, the dry land; underneath is the pit, the nether world, the cellar. Over and above us is heaven, like a huge bell. Heaven itself is divided into different levels—Jewish writings mention up to ten. But the Bible does not speak about these levels, except for Paul's mention of being "caught up to the third heaven" (2 Cor. 12:2).

The point appears to be that the higher one goes, the closer one approaches the holy God and the greater the ecstasy one experiences. When Scripture says of Jesus that he "ascended higher than all the heavens" (Eph. 4:10), we should not understand that text spatially (that he went twenty thousand feet higher than the gallery of the angels) but we should realize that height here conveys the idea of position or power. The phrase means that in his ascension Christ became most powerful. *Second,* heaven is the place where God lives. God is everywhere, but he is differently present in heaven than he is on earth. "Heaven is my throne and the earth is my footstool" (Isa. 66:1). In his prayer to dedicate the new temple, Solomon says, "Will God really dwell on earth? The heavens, even the highest heaven, cannot contain you. How much less this temple I have built!" (1 Kings 8:27).

Thus, heaven is the place from which God governs the world. It is God's residence, the seat of government. Heaven is headquarters.

Third (and this is closely related to the above), heaven is a synonym for "God." The phrase "kingdom of heaven" used by Matthew means "kingdom of God." (It is a notorious weakness of *The Scofield Reference Bible* that it insists on distinguishing between the kingdom of heaven and the kingdom of God. See its note on Matthew 6:33.)

The kingdom of heaven—or of God—is opposed to, or at least different from, any kingdom we might set up: the kingdom of Nebuchadnezzar, of Caesar Augustus, of the socialists, or of Henry Ford. The nature of God's kingdom, and the means for establishing, maintaining, and promoting it, are heavenly. But the Bible gives the great and good news that this kingdom of God—this heavenly order—is now being established on earth.

The Terms of Truth.

We don't have to accept the three-story universe as an article of faith. Yet God has given us the truth about our world and our own existence in terms of heaven and earth and the pit.

The Bible describes the history of the relationship between heaven and earth. In the beginning a natural division as well as a harmony existed between the two. The natural distance was the difference between Creator and creation. That distinction was and is ineradicable. And the harmony was symbolized by the garden of Eden, where God delighted in his creation and communed with his images.

But now, since the fall, an unnatural chasm has been added to the natural distinction between heaven and earth. Sin has caused rebellion on planet Earth. People refuse the rule of heaven. But sin also causes fear. The inhabitants of the earth do not love, but fear, the goodness of heaven. Impurity hates and fears holiness.

Besides rebellion and fear, sin is also slavery. When earth-dwellers are not ruled by heaven, they become subject to powers from the pit. Demonic forces do terrible things to God's good creation.

That's the truth of the three-story universe: we live between heaven and hell; we exist between God and the devil; we are attracted to the divine, and we are dragged by bestiality. In the cosmic play of powers we are very puny. It is not our inventions, cultures, and conquests that determine the lot of planet Earth. Our future is decided in the realm of the spirits. Our hope is in heaven, and our battle is not against flesh and blood.

The Government of Heaven.

Earth needs heaven. Without the transcendent reality of heaven, earth becomes as cold as a computer. The mind shrinks, the heart aches, and the soul is in prison. Earth is the place to be governed, and heaven is the seat of government. Where heaven does not exercise its beneficial rule, the forces from the cellar take over.

In the ages before the coming of Christ great darkness enveloped the earth. Only sporadically was there contact with heaven. A heavenly voice would come, or angels would traffic from heaven to earth, as Jacob saw them, going up and down a "stairway resting on earth, with its top reaching to heaven" (Gen. 28:12). Except for the tabernacle and temple services and the knowledge of God as it survived in Israel, the devil ruled unchained over the masses of humanity. Except for those few lanterns, there was an almost complete blackout in God's world.

Then came the wonderful invasion and the restoration of light and power. For "what does 'he ascended' mean except that he also descended to the lower, earthly regions? He who descended is the very one who ascended higher than all the heavens, in order to fill the whole universe" (Eph. 4:9-10). The rescue work of Jesus, which has its next-to-last climax in the ascension, has restored light and power to the planet earth. Men and women no longer have any excuse for being enslaved by the powers of the pit. The devil is on a chain, Jesus is Lord, and the everlasting gospel is being proclaimed in the whole world.

***Q** But isn't Christ with us until the end of the world as he promised us?*

***A** Christ is truly human and truly God. In his human nature Christ is not now on earth; but in his divinity, majesty, grace, and Spirit he is not absent from us for a moment.*

—Q & A 47

***Q** If his humanity is not present wherever his divinity is, then aren't the two natures of Christ separated from each other?*

***A** Certainly not. Since divinity is not limited and is present everywhere, it is evident that Christ's divinity is surely beyond the bounds of the humanity he has taken on, but at the same time his divinity is in and remains personally united to his humanity.*

—Q & A 48

Controversy.

We must now explain the dogmatic and philosophical detour that the Heidelberg Catechism takes in questions and answers 47 and 48. As far as I am concerned, the church and the catechism would not be any poorer if these two questions had been omitted in our modern edition. But we keep them, I suppose, because of our respect for this historical document.

The *Roman Catholic* Church teaches that the body of our Lord Jesus Christ is really, though mystically, present in the bread and wine consecrated in the eucharist (Lord's Supper). The Reformers denied it. So today Reformed churches say the *sursum corda* ("lift up your hearts") before they eat bread and drink wine. We don't embrace Christ with our jaws but with our faith, said Calvin. Lift up your hearts to heaven, where Christ is, seated at the right hand of the Father. Christ is in heaven as a glorified human being.

Luther was halfway between the Roman Catholics and the Calvinists on the Lord's Supper controversy. He did not want to say that with the tinkling of the silver bell and the priest's words of consecration the bread and wine became the real flesh and blood of Jesus, but he did not quite want to deny it either. Thus Lutherans teach that through wine and bread we commune with the literal, physical body of Jesus. And this is possible, they say, because at the ascension of Jesus his divine nature communicated omnipresence to his human nature.

That not only *seems* farfetched; it *is*. In the time of the Reformation people made as many strange constructions around the Lord's Supper as twentieth-century evangelicals have created about the return of the Lord.

Sober but Abstract.

Amid all the speculation of those days, the catechism shows good and sober sense: as a human person, Jesus is in heaven. But he is also divine, and as such he is always with us.

And if someone (a Lutheran, for instance) objected that the divine and the human nature are inseparable (the Reformed admit it in Article 19 of the Belgic Confession), then the catechism would answer that divinity cannot be limited by the bounds of humanity it has taken on. We can imagine a dot in a circle: the dot does not get out of the circle, but the circle is not confined to the point. So the divine nature (the circle) is not bound to the human nature (the dot), although the human never gets separated from the divine.

It makes sense, but it remains abstract. Perhaps we can *think* about Christ's "nature" but we cannot *see* his "nature."

Think "Person."

The church should not speak much about "natures," because they are abstractions. We think of our Lord as a person. But we have to confess that this one person is both human and divine, man and God. That's how the Bible pictures him. He is now in heaven. And he is present with us as the Holy Spirit between his ascension and his return. That's the normal, biblical way of thinking.

Perhaps questions and answers 47 and 48 are theologically correct. Today, though, they are certainly not helpful. All we need are question and answer 46 on the fact of the ascension and question and answer 49 on the benefits.

***Q** How does Christ's ascension to heaven benefit us?*

***A** First, he pleads our cause in heaven in the presence of his Father. Second, we have our own flesh in heaven—a guarantee that Christ our head will take us, his members, to himself in heaven. Third, he sends his Spirit to us on earth as a further guarantee. By the Spirit's power we make the goal of our lives, not earthly things, but the things above where Christ is, sitting at God's right hand.*

—Q & A 49

Distance?

There's always some sadness in the church because Jesus is not here. And we have our reasons to be sad. Many bad and terrible things still happen to us. We know they would not happen if Jesus were here. His absence is painful enough to make us pray for his coming.

At the same time we should listen to his Word and be comforted by the Spirit. Jesus said it explicitly: "It is for your good that I am going away" (John 16:7). If we have biblical insight into the scope of Christ's ministry, we are thankful that Jesus is now in heaven. Of course, we still long for his coming. But we understand better than Mary of Magdala why Jesus had to ascend to the Father. When Mary heard the loving voice of Jesus through the mist of her tears and sorrow, she wanted to reclaim him as her precious possession. She was probably disappointed that she was not allowed to hold on to him. But she should not have worried. Because Christ was going to a place where he could forever hold on to Mary and to all who love him. (cf. John 20:11-18).

The First Benefit.

The catechism says that Christ's intercession is the first benefit we receive from his ascent into heaven.

Christ's praying for us is mentioned in Romans 8:34 as the climax of his work on our behalf: "Christ Jesus, who died—more than that, who was raised to life—is at the right hand of God and is also interceding for us." Every one of these four steps in Christ's work is taken up in one of the church's confessions, the Apostles' Creed. Christ secured our salvation in these redemptive acts. And the last of these, his "interceding for us," speaks of the ongoing work of Christ for his own.

In 1 John 2:1 we find the word *advocate* (RSV), or "one who speaks to the Father in our defense" (NIV), to describe Christ's interceding work. First John is the Bible book that assures us that we have fellowship with the Father and his children. But sometimes we still experience an alienation caused by our sin. Yet, "if anybody does sin, we have one who speaks to the Father in our defense—Jesus Christ, the Righteous One." We must not imagine this defense by our advocate, this pleading by our intercessor, as a courtroom session in which the Son attempts to get a ruling in our favor from a reluctant Judge, God the Father. The Bible clearly teaches that the Father himself took the initiative that led to our reconciliation. Our accuser, in the language of both Testaments, is the devil, or Satan (Zech. 3:1, Rev. 12:10).

But the Bible's teaching that we have an intercessor or advocate in heaven underlines the strength of our cause in a very remarkable way. Christ is there not to add to the work he accomplished but to reap the fruits of his sacrifice. He stands before the Father and says, "Here am I, and the children God has given me" (Heb. 2:13). Christ in heaven, or his accomplished work for our salvation, is the only solid ground for our eventual victory. Our position is strong, our cause is favored, because Jesus is our defense in heaven. This is the anchor of our soul. The anchor holds "firm and secure." "It enters the inner sanctuary behind the curtain" (Heb. 6:19). The anchor lies secure in the hands of Jesus himself, who is in the holiest place, in heaven.

The Second Benefit.

"We have our own flesh in heaven [as] a guarantee" that we will get there too, says the catechism. Perhaps *flesh* is not the happiest choice (German *fleisch*, Latin *carnis*). In biblical language our "flesh" cannot inherit the kingdom (John 3:6, 1 Cor. 15:50). But the point is that our humanity is now in glory. He is of our kind, and he is now in heaven, though he is no longer in the body of his humiliation; he has been glorified. He identified with us in his humiliation; he will claim us in his exaltation. That's the confession.

This, then, is the second way that Christ's presence in heaven guarantees our destiny. First we said that he is there as the advocate, representing the accomplished work, the justification of our cause. And, second, he is there as our leader, head, forerunner.

When I served as a pastor in immigrant churches, I often met fathers or fathers and sons who had come to Canada to prepare the way for the rest of the family. They would get a job, work hard, and make a downpayment on a house, and then they would write the long-expected letter to the family in the old country: "Now all of you should come." They were the forerunners and trailblazers to the new country.

I always think of them when reading the passages in which Jesus speaks as the trailblazer: "I am going there to prepare a place for you. . . . I will come back and take you to be with me that you also may be where I am" (John 14:2-3). He also speaks this way in John 17:24: "I want those you have given me to be with me where I am."

Someday soon he is going to say, "Now all of you should come."

The Third Benefit.

The descent of the Holy Spirit is the great benefit of Christ's ascent into heaven. We'll say more about that when we discuss Lord's Day 20, which studies the words from the Apostles' Creed "I believe in the Holy Spirit." In connection with the ascension of Jesus, we need to make three remarks about the presence of the Holy Spirit on earth. First, note the connection between *the going of Jesus and the coming of the Spirit.* Jesus says in his farewell speeches (John 14-17) that his going is the necessary condition for the Spirit's coming: "If I don't go," Christ says, "he does not come; that's why, if you know what is good for you, you should be happy that I'm going" (cf. 16:7). Actually, Jesus teaches (and we must believe and experience) that his comfort, his word, and his power are now more richly present in his followers than before his ascension.

The coming of the Spirit enables the disciples to know the truth (15:26, 16:13), to know the words of Jesus (14:26, 15:26), and to do the works of Jesus (14:12). And the Spirit will be the One who makes the distinction between the disciples of Jesus and the people who belong to the world (14:17). The Spirit of Jesus in the people of God will be the reason for the world's anger (15:18-19), but the presence of the Spirit is also the guarantee that the testimony of the disciples will be effective, because the Spirit will "convict the world of guilt" or will expose the guilt of the world (16:8).

Second, *our distance from Jesus has been reduced by the Spirit because now he lives in every heart that crowns him Lord.*

The Lord demands obedience from the church, but wherever submission occurs it results from the Spirit's work in us. When he is in us, we set our minds "on things above, not on earthly things" (Col. 3:2). By "things above" the Bible means the kingship and treasures of Christ (v. 1). "Being spiritual," in biblical language, is not the opposite of being material or concrete; *spiritual* is the opposite of *sinful.* They who have Christ in the center of their lives "put to death" all actions and desires that God hates (vv. 5-10), and "as God's chosen people" (v. 12) they clothe themselves with the virtues of Christ (vv. 12-17). Far from neglecting tasks in the present world, spiritual wives (v. 18), husbands (v. 19), children (v. 20), slaves (v. 22), and masters (4:1) who have set their minds on the ascended Lord apply his lordship to marital and family relationships, education, and social responsibilities. It is in these areas that we show whether or not we have a Lord in heaven.

Finally, the presence of Christ in heaven and the presence of the Spirit on earth *form a double guarantee that heaven and earth will be united.*

The catechism teaches that a human Christ in heaven is "a guarantee that Christ our head will take us, his members, to himself." And "he sends his Spirit to us on earth as a further guarantee" of our reunion.

That's a deeply scriptural thought. Formally speaking, however, the Bible uses the word *guarantee* (in Greek, *arraboon*) not of Christ but only of the Holy Spirit, who is given as a down payment or assurance that all God's promises will be fulfilled: God "put his Spirit in our hearts as a deposit, guaranteeing what is to come" (2 Cor. 1:22, cf. 5:5). "Having believed, you were marked in him with a seal, the promised Holy Spirit, who is a deposit guaranteeing our inheritance" (Eph. 1:13-14).

But, substantially, Christ's function in heaven is very similar to the Spirit's function on earth. The Spirit is the intercessor on earth (Rom. 8:27, Rev. 22:17); Christ is the intercessor in heaven (Rom. 8:34, 1 John 2:1). Christ claims us as his own before the Father in heaven; the Spirit testifies with our spirits that we are children of God, right here and now. "They are mine," claims one, our Advocate in heaven; "you are his," assures the other, our Counselor on earth.

We are now richer and closer to the fulfillment of all God's promises than his people have ever been. Our human body is in heaven, and God's Holy Spirit is on earth. They are pledge and counterpledge. The rings have already been exchanged. Heaven longs for earth, and earth longs for heaven. There will be, there must be, a wedding. Soon.

Lord's Day 19

CHRIST'S KINGDOM

***Q** Why the next words: "and is seated at the right hand of God"?*

***A** Christ ascended to heaven, there to show that he is head of his church, and that the Father rules all things through him.*

—Q & A 50

Millennium.

The kingship of Jesus Christ is now a reality. Today Christ rules over his own people: "he is head of his church," says the catechism. But his power is not limited to the blood-bought church. The whole cosmos is our King's territory: "the Father rules all things through him [Jesus]." The ascension marks the beginning of the Messianic reign. From our point of view, *ascension* means that Jesus went from earth to heaven, from the place that is ruled to the seat of government. From another point of view, the "male child, who will rule all the nations with an iron scepter . . . was snatched up to God and to his throne" (Rev. 12:5). But when Jesus became Governor, someone else was thrown out of the driver's seat: "the great dragon was hurled down—that ancient serpent called the devil, or Satan" (v. 9).

Millennium is Latin for "one thousand years"; in the Bible the word occurs only in Revelation 20. The millennium is not a happy hope of the church or of Israel but a fulfilled expectation. It is the reign of the Son of God, who took on human nature, the Mediator, Jesus. And it is the corresponding defeat of Satan. It is a new situation that did not exist before Jesus' victory. Prior to the Son of God's loving and glorious intervention, the world was largely in darkness, and most tribes were chained by demonic tyrants. But now the devil is chained, so to speak, and Jesus is on the throne of the world. He sends his ambassadors over the globe telling all nations to surrender to Jesus. The reign of the Prince of Peace ("Prince Shalom") has begun. And he must reign forever and ever.

The Psalter Fulfilled.

The Old Testament foretold this rule of a man who would sit on the throne of God. Actually all human beings are royal; they should rule over all things and not be ruled by *anything*: "You made him ruler over the works of your hands; you put everything under his feet" (Ps. 8:6). God did not grant this to angels but to human beings. "Yet at present we do not see everything subject to him [i.e., to the human being, God's creature]" (Heb. 2:8). We still are hampered and hindered by all sorts of powers, and we live in fear of death. People are not yet as royal and noble and lifted up as they should be. "But we see Jesus, who was made a little lower than the angels, now crowned with glory and honor" (v. 9).

Jesus is *the* Man, *the* true image of God (1:3), who fulfills his mission to "taste death for everyone" (2:9) and to "free those who all their lives were held in slavery by their fear of death" (v. 15).

This is the theme of Psalm 8, as worked out in the New Testament. Jesus is God's true image, whose mission it is to set all of us free so that we may become again what the Creator wanted us to be. And this motif is coupled with the one of the Messiah, the Son and Lord of David: "The LORD says to my Lord: 'Sit at my right hand until I make your enemies a footstool for your feet'" (Ps. 110:1).

This theme of the exalted man or king, who, under God, rules in utter freedom (Ps. 8, 110), is played throughout the New Testament consistently but with rich variations. Or, to say it more prosaically, these psalms are quoted in the New Testament more often than any other psalms. The church does not listen enough to this music. We speak frequently about Jesus' coming down to serve as a slave, but we rejoice too little in his going up to be our King and to set us free. Churches make too much of Christmas and too little of the ascension. In that respect they are out of step with the New Testament.

Forever or Interim?

"He [Jesus] must reign until he [God] has put all his enemies under his feet. The last enemy to be destroyed is death" (1 Cor. 15:25-26).

The appointment of King Jesus is terminal: "he must reign until. . . ." Once the *last* anti-God power has been removed, the second stage of Christ's mission will have been accomplished. He has already accomplished his earthly ministry; he must also finish his heavenly ministry.

Luke the evangelist wrote one book on the earthly ministry of Jesus. We call it the "Gospel According to Luke." In it he "wrote about all that Jesus began to do and to teach until the day he was taken up to heaven" (Acts 1:1-2). The second book begins with the ascension and describes, as Luke himself suggests, what Jesus *continued to do and to teach.* But we call this second book of Luke the "Acts of the *Apostles.*" That's all right, of course, as long as we don't forget that what we read in this book describes the ongoing work of Jesus Christ. It tells what he did *from heaven,* by his Word and by his Spirit. The mode of the work is different, but the Worker is the same. One should not, as in a red-letter Bible, reduce the activity of the Lord Jesus to the gospels.

His heavenly ministry will end with the destruction of death, the destroyer. "When he has done this, then the Son himself will be made subject to him who put everything under him, so that God may be all in all" (1 Cor. 15:28).

This means that the work of Jesus as Mediator will then be accomplished. When all things belong to God again, when the Father's will is done on earth as it is in heaven, and when God is our one and all and we all are one in him, then he will say for the second time, "It is finished." And of the renewed creation he will say, "It is good; it is very good."

By Faith.

Christ is the head of the church and the King of the world. But for the time being the only way to the knowledge and experience of his kingship is faith.

Every Christian loves to see real, tangible, unmistakable evidences of Christ's power. As a matter of fact, the Lord has shown, does show, and may at any time show that he has all power in heaven and on earth. Sometimes he sets a prisoner free, or he takes cancer out of a sick body, or he converts people who hate him to disciples who love him. Sometimes he confirms our faith by such signs. But nobody should permit faith to rest on this evidence of Christ's lordship. Faith is always trust in the *Word* of the Lord.

The miracles in the New Testament are evidences that Jesus is Lord. They call those who see the miracle to believe in Jesus; such clear interventions by the Lord strengthen the faith of those who have believed already. The New Testament does not teach that "now the age of miracles has begun," as some evangelists say. Yet anyone who believes in God should be receptive to his wonder-working power.

Seeing the Signs of the Kingdom.

The New Testament indicates that the occurrence of "signs and wonders" decreased once the church became established. In Hebrews, a letter written to second-generation Christians, the writer recalls how the gospel, the "great salvation . . . was first announced by the Lord" himself and in the second stage "confirmed to us by those who heard him," the eye- and ear-witnesses. And he further says of the apostolic preaching of the kingdom (because the apostles were the witnesses): "God also testified to it by signs, wonders and various miracles, and gifts of the Holy Spirit distributed according to his will" (Heb. 2:3-4).

In the environment of the Jews (the "Hebrews") the expression "signs and wonders" usually refers to God's deeds that accompanied the Exodus from Egypt (see Ex. 7:3, Deut. 4:34, 6:22, 7:19, 34:11, Ps. 105:27). Now the author of Hebrews appears to say that the coming of the "great salvation," the New Testament Exodus, had similar manifestations of the power of God.

The church may not declare dogmatically that signs and wonders are limited to the apostolic era (as Benjamin B. Warfield and the old Princeton school taught). Nor should the church teach that the kingdom of Christ is present only when we sensibly experience the powers of his Spirit (as some Pentecostals teach). We must be open-minded about manifestations of the power of the Lord. We believe in miracles because we believe in a living Lord. But we may never hang the truth of the faith on the occurrence of signs. "We live by faith, not by sight" (2 Cor. 5:7).

***Q** How does this glory of Christ our head benefit us?*

***A** First, through his Holy Spirit he pours out his gifts from heaven upon us his members. Second, by his power he defends us and keeps us safe from all enemies.*

—Q & A 51

Gifts from Heaven.

In his present position Christ has all of heaven's resources at his disposal. And he supplies his church with the gifts and powers needed for endurance, growth, and victory.

In the Old Covenant, when the people of God made their wilderness journey, God supplied daily manna. The people received this supernatural food until they came to the promised land. In the same way the head of the church supplies daily strength to his people until the journey is completed.

The "gifts of the Spirit" listed in Romans 12, 1 Corinthians 12, and Ephesians 4 belong to the church's heavenly equipment. Of course, the lists in the New Testament do not claim to be a complete inventory of the church's possessions for all seasons. The Lord gives in sovereign grace, according to the need of the hour and the prayers of the saints. But the most important gifts that he supplies and that meet our need in every season are three: faith, hope, and love. And the greatest of these is love.

Our Protector.

"Second, by his power he defends us and keeps us safe from all enemies." Christ not only supplies his gifts to us, directly and inwardly, but he also controls history and restrains the enemies of the church so that they can do us no ultimate harm.

This does not mean that we will be spared the pain of persecution. But in our trials we will see the power of the Lord. Sometimes that power will be evident when the Lord breaks the chains and opens the doors of the prison (Acts 12:7-11, 16:26). And sometimes the disciple of Jesus will die a martyr's death. Even then Christ is in control: while he was being stoned to death, Stephen saw with his eyes what he believed in his heart—that the Son of Man is at the right hand of God (Acts 7:56).

World history does not run by its own laws. At the center of history is the people of God. The church is the reason why history continues. The task of the church and the goal of history coincide.

Many powers threaten to destroy the church, but it will endure forever. World history will ultimately serve church history—because the world must be saved through the church.

The End.

The present kingship of Jesus will be completely and perfectly established when he comes to judge the living and the dead. Then faith will become sight. Many will see what they never believed they would see, but Christians will see their hopes fulfilled.

We must remind ourselves and each other very often that this life and this world will soon end. The present form of existence is critically important but not everlasting. Our present possessions and positions are temporary. The kingdom of God is everlasting. Therefore we should have all our treasures in the kingdom.

***Q** How does Christ's return "to judge the living and the dead" comfort you?*

***A** In all my distress and persecution I turn my eyes to the heavens and confidently await as judge the very One who has already stood trial in my place before God and so has removed the whole curse from me. All his enemies and mine he will condemn to everlasting punishment: but me and all his chosen ones he will take along with him into the joy and the glory of heaven.*

—Q & A 52

Public and Visible.

At the present time the kingdom is hidden. In the day of his coming, the King and his glory will be openly displayed. The Bible passages that deal with his coming place much emphasis on the public character of the event: the coming is often called the "appearing" of the Lord (Titus 2:13, 1 Tim. 6:14, 2 Tim. 4:1,8), suggesting that the curtain that now hides him from mortal eyes will be torn. He will be visible to all because his "sign" will be in the sky and he will travel "on the clouds" (Matt. 24:30, 26:64; Rev. 1:7). Trumpets will announce his arrival (Matt. 24:31, 1 Cor. 15:52, 1 Thess. 4:16). When the true Lord is unveiled, everyone will hear him, everyone will see him, everyone will confess his greatness, and every knee will bow (Phil. 2:10-11).

This publicity will also extend to the deeds of people. Whatever people sowed in darkness will then be fully grown and open for inspection. "Men will have to give account . . . for every careless word they have spoken" (Matt. 12:36). There's "nothing concealed that will not be known or brought out into the open" (Luke 8:17). This removal of the covers will include the public recognition of those who gave the "cup of cold water" to Jesus' little ones (Matt. 10:42). The Lord will award those who showed kindness to the hungry, naked, and imprisoned—Christ's representatives during his absence—and he will rebuke those who failed to do so (Matt. 25:31-46). "We must all appear before the judgment seat of Christ, that each one may receive what is due him for the things done while in the body, whether good or bad" (2 Cor. 5:10).

Unimaginable.

The event is unimaginable, of course. If the living and the dead were to be lined up before a throne to be judged, there wouldn't be enough standing room on the planet. But forty years ago none of us could have imagined that it would ever be possible for the whole world to see and listen to one person at the same time—something that is now almost ordinary with the help of television and satellites. All imagination staggers and fails in view of the mighty works of God. No human imagination can remotely anticipate the greatest of all dramas, the Last Judgment.

Frightening?

The public character of the Last Judgment could be embarrassing. It does frighten children and childlike believers. We know we would lose whatever respect we have for one another if we listened to recordings of each other's family quarrels.

Radio studios have signs above their broadcasting rooms that say: "On the Air." As soon as the microphone is turned on and you are "on the air," you cannot say just anything that comes to mind, because your words go over the air, they are public. The Bible reminds us that the "On the Air" sign is always lit up. Whatever we say is "on the air"—"men will have to give account on the day of judgment for every careless word they have spoken" (Matt. 12:36). The final day will also reveal the results of deeds done in secret and of prayers uttered in the inner room. Thoughts of the Last Judgment are supposed to have a restraining influence on us. That's the pedagogical function of this revelation. In the Bible God stoops to scare us with the Last Judgment, and he encourages us with rewards in the hereafter. These are the eternally Wise One's methods to bring us to heaven. We sometimes think we are too sophisticated for such threats and promises. But we must not try to remove these conceptions from the pages of the Book.

Comfort.

"I turn my eyes to the heavens and confidently await as judge the very One who has already stood trial in my place before God and so has removed the whole curse from me," says the catechism.

The Judge is Jesus of Nazareth. And that should give us great confidence.

At one time Jesus himself stood before a judge, Pontius Pilate. That magistrate knew that Jesus was innocent, but he did not dare release him. Pilate let his soldiers play a game with the prisoner. They dressed him up as a mock king, with a purple robe and a crown of thorny twigs. Pilate wanted to arouse the contempt or pity of the people when he said, "Here is the man!" or, "Look at the man!" (John 19:5).

What Pilate said with scorn and mockery we will say in that day with sobs of joy: "Look at him; the Judge is Jesus! He is our Jesus!" Behold the Man, my Savior and my Judge!

The Vindication of the Lord.

When we think of the future, trying to anticipate what's going to happen, most of us worry about our own destiny and the eternal well-being of our loved ones. As Abraham Kuyper observed, the majority of Christians do not think beyond their own graves.

In Scripture, however, the goal of history is to establish the glory of the Lord. Christ's judgment of the world will be the climax of the exaltation that began with the resurrection: "God has made this Jesus, whom you crucified, both Lord and Christ" (Acts 2:36). "He [God] has set a day when he will judge the world with justice by the man he has appointed. He has given proof of this to all men by raising him [Jesus] from the dead" (17:31). Jesus was rejected by his people but "was vindicated by the Spirit, was seen by angels, was preached among the nations, was believed on in the world, was taken up in glory" (1 Tim. 3:16). No matter what kind of opposition (unbelief) still exalts itself against him, the Spirit and the church will testify, and finally the whole cosmos will confess, "The kingdom of the world has become the kingdom of our Lord and of his Christ, and he will reign for ever and ever" (Rev. 11:15).

When he is revealed as Judge, "even those who pierced him" (Rev. 1:7) will see to their horror that Christ is Lord. The leader of the Soviet Union, the president of the United States, and the prime minister of Canada will kneel at his feet. Pontius Pilate, Caesar Augustus, and Nero will admit that the Man of Nazareth has won.

Home of Bliss?

It is taking much longer for the Lord to return than early Christians thought it would. Whenever we read the New Testament, we are impressed by the writers' vibrant expectation of Jesus' early return to judge the living and the dead. And the longer the church has to wait, the more its attention has shifted from his coming to our going. Most people and many churches have far more to say and to sing about our going to heaven than about his coming to earth.

In the Bible, however, the vindication of the Lord, not the "home of bliss," gets center stage. The Bible has very little to say about the interim, the time between our death and Judgment Day. Most of the popular knowledge about heaven comes instead from well-meaning phrases in funeral parlors and from the poetry of sympathy with the bereaved. We hear these phrases and confessions most often while we are attending a funeral or at other occasions when it would be highly improper to argue eschatology ("teaching concerning the last things"). Therefore it is necessary that the church draw clear biblical lines.

Enemies Condemned.

"All his enemies and mine he will condemn to everlasting punishment," we confess. As the Bible says, "This will happen when the Lord Jesus is revealed from heaven in blazing fire with his powerful angels. He will punish those who do not know God and do not obey the gospel of our Lord Jesus. They will be punished with everlasting destruction and shut out from the presence of the Lord and from the majesty of his power on the day he comes to be glorified in his holy people" (2 Thess. 1:7-10).

The persecuted church makes this confession: "In all my distress and persecution I turn my eyes to the heavens. . . ." And those who make this confession are very sure that Christ's enemies are their enemies. You and I had better be sure that the Lord and we have the same enemies. And that those who love him are our friends.

The condemnation and eternal punishment of the enemies of the Lord Jesus Christ are truths taught in Scripture. Therefore they form part of the confession of the Christian church. The church may not teach universal salvation.

Nevertheless, the knowledge about the everlasting punishment of "his and my enemies" is not good news; it's a burden we carry. We must handle it with great care and convey it with discretion. Many medieval painters and, more recently, revival preachers relished pictures of the damned too much. The church can never forget that it can approach the judgment seat with confidence only because the Judge is the "One who has already stood trial in [its] place before God and so has removed the whole curse from [it]." All of us were under the curse. Therefore we must now speak to all about the One who has removed the curse.

Joy and Glory.

Although we must think of the judgment primarily as the time of Jesus' public vindication as Lord, we don't want to tone down the bliss that awaits us: "he will take [us] along with him into the joy and the glory of heaven."

Looking at Jesus and his work, I make bold to say with certainty that I will be among the number of those who share his joy and glory. But in the parable of the sheep and goats, in which (according to Reformed interpretation) the saved enter into the eternal kingdom and the condemned into eternal punishment, both groups receive their verdict with amazement (Matt. 25:31-45).

The certainty of salvation is always accompanied by amazement because we are saved by grace.

Lord's Day 20

I BELIEVE IN THE HOLY SPIRIT

***Q** What do you believe concerning "the Holy Spirit"?*

***A** First, he, as well as the Father and the Son, is eternal God.*

Second, he has been given to me personally, so that, by true faith, he makes me share in Christ and all his blessings, comforts me, and remains with me forever.

—Q & A 53

Brief But Basic.

It is true—as many have said—that this confession concerning the Holy Spirit would take up much more space in the catechism if it had been written in the twentieth century. But we should also acknowledge that the catechism refers to the Spirit and his work very frequently. We have just spoken of his work in Q & A 51, and in Q & A 54 we will again honor him.

Although Lord's Day 20 does not give a full statement of what it means to believe in the Holy Spirit, it does present the essential truths about *who he is* and *what he does.*

Who Is He?

"He, as well as the Father and the Son, is eternal God." Thus if anyone claims to know God, that person should also know the Holy Spirit.

Knowing God has more dimensions than knowing your mother. To know God means to know him as the Sovereign, the Creator, the Law-giver, the God-above-us and to know the God-for-us, the Mediator—Jesus, the Messiah. We should also know him as God-in-us. Here the knowledge of God gets under your skin. Everyone has some inkling about God, the God-at-a-distance. But just as those who have a human spirit are the only ones to know what is truly human, so only those who have God's Spirit know the deep things of God. "What God has prepared for those who love him" cannot be known through human observation or contemplation: "No eye has seen, no ear has heard, no mind has conceived" it. "But God has revealed it to us by his Spirit" (1 Cor. 2:9,10).

Spirit, Breath, Wind.

Over against bygone sects and present Jehovah's Witnesses and Mormons, the Christian church insisted and insists that the Holy Spirit is personal (a *he;* some want to say a *she*) and not an impersonal power (an *it*).

We should admit, however, that the Bible describes the Spirit of God not only as the Giver of good things (a person) but also as the Gift (an it). The gender of the Spirit in the New Testament is neither masculine nor feminine but neuter (*to pneuma*). In the Old Testament and in the New Testament the word for *Spirit* is the same as a word used for *breath* and *wind.* The *breath* of God is the *Spirit* of God. "Breathe on Me, Breath of God" is a scriptural song. God's breath is God's Spirit. And when Jesus spoke to Nicodemus of the wind that "blows wherever it pleases," teaching the Pharisee that as it is with the wind, "so it is with everyone born of the Spirit" (John 3:8), he used the same word for *wind* and for *Spirit.*

God blew the Spirit into our nostrils as the breath of life at creation (Gen. 2:7), and Jesus Christ gave us the new life by a similar action: "he breathed on them and said, 'Receive the Holy Spirit'" (John 20:22). The words and the action of Jesus are intended to remind us of creation because the descent of the Spirit at Pentecost is nothing less than a recreation.

Word and Spirit.

Thus it is natural to think of the Spirit of God as a power, an energizing force that emanates from God just as light and heat radiate from the sun. Even we creatures use our breath to give life in efforts to resuscitate accident victims. Compare this to Elisha's method, blessed by God, in the revival of the son of the Shunammite (2 Kings 4:33-35).

When the life-giving energy goes forth from God, his breath gets shape in Words that are full of his power. We think of words as letters or characters on paper or on screens. But the power of the Word, as the Bible speaks of it, is explained by the Breath that has jelled in these words. Word and Spirit are often synonymous: "By the *word* of the Lord were the heavens made, their starry host by the *breath* of his mouth" (Ps. 33:6).

Jesus and the Spirit.

The life-power of God rested on Jesus, as was promised in the Old Covenant: "A shoot will come up from the stump of Jesse. . . . The Spirit of the Lord will rest on him" (Isa. 11:1-2). "I will put my Spirit on him and he will bring justice to the nations" (42:1). "The Spirit of the Sovereign Lord is on me, because the Lord has anointed me to preach good news to the poor" (Isa. 61:1; Luke 4:18).

Jesus is the *bearer* of the Holy Spirit but also the *giver* of the Spirit: "The man on whom you see the Spirit come down and remain is he who will baptize with the Holy Spirit" (John 1:33). When Jesus had accomplished his work as earthly mediator, he began to communicate the Spirit of God to all who believed in him as the Christ: "Exalted to the right hand of God, he has received from the Father the promised Holy Spirit and has poured out what you now see and hear," said Peter on the day of Pentecost (Acts 2:33). And Paul said that Jesus, by his resurrection, became "a life-giving spirit" (1 Cor. 15:45). Between his ascension and return Christ may be identified with the Spirit: "Now the Lord is the Spirit, and where the Spirit of the Lord is, there is freedom" (2 Cor. 3:17). In our dispensation we experience the resurrection power of Jesus when we have the Holy Spirit.

That identification of the exalted Christ and the Spirit is not absolute, of course. But we must always remember the very close tie between Christ and the Holy Spirit.

Revelation of the Holy Spirit.

God is eternally three-in-one. But just as the Son of God was not unveiled as a distinct person of the trinity until the incarnation, so the Holy Spirit was not revealed as distinct from the Father and the Son (though never separated from either) until the day of Pentecost (Acts 2). Then the Age of the Spirit, prophesied in the Old Testament, became a reality on earth. God the Holy Spirit is personal, not a mere power. He does things that only persons can do: "he gives" and "he determines" (1 Cor. 12:11). We can "grieve" him (Eph. 4:30), which means to cause personal pain. We can lie against the Spirit, which would be lying against God (Acts 5:3-4), and it is possible that people commit "sin and blasphemy" against the Holy Spirit (Matt. 12:31). But next to the words that indicate the Holy Spirit as a person are those that describe him as a rain shower that is "poured out" (Acts 2:33, 10:45) or as a fire that may not be "put out" (1 Thess. 5:19). He is both Giver and Gift.

The Spirit and the Bible.

The highest good in the present life is the knowledge of God. He exists as Father, Son, and Holy Spirit. The only way to the Father is by the Son. And we come to the Son by the Spirit. But how do we meet the Spirit? He comes to us with the Word. That's why the Word is never void or empty. It "will accomplish what I desire and achieve the purpose for which I sent it" (Isa. 55:11), says the Lord. The Word of the Lord is so effective because the Word comes with God's Breath, Wind, Spirit—that is, God's life-giving power.

Thus our quest for the knowledge of God necessarily begins with the Bible. And we always return to the Book. This does not mean that the Spirit and the Bible, as a book printed and bound, are identical. But the Bible is the work of the Spirit, and by approaching it, we are, so to speak, in the room where he wants to be met. This meeting and the knowledge of God do not happen automatically. But going into the Bible is a surer way of meeting God than going into the woods, although he can be found in either or both places.

The relationship between the Spirit and the Bible is not easily defined. We should remember not to seek the one without the other. It's true that the Spirit of God must invade us. If we don't know the love of God by the Holy Spirit, we simply don't know God, even if we read ten chapters from the Bible every day. But by the same token the Spirit of Christ does not abide in us if his Word does not dwell in us.

We must take a balanced approach: we don't know God by the Bible alone, as dogmatically orthodox people are inclined to think. And we don't know God by the Spirit alone, as "hyper-spiritual" people tend to think. We know him by the Word *and* by the Spirit.

If we seek to know God by the Bible alone, we dry up. If we try to know him by the Spirit alone, we blow up. But if we know him by the Word and by the Spirit, we grow up.

What He Does.

The first part of the catechism's teaching about the Holy Spirit says who he is; the second part says what he does: "he has been given to me personally, so that, by true faith, he makes me share in Christ and all his blessings." In other words, the Holy Spirit connects us with Jesus Christ, as an electrical cord connects a lamp with a source of light and power.

The Son of God was self-effacing in his ministry: he did not speak by his own authority but by the Father's mandate; he did not do his will, but the Father's; and he did not seek his glory, but the Father's. A similar thing happens in the ministry of the Spirit of God. He glorifies the name of Jesus: when a person is born by the Spirit, that person speaks of Jesus Christ as Lord and Savior.

Pentecost was the first time the disciples officially proclaimed Jesus as the Christ. That day, standing in the stream of the poured-out Spirit, Peter did not explain who the Spirit is, but who Jesus is. And today, when the Spirit of God sets someone free, he or she does not shout, "I have the Spirit," but "I know Jesus."

Christ and All His Blessings.

Notice how the catechism says that the Spirit makes us share in Christ (first) and all his blessings (second). We cannot have the benefits of Jesus without having Jesus.

When we are physically ill, knowing the medical doctor is less important than getting the correct treatment and the right medicines. As long as we have the right medicines, we may recover even if we don't know the doctor who prescribed them. But this is not true for our spiritual malady. First the Spirit brings us to Jesus Christ, and when we personally know, accept, and love him, we can get to his treasures. We must have Christ before we can get "all his blessings."

Many of us would like to stay out of the paws of the devil without falling entirely into the hands of Jesus. It won't work. Only when our lives are "under new management" do we receive all the goodness of Christ.

"And All His Blessings."

The rich benefits in which we share when the Holy Spirit unites us with Christ are not described in this answer of the catechism. Some of the blessings follow in succeeding Lord's Days: our membership in the one holy catholic church, our part in communion of saints, the forgiveness of sins, the resurrection of the body, and everlasting life.

A benefit of the Spirit's descent mentioned in the catechism is the abiding presence of the *Paraclete*, or "Advocate," "Comforter," "Counselor." Jesus said, "I will ask the Father, and he will give you another Counselor [Comforter] to be with you forever—the Spirit of truth" (John 14:16-17; note the personal character of the Spirit: Christ does not say "counsel" or "comfort" but "another Counselor"). In the same context Jesus says that, in the coming of the Spirit, he himself rejoins his disciples: "I will not leave you as orphans; I will come to you" (v. 18). Paul also uses "the Spirit of God . . . in you," having "the Spirit of Christ," and "Christ . . . in you" (Rom. 8:9-10) interchangeably. The phrases stand for the same reality. Because of this reality we can use strong words about the future: he "remains with me forever."

The Omission of Mission.

The greatest change caused by the coming of the Holy Spirit is the movement of salvation from the small Judean nation to the whole world. Therefore we may not speak of the Holy Spirit without talking about missions.

However, mainline churches and their theologians, including those in the Reformed tradition, have been very slow to say anything about the Spirit and the mission of the church. In our seventeenth-century confessions the Holy Spirit is primarily the one who applies the work of Christ to our inner selves. He is the Builder of the church and the Edifier of the believers, but the confessions have not taught us to see him as the great Dynamo, the Life-Bringer from the One to the many. Mission is not only our proclamation of the mighty works of God; mission itself is one of the mighty works of God. It is the Spirit's undertaking.

With the coming of the Holy Spirit the good news gets wings or wheels. The Spirit uses the church to present Christ to the world; the Spirit himself is our Mover. He is the One who convicts the world (John 16:8). Although Christ mentions the testimony of the Spirit in the same breath with the testimony that is required of his followers (John 15:26-27), when we are in a pinch we will find that it is really the Spirit who is in control of the mission: "When they arrest you, do not worry about what to say or how to say it. At that time you will be given what to say, for it will not be you speaking, but the Spirit of your Father speaking through you" (Matt. 10:19-20).

The church must always be on the move. God, in the Old Testament, has a holy place and a holy land for a holy people. In the New Testament the people form the holy temple (1 Cor. 3:16) no matter where they are, because the Spirit dwells in them. The people are the vehicle of the Spirit to reach the whole world. The church itself is a preliminary result of the work of the Spirit, but the church is not his goal. The goal of the Spirit is an earth "full of the knowledge of the Lord as the waters cover the sea" (Isa. 11:9).

Spirit and Communication.

Representatives of fifteen different countries are mentioned in Acts when the Spirit is poured out (2:9-11). All of these suddenly hear "the wonders of God" declared in their own tongues. Clearly, Pentecost reverses the confusion at the tower of Babel (Gen. 11), where God came down to break up the unity of the human race because mankind was united in rebellion. But in the "last days" (Acts 2:17) he came to unite them into "one body and one Spirit" (Eph. 4:4).

The reception of the Spirit and the speech of Christians go together. In the book of Acts we read repeatedly that when the Holy Spirit descended on people, they began to speak in tongues. However, it's not the *tongue-speaking* but the *speaking* that deserves the emphasis. The Spirit stoops to use our vocal cords for the mission. So those of us who say that we cannot talk about Jesus are grieving the Spirit of God. He wants to communicate through us.

Paul considers prophecy a better gift than tongues because of its communication value: "everyone who prophesies speaks to men for their strengthening, encouragement and comfort" (1 Cor. 14:3).

The New Testament was written by missionaries and evangelists, who were always crossing borders, busy communicating the great news to new areas. Their writings aimed to equip young believers to be better witnesses to the truth. Nothing about New Testament people and situations is static. Everything and everybody is on the march: this is the mission of the Spirit.

How could we ever miss it!

The Spirit Makes Us Useful.

When our sins are forgiven, we are accepted by God. But we are not useful to him until we are led by the Spirit.

We have rich resources in the Heidelberg Catechism. We do notice, though, how the catechism teaches us well on sin and on grace but does not say enough on the work of the Holy Spirit.

Lord's Day 21

THE HOLY CATHOLIC CHURCH

Q ***What do you believe concerning the "holy catholic church"?***

A ***I believe that the Son of God, through his Spirit and Word, out of the entire human race, from the beginning of the world to its end, gathers, protects, and preserves for himself a community chosen for eternal life and united in true faith. And of this community I am and always will be a living member.***

—Q & A 54

The Catholic Church.

We must not allow the Roman Catholic Church to speak about itself exclusively as the "Catholic Church." I too am a member of the *catholic* church, the one, *universal* church of Jesus Christ. As a matter of fact, our membership in this one, universal church of Jesus Christ is the only real form of church membership that counts and lasts.

By denying the Roman Catholics their monopoly of the word *catholic* and telling them to look at the word *Roman*—because that's where their peculiarities come from—we are not only rebuking them but also claiming them. "We believe and profess one catholic or universal Church, which is a holy congregation of true Christian believers, all expecting their salvation in Jesus Christ, being washed by His blood, sanctified and sealed by the Holy Spirit" (Belgic Confession, Art. 27). We are saying that there is only one church; either one belongs to this church, or one is outside of it. The Roman Catholics claim they belong to this church; so do we make that claim. And if it is true that they belong and we belong, we had better accept each other as Christ has accepted us (cf. Rom. 15:7).

"I Believe One . . . Church."

We are not discussing here what people are doing in the church or doing to the church or saying about the church; we are stating our faith: Jesus is building his church.

We cannot say a sensible thing about the church unless and until we have seen the Son of God at work.

In the church we spend too much time staring at each other. That may keep us from seeing Christ. "Men of Israel . . . why do you stare at us?" asked Peter. An ever-growing crowd had just surrounded him and the apostle John. This happened right after a crippled beggar had been healed in the name of Jesus (Acts 3:12). "The person who is really at work here," said Peter, "is the same One you denied before Pontius Pilate" (cf. 3:13). This is nothing but the ongoing ministry of the living Jesus Christ.

We speak of the "Acts of the Apostles" and the "Careers of the Missionaries." When we read books about them, we wish that those heroes of faith would walk among us today. But we should not stare at them; we should be thinking, "That's the kind of Lord we have in the church."

There are two ways of looking at the church, and the usual way is the wrong way. Only the eyes of faith see it right: the Son of God gathers, preserves, and protects, by his Spirit and Word, a church chosen to everlasting life, says the catechism.

There are two ways of talking about the church, and most talk, by friend or foe, misses the point. But those who perceive the divine operation of which we have become a part by our church membership can scarcely contain themselves: they walk and jump and praise God like the healed beggar in the story of Acts 3.

Church and Denomination.

Someone might still ask whether the holy catholic church of our catechism is something else, something different from the denomination in which the reader holds membership. Can we be members of the one without holding membership in the other?

Thank God that the membership of the one holy catholic church is infinitely bigger than any visible, instituted church in which we may now hold membership. Even if our denomination were the biggest of all denominations, we are never permitted to see more than one little historical bit of the great company that the Son of God gathers "from the beginning of the world to its end."

But we should also stress that belonging to the Christian Reformed Church (for instance) and belonging to the one holy catholic church mean the same thing. Your church membership in the Christian Reformed Church is meaningful only if through it you give shape to your membership in the catholic church of Jesus Christ.

If you have grave doubts that your membership in the local church is membership in that one catholic church of Christ, you should reexamine both your membership and your life. Either we as a church have departed from what Jesus wants his church to be—and you must rush and join the true church—or you have not taken your church membership seriously enough.

Within this Christian Reformed Church (or whatever your denomination), Jesus Christ is the One who gathers and the One who is the Head. When Jesus admits a person, he or she is admitted, and when Jesus rejects, the council of the church must reject. What Jesus commands must be done, what he speaks must be said, and what he promises must be preached.

When we talk about the one holy catholic church, we make a confession about a work of Christ that's much bigger than what any one of us ever gets to see. But we are not talking about a work that differs from the church in which we are members. In fact, all of us should constantly strive for our own local church to reflect ever more and better the one holy catholic church. We must want nothing more and nothing less.

Elect from Every Nation

The Son of God is central in our thinking about the church. But we also acknowledge the work of the Father. All people of all times and races who are gathered by Christ are "chosen for eternal life." And the gracious choice, the election, is a work that the Bible ascribes to God the Father. "Praise be to the God and Father of our Lord Jesus Christ . . . he chose us in him before the creation of the world . . . he predestined us to be adopted as his sons through Jesus Christ" (Eph. 1:3-5).

Christ gathers the elect of God. That throws a special light on the conditions for church membership. We do not enjoy the privileges of church membership because we are qualified but because we are chosen.

If church membership depended upon our qualifications, no doubt we could think of all sorts of conditions, from the ridiculous to the sublime. We might say, for instance, that only those who have an I.Q. of more than 100 and an income of more than twenty-thousand dollars a year could join; we might insist on moral excellence or on a particular spiritual experience. Any of these conditions might be applied if church membership were a matter of qualification. But it is a matter of God's election. We become members because God loves us, not because we are lovable or have been born on the right side of the tracks.

It is not easy to discuss election as the qualification of church membership and as the fountain of salvation. But we should not shy away from it. A church that does not teach election cannot continue to teach sovereign grace. For if we are saved by anything other than God's choice, we are not saved by grace.

The Activity of the Son.

The Son of God "gathers, protects, and preserves" the church. First he "gathers." He does not lead individuals to salvation and holiness by separate ways, but he "gathers," brings us together in a community. All of us may personally know this Son of God as our Savior, but none of us gets a "personal Savior."

Those whom he *gathers* he *protects* against the evil one. In spite of their weakness and the powers of demons, he *preserves* them until the day they are promoted to the church triumphant.

This gathering, protecting, and preserving activity of Jesus Christ is the true explanation of the holy catholic church. Wherever Christ is active, the church becomes visible. And wherever the church is visible, Christ has lit a light in the world.

When we are no longer sure that the Son of God is gathering and that the church is the visible expression of his invisible presence, we are merely playing ecclesiastical games.

The Sin of Secular Churchmanship.

We North Americans must be more careful and modest in our talk about the church. Our loose remarks about "growing a church" and "starting a church" and "training some church planters" tend to make light of the mystery of the church. While the church certainly has a human side (Christ gathers; people congregate—he brings us in; we have the obligation to join), faith sees the church as the activity of the Son of God (Q & A 54). This activity results in the visible communion of saints (Q & A 55).

Obviously, then, we never really "start" a church. We join. And we *must* join. We are not free to be Christians in any other way because Christ gathers us and protects and preserves us in the togetherness of his church. "We believe . . . that no person of whatsoever state or condition he may be, ought to withdraw from it . . . but that all men are in duty bound to join and unite themselves with" the true church, "submitting themselves to the doctrine and discipline thereof; bowing their necks under the yoke of Jesus Christ" (Belgic Confession, Art. 28).

The multitude of sects, religious groups, denominations, and whatever else goes by the name of "church," has certainly cheapened our church concept. But the Scriptures teach that there is only one church of Jesus Christ. We must find and honor her, because this church is his church.

Through His Spirit and Word.

The Son of God gathers the church. But he performs his activities through his Spirit. This is how Christ does his universal work. The age of Christ's reign is also the age of the Spirit. The Son of God is now among us as the Holy Spirit (see our discussion of Lord's Day 20).

The success of church gathering and church building depends on the tools of Spirit and Word. One might gather crowds and even form communities with other means of communication and attraction. But churches are built by God's Word and God's Spirit. All who have received an assignment within the church of Jesus Christ must learn to value these two tools and to have a healthy suspicion of all other instruments for church growth.

The Trinity and the Church.

All the works of God are works of Father, Son, and Spirit. And the church is God's masterwork. The one holy church was "chosen according to the foreknowledge of the Father," is holy by "the sanctifying work of the Spirit," and exists to serve its Lord and Savior: it was chosen "for obedience to Jesus Christ and sprinkling by his blood" (1 Pet. 1:2).

Therefore, a careful look at "Zion" (that's a love name for the church) requires a view from at least three angles: we should see God's church as the people of God, the body of Christ, and the temple of the Spirit.

People of God.

Here we must speak of the biblical themes of election, calling, and covenant making. Usually we begin with the calling of Abraham (Gen. 12), but it would not be wrong to go back to Abel, who may be called "righteous by faith" (Heb. 11:4), and to the line of Seth, whose children called on the name of the Lord (Gen. 4:26).

When we study the church from this angle, we confess that it is a covenant people, bound to God through all ages by the one covenant of grace that God established with Abraham and his seed. Historically, this covenant goes through two dispensations: the time of the shadows, when the pact of Sinai was binding, and the era of fulfillment, in which the covenant people live under the blood and by the Spirit of Jesus Christ.

Wherever this biblical insight prevails, people hear God's Word in the Old Testament much better than in congregations where this insight is lacking. The consciousness of being God's covenant people makes for a profound sense of historical continuity: David is no stranger, and Abraham is our father; the *shalom* of the promised land is still the goal of the journey. These people regard the congregation as a blood-bound, covenanted unity. Life's highest privilege is to belong to the congregation, and life's worst fate is to be cut off from it. And the people of God have no doubt about the standing of children and babies (they belong!) or about the obligations that the covenant community has toward them.

Yet even this grand view of "Zion" may obscure other biblical vistas.

Body of Christ.

Especially through the apostle Paul, God taught us to look at the church as the body of Christ: "in Christ we who are many form one body" (Rom. 12:5); "now you are the body of Christ, and each one of you is a part of it" (1 Cor. 12:27).

When the Bible calls us the "body" of Christ, God instructs us about the relationship all of us have to Jesus and, second, the relationship we have to each other.

In understanding our common relationship to Jesus, it is not helpful to think of ourselves as a human body or trunk or torso of which Christ is the "head." The idea is that we are the *corpus* or corporation of which he is the representative head. Whatever he did, we did; whatever happened to him, happened to us. All of us are in the One. Being "in Christ" is a short way of saying that we are no longer "in Adam" but that we have died to one form of life and risen into another. Henceforth we are "in Christ" (Eph. 1:12-13), and we do all our work and ordinary living "in the Lord," as his body. We even marry in him (1 Cor. 7:39), and finally we die in him (1 Thess. 4:16). The church exists in her Lord because she is the body of Christ.

The expression *body of Christ* also teaches us about the intimate relationship we have with one another. Used this way, *body* means a human body, an organism with "members." And this figure of speech includes the head as a part of the human body (1 Cor. 12:21). The Lord teaches us not to think of ourselves as being more useful or more important than other church members, because the foot needs the hand and all the members of the body form one harmonious unit (Rom. 12:4-8, 1 Cor. 12:14-31).

Temple of the Spirit.

Finally, we should also view the church (believers) as the dwelling place of God. We are communally God's temple, although each of us has the Spirit. The New Testament does not allow us to think of the people of God as a *bunch* of temples, but as *the* temple (1 Cor. 3:16, Eph. 2:22).

The new era that began with the coming of the Spirit signified the end of a period during which God lived in buildings or tents. God never lived visibly in these buildings; nevertheless, these were once his divine residences. The temple in Jerusalem was his earthly address, and those who sought the Lord had to go there. Now that period is past.

***Q** What do you understand by "the communion of saints"?*

***A** First, that believers one and all, as members of this community, share in Christ and in all his treasures and gifts. Second, that each member should consider it a duty to use these gifts readily and cheerfully for the service and enrichment of the other members.*

—Q & A 55

The church is always tempted to return to the Old Testament, not only to works and law rather than living by faith and grace but also to its building-centeredness. It's a continuing temptation for "pious" people to enclose God in shrines and buildings and to call these places sanctuaries.

Perhaps God can be glorified by a nice church building. Usually, however, people take the glory from the real temple and give it to the building. *You* are God's holy ground!

The Creation of Community.

The first result of the work of the Savior is the communion of saints. There is no private Christianity. When we are saved by the Lord, we are given to each other. No one is called by Christ without being recruited into his army. One cannot be a Christian without being a part of the body of Christ.

We Share in Christ.

All members of the holy community "share in Christ and in all his measures and gifts." This means that all of us have at least three gifts in common: faith, hope, and love. Faith needs to be fed, hope must be quickened, and love should be deepened, but one could not be a member of the church of Christ without having in some measure the gifts of faith and hope and love. After all, we share in Christ. And it is by faith that we have received him, by hope that we reach forward to meeting him, and by love that he is present within us. Therefore love is the greatest of the church's possessions (1 Cor. 13:13). Love is the cement that holds the church together. If we do not love, we have no part in Christ, and the "communion of saints" falls apart. Love is a gift and a calling; *every* gift from Christ is at the same time a calling.

For Cheerful Service.

In addition to faith, hope, and love, the communion of saints has a variety of gifts that the Spirit divides as he sees fit. God entrusts us with these gifts for the enrichment of other members. Each *must* help the other within the communion of saints. That's not optional or "nice" but our duty. God gave the gifts for this purpose, and God will punish those who use them for self-aggrandizement. Neither are we free to merely "mind our own business" within the communion of saints. Another's welfare is our concern, another's poverty—economic or spiritual—is our challenge, another's laughter is our reason for joy, and another's sorrow costs us tears.

The payment of love that the Scriptures say we owe to one another is much bigger than we teach or practice in the life of the church. Certainly, each and all of us must have had some moving and rich experiences of the communion of saints. But we do not feel sufficiently responsible for each other's spiritual enrichment. Yet this is one of the strongest biblical themes—one that recurs in every Bible book.

Forgiven Sinners.

In the Apostles' Creed the article about the forgiveness of sins follows the one about the holy catholic church and the communion of saints. It is fitting to keep words about forgiveness close to the confession about the saints: human saints are moral heroes, but God's saints are forgiven sinners.

Forgiveness is the bottom line of all church talk. I believe in the unity, holiness, and catholicity of the church, but it is painfully torn, fragmented, and parochial. I also believe in the forgiveness of sins.

I believe in the communion of saints, but sometimes we do each other more harm than good. And I believe in the forgiveness of sins.

***Q** What do you believe concerning "the forgiveness of sins"?*

***A** I believe that God, because of Christ's atonement, will never hold against me any of my sins nor my sinful nature which I need to struggle against all my life. Rather, in his grace God grants me the righteousness of Christ to free me forever from judgment.*

—Q & A 56

Forgiveness Measured Out.

The catechism often speaks of God's forgiveness. As a matter of fact, the main motifs of the document are the forgiveness of sinners for Jesus' sake and our righteousness through Christ's merits. Note how carefully forgiveness is spelled out in this answer:

Why does God forgive? "Because of Christ's atonement." Not because we have repented and believed, though that's essential. Not because I am now doing better, although that, too, is an indispensable turn. And not because of anything I have done, but "because of Christ's atonement."

What does God forgive? "My sins"—that's what I've done. And "my sinful nature"—that's my character and my condition. I may not use my sinful nature as an excuse for my sinning ("too bad, but that's the way I am"). That sinful nature is an enemy "which I need to struggle against all my life." And my sinful nature is in need of God's forgiveness.

Notice *how God forgives:* He "will never hold against me" what I did and what I am. That's beautiful: that's royal forgiveness, ugliness put as far out of sight as east is from west.

That's how a husband and wife must forgive—"never hold it against her." Never bring it up again! That's how the communion of saints must forgive and can forgive.

The *goal of forgiveness* is "the righteousness of Christ" and being "free . . . forever from judgment." Our righteousness and uprightness are the goal of Christ's work, and the guarantee of his blood is that we shall never come into condemnation. We are free at last and free forever.

The church is the first result of forgiveness. The church lives by forgiveness; it practices and proclaims forgiveness in Jesus' name.

Lord's Day 22

THIS IS THE LIFE

***Q** How does "the resurrection of the body" comfort you?*

***A** Not only my soul will be taken immediately after this life to Christ its head, but even my very flesh, raised by the power of Christ, will be reunited with my soul and made like Christ's glorious body.*

—Q & A 57

Comfort.

Each question of Lord's Day 22 asks how a particular article of the Apostles' Creed *comforts* us. All of the catechism wants to teach us how we should live and die in the joy of the only comfort (Q. 2). The Christian faith gives much food to philosophers and theologians, but we study it properly only when we use it for God's glory and for human comfort.

Unless we know our need for comfort, the catechism's teachings about the resurrection of the body and everlasting life are probably wasted on us. We live among thousands of people whose basic conviction is that life is eating cake and that some good pieces are still left for them. Some of these people listen to sermons about the resurrection of the body and life everlasting. Then they go back to cake eating, girl watching, car polishing. They have no need of Christian comfort.

Eye Salve.

Jesus once wrote a letter to a congregation that was well settled, well established, and unaware that they needed his comfort: "You say, 'I am rich . . . and do not need a thing.' But you do not realize that you are wretched, pitiful, poor, blind and naked. I counsel you to buy from me . . . salve to put on your eyes, so you can see" (Rev. 3:17-18).

Some of us are not going to be very excited about the great truths of the resurrection of the body and life everlasting because it is impossible for us to see our own pitiful condition. That's why we should say a prayer for eye salve before we study the catechism.

Beyond Imagination.

The teaching of the resurrection of the body is the most mind stretching and faith demanding of all Christian doctrines. Some people have difficulty believing in creation—the act by which God made the world out of nothing by the word of his power. But compared to the resurrection of the body, creation is easy to believe. The mystery of living, the riddle of dying, and the amazing wonders we observe on planet Earth confirm a faith in an omnipotent Creator. The daily and nightly speech of creation makes a faith in chemical accidents and mere mechanical processes hard to maintain.

But now think of the resurrection of the body: so many thousands and millions of human bodies have been mangled by accidents and wars, and billions have been buried or burned or gassed or drowned. All have returned to dust or into other living organisms, which again died and became parts of the same cycle. And the church teaches us to say, "Not only my soul will be taken immediately after this life to Christ its head, but even my very flesh, raised by the power of Christ, will be reunited with my soul and made like Christ's glorious body." "My . . . flesh" is this fragile human existence that must be kept going with food and exercise and medicine until it is worn out. "All men are like grass, and all their glory [their genius, brilliant theology, and heroism] is like the flowers of the field; the grass withers and the flowers fall"—and then it's all over. Except that "the Word of the Lord stands forever," and therefore the church dares to make the unimaginable confession of a resurrection (1 Pet. 1:24-25).

Language of the Catechism.

Today we no longer talk in terms of "soul" and "flesh," though we still admire the carefulness and brevity of the catechism.

In the New Testament *flesh* usually indicates humanity in its unredeemed state, doomed to lose the struggle against sin and death. *Flesh* is not opposed to *soul* in the Bible. But *flesh* is contrasted with (Holy) *Spirit.* However, the catechism uses *flesh* as a synonym for the human body, our present form of existence. At death (the end of our present form of living) life, or soul, leaves the body: it "will be taken immediately . . . to Christ its head." The catechism does not say that the soul goes to heaven but that it will be taken to Christ. Next it teaches us to confess that "even my very flesh" will be raised in the last day by the power of Christ and "reunited with my soul." This is the resurrection of the body. After this event I will live as a transformed human being, with a body "like Christ's glorious body."

Soul and Body.

In trying to say what human beings are, what happens to them when they die, and what awaits them at the last trumpet, the Christian church has always followed two streams of thought. One emphasized the "immortality of the soul," and the other, the "resurrection of the body."

Emphasis on the immortality of the soul has usually not been good for the Christian community. It has led to a disregard for the body and all things temporal. The teaching of an immortal soul in an inferior body is found in many non-Christian religions. This teaching—that a person's soul is a bird jailed in the cage of a temporary body—used to tie in with Greek philosophy and now finds a kinship in Asian religions. It is not biblical, but sometimes it sounds biblical.

In the Bible "the Lord God formed man from the dust of the ground and breathed into his nostrils the breath of life, and man became a living being" (Gen. 2:7), a servant of God who must love God with body and soul, muscle and imagination.

What Happens When We Die?

Soul and body belong together, and neither one, all by itself, is "me." When physical death occurs, these two, body and soul, are wrenched apart, and I die. But that's not the whole story.

When your father's (or mother's) body is lifeless, the physician pronounces him dead. We say, "He is dead," and we weep. But we also say, "He lives!" and we are comforted. The doctor tells the truth when he says that your father is dead. But the Scriptures don't lie, either, when they teach that your dad is living.

If we continue to press the question by asking, "*How* does dad live now? Does he see Jesus? Can he see us? Is he fully happy even without a body? Is he fully conscious, and, if so, of what is he conscious?" then we must admit that we don't have many answers. We know that he lives, because the Bible says so. We know that he was immediately transferred to live with Christ his head, because God says so.

"I tell you the truth, today you will be with me in paradise." In that famous saying on the cross (Luke 23:43) Jesus promised an early meeting ("today") with the thief who hung next to him. The meeting would occur in a place of bliss called "paradise."

"I desire to depart and be with Christ, which is better by far" said Paul (Phil. 1:23). All who know that dying is "gain" when living is "Christ" (v. 21) will understand his sentiment. "To depart and be with Christ" refers to a move from the present address to the other one. The same thought is in another of Paul's sayings: "We . . . would prefer to be away from the body and at home with the Lord" (2 Cor. 5:8). Such language does not contemplate a prolonged state of unconsciousness between death and the resurrection of the body.

The Old Testament teaches very little about life after death. Those who want a picture of the future state and the future home don't get much. But the assurance that God's power rescues his loved ones from the grave and holds on to them beyond the realm of death pervades Old Testament writings. It seems that all of us, like sheep, are destined for the grave, but God will surely take us to himself (Ps. 49:14-15). God guides us with his counsel through this life, and afterward he will take us to glory (Ps. 73:24). "You will not abandon me to the grave, nor will you let your Holy One see decay. You have made known to me the path of life; you will fill me with joy in your presence, with eternal pleasures at your right hand" (Ps. 16:10-11).

Crucial Consideration.

True, the church has always debated these texts. The Jehovah's Witnesses are not the only ones who deny the continued existence of human beings after death. The "intermediate state," the time between our physical death and the resurrection of the body, receives only indirect attention in the Scriptures. Therefore many believe in some kind of "soul sleep": the soul plunges into a dark and dreamless sleep without any awareness of time or place until the alarm clock goes off for the great getting-up morning. And that theory has many attractive points.

We maintain, however, with our confession, that we will be with Christ as soon as life leaves our bodies. The crucial consideration is not merely our exegesis of the texts mentioned above and debated so frequently. The argument finally comes down to an understanding of the *faithfulness of God himself.* When Jesus debated with the Sadducees, who did not believe in angels and who said that there was no resurrection, he showed that Scripture teaches a continued life after death with a text you or I would never have used. Jesus said, "Have you not read what God said to you, 'I am the God of Abraham, the God of Isaac, and the God of Jacob'? He is not the God of the dead but of the living" (Matt. 22:31-32).

Once God has covenanted with Abraham (or John or Dick or Mary), he never lets go of such a covenant or of his covenant partner. Once God has established communion with us, it is necessarily an eternal communion. A covenant with God is more than a faithful marriage that endures until death parts the husband and wife. God's faithful covenant is not interrupted. Death cannot break up a union forged by the love of God (see Rom. 8:39).

Yes, what the doctor says is true. When your father or mother has died, the body is lifeless. Your hand feels it, the doctor says it, and the truth comes slowly home: this is no longer your father. Life is gone. Respectfully we bury the remains of our loved ones in the sure expectation of the resurrection of the body. For God will redeem all of his creation.

At the same time it is true that your departed mother lives. Death was gain for her. She moved immediately to be with Christ, her head. You must not press for answers about the circumstances and about how she can live before the Lord gives her a new body. We know that she is kept with the Lord and by the Lord. For the Lord was her God all these years, and her God is not a God of the dead but of the living.

1 Corinthians 15.

Paul's treatise on the resurrection of the body (1 Cor. 15) never fails to affirm our faith in what God has done and to make us eager to see his new creation. All of us should read this chapter frequently.

Paul begins with an impressive restatement of the apostolic tradition, the saving gospel, which is the foundation of the Christian church: "I want to remind you. . . . What I received I passed on to you . . . that Christ died for our sins . . . was raised on the third day . . . appeared to [many witnesses]. . . . This is what we preach, and this is what you believed" (vv. 1-11). Then Paul takes on the people who deny the resurrection (v. 12). Forcefully he maintains first *that* the dead are raised (v. 12) and later answers the question of *how* they are raised (v. 35). In the first part he argues that denying the resurrection of the body would involve a rejection of Jesus' resurrection. Evidently, people in Corinth who denied the resurrection in general did not deny that Jesus was raised to life. Paul shows that denying the resurrection repudiates the whole content of the Christian faith.

Turning to the question "How are the dead raised?" (v. 35), he begins his answer by saying to the questioner, "Fool!" or "How foolish!" (v. 36) which sounds strange and discourteous to us. But in the Bible a fool is someone who does not know God. And in discussing the resurrection of the body, Paul shows that the doctrine hangs on the power of God and on the resources God has at his disposal.

Our Bodies Are Sown.

The analogy of the seed has at least two applications. The first is that—for the seed and for us—the only way to a new life is through "death." The second is that what comes out is quite different from what goes in (vv. 36-37), both for the seed that goes into the ground and for our earthly bodies that are to be buried. "God gives [the seed] a body as he has determined, and to each kind of seed he gives its own body" (v. 38).

God demonstrates his freedom and power in creating an astounding assortment of (new) bodies. Not only do a great variety of "bodies" come from buried seeds, but also "all flesh is not the same" (v. 39): people, birds, fish, and animals have their own "flesh," their own forms of existence on earth. And this variety is not limited to what is on earth but extends to the "heavenly bodies" that are discernible to us. All these heavenly "bodies" have splendor, but their radiance is not the same: "The sun has one kind of splendor, the moon another and the stars another; and star differs from star in splendor" (v. 41).

From Adam's Weakness to Christ's Glory.

From the analogy of the seed Paul moves to the great comparison between heavenly and earthly man. He makes that move through a fourfold comparison of great literary power (vv. 42-44):

> The body that is sown is perishable, it is raised imperishable; it is sown in dishonor, it is raised in glory; it is sown in weakness, it is raised in power; it is sown a natural body, it is raised a spiritual body.

The comparison of the natural ("psychic") and the spiritual ("pneumatic") is anchored in the comparison between Adam and Christ. When Paul says that the natural comes first and then the spiritual (v. 46), he refers to the era of Adam that precedes the era of Christ. First we live in a form of existence that is qualified by Adam: it's a "flesh and blood" kind of existence (v. 51) that's incapable of entering into the other world. The Adamic kind of life must be changed through death or "in the twinkling of an eye, at the last trumpet" (v. 52), but change it must. The descendants of Adam are all mortal and perishable because they are all "of the earth." They received the breath of life into their nostrils, but some day they must breathe their last (vv. 45, 48; cf. Gen. 2:7).

The new life and the other form of human existence come from the "last Adam, a life-giving spirit" (v. 45). By his resurrection Christ inaugurates the new creation in the "spiritual" human body. By his Spirit he gives imperishable and glorious life to us. In principle we receive this new life when the Spirit dwells in us as the pledge or first payment of the world to come. The full reality will be ours when God's kingdom comes in full force and death is abolished (vv. 24-26).

The Spiritual Body.

We will have spiritual bodies. That does not mean nonmaterial bodies. *Spiritual* does not stand over against *material* in 1 Corinthians 15 but contrasts with what is weak, sinful, mortal. A spiritual body is still a body. It is a form of existence totally qualified by the Holy Spirit. A spiritual body is a Christ-like body, whereas a "natural" or "physical" body is an Adam-like body.

The new life will be quite different from the kind of life we know. None of us will be handicapped. We will need no health insurance. Work will be worship. Living will be as good as God intended it to be.

The new life and the new world will be shockingly different from the present world. But there is also going to be a continuation from the present to the future, from here to there. That's because eternal life begins here and now. And the future will be the completion of what God has now begun in us.

The Joy Is in My Heart to Stay.

Christ redeems us for eternal joy, and today he gives us the beginning of that joy. It's a joy in body and soul. We have it at the Lord's Supper and at work, during the prayer meeting and at the baseball game. We experience joy because we have smallpox vaccinations and a serum against measles, but also because we are steadfast against temptation. These joyful experiences are harbingers of victory, messages of shalom. We participate in the joy because we have received eternal life—already!

"Whoever believes in the Son has eternal life" (John 3:36). This does not say that the believer "will have" eternal life, nor that he or she "might get" eternal life, but that he or she *has* eternal life.

Q ***How does the article concerning "life everlasting" comfort you?***

A ***Even as I already now experience in my heart the beginning of eternal joy, so after this life I will have perfect blessedness such as no eye has seen, no ear has heard, no human heart has ever imagined: a blessedness in which to praise God eternally.***

—Q & A 58

Life of a Different Quality.

In church school we learned that *eternal* means "without beginning and without end." Therefore we might think that we go on living forever when we get "eternal life." But "eternal life" is much more than prolonged human life.

When the Bible says we inherit or receive "life everlasting," or "eternal life," it means we participate in the life of God by his redeeming love. We should not think of this kind of life as "life that never ends." The emphasis should be on the quality of eternal life as life that comes to us from God through the Holy Spirit when we believe in Christ. And since this life is nothing less than the life of God, we logically conclude that it has no end.

By biblical standards, only those who have this kind of life are really living, and those who do not (yet) have this life are actually dead. They who believe in Christ live, even when they die. But those who refuse to accept Jesus Christ are dead, even if they claim to be living. In that sense, "to have life" and "to have eternal life" are the same thing in the Bible.

"God has given us eternal life, and this life is in his Son. He who has the Son has life; he who does not have the Son of God does not have life" (1 John 5:11-12). The message of that text is clear enough. The question is not whether we hear what it says; the question is whether we want to *believe* that Jesus is the difference between life and death. Knowing that others are dead—yet refuse to come to the Tree of Life—makes our present joy less than perfect.

Future Blessedness.

"After this life," says the catechism, "I will have perfect blessedness such as no eye has seen, no ear has heard, no man has ever imagined."

First Corinthians 2:9 tells us, "No eye has seen, no ear has heard, no mind has conceived what God has prepared for those who love him." Paul says that he is quoting from the Old Testament (Isaiah 64:4), but the origin of that quote has given all interpreters difficulties. Paul's point is that the mystery of salvation is not discoverable by human investigation (no eye has seen; no ear has heard) or by human philosophy. Only those who love God know this mystery, and they know it only because God has revealed it to them by the Spirit.

The catechism uses this verse to refer not to the salvation that has been revealed in the fullness of time but to the full salvation to be unveiled at the end of time. The blessedness will be beyond anything human senses can predict or imagine. That's the meaning the catechism gives to the words of 1 Corinthians 2:9. Of course, nobody can deny that "what God has prepared for those who love him" involves more than we have received thus far. That's probably why the writers of the Heidelberg Catechism chose the text; the blessedness prepared by our heavenly Father is more than we have and more than we can imagine.

To Praise God Eternally.

Some non-Christian religions offer lively descriptions of the delights that await the faithful in the hereafter. The Bible describes the delights rather soberly, usually in negative terms: the *absence* of pain, weakness, death, illness; an inheritance that *cannot* perish, spoil, or fade; *no* darkness, *no* injustice, and *no* tears. In positive terms, we will be like Jesus, and we will praise God eternally.

At the end of the journey we reach the goal. And the goal of life is the glory of God.

Then we will thank and praise him not only for what he has done but for what he is. We will rejoice not merely in the gifts but in the Giver, whom we embrace. He will be everything for everybody, "all in all" (1 Cor. 15:28).

Today one valid test to see if we have received the true life from God is to ask ourselves what place God occupies in our lives. As long as we are in this body it remains a struggle to keep our priorities in the right order. "Seek first his kingdom and his righteousness" (Matt. 6:33). We do want that. We have also learned that the way of obedience is the road of happiness. "Take my yoke upon you . . . and you will find rest for your souls" (Matt. 11:29). It's the only way to live. "Let us fix our eyes on Jesus . . . who for the joy set before him endured the cross" (Heb. 12:2). It's the only way to run the race and to reach the finish.

We are on our way to Jerusalem. "My soul yearns, even faints for the courts of the Lord" (Ps. 84:2). Because all my fountains are in him (Ps. 87:7).

Lord's Day 23

RIGHT WITH GOD

Q *What good does it do you, however, to believe all this?*

A *In Christ I am right with God and heir to life everlasting.*

—Q & A 59

What Gives?

With the church of all times and places we have now confessed our faith in God the Father and our creation, God the Son and our redemption, and God the Spirit and our sanctification. And every time our teacher, the catechism, has stopped us to ask, What's the use? What's the profit? What good does it do? "How does the knowledge of God's creation and providence *help* us?" (Q. 28). "How do the holy conception and birth of Christ *benefit* you?" (Q. 36). "What further *advantage* do we receive from Christ's sacrifice and death on the cross?" (Q. 43). "How does Christ's resurrection *benefit* us?" (Q. 45). "How does Christ's ascension into heaven *benefit* us?" (Q. 49). "How does this glory of Christ our Head *benefit* us?" (Q. 51). "How does Christ's return . . . *comfort* you?" (Q. 52). "How does 'the resurrection of the body' *comfort* you?" (Q. 57). "How does the article concerning 'life everlasting' *comfort* you?" (Q. 58).

So we conclude the study of the content of the Christian faith by answering this question: "What *good does it do you* . . . to believe *all* this?" What gives? What's in it?

It is not wrong—not too "utilitarian"—to ask ourselves what profit we realize by going to church and studying the Bible. We ought to be able to state the benefit of a particular belief or of a certain sermon. But the benefits and the advantages are clear only to those who have spiritual discernment (cf. 1 Cor. 2:14).

Not for Atheists.

The benefit of believing God's revelation is that "in Christ I am right with God and heir to life everlasting."

This answer disappoints many people because it describes an intangible benefit that presupposes both faith and fear. "Being right with God" is important only to those who are convinced that God exists. And if he exists as the Judge of all, there is no more important question than how we are related to him: are we the objects of his anger or the recipients of his grace? However, if we are uncertain whether creation has a Creator and humanity a Lord and we have never asked whether we are under God's wrath or favor, this whole teaching about "justification by grace through faith" remains a strange, irrelevant dogma.

Very few people are atheists by conviction. But millions are practical atheists. They live from day to day in ignorance of God. They make no conscious efforts to find him, because they don't care to get to know him. They are indifferent toward God, although many think that churches and religions are all right. A countless number of our contemporaries live and die without knowing God's law and God's grace.

Not for Materialists.

Our North American culture is thoroughly materialistic. It cannot think of goodness and happiness without thinking of *things*. Therefore even today's Bible-believing Christians tend to seek the benefits of believing in something other than "being right with God." Deeply influenced by contemporary culture, too many evangelists present the gospel in terms of extravagant promises: "accepting Christ" stands for delivery from all sorts of nasty habits and situations, while, positively, it stands for joy, happiness, prosperity, wholeness, good relationships, and so on. By embracing the Christian faith, people will find their self-worth, we are told. By being active in giving and praying, we will experience many tangible benefits, preachers promise. And, tired of the old testimonies about "being right with God in Christ," we hear of people who win a golf tournament by the power of prayer. Now that's where people begin to take note. There's a faith that pays dividends!

No Condemnation.

The biblical message is that all of us are by nature "objects of [God's] wrath" (Eph. 2:3). That's a hard message for all human ears, but it is especially hard for people who live relatively rich lives and who have the feeling that they govern a good part of their own destiny. When living is a struggle—from day to day, from generation to generation—a continuous effort to keep body and soul together, it is easier to believe that humanity has fallen short of God's goals and that we are objects of divine anger.

Actually it is not correct to say that the message of the Bible is the wrath of God over sin and sinful people. The message is how we can be forgiven, how God's holy anger was burned out, and what God has done with our sins in Jesus Christ. Our sinful and hopeless condition is the background against which we must understand the message of the Bible. But the message *cannot* be understood if our state of condemnation, the biblical context, is denied.

The good news is "Whoever believes in him is not condemned" (John 3:18). The reason why this is *good* news lies in the second part of the same verse: "whoever does not believe stands condemned already."

The Bible assumes that the natural way is the way to hell, the road to perdition. In biblical language all of us are traveling along that way. And

Q ***How are you right with God?***

A ***Only by true faith in Jesus Christ.***

Even though my conscience accuses me of having grievously sinned against all God's commandments and of never having kept any of them, and even though I am still inclined toward all evil, nevertheless, without my deserving it at all, out of sheer grace, God grants and credits to me the perfect satisfaction, righteousness and holiness of Christ, as if I had never sinned nor been a sinner, as if I had been as perfectly obedient as Christ was obedient for me.

All I need to do is to accept this gift of God with a believing heart.

—Q & A 60

our only hope is God's loving solution: "Whoever believes in him [God's Son] shall not perish but have eternal life" (v. 16).

The great benefit of believing is, negatively, that we will not be condemned in the final judgment. And, positively, we will inherit life everlasting, which is the opposite of what we deserve.

Justification by Faith.

This teaching is the heart of the matter, as far as the Heidelberg Catechism is concerned. Christian comfort actually consists of this: that we are righteous in God's sight by grace through faith. This was Martin Luther's life-changing and church-reforming discovery. And this biblical teaching was equally important to John Calvin, who says that justification by faith "is the main hinge on which religion turns" (*Institutes;* III, xi, 1).

It's not the first time the catechism wants us to think about this doctrine, but this time it is described more explicitly and carefully than before. We must now learn—each and every member of the church—to confess how we are right with God. The confession begins with a humble, self-denigrating admission of guilt: "Even though my conscience accuses me of having grievously sinned. . . ."

Not everybody's conscience speaks so accusingly. Only the enlightened, God-instructed conscience talks this way. Faith does not deny what conscience says. Yet we "set our hearts at rest in his presence whenever our hearts condemn us. For God is greater than our hearts" (1 John 3:19-20).

Faith and Failure.

The catechism teaches us, first, to admit that we are failures. This admission is part of the faith language of the church; it is a response to God's revelation.

I have "sinned against all God's commandments"—this means that I have done what he has forbidden—and I have not "kept any of them," which means I have failed to adore him and to love my neighbors as God requires.

Later, when we discuss Lord's Day 44, we should face the question of whether the catechism does not overestimate the power of sin—or, perhaps, underestimate the power of the Holy Spirit in those who have received redemption and renewal in Christ. The radical words of this answer ("never having kept any of [the commandments]" and "I am still inclined toward all evil") are echoes from the letter to the Romans, to which the church must always go to learn what it means to be righteous before God.

In Paul's letter to the Romans the teaching of justification by faith is preceded by a discourse on human failures so that the readers might appreciate how righteousness by faith is the only possible way. So the first part of the letter concludes this way: "Jews and Gentiles alike are all under sin" (3:9); "there is no one righteous, not even one" (3:10); the word of the law brings condemnation to all "who are under the law, so that every mouth may be silenced and the whole world held accountable to God" (3:19); and "no one will be declared righteous in his sight by observing the law" (3:20).

The Word of God convinces us of the impossibility of traveling any other way, thus urging us to go the way God opened. The Spirit destroys our spiritual pride and self-confidence so that we might boast in the cross and place our confidence in Christ alone. The Spirit shows our unrighteousness so that we desire to be clothed in Christ's righteousness. Accepting this "negative" teaching is essential for receiving the comfort of the gospel. Unless our hands are emptied, they cannot be filled.

"Nevertheless!"

The word *nevertheless* in the middle of this confession (A. 60) is crucial. The good news is an impossible possibility. It is something that happens in spite of all reasonable expectations. It is a "nevertheless" of grace, God's great surprise, unveiled in the fullness of time: "But now a righteousness from God, apart from law, has been made known. . . . This righteousness from God comes through faith in Jesus Christ to all who believe. There is no difference, for all have sinned and fall short of the glory of God, and are justified freely by his grace through the redemption that came by Christ Jesus" (Rom. 3:21-24).

All differences, no matter how old and deep or how recent and painful, are removed in this apostolic teaching of the New Testament: "there is no difference!" All people are guilty before God, and all are justified freely by his grace. Only believe!

No matter what terrible sin you may have committed, you are declared righteous by the Judge; you are clean and innocent when you have placed your faith and hope in Jesus.

This is the "nevertheless" of the gospel proclaimed by God's church. We all must learn to repeat it against the accusations of Satan, of our own consciences, and, sometimes, of fellow believers: "nevertheless," I am righteous "as if I had never sinned nor been a sinner, as if I had been as perfectly obedient" as Christ himself.

Faith triumphs over our failures as long as we know the "nevertheless" of justification by faith in Christ. Everyone who humbles himself and cries "God, have mercy on me, a sinner" will go home "justified" (Luke 18:13-14).

The Protestant "Solo."

"We maintain that a man is justified by faith apart from observing the law" (Rom. 3:28). When Martin Luther translated this verse, he inserted a word that is not really in the original—the word *alone*. A person is justified "by faith alone." But with that extra word Luther did catch the thrust of Paul's argument. Henceforth *sola fide*, "by faith alone," became a motto of the children of the Reformation.

Most Lutheran and Reformed Christians have learned three short Latin expressions, and all three have the word *alone* in them: *sola fide*, "by faith alone"; *sola gratia*, "by grace alone"; and *soli Deo gloria*, "to God alone the glory." Sometimes we add a fourth one: *sola Scriptura*, "only the Scriptures."

***Q** Why do you say that by faith alone you are right with God?*

***A** It is not because of any value my faith has that God is pleased with me. Only Christ's satisfaction, righteousness, and holiness make me right with God. And I can receive this righteousness and make it mine in no other way than by faith alone.*

—Q & A 61

Christ Alone.

These "solo" words still get to the heart of the conflict with Rome. The Roman Catholics did not and do not deny that we are redeemed by the work of Christ and that this great benefit must be received by faith. But, they say, a person is saved by faith *and* works, or faith *and* charity (Council of Trent).

Karl Barth has correctly observed that the word *and* describes the errors of Rome. We say that we have only one infallible source of revelation: the Scriptures. They say that we have the Scriptures *and* tradition. We say there is only one mediator between God and man: Christ. They say that Christ *and* Mary (and other "saints") will help us. We depend on Christ alone, faith alone, and grace alone. But they add love and works and saints and the church.

For that reason our conversations with Roman Catholics ought to continue. At one time we did not talk; we killed each other over *both . . . and* or *alone*! Today we have become too polite to debate, and nobody would wish us back in the age of the killings, unless his name is Ian Paisley. But one cannot deny that in those days the honor of Christ weighed more heavily on the consciences of preachers and princes. Today the big issue should not be whether we look kind and humane and enlightened but whether we are zealous for the honor of him who loves us and them.

Faith Is Not Work.

The word *faith* does not have the same meaning throughout the Scriptures. But when we speak about "justification by faith," we should have no doubt what the Bible and the catechism mean by *faith*. Paul uses *faith* as the opposite of *law* or *works*. Therefore it would be perverse to regard faith as another kind of work—the one kind that pleases God. The work of Christ is the only ground of our righteousness before God. Faith is the hand that receives this gift. Faith is indeed indispensable, but we do not give credit to the hand of the beggar for the generous gift someone else has placed in that hand. We believe in Christ, but we are not justified *because* of our belief. Faith is the instrument, or means, but never the ground of our rightness before God.

In two ways people may miss out on the great love and generosity of God in Christ Jesus. The first is by "passing by his cross." This does not even have to be rejection as much as neglecting to pay attention ("how shall we escape if we ignore such a great salvation?" Heb. 2:3). The second way in which we fail to receive God's grace is by trusting in our own works, our faithfulness.

Some people believe in their beliefs. Once I counseled a woman of eighty who had been converted when she was forty-six. She was always trying to determine whether she had the right kind of faith at the time of her conversion. Her teacher had said that besides true faith there was also a historical faith and a miracle faith. So she was continually attempting to convince herself (and me) that her faith and her commitment had been genuine. She was trying to strengthen her belief in her faith!

It is true, of course, that faith is more than knowing a theory about Jesus' death for our sins. Faith embraces Jesus. James (2:14-24) fights the notion that faith can ever be a mere abstract knowledge. The Catechism discusses that in the next Lord's Day.

It's All by Grace.

"Only Christ's satisfaction, righteousness, and holiness make me right with God," says our confession. "I can . . . make it mine in no other way than by faith alone." But I should not take credit for the faith as if it were responsible for the gift. Faith itself is a gift, although it is also a responsibility.

Faith is nothing but accepting the golden coins from the generous one.

Faith means getting out of our own house and walking in God's rain. Or as the old form for public profession of faith has it, "Do you confess . . . that you seek your life not in yourselves, but only in Jesus Christ your Savior?"

Faith means bathing in God's golden sunlight. It is to let yourself be loved.

Certainly our loving and our doing will necessarily result from being declared righteous, forgiven, and loved. But watch out: the response to God's love may never become a New Covenant law—a condition for entering the kingdom. "Christ is the end of the law so that there may be righteousness for everyone who believes" (Rom. 10:4). This is the era of grace. Now all of us must believe, only believe: all we need to do is believe. "The righteous will live by faith" (Hab. 2:4, Rom. 1:17, etc.).

Lord's Day 24

WORKS WITHOUT WAGES

***Q** Why can't the good we do make us right with God, or at least help make us right with him?*

***A** Because the righteousness which can pass God's scrutiny must be entirely perfect and must in every way measure up to the divine law. Even the very best we do in this life is imperfect and stained with sin.*

—Q & A 62

Grace Without Merit.

In Lord's Day 24 we continue to confess how we are right with God because of the work of Christ and without any work of ours. We might summarize the teaching of this Lord's Day in three propositions:

—We are saved by grace and not by works.
—Yet we will be judged according to our works.
—They who do not work have not believed.

Why Not?

Why can't our works at least contribute to our salvation? The question is formulated by someone who knows the teaching and practice of the Roman Catholics. They do not teach that a person can save himself or herself, but they say that without our doing we cannot be saved either. God does his gracious work, but we must do our share. This kind of cooperation between God and man is popular and is taught by many Christians. (We call these teachings Pelagian, semi-Pelagian, or Arminian.)

The catechism resolutely denies such a possibility: "No one will be declared righteous in [God's] sight by observing the law" (Rom. 3:20). "All who rely on observing the law are under a curse" (Gal. 3:10). God demands a perfection that no one can render, because "all our righteous acts are like filthy rags" (Isa. 64:6).

We cannot present the kind of work God demands, says the catechism. We can also turn that around: Christ has presented the only kind of work that meets God's demands. Therefore people who think they have to add to the work of Christ offend God. This was precisely the issue Paul addressed in the letter to the Galatians. The false teachers among the Galatians were not saying that they could be saved without Christ, but they taught that something had to be added. Then Paul exclaimed, "If you let yourselves be circumcised, Christ will be of no value to you at all" (Gal. 5:2).

If our work must complement the work of Jesus, his work is neither perfect nor complete. And if anyone can be saved by being good and honest, God should have spared his Son the pain of the cross.

Soli Deo Gloria.

The deepest reason why it is everlastingly impossible for us to contribute to our own salvation is stated in these words: "It is by grace you have been saved, through faith—and this not from yourselves, it is the gift of God—not by works, so that no one can boast" (Eph. 2:8-9). Salvation is totally God's work "*so that no one can boast.*" God has so ordained the way of salvation that no human being will ever stand before him and boast. The "flesh" shall not boast. But all flesh shall praise God, for of him, through him, and unto him are all things in creation and redemption.

The Paradox.

We are not saved by good works, and we are not saved without them. That's the paradox. The Bible teaches clearly that good works are rewarded by God in this life and in the life to come. Therefore we should not be wiser than God, who stimulates us to do good works by promising rewards. *And* we ought not read this teaching about rewards as if it introduces a theme of merits in the melody of grace.

***Q** How can you say that the good we do doesn't earn anything when God promises to reward it in this life and the next?*

***A** This reward is not earned; it is a gift of grace.*

—Q & A 63

The Coming Reward.

Why did Moses reject the easy life and the riches of Egypt? Why did he choose "to be mistreated along with the people of God rather than to enjoy the pleasures of sin for a short time"? Because "he regarded disgrace for the sake of Christ as of greater value than the treasures of Egypt, *because he was looking ahead to his reward"* (Heb. 11:25-26).

Such a choice to go one way and not another is based (first) on the faith that God's and Christ's promises are reliable. And, in making the choice, a person (second) contemplates the reward. In fact, the Lord encourages us to do so. When the "rich young man" came to Jesus, he could not bring himself to make the right choice; "he went away sad, because he had great wealth" (Matt. 19:22). He is the only one in the Bible who came to Jesus and then sadly went away again.

Next, Peter, always quick on the draw, said, "We have left everything to follow you! What then will there be for us?" One would almost expect the Master to rebuke Peter because he and the other disciples were frequently too greedy for honor and rewards. However, Jesus enumerated the disciples' rewards with great generosity: his special disciples, the twelve, would have a kingly role on judges' thrones. "Everyone who has left houses or brothers or sisters or father or mother or children or fields for my sake will receive a hundred times as much and will inherit eternal life" (19:29).

Thus we may encourage everyone who faces the choice of the two roads: the richest rewards are found on the road we travel with Jesus. It is quite sound, biblically and doctrinally, that we encourage each other to invest ourselves and all that we have in Christ and his cause. As investments go, we couldn't do better anywhere else.

However, the reward offered and the investments made may never lead to a worldly ledger keeping. That would spoil the relationship.

God Gives Rewards.

The Bible speaks freely of rewards for God's servants. If we are "faithful with a few things," says the Lord, we will be "put . . . in charge of many things" when accounts are settled (Matt. 25:21,23). If we learn how to use our money to advance God's cause in this world, we will reap the results in the next (Luke 16:9, 1 Tim. 6:17-19). If any person's temple-building work is of enduring quality, "he will receive his reward" (1 Cor. 3:14). "Behold, I am coming soon!" says Christ. "My reward is with me, and I will give to everyone according to what he has done" (Rev. 22:12).

Thus the New Testament has much to say about the rewards that God (Christ) will give the faithful at the final judgment. The Old Testament has even more teaching about rewards for God-fearing people. These rewards are mostly related to the present life. Therefore the Christian church cannot ignore the Bible's teaching on rewards.

Rewards by Grace?

The Reformers were quite right, however, in not making any concession to the Roman Catholic concepts of merit and compensation as these ideas had developed in the church of the Middle Ages. We do not deny that work and reward are related. But as soon as we teach the churches that God must deliver when the faithful submit their claims, the church has poisoned the gospel. The relationship of saved sinners to a God who gives rewards remains one without claims or rights on our part. We live and work in the shadow of the cross of his Son. In life and death we depend on his mercy.

It is a bid odd,we admit, to call our reward "a gift of grace." A reward is some form of recompense, return, or requital. When such a thing is a "reward of grace," it hardly deserves the name "reward."

Reformed teachers have attempted to defend the terminology of Answer 63. It's the kind of reward a father gives to his children, they have said. Actually, said one of the best catechism teachers (Herman Veltkamp), what God is rewarding is the works of Christ credited to the account of believers; that's why it is a reward of grace. But it remains a strange way of handling very ordinary words.

The issue, though, is free grace. And that's important.

The Freedom of God.

Even while he makes payments or rewards to those who work for him, God remains free to be gracious and merciful. This truth is probably best illustrated in the parable of the workers in the vineyard (Matt. 20:1-16). The story likens the rewards of the kingdom of heaven to the pay of people working in an orchard. The boss hired them at 6 A.M., 9 A.M., noon, 3 P.M., and 5 P.M. Quitting time was generally at sunset, or 6 P.M. When they left work for the day, each got a denarius, although those who had been hired at dawn complained that it wasn't fair that people who worked for an hour got the same pay as those who had "borne the burden of the work and the heat of the day" (v. 12). And, indeed, in this story Jesus is not giving a model for a fair labor contract. He teaches that in the kingdom the latecomers, "the last," shall be frontrunners, "the first" (v. 16). As it turned out, the Gentile latecomers have replaced the Jewish frontrunners.

But the story has a special message for those of us who have been slaving away in the vineyard for some time. We "have borne the burden of the work and the heat of the day." Sometimes we wonder what the vineyard would look like if *we* had not taken care of it. Then someone comes into the kingdom who is not yet dry behind the ears. She makes all the baby sounds of one just born again. But do you know what the Master pays her? A denarius. And do you realize what we are going to get? A denarius.

Thus Jesus teaches us the generosity and the freedom of God. It's also a lesson in interpersonal relations for kingdom workers. There may be no envy or pride of seniority among us. We are in the kingdom by grace, or we do not belong here at all. Once I baptized a young man who six months earlier did not know Christ. After the service an elderly man of about 80 shook the young member's hand. The elderly man was a leader in this church. The very church building might not have been there but for this man's devotion.

But when he shook hands with the newly born he said, "You have the same rights and privileges here as I have." And I saw that he understood the nature of the grace that gives us our place in God's church.

Certainly grace teaches obedience, and obedience will be rewarded by the Master. But those who obey are not doing it in order to have bargaining power with the Lord. "So you also, when you have done everything you were told to do, should say, 'We are unworthy servants; we have only done our duty' " (Luke 17:10).

The Reformation was founded on astonishment at God's goodness (says G. C. Berkouwer). Even the holiest of us has no bargaining position with God. But by grace even latecomers and sinners may get in.

Work Religion Versus Grace Religion.

The question whether the gospel of grace does not make for a cheap religion is as old as the days of the apostle Paul: "Shall we go on sinning so that grace may increase?" (Rom. 6:1). The question betrays misunderstanding of the gospel and ignorance of Christ's Spirit: grace is not intended to eliminate good works but to make them possible. Work religion and grace religion agree on the necessity of being good and doing good. But work religion says that by being good and doing good, we will be saved. Grace religion says that it's impossible to be saved by works but that once we are saved by grace, it is impossible not to do good works.

***Q** But doesn't this teaching make people indifferent and wicked?*

***A** No. It is impossible for those grafted into Christ by true faith not to produce fruits of gratitude.*

—Q & A 64

Notice how the word *work* is used in the following well-known gospel-of-grace text: "it is by grace you have been saved, through faith—and this not from yourselves, it is the gift of God—not by *works*, so that no one can boast. For we are God's *work*manship, created in Christ Jesus to do good *works*, which God prepared in advance for us to do" (Eph. 2:8-10).

The Impossibilities.

The Scriptures teach us to confess certain impossibilities that the catechisms and instruction books of any Christian church must faithfully repeat: it is *impossible* for us to love God and our neighbors unless we are born again (Heidelberg Catechism, Q & A 5 and 8); it is *impossible* for us to pay our debts and gain favor with God (Q & A 13) outside of Jesus Christ; and it is *impossible* "for those grafted into Christ by true faith not to produce fruits of gratitude" (A. 64).

For a Christian, doing good works is not only a task, a matter of obedience to the law of God: it is *impossible* to be a Christian without doing good works. Those who have a life void of good works should not merely be asked to try a little harder; they should be asked whether or not they are "in Christ." For it is *impossible* to be in him and "not to produce fruits of gratitude."

The Cheapening of Our Faith.

The greatest error of Christians in general and of orthodox Christians in particular may well be that we think we are saved by subscribing to the right theory. That must be the impression that many of us teachers and preachers have created. And woe to us if we don't clarify and correct ourselves.

You cannot have the righteousness of Christ by subscribing to the right theory of the atonement—merely as a theory in a catechism book. You cannot have *it* without having *him*. Christ cannot be *for* you without being *with* you and *in* you. He cannot be your Savior unless he is also your Lord. You were not bought by him unless you are now owned by him. It's "impossible!" to have anything of him without being in him, to share in the death he died without having a part in the life he lives.

The Judge is coming, and he will reward us for what we have done. Why is there, both now and at his coming, "no condemnation for those who are in Christ Jesus"? Because they happen to be in the right church, where they subscribe to the right formula? No; it's because "in Christ Jesus . . . the law of the Spirit of life set [them] free from the law of sin and death" (Rom. 8:1-2). Of course it is essential to be in the true church and to have the apostolic doctrine rightly taught. Nothing is more tragic than to have a false teaching believed and spread by a fake church. It's worse than having a quack prescribe medicines that aggravate an illness.

But when orthodox churches make it their main concern to set their doctrine straight instead of to meet the person of Christ himself, sermons are mere words—powerless explanations of theories. The transition from death to life takes place when we embrace Christ by faith.

The Church's Practice.

Every generation seems to face a situation in which the church either makes the gospel sound so easy that its "teaching makes people indifferent and wicked," as the catechism says, or, in trying to get people to pay and pray and work, it teaches that good works are a necessary condition for salvation. The Roman Catholics taught salvation by good works; the Lutherans ended up peddling cheap grace, said Dietrich Bonhoeffer. Soren Kierkegaard spoke of Lutheran Denmark as a country of baptized pagans.

The various Reformed churches tend to accuse each other (but not to each other's faces) of drawing the circle of salvation too small or too large. Some say that others will allow only the spiritual elite to sit at the Lord's Supper. Others say that some, at funerals, talk everyone into heaven and speak of "grace" too often and of "obedience" too seldom. Meanwhile, every one of these Reformed groups tends to have its own saintly writers (now dead) who have gotten the relationship between salvation and its evidences "just right."

It may be difficult to put the relationship between grace and works into words, but God's children have no trouble getting the connection.

In the churches' (and the preachers') practice, the tendency to be scared of free grace is usually stronger than concern about teaching decent "Christian" living without much knowledge of Jesus and his love. All of us must learn again and anew that God's grace, the gospel of forgiveness and love, is God's way of bringing all of us to works of obedience. Because without faith we do not have Christ, and without Christ there simply are no good works.

Lord's Day 25

THE MEANS OF GRACE

***Q** It is by faith alone that we share in Christ and all his blessings: where then does that faith come from?*

***A** The Holy Spirit produces it in our hearts by the preaching of the holy gospel, and confirms it through our use of the holy sacraments.*

—Q & A 65

God's Channels.

We confess that the Holy Spirit creates faith in us by means of the Word and that he strengthens that faith by means of baptism and the Lord's Supper. That's why we call the Word and sacraments the "means of grace."

God is perfectly free, of course, to use any thing, any event, and any person to bring his grace into people's lives. A kind word to a visitor at church may be (and has often been) God's driveway to that person's heart. As a matter of fact, nothing is nicer than to be used as God's channel of grace to another person.

God also uses events as means of grace. He may use any wedding feast (but more often he uses a funeral) as a means of grace. He may use any gift of money (but more often the lack of money) or the gift of health (but more often the lack of health) as a means to make himself known as the God of hope and comfort.

But we are not talking about means of grace in general. We are saying that saving faith comes from God, that he gives it to us by means of the Word, and that he strengthens our faith by means of the sacraments.

No Theology of the Word.

The writers of the Heidelberg Catechism intended to teach about the sacraments in Lord's Days 25 through 30. They did not intend to discuss proclaiming the Word. Although the creation of faith through the preaching of the gospel was an important part in the teachings of the Reformers, this doctrine did not get a place in the catechism. That's one of the reasons why we children of the Reformation have, until this day, a common theory about sacraments (the "signs and seals") but are less definite in our theories about the Word. Recently the massive and controversial works of Karl Barth have made all Reformed people (at least) think about the different forms of the Word and about the works that God accomplishes by his Word.

Mysterious.

The creation of faith in human hearts remains a miraculous work which is performed by the Spirit of God.

The first European convert to Christ was a businesswoman named Lydia. She became a Christian when "the Lord opened her heart to respond to Paul's message" (Acts 16:14). No man or woman ever came to faith by another route: it was always the Spirit creating faith by means of the Word.

No Uniformity.

Although the creation-and-growth of faith is always a mystery and always Word related, we don't all come to faith in Christ by the same route. He who made every tree different from the next should not be expected to limit himself to Baptist, Reformed, or Episcopalian patterns in generating and rearing his children.

Neither does the Spirit usually strike like lightning, bypassing created relationships. Some of us learned from the Bible before we could read, and we were taught how to pray while we were learning to talk. God was already teaching us through our fathers and mothers.

Paul had his Damascus-road experience, of course. But Paul's encounter with the Light and the Voice does not constitute the whole story of his faith or of the Spirit's work in him: it started much earlier. Living and working as a Christian missionary, he said that he served God "as [his] forefathers did, with a clear conscience" (2 Tim. 1:3). By such testimony he acknowledged the continuity of the Spirit's work from the faith of his fathers to his personal faith. And he would say the same thing about the faith of our mothers: young evangelist Timothy's "sincere faith . . . first lived in [his] grandmother Lois and in [his] mother Eunice" (1:5).

Parental Patterns.

When they are asked why they believe in God, Christ, and the Bible, some shy and honest people will say, "Because I was brought up that way." That answer is not as bad and fatalistic as some make it out to be. When we are raised by Christian parents and grandparents, God's goodness reaches us with porridge and prayers. We learn the Christian religion—like everything else—by imitation.

Faith is covenantal: it is a communal response to God's love in Christ, shown by obedience to his revealed will. A Christian must necessarily share in the faith experience of a believing community.

But faith, like love, is also intensely personal. By his Spirit and through his love Word, God gives us personal trust in Christ. He also expects us to be biblically critical of the faith we inherit. Biblical checking of the faith of fathers and mothers is more important than an unquestioning loyalty to those who taught us in Christ.

Both Paul and Timothy owed spiritual debts to the teachers of their youth. So do most of us. But their debt is the more remarkable because Paul's and Timothy's forebears lived in the pre-Christian era. (Incidentally, the mention of Paul's and Timothy's ancestors in 2 Timothy 1 shows an understanding of the continuation between Israel and the church, an understanding that has been lost by most Jews and Christians today.) Though the Spirit by the gospel did great works in Paul and Timothy, even they received the faith first through their fathers and mothers.

God's Workshop and Tools.

Ordinarily we find and strengthen faith by exposing ourselves to the tools God uses: Word and sacraments. Therefore we must come to God's workshop, the church of Jesus Christ. Here God's children are born and nourished. We may not doubt that God can do this work to his children anywhere and anytime. But we would be reckless not to go where he does it normally and all the time: his church. Sometimes Reformed people have taken too formally the axiom that God creates and builds faith in his church. God does *not* do this work only when a congregation is gathered officially for worship and when an educated and ordained servant of his is preaching. Important as these occasions are, we don't need to think merely of official worship services when we speak of God's faith-creating and strengthening activity. When we say that the church is his workshop, we mean the community of his own, the household of God, where instruction and mutual edification take place in all kinds of settings. In this temple the Spirit dwells (1 Cor. 3:16, Eph. 2:22). He "builds" us, and he uses the Lord's own instruments: Word, baptism, Lord's Supper.

Primacy of the Word.

"The Holy Spirit produces [faith] in our hearts by the preaching of the holy gospel." We don't say the same thing concerning the sacraments. Gospel proclamation is primary in the saving and sanctifying work of God. The sacraments do not produce faith but confirm or strengthen it. Therefore the sacraments are for believers, but the Word is for believers *and* unbelievers. The proclamation of the Word is "public," but the administration of the sacraments belongs to the household of believers.

Word proclamation not only produces but also confirms faith. Answer 65 could be improved by a reading which says that the Spirit creates faith by the Word *and* strengthens faith by the Word and sacraments. But the emphasis of the catechism is on the primacy of the Word. Roman Catholics go to their church buildings to attend Mass; Reformed people go mainly to hear a sermon. The central liturgical piece of furniture in the Roman church is the altar; for the Reformed it is the pulpit or lectern with an open Bible, and the communion table and baptismal font stand to the side of or below the pulpit.

***Q** What are sacraments?*

***A** Sacraments are holy signs and seals for us to see. They were instituted by God so that by our use of them he might make us understand more clearly the promise of the gospel, and might put his seal on that promise. And this is God's gospel promise: to forgive our sins and give us eternal life by grace alone because of Christ's one sacrifice finished on the cross.*

—Q & A 66

Changing Characters?

Today a reform movement among Roman Catholics demands centrality for Word proclamation and Bible study. And a liturgical movement among Reformed people wants not only more frequent communion but also more prominence for forms of worship, prayer, seasonal colors, and many other matters that fit most naturally in a sacramental environment. The Roman Catholic Church would be re-formed if Word proclamation regained supremacy. And the Reformed cannot remain Reformed unless the "preaching of the holy gospel" remains central.

The Name and the Thing.

Sacrament is a Latin word that means "a holy thing with a hidden meaning." This word has a long and unhappy history in the church. We would love to get rid of it, but we cannot. My sympathy is with Anabaptist purists who try to replace sacraments with ordinances (e.g., Vernard Eller, *In Place of Sacraments*). However, if we wish to join the worldwide, agelong conversation inside the one holy catholic and apostolic church, we will have to use the terms of the household, and *sacrament* is one of them.

What *thing* we mean when using the word *sacrament* is most important. The catechism says that sacraments are "holy signs and seals" to "make us understand more clearly the promise of the gospel." With this simple description the Reformation freed baptism and the Lord's Supper from all sacred secrecy and gave these rites their God-appointed place as aids to the gospel.

Signs and Seals.

The two key words in answer 66, *signs* and *seals,* are taken from Romans 4:11, where they describe circumcision: "And [Abraham] received the sign of circumcision, a seal of the righteousness that he had by faith while he was still uncircumcised." When Abraham received the painful sign of circumcision (Gen. 17:26), God sealed the righteousness that Abraham received because Abraham had believed God's promise (Gen. 15:6). Circumcision did not add any holiness or righteousness to Abraham, but the sacred rite clarified and certified that Abraham was righteous by faith. "So then, he is the father of all who believe" (Rom. 4:11), whether they have been circumcised or not.

When believers receive the sacraments, says the catechism, God does to us what he did to Abraham: he gives us a visible, tangible sign and a touchable assurance (seal) that his promises are true for us, "to forgive our sins and give us eternal life by grace alone because of Christ's one sacrifice finished on the cross."

One Message.

What God says in the gospel is confirmed by baptism and the Lord's Supper. Word and sacraments bring one message from God to us: "he assures us that our entire salvation rests on Christ's one sacrifice for us on the cross." The writers of the catechism were not afraid to sum up the biblical message in one gospel line. And they found the core of the gospel in Christ's sacrifice on the cross.

Our practice has not always underlined this teaching that there is nothing *extra* to be had in the sacraments. In several branches of the Reformed tradition participation in holy communion, or the Lord's Supper, carries much greater weight than the reception of the Word.

***Q** Are both the word and the sacraments then intended to focus our faith on the sacrifice of Jesus Christ on the cross as the only ground of our salvation?*

***A** Right! In the gospel the Holy Spirit teaches us and through the holy sacraments he assures us that our entire salvation rests on Christ's one sacrifice for us on the cross.*

—Q & A 67

For Slow Learners.

If, then, the sacraments add nothing to the Word, why did God give them to us?

In Answer 66 the catechism says that "they were instituted by God so that by our use of them he might make us understand more clearly the promise of the gospel and might put his seal on that promise." The Reformed churches stress that God's giving of the sacraments shows his compassion with human frailty. According to Article 33 of the Belgic Confession, God added the sacraments to the gospel, "mindful of our crudeness and weakness." He wanted to "represent better to our external senses both what he enables us to understand by his Word and what he does inwardly in our hearts."

Sacraments are special measures devised by a loving Teacher for slow learners.

Word and Oath.

A word is only as reliable as the one who utters it. God's Word is utterly reliable because the Speaker is the faithful Maker of the covenant. He will eternally back up what he has said. And yet we are always inclined to be unsure and doubtful.

Sometimes God is irritated and distressed by his people's disobedience and lack of trust. But he also condescends to help us get over our weakness: "When God made his promise to Abraham, since there was no one greater for him to swear by, he yet swore by himself, saying, 'I will surely bless you and give you many descendants'" (Heb. 6:13-14, a reference to Gen. 22:16: "I swear by myself, declares the LORD").

An oath is an ultimate recourse in human society. Human beings are notoriously unreliable. Therefore when an affirmation needs to be anchored in truth, people place themselves before the face of the eternal One who cannot lie: they swear an oath (cf. 6:16). God, who does not need such ultimate recourse, yet swore an oath "by himself." And "God did this so that, by two unchangeable things [Word and oath] in which it is impossible for God to lie, we who have fled to take hold of the hope offered to us [by the gospel] may be greatly encouraged" (v. 18).

I am not saying that the writer of Hebrews is speaking of Word and sacraments when he speaks of Word and oath. But in the church of Christ the sacraments do, indeed, represent the oath of God, which adds an unchangeable thing to an unchangeable truth. Now "we have this hope [of the gospel] as an anchor for the soul, firm and secure. It [our anchor of hope] enters the inner sanctuary behind the curtain, where Jesus, who went before us, has entered on our behalf" (vv. 19-20).

Our faith is anchored in Christ. He is the focus of Word and sacraments.

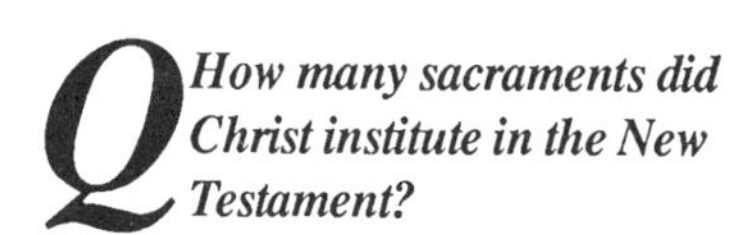

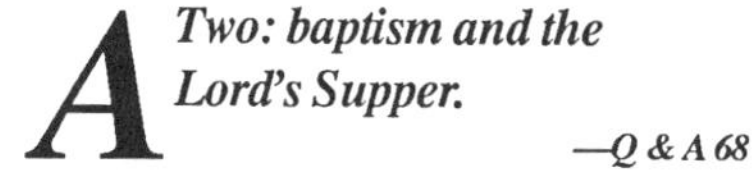

—Q & A 68

Two Sacraments.

Trying to understand the sacraments causes many divisions and much strife among Christians. Let's therefore be grateful that God gave us no more than two—and not seven, as the official Roman Catholic doctrine has it.

Although the New Testament has no word for "the sacraments" (and I admitted earlier that I regret having to use the term), its writers occasionally use baptism and the Lord's Supper in combinations that show their relatedness.

Thus Paul warns that participation in the life of the covenant people does not guarantee the truth of our faith. Of old Israel he says, "They were all baptized into Moses. . . . They all ate the same spiritual food and drank the same spiritual drink." So, in a manner of speaking, they had the two sacraments. "Nevertheless, God was not pleased with most of them" (1 Cor. 10:2-5).

In 1 Corinthians 12:13 Paul says that by our incorporation into the church all of us are baptized by and made to drink of one Spirit—which is another one-sentence reference to the two sacraments.

The writings of John have often been read "sacramentally." Think of such expressions as "born of water and the Spirit" (John 3:5); "my flesh is real food and my blood is real drink" (6:55); "the soldiers pierced Jesus' side with a spear, bringing a sudden flow of blood and water" (19:34); and "this is the one who came by water and blood—Jesus Christ" (1 John 5:6). Thus we receive by faith his coming through the Word and in the two sacraments: baptism and the Lord's Supper.

Lord's Day 26 and 27

BAPTISM

Note on Procedure.

A contemporary preacher who uses the Heidelberg Catechism to teach God's Word to a Christian congregation should pause and decide on procedure before wading into the fourteen questions and answers, fitted into five Lord's Days, that deal with baptism and the Lord's Supper. The explanation in the catechism is heavily slanted by the conflicts in which the Reformers of the sixteenth century were involved. In dealing with baptism, one might wish to follow the order of the Heidelberger and preach baptism in general (Q&A 69-73) and follow with a sermon on Question 74, "Should infants, too, be baptized?" But this treatment strengthens a wrong notion, already too prevalent, that there are two kinds of baptism practiced in our church: one for adults and one for the children of believers. Some ministers announce, "We will now administer the sacrament of infant baptism," as if it were a third sacrament instituted by Christ. We have only one ritual of baptism, of course. We affirm that believers *and* their children should receive this one baptism. The forms we use for baptism—which do more to teach the church's doctrine than do the confessions—should be (virtually) identical for adults and children; only the questions ought to be different, for obvious reasons.

At one time I attempted two sermons on the topic of baptism, according to the division of the Heidelberg Catechism, but I found that repetition was unavoidable and that interest was hard to maintain. Today I would preach one sermon on baptism. Such a sermon should answer three questions: WHAT is the meaning of baptism? HOW is it to be administered? WHO are legitimate candidates for baptism?

The *meaning* of baptism we learn quite adequately by going through the questions and answers of Lord's Days 26 and 27. The *mode* of baptism is not discussed by the catechism. But the question of the legitimate *candidates* is addressed (in Question 74).

Reminded and Assured.

This is a characteristically Reformed approach to baptism: by baptism God comes to the congregation and to each member with a reminder and an assurance. This is the way Paul speaks of baptism whenever the subject comes up in his letters.

***Q** How does baptism remind you and assure you that Christ's one sacrifice on the cross is for you personally?*

***A** In this way: Christ instituted this outward washing and with it gave the promise that, as surely as water washes away the dirt from the body, so certainly his blood and his Spirit wash away my soul's impurity, in other words, all my sins.*

—Q & A 69

Paul on Baptism.

Although thousands of treatises have been written on baptism throughout the history of the church—and most of these are controversial—the Bible contains no essay on the topic. The Spirit of God has given us thirteen letters written by Paul to young Christian churches or preachers, and half a dozen times Paul refers to baptism. As a rule Paul brings up baptism to *remind and assure the congregation of its riches in Christ.*

In Romans 6 Paul answers the oldest objection to the gospel of grace: Shall we go on sinning because we are saved by grace anyway? (cf. v. 1). The answer is a reminder ("don't you know?" v. 3) that the church has been baptized into the death and resurrection of Jesus Christ. And it's because we are identified with Christ in baptism that we cannot go on sinning: "Count yourselves dead to sin but alive to God in Christ Jesus" (v. 11). In 1 Corinthians 1:12-13 Paul reminds a divided church of its baptism: how can you possibly say that you belong to Paul or to Apollos or to Peter? By your baptism you were once and for all identified with Christ!

In Galatians Paul introduces baptism again as a reminder of the true identity of the community: "You who were baptized into Christ have clothed yourselves with Christ" (3:27). Therefore we cannot return to a pre-Christian era; we must enjoy the full riches and rights of God's own children.

In Colossians the apostle again mentions baptism as that which decisively pictures who we are in Christ: baptism incorporates us into the "circumcision" of Christ. Therefore we should not even consider circumcising the flesh (2:12-15).

Remember and Believe.

Although we immediately associate the words "remember and believe" with the Lord's Supper, they could serve appropriately whenever the church administers baptism. Baptism is not only a once-and-for-all incorporation into Christ but also a continual visible reminder of our true identity. Every time someone is "baptized into the body" (1 Cor. 12:13) to which we belong already, we must remember and believe that we are the baptized congregation, dead to sin and alive to God in Christ. Baptism assures us of our nobility and encourages us to live up to our high calling. Every baptismal ceremony reminds us to be what we are.

"Improving Our Baptism."

This term comes from Calvinists who grew up with the Westminster Catechism. It is regrettable that the idea disappeared when the influence of evangelical movements increased in Reformed churches. The thought is in harmony with an original Reformation teaching of both the Lutherans and the Calvinists: that the remembrance of one's baptism must be made determinative throughout one's later life.

Made Clean.

Christ has accomplished all things necessary for our salvation. Baptism is one of the witnesses to that completed work. When I think of my own baptism or when I watch the water sprinkled or poured on a new member of the church, I am "reminded and assured" that I am clean! As surely as water washes, God has washed us by Christ's blood and Spirit. I have been washed, and now I am clean!

***Q** What does it mean to be washed with Christ's blood and Spirit?*

***A** To be washed with Christ's blood means that God, by grace, has forgiven my sins because of Christ's blood poured out for me by his sacrifice on the cross. To be washed with Christ's Spirit means that the Holy Spirit has renewed me and set me apart to be a member of Christ so that more and more I become dead to sin and increasingly live a holy and blameless life.*

—Q and A 70

***Q** Where does Christ promise that we are washed with his blood and Spirit as surely as we are washed with the water of baptism?*

***A** In the institution of baptism where he says: "Therefore go and make disciples of all nations, baptizing them in the name of the Father and of the Son and of the Holy Spirit." "Whoever believes and is baptized will be saved, but whoever does not believe will be condemned." This promise is repeated when Scripture calls baptism the washing of rebirth and the washing away of sins.*

—Q & A 71

Blood and Spirit.

The washing by blood and Spirit erases our sin and consecrates us to God. The blood cleanses us from sin, and the Spirit makes us holy.

We "have been washed," and we "have been renewed." These events have happened. But my dying to sin is a process ("more and more I become dead to sin"). Holy living is a daily assignment: "increasingly" I live a holy life.

Baptism reminds me of what has happened already and encourages me to become what by faith in Christ I am: holy and blameless before God.

The Washing.

This question and answer do not seem to match very well. The questioner says, "Show me a text from Scripture in which Christ promises that in baptism we are washed by blood and Spirit as surely as water washes the body." But the answerer addresses a double question: first, where did the Lord say that we should be baptized? Second, where does Scripture say that *washing* is the main point of baptizing?

For the institution of baptism (the time that the Lord authorized the church to baptize) the catechism refers us to the "Great Commission" of Matthew 28:19: "Make disciples . . . baptizing them in the name [singular] of the Father and of the Son and of the Holy Spirit"—the three names that are one. The catechism also mentions Mark 16:16, but the church is no longer convinced that Mark 16:9-20 belongs to the sacred canon, or inspired Bible. Nearly all Bible translations made after the seventeenth century have a note to this effect in the last chapter of Mark's gospel.

Many scholars have also argued that in Matthew 28:19 the command to baptize in the name of the triune God must have been added later. But no one has given good grounds to doubt the genuineness of this passage. It remains remarkable, of course, that the New Testament recounts no instance of baptism in the name of the triune God. All baptisms mentioned in the book of Acts seem to have been performed in the name of Christ.

The catechism is correct to identify Jesus' commissioning of his disciples as the place of the institution of baptism. Many Bible teachers (including Karl Barth) trace the origin of Christian baptism to Jesus' own baptism in the Jordan. But this event didn't give the church authorization to baptize.

To show that washing is the main point of baptism, the catechism quotes part of Titus 3:5: ". . . he saved us, not because of righteous things we had done, but because of his mercy. He saves us through the washing of rebirth and renewal by the Holy Spirit." God's mercy, Paul says here, is the ground or motivation of our salvation. Then follows the means by which God saved: "through the bath of rebirth, that is, renovation by the Holy Spirit." This refers to baptism as God's way to bring sinners into renewed humanity. Baptism is the passage from old to new. Then Paul describes this transition more closely as "renewed by the Holy Spirit." These additional words warn us that mere use of water does not accomplish the inner change.

The catechism could have mentioned Ephesians 5:26—"[Christ made the church] holy, cleansing her by the washing with water through the word"—which is parallel to Titus 3:5.

Finally, Answer 71 refers to Acts 22:16, where Ananias says to Saul (Paul), "Get up, be baptized and wash your sins away, calling on his name." This expression is evidence that we must regard the water of baptism as the outward sign of inward cleansing.

In the next two questions and answers the catechism warns the church that it is not baptism but the blood and Spirit of Christ that save us from death.

Faith and Superstition.

The "washing of rebirth" (Titus 3:5) is a name for the ritual of baptism. But rituals can never remove our sins, no matter how holy the people and how solemn the ceremony.

Sacramentalists (Roman Catholics, Anglicans, Episcopalians) tend to believe that the ritual can take away sins as long as the right people do it in the right manner. Baptists must resist the temptation to think that the volume of water influences the effect of the cleansing. Upon reflection, however, all Christians admit that no solemn words and no drops or oceans of water can wash away our sins. Only Jesus Christ and his Holy Spirit can cleanse us. And neither the Word nor the baptism has the desired effect unless we *believe* what God is saying or signaling. I fear that superstition precedes and outlives faith. Tribes that have not yet heard and accepted the gospel of Christ live in fear of gods and pin their hopes on magic, as taught by their traditions. And post-Christian tribes that have lost a living faith often retain some forms of superstition. Although they live secular lives, they value the water of baptism for their children (also, in many cases, the wedding and burial rites of the church). Clergymen who administer such magic, who perform rituals to give people a false sense of security, bring dishonor to their God and do a disservice to those who seek their help.

The Mode of Baptism.

The catechism does not discuss the manner in

Q ***Does this outward washing with water itself wash away sins?***

A ***No, only Jesus Christ's blood and the Holy Spirit cleanse us from all sins.***

—Q & A 72

Q ***Why then does the Holy Spirit call baptism the washing of rebirth and the washing away of sins?***

A ***God has good reason for these words. He wants to teach us that the blood and Spirit of Christ wash away our sins just as water washes away dirt from our bodies. But more important, he wants to assure us, by this divine pledge and sign, that the washing away of our sins spiritually is as real as physical washing with water.***

—Q & A 73

which the church should administer baptism. Nevertheless, we ought to devote some attention to this question and derive a few rules from the Scriptures.

1. *In church.* Baptism means incorporation into the body of Christ, the church. Therefore it should take place while the church is assembled, at least in all normal events. And it ought to be administered by those whom the church authorizes.

2. *With the use of forms.* The church order of the (Christian) Reformed churches prescribes the use of particular liturgical forms during baptisms. Originally the forms were written to educate the congregations. By the required reading of a historical, widely accepted explanation of the meaning of baptism, a congregation is spared the peculiarities of individual views. It is a good rule. The church must guard the right understanding of baptism. The rule has been followed too slavishly, however—in churches where baptism occurs frequently, the reading brings more boredom than edification.

The main task of the church in teaching about baptism is not to read forms but to make certain that those who request baptism understand its meaning.

3. *With the use of water.* Perhaps the catechism emphasizes too exclusively the cleansing signified by baptism. Other aspects of its meaning (such as incorporation into Christ) could have been mentioned and explained. Nevertheless, the only symbol prescribed for baptism is water, and it stands for washing.

Although all (make that "nearly all") Christians agree that the Lord requires us to use water in baptism, we don't agree on whether this water should envelop or be poured or sprinkled on the one to be baptized. Reformed Christians approve of all these modes and don't believe that the way of using the sign is very significant as long as water is used.

The Baptists' argument that immersion is essential because baptism is supposed to picture our burial and resurrection with Christ rests on a misreading of Romans 6:3-4. We were "buried with [Christ] through baptism into death," Paul says there. But that has nothing to do, I believe, with going under water. When speaking about our being buried and raised with Christ, Paul refers to the meaning, not the mode, of baptism (Col. 2:12). He is stressing our incorporation, our unity with Christ, of which baptism is the sign. Now we are new and different, he says, because the death and resurrection of Jesus apply to us. Immersion in water is a valid and a more dramatic form of Christian baptism than sprinkling or pouring water. But it is wrong to attach special religious value to "going under all the way" or to think that immersion is a biblically prescribed symbol.

Holy Spirit Baptism.

The symbolism of water baptism as washing hails from John the Baptizer. It was made complete in Christian baptism. John's baptism stood for a sign of repentance and washing—a farewell to the old and a necessary cleansing in order to meet the coming Judge (Matt. 3, Mark 1, Luke 3). Christian baptism in the name of Christ seals to us not only the forgiveness of sins but also our reception of the Holy Spirit (Acts 2:38). It is therefore much richer than the baptism of John (Acts 19:1-6) because it seals and confirms to us the forgiving grace and the new life God has promised his children.

Formulating the Question.

In our discussions about baptism with Baptist brothers and sisters, we should formulate the question correctly; otherwise our conversations will be fruitless. The question should be, How does the Bible regard the sons and daughters of believers? Are they "in Christ" or are they "in limbo," neither saved nor lost until they themselves make a decision? In talking with Baptists, I would even hesitate to address the catechism's question whether infants should be baptized. We certainly do not baptize infants because they are so nice and innocent looking; neither do we propose to baptize all babies on the block. Reformed people baptize the sons and daughters of believers because these children belong to the covenant. So in our discussions with Baptist friends, *they* would have to show us that Scripture excludes the children of believers from baptism.

***Q** Should infants, too, be baptized?*

***A** Yes. Infants as well as adults are in God's covenant and are his people. They, no less than adults, are promised the forgiveness of sin through Christ's blood and the Holy Spirit who produces faith. Therefore, by baptism, the mark of the covenant, infants should be received into the Christian church and should be distinguished from the children of unbelievers. This was done in the Old Testament by circumcision, which was replaced in the New Testament by baptism.*

—Q & A 74

Part of Truth.

Baptists rightly rail against a *corpus Christianum* ("Christian society"), in which everyone receives baptism as a sign of membership in good and regular standing. In Israel the church family and the nation were identical. But the members of the New Testament church are separated from the nation of their temporary citizenship by their identity in Jesus Christ. That's the historical Anabaptist position for "believers' baptism." We agree with their opposition to the idea of a Christian nation. Yet we baptize the sons and daughters of those who profess their faith. We also admit that the baptism of a child of believers is "incomplete": we insist that baptized children make a personal and public profession of faith when they can speak for themselves.

Baptists also testify to the "incompleteness" of their position. They refuse to think of their children as being outside of Christ. They cannot regard them that way, and they don't raise them in that manner. Therefore they "dedicate" them in a ceremony that resembles the baptism of infants.

The Reformed may be in danger of neglecting the individual responsibility to confess and to witness. But they glory in the grace of God in Jesus Christ that precedes anything they do and that enables them to do anything good at all.

The Baptists are in danger of paying much more attention to the unreliable words of people than to the reliable words and deeds of God. But they are set on saving souls.

The One Covenant.

We read the Bible as one story of God's dealing with his people. God made one covenant of grace with Abraham, and he continued it with all those who now belong to Jesus Christ. Jesus is the great Son of Abraham, through whom the blessing of the covenant is extended to all the families of the earth (Gen. 12:3, 17:7, Rom. 4:11, Gal. 3:14, 29). According to God's plan, this one covenant of grace has two dispensations, commonly called the Old and the New Covenants, or Testaments. The old was established at

Sinai, and the new was instituted through the blood and the Spirit of Christ (Ex. 19:4-8, Jer. 31:31-34, 1 Cor. 11:25, 2 Cor. 3:6, 14-17, Heb. 8-10). "The new was in the old concealed; the old is in the new revealed."

Enduring Promises.

The heart of God's unchanging covenant vow is this: I will be your God and the God of your children; you will be my people (Gen. 17:7, Ex. 29:45, Lev. 26:12, Ezek. 37:27, John 14:23, 2 Cor. 6:16, Rev. 21:3). The proper response to God's promise is belief and obedience. The suggestion that children are excluded from this covenant of grace is foreign to the whole biblical way of thinking. When on the day of Pentecost the stream of mercy began to rush from Jerusalem to the ends of the earth, Peter said, "Repent and be baptized, every one of you. . . . You will receive the gift of the Holy Spirit. . . . The promise is for you and your children" (Acts 2:38-39). Peter's use of the formula "you and your children" does not prove that children were included in the Christian baptisms on the day of Pentecost. Peter says that the promise of the new age is for his hearers, for their children, and for the worldwide community God would call. But his use of the old covenant formula "you and your children" on the birthday of the new dispensation is very significant.

You and Yours.

God used either the expression "you and your children" or "you and your household" in establishing his covenant with the patriarchs and when he gave the signs of his covenant. The apostles used the same words in bringing the message of the New Covenant (e.g., Acts 16:31). It is remarkable, but not surprising, that the expression "and your household" is used five times in connection with New Testament baptisms (Acts 11:14, 16:15, 33, 18:8, 1 Cor. 1:16). Debates about the ages of these household members miss the point. The point is that the apostles could not have used the "you and your household" formula in preaching and baptizing if God's approach to the family unit had changed since the Old Testament.

Our relationship to Jesus Christ is personal but not individualistic. We are baptized, saved, redeemed, nourished, trained, and used within the covenant community.

Lord's Day 28, 29, and 30

THE LORD'S SUPPER

A Dated Discussion.

By baptism the Lord brings us into fellowship with himself and his children. Through the Lord's Supper he strengthens and maintains that fellowship.

The confession concerning the Lord's Supper in the Heidelberg Catechism is deeply marked by the doctrinal disputes of the sixteenth century. The Reformers' criticism of Rome was nowhere more evident than in their teaching about the Lord's Supper as compared to Roman Catholic ideas about the mass. But the Reformers also differed among themselves when they tried to formulate what God does in the supper. Luther was the closest to Rome, Zwingli was the furthest removed, and Calvin was between Luther and Zwingli.

***Q** How does the Lord's Supper remind you and assure you that you share in Christ's one sacrifice on the cross and in all his gifts?*

***A** In this way: Christ has commanded me and all believers to eat this broken bread and to drink this cup. With this command he gave the promise: First, as surely as I see with my eyes the bread of the Lord broken for me and the cup given to me, so surely his body was offered and broken for me and his blood poured out for me on the cross. Second, as surely as I receive from the hand of the one who serves, and taste with my mouth the bread and cup of the Lord, given me as sure signs of Christ's body and blood, so surely he nourishes and refreshes my soul for eternal life with his crucified body and poured-out blood.*

—Q & A 75

From the perspective of church history, the quarrels and problems of the Reformers are significant. The central question of those days, "*How* is Christ present in the supper?" must still be answered for every newcomer to the faith. By and large, however, the attention and interest of the church universal have shifted to different aspects of holy communion. Few among us worry about "transubstantiation" and "consubstantiation," but many want to know if covenant children should attend the Lord's Supper and whether the feast may be observed in a retreat or an ecumenical gathering.

Outline.

I will quote the eight questions and (long) answers of Lord's Days 28, 29, and 30 and comment briefly. Four aspects of the Lord's Supper should get our attention: (1) it is a memorial to a past event, (2) it is a table at which the Lord feeds his children, (3) it is a pledge of a future communion, and (4) we should know who may sit at this table.

Christ's Command.

God gave us baptism and the Lord's Supper to "remind and assure" us that we belong to Christ and that his gifts are ours. The catechism's approach is typically Reformed (cf. Q & A 69): the sacraments assure us of what we have and what we are, but they do not by themselves bring us new riches in addition to the gospel.

"Christ has commanded me and all believers to eat . . . and to drink." In healthy Christian churches the *command* of Christ to participate in the Lord's Supper ("do this in remembrance of me") has played a major role in persuading believers that they have their place at the table. In less healthy churches and traditions, believers find their worthiness to partake of the Lord's Supper not in the command and call of the Lord but in an inner freedom and degree of sanctification that they discover in examining themselves.

***Q** What does it mean to eat the crucified body of Christ and to drink his poured-out blood?*

***A** It means to accept with a believing heart the entire suffering and death of Christ and by believing to receive forgiveness of sins and eternal life.*

But it means more. Through the Holy Spirit, who lives both in Christ and in us, we are united more and more to Christ's blessed body. And so, although he is in heaven and we are on earth, we are flesh of his flesh and bone of his bone. And we forever live on and are governed by one Spirit, as members of our body are by one soul.

—Q & A 76

Breaking Bread.

Unfortunately the catechism makes much of the *broken bread* that I receive to eat: "I see with my eyes the bread of the Lord broken for me," which assures me that "his body was . . . broken for me . . . on the cross." Actually the Scriptures emphasize that his body was *not* broken (John 19:33-37). The Lord died as the passover lamb; his body was not torn apart. The point of the breaking of the bread is the sharing and distributing. The "broken body" idea rests on a word someone once inserted into 1 Corinthians 11:24, which reads "This is my body, which is for you." But it was made to read: "This is my body which is *broken* for you" (see the King James Version and footnotes in some versions). The thought of a "broken body" is now familiar to the church (through songs and forms for the observance of the Lord's Supper), and it's hard to bring our ideas back to the biblical message.

The Memorial.

The Lord's Supper was instituted at an occasion that was itself a memorial: the passover meal. Therefore the supper is, first and foremost, a memorial dinner, such as we have at anniversaries. We eat and commemorate a past event.

Christ and the disciples were together to eat the meal in remembrance of the night when they were led out of Egypt by God's mighty arm. They ate the passover lamb. The blood of that lamb had marked their houses so that they were *passed over* by the angel of death. And now it was the night in which Jesus was being betrayed.

After they had commemorated the old deliverance, Jesus took bread, and he broke it—that is, he shared it with his disciples. Then he shocked them by saying, "This is my body, which is for you." And he told them to eat the bread. Then he passed a cup of wine. It was the goblet that used to go around as the "cup of thanksgiving" (hence the word *eucharist*). He said that it was his blood, covenant blood, and that it meant forgiveness "for many" (Matt. 26:28). And this, he said, is how we must remember him.

Thus the Lord's Supper became the covenant meal of the restored Israel, built on twelve (not tribes but) apostles. It is the new people's celebrative supper in remembrance of the atoning death by which they came to life. Jesus did not die when he instituted the Lord's Supper, but he applied the fruits of his death: his body and blood are freedom and life for his own.

Past and Present.

All of us must be able to confess not only what the Lord's Supper says about the *past*—how Jesus' suffering became our joy, and his death our life—but also what it says about the *present.*

Answer 76 is the classic statement of the Reformed understanding of the meeting of grace and faith in the mysterious event of holy communion. By coming to the table in faith and obedience, says the first part of the answer, I accept Christ's work for my salvation. Then comes the part about nourishment in the present: Christ comes and pulls me close to himself, like a lover embracing the beloved, so that one spirit, his Spirit, rules in him and in us.

***Q** Where does Christ promise to nourish and refresh believers with his body and blood as surely as they eat this broken bread and drink this cup?*

***A** In the institution of the Lord's Supper: "The Lord Jesus on the night he was betrayed, took bread, and when he had given thanks, he broke it and said, 'This is my body, which is for you; do this in remembrance of me.' In the same way, after supper he took the cup, saying, 'This cup is the new covenant in my blood; do this, whenever you drink it, in remembrance of me.' For whenever you eat this bread and drink this cup, you proclaim the Lord's death until he comes" [1 Cor. 11:23-26].*

This promise is repeated by Paul in these words: "Is not the cup of thanksgiving for which we give thanks a participation in the blood of Christ? And is not the bread that we break a participation in the body of Christ? Because there is one loaf, we, who are many, are one body, for we all partake of the one loaf." [1 Cor. 10:16-17].

—Q & A 77

Jesus Christ lives, and he meets us at the table, as he promised. He "nourishes" us, we say. That happens by his Spirit, we explain. And we admit that it is difficult to find the right language and that most of our words are used figuratively or metaphorically because that's the only language we have to describe what happens when we meet Jesus in his grace at the communion table.

The next question and answer give two texts from 1 Corinthians to emphasize, apparently, that it was the Lord himself (and not church tradition) who instituted the supper and told us to observe it.

Notice that the Bible text quoted reads, "this is my body which is for you" and *not* "this is my body which is *broken* for you." Although we have had this (correct) text in the printed version of the catechism since 1934, many liturgists continue to ignore it.

We should pay attention to two more points in the meaning of the supper and in the words of its institution. These are its communal aspect—"we who are many are one body"—and its eschatological, or future, aspect—"you proclaim the Lord's death *until he comes.*"

All One Body.

The oneness of Christians is more graphically expressed in the Lord's Supper than at any other occasion. "We who are many are one body, for we all partake of the one loaf."

Elders or deacons in the ancient church used to carry the bread and the wine to the sick. Although this was soon associated with superstitious ideas, originally it meant to say, "You too belong to the body."

When Paul discusses the improper behavior of the Corinthian church at lovefeast and holy supper, he closes the section with a serious warning: "Anyone who eats and drinks without recognizing the body of the Lord eats and drinks judgment on himself" (1 Cor. 11:29). It is almost impossible to say with certainty if in this well-known sentence "discerning the body" means "knowing that the bread stands for the body of Jesus" or "recognizing the body of the Lord as the unity of believers." The very fact that the two meanings have been convincingly defended indicates how in the Lord's Supper the Lord and his church are one.

Future.

In the gospels the last supper takes place against the background of the approaching establishment of the kingdom: "I will not drink of this fruit of the vine from now on until that day when I drink it anew with you in my Father's kingdom" (Matt. 26:29, Mark 14:25). "I will not eat [this meal] again until it finds fulfillment in the kingdom of God" (Luke 22:16). "You are those who have stood by me in my trials. And I confer on you a kingdom, just as my Father conferred one on me, so that you may eat and drink at my table in my kingdom and sit on thrones, judging the twelve tribes of Israel" (Luke 22:28-30).

Thus the Lord's Supper is, first, a memorial to the once-for-all event of the past; it is, second, a table at which the Lord graciously feeds and refreshes us with himself in the present; and it is, third, a pledge for the future. The invitation to the Lord's Supper in your church is good also for the banquet in God's kingdom.

Historical Argument.

One of the stated reasons why synods of the Christian Reformed Church have declined to change the catechism or to take out Q & A 80 has been their desire to preserve the historical character of the document. That may be a good reason. It's odd and unsightly to put modern patches on ancient fabric or to remove marks of age from monuments. But this historical document was written in the heat of a historical argument about the Lord's Supper. And in a debate the issues are shaped as much by the opposition as by one's own insight. The fathers (I don't know about the mothers) of the sixteenth century focused the debate on the interpretation of the words "This is

Q ***Are the bread and wine changed into real body and blood of Christ?***

A ***No. Just as the water of baptism is not changed into Christ's blood and does not itself wash away sins but is simply God's sign and assurance, so too the bread of the Lord's Supper is not changed into the actual body of Christ even though it is called the body of Christ in keeping with the nature and language of the sacraments.***

—Q & A 78

Q ***Why then does Christ call the bread his body and the cup his blood, or the new covenant in his blood? (Paul uses the words, a participation in Christ's body and blood.)***

A ***Christ has good reason for these words. He wants to teach us that as bread and wine nourish our temporal life, so too his crucified body and poured-out blood truly nourish our souls for eternal life. But more important, he wants to assure us, by this visible sign and pledge, that we, through the Holy Spirit's work, share in his true body and blood as surely as our mouths receive these holy signs in his remembrance, and that all of his suffering and obedience are as definitely ours as if we personally had suffered and paid for our sins.***

—Q & A 79

***Q** How does the Lord's Supper differ from the Roman Catholic Mass?**

***A** The Lord's Supper declares to us that our sins have been completely forgiven through the one sacrifice of Jesus Christ which he himself finished on the cross once for all. It also declares to us that the Holy Spirit grafts us into Christ, who with his very body is now in heaven at the right hand of the Father where he wants us to worship him. But the Mass teaches that the living and the dead do not have their sins forgiven through the suffering of Christ unless Christ is still offered for them daily by the priests. It also teaches that Christ is bodily present in the form of bread and wine where Christ is therefore to be worshiped. Thus the Mass is basically nothing but a denial of the one sacrifice and suffering of Jesus Christ and a condemnable idolatry.*

—Q & A 80

*See note on page 186 regarding a change to Q&A 80.

my body." And these ancestors of ours concluded and confessed that the interpretation of these words should be "in keeping with the nature and language of sacraments" (A. 78).

With respect to Q & A 80, the argument that historical documents should be left intact has a weakness: the original document did not have this explicit statement on the Roman Catholic mass. Our present Q & A 80 appeared only in the third edition of the German version of the catechism. Therefore one might rightly say that respect for historicity should require us to return to the first edition. (With respect to the whole of our confessional writings, the argument that we ought not tamper with historical documents strengthens our appreciation of history but weakens the relevance of the confession.)

Relevance.

When I study the catechism and especially when I read its long and somewhat repetitive answers on the Lord's Supper, I feel the need for a fresh expression of the Reformed confession. Yet I do not deny the truth or relevance of its position. The writers of the catechism refuse to interpret "This is my body" literally, but they want to take the reality of communion with Christ as literally as anybody: we are united with our Lord in the supper, but it happens "through the Holy Spirit." "Although he is in heaven and we are on earth, we are flesh of his flesh and bone of his bone" (A. 76). We receive him by faith, not with our mouths, yet our mouths are involved when the sacrament teaches us that his body and blood "truly nourish our souls for eternal life." "As surely as our mouths receive these holy signs," so it is that "his suffering and obedience are . . . ours." When we eat and drink, we are as intensely united with the fruits of Christ's work "as if we personally had suffered and paid for our sins" (A. 79).

This is (again) justification by faith in Christ, the core teaching of our only comfort. The Reformers were gripped by the joy of that confession. Therefore Q & A 80 speak harsh words about the mass.

Indignant Tone.

If Roman Catholics think that Christ must become flesh and blood every day in order to be sacrificed in the mass every day, they deny the finality of the cross. And if they think that the faithful should worship a Christ laid on the altars in their churches instead of the Christ who sits on the throne of his Father in heaven, they are guilty of idolatry! That's the catechism's outburst.

It may not help us to have this outburst preserved and proclaimed as part of the Reformed confession. But two things are *still* necessary:

First, we, like the Reformers, must be gripped by the teaching and texts of the epistle to the Hebrews, so often quoted by the Reformers: *we have one high priest, only one, for all sinners and one, only one, all-sufficient sacrifice for all sins.* Those who rediscovered this liberating gospel shook their fists at the mass, pointed at Golgotha, and quoted from Hebrews: Christ's offering is "once for all" (7:27, 9:26, 10:10), only "once" (9:28), "for all time one sacrifice" (10:12).

Second, the reformation of the Roman Catholic Church is unfinished: the denial of the uniqueness of the Bible and of the finality of the work of Christ are built into a system that gives equal authority to the Bible and to its own tradition.

A Personal Confession.

Every member of the church of Christ makes a personal confession by participating in the Lord's Supper: we "proclaim the Lord's death" (1 Cor. 11:26). Participation also has lasting consequences for daily living. Saying *yes* to this Lord is saying *no* to all other spiritual lords: "You cannot have a part in both the Lord's table and the table of demons" (1 Cor. 10:21). Therefore those who come to the Lord's Supper must answer about their relationship to Jesus Christ.

The catechism has a simple answer to the important question, Who may come to the table of the Lord?: those who (a) hate sin, (b) love Jesus, and (c) want to do his will. This is no new teaching. It's the a-b-c of Christian comfort: I must know my sin, my Savior, and how I should serve him.

A Communal Responsibility.

All Christians agree that coming or not coming to the Lord's Supper is a matter between God and each individual. But the Reformed churches also teach that the session, council, or consistory has a responsibility to admit or not to admit. The question is not only, Who are to come? (Q. 81) but also, Who are to be admitted? (Q. 82).

We are one body. Together we have covenanted to live as God's people. God blesses us together, and God punishes us together. Just as the Israelites could not win their battles as long as Achan's theft was hidden in his tent (Josh. 7) and just as God's judgment came over the church of Corinth because of its misconduct at love feasts and the Lord's Supper (1 Cor. 11:17-34), so, we believe, the church *as a whole* bears responsibility for how we observe the Lord's Supper and for the people who partake. (Of course, that's only part of our responsibility for the

***Q** Who are to come to the Lord's table?*

***A** Those who are displeased with themselves because of their sins, but who nevertheless trust that their sins are pardoned and that their continuing weakness is covered by the suffering and death of Christ, and who also desire more and more to strengthen their faith and to lead a better life. Hypocrites and those who are unrepentant, however, eat and drink judgment on themselves.*

—Q & A 81

***Q** Are those to be admitted to the Lord's Supper who show by what they say and do that they are unbelieving and ungodly?*

***A** No, that would dishonor God's covenant and bring down God's anger upon the entire congregation. Therefore, according to the instruction of Christ and his apostles, the Christian church is duty-bound to exclude such people, by the official use of the keys of the kingdom, until they reform their lives.*

—Q & A 82

body. We must also prevent poverty among our members. And we must assist each other in growing and correcting.)

Worthy Participants.

Most of us agree that the communion table is not for a cafeteria-style encounter but for the family meal of God's children. Supervising this meal is not easy, though—it has led to a host of difficulties, embarrassments, sins. Yet it would be better to make the supervised table a matter of constant pursuit and learning, even if we make mistakes now and then, than to abandon the ideal all together.

We must shun the search for "marks" and mystical experiences that would prove our worthiness to be admitted to the supper. We must not go back to the preparatory sermons that encourage wailing about sins rather than boasting in Christ. In the Presbyterian Calvinist tradition elders used to issue coins and cards to those they deemed worthy to be guests at the Lord's Supper. But such a custom tolerates and perpetuates two kinds of church membership—those who may take communion and those who may not. We must avoid many pitfalls, but we should practice what Christ commands to all, especially to those whom he appoints: encourage the little ones, that is, those who have "little faith and contrite hearts" to come to the Lord's Supper. And keep away those who, by life and teaching, show that they have no part in the kingdom. But strive to get all of them to the Lord, to his table, and to heaven. This kind of discipline aims not to get the dirty ones out but to get them washed.

No rules exist that cover all situations. We don't have to do all things perfectly, as long as we do them lovingly and in an orderly way. (See "Supervision of Guests at the Lord's Table," *Acts of the Synod of the Christian Reformed Church, 1975*, pp. 102, 471-487.)

Credible Confession.

No one may lord it over someone else's conscience. Everyone must respect everyone else's freedom in Christ and their secrets before God. Consistories may not measure by standards of topical spirituality ("Is he really born again?") or activity ("How often does she go, and how much does she pay?"). Certainly we don't need to avoid these matters in conversation. But our temporary spiritual supervisors must respect God's prerogatives. God alone is your and my Judge. He alone knows what's in the heart of the person who gives the testimony. He reads our thoughts, and he knows our motives. The church may only insist on a credible confession: that is, a Christian confession of who the Lord is and what the person's relationship is to him. And the church may expect a life-style that makes the confession credible, believable, and plausible.

Without the requirement of a credible confession, the members of a church are uncertain of their creed and of how they should behave. But in communities where supervisors go beyond the rule of a credible confession, a spiritual tyranny results.

Please note:

Synod 2006 of the Christian Reformed Church decided that part of answer 80—from "But the Mass teaches . . ." through ". . . a condemnable idolatry"—be placed in brackets. These words no longer represent the official teaching and liturgical practice of the Roman Catholic Church. This conclusion was reached after six years of study and conversations with Roman Catholic representatives (*Acts of Synod 2006,* Christian Reformed Church in North America, p. 711).

Lord's Day 31

THE KEYS OF THE KINGDOM

Q ***What are the keys of the kingdom?***

A ***The preaching of the holy gospel and Christian discipline toward repentance. Both preaching and discipline open the kingdom of heaven to believers and close it to unbelievers.***

—Q & A 83

What Are the Keys?

Keys are means to open and to lock doors. The keys of which we speak give access to the *kingdom of heaven.* The kingdom of heaven is the same as the kingdom of God (Matthew uses *heaven* as a typically Jewish way of indicating the Almighty One). God's kingdom includes heaven but is not limited to the hereafter. The kingdom came to earth when its King—incognito as the suffering servant and crucified criminal—came to earth. We enter God's kingdom while on earth, not merely when we depart this life. Christians already enjoy the power, peace, grace of the new order. But the full glory of kingdom citizens will be unveiled when the kingdom has fully come.

We are now asking, What power or authority gives us entrance into this kingdom? Where and what is the key? And the catechism answers, gospel preaching and the exercise of discipline. It could have answered using one term: *the gospel.* After all, Christian discipline is nothing but applying the gospel to life.

Fake Keys.

By saying that the gospel gives entrance to the kingdom, we reject the notion that the key could be a mysterious code that some guru discovered. Every year a cult springs up around some leader who claims he has found "the key."

We also reject the idea that the power to open and close the kingdom could be in a particular office or person. The authority does not rest in people; the power is in the (preaching of the) gospel. The apostolic witness about the death and resurrection of Jesus Christ is the key.

To Whom Did Christ Entrust the Keys?

The words "keys of the kingdom of heaven" come from Matthew 16:19, where Jesus says to Simon Peter, "*I will give you the keys of the kingdom of heaven; whatever you bind on earth will be bound in heaven, and whatever you loose on earth will be loosed in heaven.*" The expression about binding and loosing means this: I give to you the authority to make statements on earth that hold true in heaven.

This authority, then, which belongs exclusively to Jesus Christ as the Son of the Father, he entrusted to others, just as a master of a house leaves the key with his steward while he goes on a long journey (a number of Jesus' parables have this theme). In the Matthew 16 passage just mentioned, the Lord gave the keys to Peter right after Peter confessed Jesus as the Messiah and after Jesus promised, "On this rock [*petra*] I will build my church." But in Matthew 18:18 Christ entrusts this power to "the church," and in John 20:23 he gives to the apostles the authority to forgive and to withhold forgiveness.

Conclusion Based on the Gospels. The gospels teach that the power of the keys is to make authoritative declarations on earth that hold true in the judgment halls of heaven. The keys are entrusted to the church that Jesus will build and especially to the apostles, to whom he assigns a special function, and to Peter—if not as their leader, then at least as their spokesman.

Admitting to or excluding from the kingdom remains the privilege of Christ. Yet, as the Lord explains in Matthew 18:19-20, his church wields this power while Jesus is in heaven. In order to do so properly, the church must be in prayer, and the members must agree on what to ask. The church can wield heavenly power on earth because the heavenly Lord himself is present with those who gather in his name.

The Apostles and After.

The qualifications of an apostle are stated in Acts when Matthias is chosen to replace Judas (1:21-23): an apostle had to be an earwitness of Jesus' teaching and, especially, an eyewitness that Jesus came back to life after he died. That's also why Paul qualified as an apostle ("Am I not an apostle? Have I not seen Jesus our Lord?" 1 Cor. 9:1), although, as an apostle, he did have an abnormal birth (1 Cor. 15:8).

The Apostolic Church.

The idea of an apostolic succession—as if a Peter the First gave the power to a Peter the Second and he to a Third and so on, until the present pope received it—is a myth, historically speaking, because it did not happen this way. And in biblical language *apostolic succession* is a contradiction in terms. An apostle is an authorized missionary only if he (and she, if the Junias of Romans 16:7 was a female) is an eye and earwitness. Such witnesses do not have successors. The time of the apostles is the unique, foundation-laying era in the church of Christ. The church did not appoint successors to its apostles when they died. But the church guarded the teachings of the apostles not *as if* but *because* the church's life depends on preserving the "faith once for all entrusted to the saints" (Jude 3). Paul's last will and testament (2 Timothy) has one main concern: guard the gospel. And God himself inspired writers to make a permanent record of the gospel in what we now call the New Testament. This is the foundation of the church.

The proclamation of this gospel opens the kingdom. The main task of the church is the administration of the keys of the kingdom. God has appointed the holy catholic and apostolic church of Jesus Christ as the guardian of the keys and as the steward of the Bible.

The Word Disciplines.

All people will be judged by their response to the gospel; the church is here to tell them so. The gospel, the good news, is that God has sent his Son to the cross—a story that's folly to those who perish but power to those who believe (see 1 Cor. 1:18). It's not what the Jews wanted, and it's not what the

Q How does preaching the gospel open and close the kingdom of heaven?

A According to the command of Christ: The kingdom of heaven is opened by proclaiming and publicly declaring to all believers, each and every one, that, as often as they accept the gospel promise in true faith, God, because of what Christ has done, truly forgives all their sins. The kingdom of heaven is closed, however, by proclaiming and publicly declaring to unbelievers and hypocrites that, as long as they do not repent, the anger of God and eternal condemnation rest on them. God's judgment, both in this life and in the life to come, is based on this gospel testimony.

—Q & A 84

Greeks desired (1 Cor. 1:22), but the cross is the door, and the gospel calls, invites, demands that all people enter.

The Whole Counsel of God.

The faithful church proclaims the whole counsel, or will, of God. This expression does *not* mean (as people in the Reformed tradition are often given to understand) that the church should, in addition to the simple gospel, preach the "deeper" things: predestination, election, reprobation, and so on. It actually means that the church must warn the wicked that unless they repent, they will pay the price when they perish. If the church does not warn the wicked, God will hold it accountable for the blood of perishing sinners. That was the word to an Old Testament prophet (Ezek. 3:16-21). But a New Testament apostle knew that it also applied to him. Therefore he said in one of his most moving recorded speeches that he was "innocent of the blood of all men" because he had "not hesitated to proclaim . . . the whole will of God" (Acts 20:26-27).

The preaching of the gospel, if it is a faithful handling of the keys, opens *and* closes the door. The public proclamation should inform all hearers where they are—in or out.

The Difficulty with Discipline.

The church does not censure those who fall into sin; the church helps them to get up. The censure of which the confession speaks is for stubborn sinners. And its purpose is to save them from the final judgment.

These confessional statements on discipline (as well as the forms and procedures we use to apply them) were composed in an age when the church had a monopoly within the state. Today, though, everyone enjoys the choice of a vast array of denominations. And because people switch churches rather easily, discipline loses its desired effect before the procedure can run its course. In the ancient church a person who was cut off from the fellowship was convinced that he or she was without grace, handed over to Satan (1 Cor. 5:1-5). In medieval times and also during the age of the Reformation, when there was one church to one state, this picture was still meaningful. But today a sinner who feels harassed switches to another church.

A second difficulty concerns the kind of sinner our confessions and church-orderly documents anticipate. These writings seem to visualize a sinner as one who espouses an unbiblical teaching or lives an immoral life. Occasionally today's elders still have to deal with such a sinner. But most candidates for disciplinary action are the lax and the indifferent.

The Need for Discipline.

While the changed situation of the church and of its objects of discipline might dictate that we rewrite the manual, we ought not to neglect discipline.

Only churches in which people don't really believe that Christ saves us from everlasting damnation neglect discipline.

Church people who take the gospel seriously don't allow each other to live and die quietly in sin. Christians who love each other have the courage to warn each other against the fires of hell. People who really care wouldn't mind dragging each other into the kingdom, if that were possible. Discipline in the church is the sure signal of Christian love.

The Three Levels of Discipline.

But church discipline cannot be a police action by a few chosen officials, the elders. It must begin with *self-discipline* ("If your hand or your foot causes you to sin, cut it off . . ." Matt. 18:7-9), and it must be followed and sustained by *mutual discipline* ("if your brother sins against you, go and show him his fault . . ." vv. 15-16). The last earthly action is by the *church officials* (vv. 17-20).

A stream cannot rise higher than its source. By the same principle, one cannot expect discipline to function in a church where people don't practice self-discipline and don't even dare to admonish each other. But whenever the church believes the gospel with renewed seriousness, it will practice discipline at all levels.

***Q** How is the kingdom of heaven closed and opened by Christian discipline?*

***A** According to the command of Christ: Those who, though called Christians, profess unchristian teachings or live unchristian lives, and after repeated and loving counsel refuse to abandon their errors and wickedness, and after being reported to the church, that is, to its officers, fail to respond also to their admonition—such persons the officers exclude from the Christian fellowship by withholding the sacraments from them, and God himself excludes them from the kingdom of Christ. Such persons, when promising and demonstrating genuine reform, are received again as members of Christ and of his church.*

—Q & A 85

Lord's Day 32

SAVED TO SERVE

***Q** We have been delivered from our misery by God's grace alone through Christ and not because we have earned it: why then must we still do good?*

***A** To be sure, Christ has redeemed us by his blood. But we do good because Christ by his Spirit is also renewing us to be like himself, so that in all our living we may show that we are thankful to God for all he has done for us, and so that he may be praised through us.*

And we do good so that we may be assured of our faith by its fruits, and so that by our godly living our neighbors may be won over to Christ.

—Q & A 86

The Goal of Redemption.

Question 86 summarizes the second part of the Heidelberg Catechism, which teaches redemption. The question also introduces the third part, which is about our gratitude: "We have been delivered . . . by God's grace alone . . . not because we have earned it: why then must we still do good?" Every translation except the Christian Reformed Church's new one asks, Why must we still do *good works*? (in German, *gute Werke tun*; in Latin, *bona opera faciamus*). But to us the expression "good works" has a special (bad) odor. And the writers of the catechism did not have in mind any extraordinary acts of kindness or holiness: they were thinking of obedience to God's commandments, as the wider context shows. The question is this: If we are saved only and wholly by grace, why must we be so careful to obey God's will? And here is the answer: We obey not to earn salvation, but we obey as the beautiful fruit of salvation.

The goal of God's salvation is a gratefully obedient people: "'This is the covenant I will make with the house of Israel after that time,' declares the Lord, 'I will put my law in their minds and write it on their hearts'" (Jer. 31:33). "Our great God and Savior, Jesus Christ . . . gave himself for us to redeem us from all wickedness and to purify for himself a people that are his very own, eager to do what is good" (Titus 2:13-14). "For we are God's workmanship, created in Christ Jesus to do good works, which God prepared in advance for us to do" (Eph. 2:10).

The Blood and the Spirit of Christ.

The blood of Jesus Christ—his death on the cross—delivers us from the curse of sin. The Spirit of Jesus Christ delivers us from the power of sin. Christ redeems us by his blood; he purifies us by his Spirit. We cannot have the one without the other. Or, to say the same thing in different words, we cannot have Jesus as Savior if we refuse to honor him as Lord.

We are justified by faith in Christ, justified wholly by the grace of God. From that moment on, we exist only "in Christ," and outside of Christ we have no existence. "We died to sin; how can we live in it any longer?" (Rom. 6:2). In Christ we are a part of the new creation that has been restored to love and glorify the Lord. "He chose to give us birth through the word of truth, that we might be a kind of firstfruits of all he created" (James 1:18).

To God's Glory.

The Spirit of Christ renews us "so that in all our living we may show that we are thankful to God." The result of redemption is thankful living. Thankfulness is impossible for those who are outside of Christ's renewing influence. Their lack of gratitude is not only evidence of their bondage but also is the reason for their condemnation. Every person has an inkling of God's existence and power simply by living in his world (Rom. 1:20, Acts 14:17). However, human beings react negatively to this "general revelation." Their urge to worship turns from the Creator to the creature. "For although they knew God, they neither glorified him as God nor gave thanks to him" (Rom. 1:21). But when we are renewed by the blood and the Spirit, we can begin to fulfill our original assignment: to give God his due and to thank him who owns us because he made us and he bought us back.

"Thankfulness is the attitude of the man who lives by grace and does not plunge again into the abyss from which he has been saved," said Karl Barth.

All of life becomes a grateful response to God when the love of God has changed my *heart*, the center of my being. My words and works are now done for God's glory because all my actions have their wellspring in my heart's gratitude.

Horizontal Benefits.

Not only the Father in heaven but also the child on earth benefit from obedient and grateful living: "We do good so that we may be assured of our faith by its fruits," says the catechism.

Does this answer teach that we find assurance of the genuineness of our faith when our deeds are good, true, and beautiful? That could be a dangerous line. It is true that the tree is known by its fruit (Matt. 7:17-20) and that the fruit of the Spirit is observable (Gal. 5:22-24). But our lives will never convince us that our faith is real. Someone else's life may encourage our faith and be worth telling others about. But my own faith remains anchored in God's Word, and I had better be very critical of my own performance.

With this answer the catechism probably wishes to state the simple truth that our faith grows when our Christian activity increases. If I go out on a limb for Jesus, I receive a deep sense of his presence. On the other hand, I stunt the growth of my faith if I confess that outside of Christ is no life but have no problem living, working, talking with people who deny the Savior. We find the peace of Christ in our souls when we take up his yoke (Matt. 11:28-30), not when we merely talk about him. When we refuse discipleship, our talk about Christ remains hollow. Until and unless we join faith and action, faith is a widow. In fact, according to James, if faith is not accompanied by action, it *is dead* (2:17).

It's the tragedy of many church members that they say they believe but have never done anything to back it up.

Three Directions.

The good report of a grateful and obedient life goes in three directions, says the catechism. First, the fruits of such a life please our Father in heaven. Just as the trees reflect favorably on the owner of an orchard when they bear fruit, so our lives glorify God when they produce what he intended (see John 15:1-8).

Second, we ourselves benefit from work we perform to God's honor. A consistent Christian life in which confession and performance harmonize happily is a calm and assured kind of life. It's a benefit any Christian may enjoy in the present age.

And, third, says the catechism, the good report of my redeemed life should go to my neighbor.

Evangelism.

Here's one of the few points at which the "Heidelberger" speaks of evangelism: we do good so that "our neighbors may be won over to Christ."

The gain from our works is supposed to go to Christ, or to God. Many of us are inclined to do nice deeds to gain points with other people. Then we are the ones to whom our neighbors are "won over." But the catechism speaks of *winning neighbors over to Christ*. Evangelism is not only different from but the opposite of proselytizing or group extension.

Word and Deed in Matthew 5:16.

"Let your light shine before men, that they may see your good deeds and praise your Father in heaven." The people who are looking at me are supposed to praise my Father. If they keep staring at me or talking about me or my family or my church, the goal of good works has not yet been reached. The praise must go up! Only then will Christ, God, and the neighbor(!) be the winners. Obviously, then, these neighbors would have known already what relationship exists between Christ and me. They heard it before they saw it.

In 1 Peter 2:12.

This text also presupposes that a word precedes the deed: "Live such good lives among the pagans that, though they accuse you of doing wrong, they may see your good deeds and glorify God. . . ." Note again that the people who are told to live "good lives" are already known as Christians. Moreover, they are falsely accused of "doing wrong." Hatred has spoken evil of these Christians. Now Peter says that they should deny the rumors with their lives. Then the pagans will have a second look (a careful look, the verb implies) and conclude that the God of these people is good and great.

In both cases the onlooker knows already that Christ owns the one who does the good works. Then the works convince the neighbor of the goodness and greatness of Christ and God.

In 1 Peter 3:1-2.

In a third instance the word had been ineffective in evangelism, and the deed became the only weapon: "Wives, in the same way be submissive to your husbands so that, if any of them do not believe the word, they may be won over without words by the behavior of their wives, when they see the purity and reverence of your lives."

These women had believed the gospel, but their husbands had not accepted Christ. The wives could not keep silent about their new riches. But all their talk was merely a nagging nuisance to the husbands. Keep still now, writes Peter. Preach with your lives.

There is a time when we must stop talking, but we may never stop doing.

God's Love for the Bad Ones.

A Calvinist and an Arminian once met an unchaste drunkard convicted of robbery. The Arminian said, "Friend, God loves you." And the Calvinist added, "Yeah, and he loves to change you."

To the great irritation of decent, religious, law-abiding people in the days of Jesus, our Lord announced that he came to save unchaste persons, adulterers, and other bad folk. He even came to save people who were rich and crooked (Luke 19:9-10). So he loved them, and he still loves them. Otherwise he would not have gone through all the pain of saving them (1 Tim. 1:15).

But salvation involves conversion. And those who don't get converted have not been saved.

Conversion is like the adoption of a child who lives in a hopelessly decadent milieu. The parents adopt the child because they love him or her. But as soon as the child moves into the new home, with loving parents and a wholesome environment, a big change must be worked out in that beloved and adopted child. The adoptive parents love the child too much to allow her or him to grow up crooked, decadent, and unchanged.

Salvation involves conversion. "Jesus loves you, friend!" "Yeah, and that's why he is going to change you."

***Q** Can those be saved who do not turn to God from their ungrateful and impenitent ways?*

***A** By no means. Scripture tells us that no unchaste person, no idolater, adulterer, thief, no covetous person, no drunkard, slanderer, robber, or the like is going to inherit the kingdom of God.*

—Q & A 87

Lord's Day 33

CONVERSION

***Q** What is involved in genuine repentance or conversion?*

***A** Two things: the dying-away of the old self, and the coming-to-life of the new.*

—Q & A 88

Conversion Is Change of Direction.

Conversion is like a U-turn: people who become aware that they are traveling in the wrong direction turn around. They change because they know they are on the wrong road. Conversion results from an altered relationship to God. A converted person is no longer estranged from the Father but learns to behave as a child of God.

Because every human being is a sinner and estranged from God, everyone must be converted. Thus, John the Baptist, Jesus himself, and also his disciples demanded repentance, or conversion, when they proclaimed the gospel of the kingdom (Mark 1:5, 15, 6:12). "Repent or perish" is an essential part of the New Testament message (Acts 3:19, Rev. 3:19).

In this part of the catechism, however, we do not discuss the initial, direction-changing turn, but we speak of conversion as the ongoing pain and joy of breaking down and growing up. We are not thinking of the conversion of the prodigal son, who "came to his senses" while feeding the hogs and decided, "I will set out and go back to my father" (Luke 15:17-18). That remains the classic example of the decision every lost child should make. But we are thinking about the life of obedience as God's children live it once they have come home.

Lifelong Repentance.

The first of Martin Luther's Ninety-five Theses (which he posted on the door of the Castle Church in Wittenberg on October 31, 1517) says that "our Master Jesus Christ, in saying 'Repent ye, etc.,' meant the whole life of the faithful to be an act of repentance."

Wherever biblical teaching has been restored, Christians know that change is a daily order and that conversion is not finished until we are completely new, inside and outside. As C.S. Lewis has said, many Christians first call on the Lord to do some little fixing in their lives, like homeowners who call on the repairman to mend the plumbing. But once *this* Repairman comes into the house, he does not merely fix a leaky valve and a broken pipe but remodels the whole house! He installs new windows and doors and does not cease rebuilding until the shack has become a mansion.

Conversion is the ongoing "dying-away of the old self" and the steady "coming-to-life of the new," until we are "clothed with our heavenly dwelling" and our mortality itself has been "swallowed up by life" (2 Cor. 5:1-5).

Conversion Accomplished.

The "old self" is the unregenerated you and me. It's the "old man," which is not a disrepectful way of talking about your dad but a reference to the fallen Adam.

This old self, the Adamic man, was put on the cross. He died. On Golgotha old Adam died. And on the first day of the week the new Man arose. He is the last Adam, and he is the life-giving Spirit (1 Cor. 15:45).

"Our old self was crucified with him so that the body of sin might be rendered powerless" (Rom. 6:6). That's the end of the old sinful, selfish way of death. That's the end of old Andrew and Cathy, Harry and Joan, the end of old you and me. When he died, I died. If you ask me when I was converted, I will answer that it happened on Golgotha. There my old self was killed. And when you ask me when I came to life, when my new self that lives for God was born, I must tell you that it happened when Jesus arose. Since Christ died for the old world and arose to inaugurate a new world, you too must "count yourselves dead to sin but alive to God in Christ Jesus" (6:11). You and I and the whole church may apply this judgment of faith to ourselves. By faith we know that we have died and that we have risen, because Christ died to sin and arose to live for God. And we are in Christ.

Q *What is the dying-away of the old self?*

A ***It is to be genuinely sorry for sin, to hate it more and more, and to run away from it.***

—Q & A 89

Q *What is the coming-to-life of the new self?*

A ***It is wholehearted joy in God through Christ and a delight to do every kind of good as God wants us to.***

—Q & A 90

Conversion Applied.

These once-for-all events are, second, applied to us in baptism. Baptism is the sign and seal that a particular person has been washed by the blood and revived by the Spirit of Jesus. Baptism shows incorporation into Christ Jesus (*incorporation* means "being made part of the *corpus,* or body," of Christ). Whatever happened to Christ happened to those who are in Christ. We are baptized into his death. "We died to sin; how can we live in it any longer?" (6:2). And "just as Christ was raised from the dead through the glory of the Father, we too may live a new life" (6:4).

The end of the old and the beginning of the new took place on Golgotha and on resurrection morning. I participate in these great events because I am a part of the body.

Conversion Carried Out.

Conversion is a fact, accomplished for us and applied to us, but also a command to be carried out by us: "Set your hearts on things above" (Col. 3:1). "Put to death . . . whatever belongs to your earthly nature," and "as God's chosen people . . . clothe yourselves" with Christian virtues (3:5-14).

If we don't believe our conversion in Christ, we cannot obey. And it is only by obeying the command that we can show our faith in the gospel.

Faith and Experience.

Our conversion was *accomplished* in Christ, our head: with him we died and arose to a new life.

Baptism *signifies* that conversion. Our baptism says that we are no longer under the curse of Adam but that we share the righteousness of Christ.

Conversion is *effected by* the Holy Spirit. The Spirit gets under our skin, he dwells in our hearts, and he makes the work of Jesus real in our daily living.

And conversion *is realized* in good works, which are the fruit of the Spirit and the observable results of a converted life.

Dying to Sin.

The catechism explains our mortification (that is the old word for *dying-away*) as sorrow for sin. Indeed, being sorry for one's sins is a necessary part of conversion. "Godly sorrow brings repentance that leads to salvation" (2 Cor. 7:10). The inaccessible heavens *and* repentant people form the residence of God Almighty: "For this is what the high and lofty One says—he who lives forever, whose name is holy: 'I live in a high and holy place, but also with him who is contrite and lowly in spirit, to revive the spirit of the lowly and to revive the heart of the contrite'" (Isa. 57:15).

Our pious forebears moved forth and back from this sorrow and contrition to new hope and "joy in God through Christ." They struck this theme constantly. They made strong confessions of their sinfulness—so strong that we who read their prayers and confessions wonder whether they dared to believe that they had gone over from darkness to light, from death to life. (See, for example, "A Public Confession of Sins and Prayer Before the Sermon" in the *Psalter Hymnal* used by the Christian Reformed Church until 1988. The hymnal's prayers date back to the sixteenth century; nobody seemed to use them in the twentieth century.)

A life lived between sorrow for sin and reception of God's forgiveness is the main evidence of an ongoing conversion, according to the catechism. This teaching is backed up by biblical references printed as footnotes to Answers 89 and 90. Notice that no fewer than five verses from Psalm 51 are used.

We may not lose this religious tone and awareness. Our ancestors were more deeply conscious than are we of the spotless holiness of God and the fact that he is always right and we are usually wrong.

Discipleship.

But Christian conversion is more than sorrow for sin and hope for forgiveness. It's also a school of *discipleship* and *cross-bearing*. In this school we learn to take leave of the old way, and we train daily in living as citizens of the new world.

Once we have been called to Christ and to his kingdom, we must reorder our lives. Our Master wants us to let go of much so that he may give us more. And if we cannot let go, we may lose the pearl while we play with the beads. This "giving up" and "letting go" involves suffering. It is the unavoidable conversion and reordering of a natural, sinful human life of which Jesus has become Lord. The natural person (that is, the sinful self) must die. Our worldly ambitions must perish. This must happen in this present life and world, and it cannot happen without pain. We need instruction in living the converted life. Otherwise, we say and sing the right things when we pray and worship, but in "our own time" and with "our own money," we are acting no different than the unconverted.

I am not saying that this reordering and rebuilding of our lives does not get attention in the "Heidelberger." It certainly does in Lord's Days 34 through 52. But I am saying that when we think of daily conversion, it is not enough to think of being sorry for bad things, believing that Jesus died for our sins, and trying to do a little better tomorrow. Conversion is the renovation of a life that has become the sole property of God, who created it, who bought it back through his Son's blood, and who now governs it by his Spirit. Conversion is the steadfast transformation of a child of this present world into a citizen of the kingdom of our Lord Jesus Christ. This transformation is not completed until—either by death or in the twinkling of an eye at the last trumpet—the final shock treatment has been administered by the great Doctor. But the first results of God's work must be evident here and now in our lives.

Joy in God.

When we really come alive, says the catechism, we will have "wholehearted joy in God . . . and a delight to do . . . as God wants us to."

This is the secret, of course. It's the key to overcoming the ordinary temptation to worldliness, and it's the clue to the big overhaul of life itself.

The desire for evil diminishes when good becomes the more powerful attraction.

Oak trees will not let go of some of their old leaves even when winds blow and snow flies. But in the spring an old leaf will fall without any wind or blast, because a new leaf sprouts!

We don't overcome evil merely by fighting it. We change when we have a taste for doing good, a taste given by the Holy Spirit.

The Definition.

Whatever is truly good, says our confession, must proceed from faith, conform to God's law, and aim at his glory. That's a very strict, God-centered definition of a good work. And the catechism adds that the things we do are not necessarily right because we think they are or because human tradition considers them so. Thereby our teacher is preparing us to consider God's law (Lord's Day 34-44) and our prayers (45-52).

A good work is like a young tree: it grows out of the soil of faith, it is kept straight by a stake representing the law, and it shoots up and up to heaven.

***Q** What do we do that is good?*

***A** Only that which arises out of true faith, conforms to God's law, and is done for his glory; and not that which is based on what we think is right or on established human tradition.*

—Q & A 91

A God-created Response.

The catechism is no stricter than the Scriptures. At the close of his discussion of Christian freedom and the differences between strong and weak Christians, Paul writes, "Everything that does not come from faith is sin" (Rom. 14:23). Here he uses *faith* to mean our relationship to Jesus Christ. We sin when we make decisions outside of that relationship.

When it comes to living a God-pleasing life, Jesus' prescription is very clear: "I am the vine; you are the branches. If a man remains in me and I in him, he will bear much fruit; apart from me you can do nothing" (John 15:5). He did not say that when we go it alone we are bound to miss the mark now and then; he said, "Apart from me you can do *nothing*."

Only when we abide in Christ are our words and deeds and we ourselves acceptable to God.

Law-directed Behavior.

King Saul claimed that he had kept the best of the Amalekite cattle for a sacrifice to the Lord. But Samuel told Saul, "To obey is better than sacrifice," and "you have rejected the word of the Lord" with the just but terrible result that "he has rejected you as king" (1 Sam. 15:22-23).

We are always inclined to give our selfish behavior a pious twist. But we should never let it come to the point that we defend taking our self-willed byways. Instead we must concentrate on doing God's will. Let's stay on the highway of faith and obedience because that is the essence of covenant living.

To God's Glory.

When, in their pagan society, the early Christians attempted to find God's will for everyday living, the apostle Paul gave them a number of principles. In Romans 14 (mentioned above) he said that if you act outside of your faith relationship to God, you sin. In 1 Corinthians 10 he added that in our doing or not doing, eating or not eating, participating or not participating, our highest aim is the glory of God (v. 31). If our behavior glorifies God's name, we are doing good. If what we say or do dishonors his name, we are entirely wrong, even when we think we can defend ourselves.

It Is Possible.

The Bible stresses the *possibility* that the redeemed can do good works. But we are inclined to stress the *difficulty* of doing good works. And although we will have to maintain over against arrogant and/or superficial people that a good and obedient life is not perfect here below, we don't honor Christ by always telling each other how hard it is to do his will. After all, doing good works is a labor of love. And to love is not hard for those whom God loves.

Our good works and obedient lives are the goals of Christ's redeeming work. If we keep saying that it's so hard to do good, we are actually saying that Christ's work is imperfect.

Christ died to set us free to do good works. He arose to empower us to live the new life. He gave us his Spirit so that we desire what he himself wants. Therefore we may, we can, we want to do good works.

Excluded by Definition.

By its definition of *good*, the catechism excludes the possibility that your unbelieving but friendly neighbor does what is good in God's sight. We do not mean to say, however, that unbelievers and believers cannot cooperate in good programs and projects, and we don't deny that many unbelievers (or those who have a false faith) deserve to be held up as examples to those who know Christ. Jesus himself frequently referred to the Samaritans (see Luke 10:33, 17:16) as examples of neighborly love and gratitude. And every one of us has experienced the disappointing behavior of fellow Christians as well as some surprising goodness on the part of those who deny our Lord.

The church has often debated what to think of the goodness of the ungodly. We have taught that unbelievers are capable of doing civil and moral good, and we have said that only Christians can render spiritual good. These distinctions may be helpful. At any rate, God is a righteous judge, and he will not do evil to those who do good. Leave it to him.

The Source of Goodness.

God is the "overflowing fountain of all good" (Belgic Confession, Art. 1). "Every good and perfect gift is from above, coming down from the father of the heavenly lights" (James 1:17). Nobody has anything good unless it comes from God. And nobody can do anything that's good in God's eyes if he or she neglects or denies God. The Lord must be loved above all, otherwise nothing is good.

Our greatest sin is our estrangement from God. Only regeneration makes us good. For goodness is God-centered. And the goodness we perform comes from God.

Lord's Day 34

THE TEN WORDS

Q *What does the Lord say in his law?*

A *God spoke all these words: I am the LORD your God, who brought you out of the land of Egypt, out of the land of slavery. You shall have no other gods before me . . . (this answer of the Heidelberg Catechism quotes Exodus 20:1-17).*

—Q & A 92

The Introduction to the Ten Words.

God addressed the Ten Commandments (or Words, as the Jews say) to the former slaves of Egypt, camped at Sinai, where he made a treaty, or covenant, with them.

The Lord addressed these people as those who were free from bondage and set apart as his own. The address is very significant, and nearly every expositor of the Heidelberg Catechism regrets that the catechism does not comment on the introduction to the law.

The Westminster Catechism does address the introduction in a separate question (44), which asks, "What doth the preface to the ten commandments teach us?" The answer: "The preface to the ten commandments teacheth us, That because God is the Lord, and our God, and Redeemer, therefore we are bound to keep all his commandments."

The Heidelberg Catechism does show that it understands the meaning of the introduction by addressing the law in the third part, the part about gratitude: the law comes to God's people *after* he has delivered them. We obey our Lord *because* he has set us free.

Law and Gospel.

The introduction to the Ten Commandments, says one able expositor (B. Holwerda), forces us to make sure we understand the connection between the law and the gospel. The gospel comes first: I am the Lord, who set you free. And the law is the rule for grateful living: now keep my commandments.

The Road Map.

In order to grasp the crucial connection between gospel and law, a person should always call to mind *when* and *where* God gave the commandments. He gave them *after* the great deliverance. The people were delivered from Egypt not by obedience but by grace. And the Lord gave the law to them *before* they reached the Promised Land.

This is how the law functions in our lives: we were not redeemed by law-keeping but set free by God's sovereign grace. We begin with the gospel and not with the law. Yet between our redemption from the bondage to sin and our arrival in the land beyond the Jordan, we travel by the road map of God's law. God's law is the guide for our pilgrimage.

Free to Obey.

"I am the Lord your God, who brought you out of the land of Egypt." In New Testament language the introduction would read, "I am the Lord your God, who set you free through the death and resurrection of my Son." Now you enter the school of discipleship, the instruction in Christian living, the keeping of the law, the walk by the Spirit.

In both the Old and New Testaments, freedom is not only a *freedom from* but a *freedom to*. We are free *from* bondage, from Egypt, from the guilt and power of sin, *to* obey the Lord.

Covenant Keeping.

The lawgiver introduces himself as the covenant God. The ten rules spell out how the people who have been delivered by Jahweh must live. For them, law keeping means adhering to the conditions of the covenant. Obedience by God's people under the old (Sinai) covenant and in the New Covenant dispensation is not slave-like but child-like. Law keeping is covenant keeping. But in the New Testament this obedience is possible for us and acceptable to God because the Spirit lives in us and works through us.

Those who say that the law of Sinai has been replaced by the law of love in the New Covenant misunderstand the teaching of God's Word. The New Covenant does not bring a new law but a new obedience (Jer. 31:33). However, the Old Covenant law is deepened and "filled full," or "fulfilled," by Jesus. The full meaning of the law proclaimed on the first mountain (Sinai) is expounded from the other mountain (the Sermon on the Mount, Matt. 5-7) by Jesus, who came to fulfill the law and the prophets (5:17). This means that by his life and teaching he brings the fullest and deepest meaning of the law and the prophets to light.

Centrality of the Ten.

The Sinai covenant consisted of many more obligations and privileges than the ten rules that have become so familiar to us. But the Ten Commandments were central to the covenant made at Sinai: this law was repeated (Ex. 20, Deut. 5), these commandments were recited by God's own voice and written by God's own fingers (Ex. 20:22, 31:18, 34:1, 28), and the stone tablets on which this law was inscribed were kept in the ark (40:20). These two tablets, containing the Ten Words, were known as the "Testimony" (16:34, 25:16, 31:18), because the Ten Commandments set forth the basic stipulation of Israel's covenant with the Lord, the God of Israel.

In the New Covenant.

The New Testament maintains and deepens the commandments on the second tablet—those relating to the neighbor. But the commandments on the first tablet, regulating our relationship to God, the New Testament reinterprets in the light of the appearance of Jesus Christ.

The Ten Commandments definitely belong to the Sinai covenant, and we belong to a covenant in which everything is "better," as Hebrews says (1:4; 6:9; 7:7, 19, 22; 8:6; 9:23; 10:34; 11:16, 35, 40; 12:24). Yet the church has found that the Ten Commandments supply the best tools for explaining the will of God to the New Testament congregation.

***Q** How are these commandments divided?*

***A** Into two tables. The first has four commandments, teaching us what our relation to God should be. The second has six commandments, teaching us what we owe our neighbor.*

—Q & A 93

Dividing the Ten.

We are used to seeing pictures of the tablets of the Ten Commandments in the hands of Moses. In these pictures the two tablets always resemble grave markers. Actually, we don't know what the tablets looked like, how much was written on either one, and how the Ten were divided.

In studying the commandments, the first question is how one should count them. One tradition, followed by Roman Catholics and Lutherans, combines our first and second commandments and splits our tenth. Therefore a recent novel, *The Sixth Commandment*, deals with the seventh, and thus with adultery (as do most novels).

Both traditions—it is safe to say—will continue to number the commandments as they have always done.

Second, we ask what words were engraved on the original tablets that Moses carried from the mountain. The text in Exodus 20 differs a bit from the one in Deuteronomy 5: they present different reasons why God wants his people to keep the Sabbath day holy. God revealed both reasons to his people, we believe. But he did not include on the stone tablet both motivations for keeping the Sabbath. Some scholars and teachers say that the Exodus text is the original. Others maintain that the original commandments came *without* the "reasons" or "motivations." These embellishments of, for example, the second and fourth commandments do seem to fit better in the context of covenantal instruction than in law proclamation.

Two Relationships.

The first four commandments teach us (1) our relationship to God, (2) to worship him, (3) how we may use his name, and (4) to observe his day.

The fifth commandment, about honor for parents and respect for authority, is set between the first and the second group. It does not regulate the vertical, or "God-ward," relationship, and yet it speaks of more than the horizontal, the neighborly, relationships, regulated by the second group.

In horizontal relationships God teaches us to respect (6) the neighbor's life, (7) the neighbor's marriage, (8) the neighbor's possessions, and (9) the neighbor's name. We understand the tenth commandment to address the root cause (coveting) of all transgressions named in the second group.

Your Commands Are Boundless (Ps. 119:96).

These commands are terse statements, and most of them are negative, telling us what we may *not* do. Of course, the New Testament exposition of Christian love as the fulfillment of all of God's commands far exceeds the elementary teaching of the Ten Words. Yet disparaging talk about the "thou-shalt-nots" betrays great ignorance. The reverence for God and the respect for the neighbor commanded by the Ten Words is foundational to all social ethics. William Barclay calls it "the law without which nationhood is impossible."

The majesty of God (the first table) and the rights of human personality (the second table) must be held in tandem. Both are destroyed when one is forgotten. Therefore a materialistic society has no chance of survival, because it erases the first table of the law. And "religious fanatics" who kill people of another faith destroy the whole law of God, because they sacrifice the second table in the name of the first.

We also see the wide reach of the commandments when we remember that all ten address principles rather than details and that this is how the catechism expounds them. Properly understood (reading the Ten Words through the spectacles of the New Testament), the Ten Commandments cover the whole width and depth of human living in all our relationships. And their fulfillment is nothing less than a whole-life response of love to God's love.

The Only God.

The first commandment says, "You shall have no gods except me," or, "you shall have no gods against me." This is the sense of the first commandment, even if its translations differ somewhat. Parallel to this command is the confession recited thrice daily by every pious Israelite: "Hear, O Israel: The Lord our God, the Lord is one" (Deut. 6:4).

Does the Bible assume the reality of "other gods"? The Bible assumes that people worship many gods and lords (Ps. 95:3, 1 Cor. 8:5). But it teaches that other gods are "nothings." And God demands that his people worship no other than the One who delivered them.

This command comes to a covenant people. Translated into New Testament language, it requires that the Father of our Lord Jesus Christ—and no one else—receive the wholehearted worship, love, and trust of all of his people and that we teach the world to believe in him likewise.

Q *What does the Lord require in the first commandment?*

A *That I, not wanting to endanger my very salvation, avoid and shun all idolatry, magic, superstitious rites, and prayer to saints and to other creatures. That I sincerely acknowledge the only true God, trust him alone, look to him for every good thing humbly and patiently, love him, fear him, and honor him with all my heart. In short, that I give up anything rather than go against his will in any way.*

—*Q & A 94*

Most Fundamental.

The Ten Commandments may be compared to a ten story building. The first and main level is the one on which all others rest. Unless God is Lord, the other rules cannot be maintained. There's no way to safeguard obedience to the rules that protect the neighbor's life, wife, and goods if the most fundamental rule is disobeyed. The ten stories collapse if the first falls.

A redeemed community and a redeemed life that is reformed according to God's Word is no longer idolatrous. In such a community, the God of the Scriptures is honored as the only Lord. This is the most characteristic feature of redeemed lives: true priority has been reestablished. We seek the kingdom of God first. Our first concern, our prayer, has become "hallowed be your name." Our obedience to God's law begins with obedience to the first commandment. Otherwise the new life's building does not get off the ground.

Q *What is idolatry?*

A *Idolatry is having or inventing something in which one trusts in place of or alongside of the only true God, who has revealed himself in his Word.*

—*Q & A 95*

Either-Or.

The catechism says that magic, superstitious rites, and prayers to saints are sins against the first commandment: they place our salvation in jeopardy. God alone is the fountain of all good things. We must trust him completely, but we don't trust and honor him if we seek the protection of saints and the power of magic words and incantations. No matter how well-meaning may be the people who bow before Mary and the saints, they insult God. Just as it would be a bitter insult to an earthly father if his children went to the neighbors for protection and help, so our Father in heaven cannot stand it when we bypass him and go to others. A church that teaches people to go to the saints because they are supposed to be our lobbyists in the throne room of the Almighty departs from the teaching of God's Word and transgresses the very first commandment.

If God is our God, we trust him completely. But if we trust in something "in place of or alongside of the only true God," we have committed idolatry. Trusting and honoring God as the Father of our Lord Jesus Christ is the first commandment. And idolatry is the most basic temptation of the human heart.

The First Temptation.

When the Father had appointed Jesus as Messiah and the Spirit had anointed the Son at his baptism in the Jordan River, "Jesus was led by the Spirit into the desert to be tempted by the devil" (Matt. 4:1). This was the beginning of the great confrontation between these two. The stakes of the battle were "all the kingdoms of the world and their splendor," (4:8) and the battle could be won only by obedience—unwavering allegiance to the first commandment. In the first temptation Jesus had to answer whether he would trust God even if he had to suffer (4:4, Luke 4:4). He passed the test that Israel had failed: Israel had thought that unless it had bread, life was not worth living (Deut. 8:3). Jesus knew with his whole being that a person does not yet have life when he has something to put *into* his mouth. We live when we obey what comes *out of* the mouth of the Lord. Obedience to the Word of God: this is life!

This remains one of the most basic tests that all of us must pass. A job is *not* the most important thing in life. Food is not the most important thing. School isn't. Our lives aren't most important. But God *is* most important. If we obey him, we cannot lose. But if we have everything else and disobey him, we have nothing. All things have the capacity to become your and my idols, especially things and people on which our lives seem to depend partly or completely. And you and I must learn the way of obedience, says the catechism, which means that we give up anything rather than go against his will in any way. We must trust God so much that we know, deep down, that ultimately we cannot lose, even if we lose all the respect of people, all our money, even the love of relatives, as long as we put God first.

Fulfillment of the First Commandment.

In order to obey the first commandment, we have to get rid of all other gods, such as nation, clan, husband, wife, children, money, security, academic degree, or whoever or whatever tends to take first place in our lives. Only the God of the Scriptures may have the first place in our lives; whatever has the first place in our lives, that is our god.

Not all idols are ugly. Some people live for art or music, and both these things are from God. But they are idols when we give them what is due to God alone.

However, even if we have had an idol-removal exercise such as the patriarchs used to have (see Gen. 35:1-5)—and as is required of us periodically—we have not yet fully obeyed the first commandment. The fulfillment of the first commandment consists of loving God with all our heart and soul and mind and strength. Only when we completely love him and therefore completely trust him have we obeyed the most basic command the Lord gave us.

When we love him, we know that the worst we can do to the Beloved is to lean on an idol. And suddenly it makes sense that the last word in the epistle of love reads, "Dear children, keep yourselves from idols" (1 John 5:21).

Lord's Day 35

HOW TO WORSHIP GOD

***Q** What is God's will for us in the second commandment?*

***A** That we in no way make any image of God nor worship him in any other way than he has commanded in his Word.*

—Q & A 96

***Q** May we then not make any image at all?*

***A** God can not and may not be visibly portrayed in any way. Although creatures may be portrayed, yet God forbids making or having such images if one's intention is to worship them or to serve God through them.*

—Q & A 97

Second Commandment.

In the first of the ten commandments God insists that we should worship him and him alone as the only true God: have no other gods. In the second commandment our Lawgiver speaks of the way in which we may not worship: have no graven images (RSV). The first commandment says *whom* we should worship; the second teaches *how* we should worship. We may not do it in our self-willed ways; we must bring our adoration in a manner that is right and pleasing to God.

Our study of the second commandment should yield answers to at least three questions: What exactly does God forbid? What does he command? And how do we fulfill God's requirement in the second commandment?

What God Forbids.

We may not make any image of God, says the catechism. But Exodus 20:4 (and Deut. 5:8) tells us only that we may not make "a graven image, or any likeness of anything that is in heaven above" or on the earth or under the earth (RSV).

The New International Version (NIV) of the Bible has broken with a long tradition by translating the second commandment this way: "You shall not make for yourself an idol in the form of anything in heaven above or on the earth beneath or in the waters below." An editor of the NIV told me that the word *idol* was chosen over *graven image* for easier recognition by English readers. *Idol,* in common usage, now means any physical representation of deity, the editor said. (The Hebrew word that was always translated as "graven image" is *pesel,* from a verb meaning to cut or carve. A *pesel* is not [yet] an idol that takes the place of the living God.) A graven (engraved or carved-out) image as well as a molten image are visual and tangible representations of something or somebody else. But in Bible times when an image was set up as an object of worship, people didn't believe that the image was a picture or look-alike of a deity, as we are inclined to think. They believed that in the shape of the object resided the supra-natural power of the deity. Having such an image or idol would therefore put people in contact with that power. And if one knew how to use that power to one's advantage or if one had a priest who knew how to manipulate the power, one had favor and fortune at one's disposal (see Judg. 17:18).

***Q** But may not images be permitted in the churches as teaching aids for the unlearned?*

***A** No, we should not try to be wiser than God. He wants his people instructed by the living preaching of his Word—not by idols that cannot even talk.*

—Q & A 98

Illegitimate Worship of God.

I believe that in reading the second commandment we should not think in the first place of the worship of a false god. Rather, God tells his people how they may not worship *him*. He decrees that Israel's worship must differ from the religious practice of all nations. Israel worships an *invisible* God, whose *Word* (first spoken, then written and spoken) is law.

At Sinai (Horeb) the Israelites had not seen, only heard, their God: "You saw no form of any kind the day the Lord spoke to you at Horeb out of the fire. Therefore watch yourselves very carefully, so that you do not become corrupt and make for yourselves an idol, an image of any shape, whether formed like a man or a woman, or like any animal on earth or any bird that flies in the air, or like any creature that moves along the ground or any fish in the water below." (Deut. 4:15-18; the whole section, vv. 15-31, is very appropriate for understanding the meaning of the second commandment, the temptation this forbidden practice presented to Israel, and the lasting consequences of obedience and disobedience to this law.)

The Sin of Jeroboam.

The human yearning to see God and to "have" his power is evident in Israel's history of image carving; image making leads to idolatry. Those who transgress the second commandment will also break the first commandment even if they never intended to do so.

Israel did not mean to choose another god when it constructed golden calves under Aaron (Ex. 32) and Jeroboam (1 Kings 12). In fact, in both events the leaders emphatically stated, "Here are your gods, O Israel, who brought you up out of Egypt" (1 Kings 12:28, cf. Ex. 32:4, 8). Neither did the people think that these calves were a portrait of Jehovah. But they did see the images as pedestals or chariots on which the Power would dwell or ride. And this sin against the second commandment became the downfall of Israel. More than twenty times the books of Kings speak of "the sins Jeroboam had committed and had caused Israel to commit" as the cause of the curse on the nation (from 1 Kings 14:16 to 2 Kings 23:15).

When the followers of the Roman pope colonized the Philippines and Central and South America by the sword and in the name of the cross, they taught the people a wrong worship of the living Lord. Today one may still view the frightening results of their transgression of the second commandment. Millions in these lands are estranged from God and from Christ because they learned to worship the Lord by illegitimate means.

In his covenant relationship with his people God makes himself known by his Word. And in the fullness of time that Word became flesh: Jesus is the perfect image of the Father.

Images That Steal the Devotion.

God himself taught his people by monuments, rites, and symbols to worship him as God. The twelve stones from the Jordan were supposed to tell the story of the crossing of that river (Josh. 4:8-9). The calendar of Israel was loaded with events of commemoration (Lev. 23-25), and the whole liturgy of Israel was filled with symbols that pointed to God and to realities still to be revealed (compare Leviticus with Hebrews).

Yet history witnesses that the patterns and symbols of a religion may outlast their spiritual content. Patterns of worship affect the third and the fourth generations, for better or for worse, and sometimes the adherents of a faith shift the power of their god to the objects by which they worship.

During their wandering through the wilderness, the Israelites once became so impatient that they despised God's great acts of salvation. God punished them with an attack of venomous serpents. Many who were bitten died. But after Moses' intercession, God allowed him to make a bronze serpent and to place it on a pole. "Then when anyone was bitten by a snake and looked at the bronze snake, he lived" (Num. 21:4-9). But centuries later, when the people of Israel had forsaken the true worship of the real God, they worshiped the bronze serpent. Then Hezekiah destroyed the snake (2 Kings 18:4).

Iconoclasts.

Hezekiah was an iconoclast ("one who destroys an image") for the glory of God. His counterparts in the sixteenth century were Protestants who took their hammers and axes into Roman churches and smashed countless images. In their own barren church buildings they made the Bible central: the Reformed-and-Presbyterian tradition would allow little else than the Word and the lectern (pulpit) at the liturgical center. The Lord's table and the baptismal font received honorable but lower places.

The Heidelberg Catechism hails from that iconoclastic era: don't "try to be wiser than God," it says. "He wants his people instructed by the living preaching of his Word—not by idols that cannot even talk." And we see that the use of images in the Roman and Orthodox traditions has been detrimental to the true worship of God. If the pope, the cardinals, and the patriarchs were truly zealous for the honor of God, they would smash many a madonna and icon today. For whenever people transfer the fear and reverence due to God to an image, a holy site, or a holy shrine, these symbols and images do not advance but destroy true religion.

Protestant Golden Calves.

But Roman and Orthodox churches are not alone in their idolatry. Denominations and denominational saints (the founders) also often demand a loyalty that may conflict with the honor and authority of God. By giving such loyalty, Protestant Christians might be bowing to a "graven image." In numerous Protestant denominations the Lord God is reduced to the patron saint of a particular church: the church's history is regarded as salvation history, and people spend their religious energy dancing around this golden calf.

Threat and Promise.

God is intolerant of competition. "I am the Lord; that is my name! I will not give my glory to another or my praise to idols" (Isa. 42:8). "I, the Lord your God, am a jealous God, punishing the children for the sin of the fathers to the third and fourth generation of those who hate me, but showing love to thousands who love me and keep my commandments" (Ex. 20:5-6).

As a rule, children see God through the eyes of their parents. That's why there's nothing more important than giving the right teaching about God to the next generation. Most of us will admit that our concept of God has much to do with the way God was experienced by our parents. A sickly or false idea of God becomes a scourge of generations. But a "pattern of sound teaching, with faith and love in Christ Jesus" (2 Tim. 1:13), can endure among one's children's children.

That we learn our faith from our parents may not be used as an excuse, however, for the spiritual poverty of one's own generation. When a generation justified its failures by saying, "The fathers have eaten sour grapes, and the children's teeth are set on edge," the prophets answered, "Everyone will die for his own sin," and "the soul who sins is the one who will die" (Jer. 31:29-30, Ezek. 18:2-4). Thereby the prophets did not deny the general validity of the law, but they did deny a sort of fatalism, and they affirmed personal responsibility.

Therefore it remains every generation's duty to rediscover God and Christ by the Word and the Spirit and not to freewheel on the impetus of former generations.

Today it is widely said and believed that as long as we all believe in the same God, it is not important in what church we worship him. That's a serious error. For the way in which we worship God is mostly determined by the church to which we belong. Here his will is made concrete, and his worship gets shape. This is the area governed by the second commandment.

Spirit and Truth.

When we want to say what the second commandment's positive teaching is, we usually quote John 4:24: "God is spirit, and his worshipers must worship in spirit and in truth." Most people understand this text to say that God is not material but "spirit" and that therefore our worship should correspond to his nature: worship must not consist of mere rituals or rely on crude objects. It must be inward, spiritual, sincere, and according to God's revealed truth.

Although this understanding of John 4:24 catches much of the message, it misses the newness that this text adds to Old Testament statements to the same effect. Throughout the Bible, God warns his people that they should not try to satisfy him with the outward display of rituals and sacrifices. He says through his prophets that he hates the empty sounds of worship and that he does not need all those sacrifices because he owns every beast and all the cattle anyway. He calls, rather, for a contrite heart and a humble spirit. (In his commentary on John 4:24, John Calvin mentions Psalm 50; Isaiah 1, 58, and 66; Micah 6; and Amos 5 as "the most remarkable passages.")

In John 4 Jesus answers the question of the Samaritan woman at the well about the place of worship: Is it right to worship on Mount Gerizim, as the Samaritans want it, or should one worship in Jerusalem, as the Jews say? Jesus knew that the Jews were right (v. 22), but he had something much more radical to say to the woman and to us.

Worship in the New Age.

I am the Messiah, said Jesus to the woman at the well (v. 26). A new time "is coming and has now come," he said (v. 23), when the creation no longer has particular holy places. The question is now no longer *where* but *how* we shall worship God. And God says that "his worshipers must worship in spirit and in truth." That means more than the sincerity and inwardness that were always required. "Spirit" and "truth" now mean this: worship in and by the Spirit of Jesus, who is the truth. Authentic worship in the new dispensation is worship "in Christ." Worship that ignores or denies Christ is not acceptable to the Father. "Through Jesus, therefore, let us continuously offer to God a sacrifice of praise—the fruit of lips that confess his name" (Heb. 13:15).

God Is Still Strict.

The book of Leviticus is almost entirely devoted to the question of how a sinful but elect people can worship a holy, covenant God. It sets the liturgical standards for the old, or Sinai, covenant. God's demands for purity, the divine regulations of minute details of acceptable worship, and God's harsh punishment of those who broke the rules (the death of Nadab and Abihu, Lev. 10) continue to amaze us. Is our God that picky?

The book of Hebrews may be regarded as a New-Covenant commentary on the book of Leviticus. It teaches how a sinful people should worship a holy God. Basically it offers one requirement: faith in the last Word for the last days. This gospel of the last days is Jesus, mediator of a better covenant, priest whose sacrificial death is our once-and-forever covering, forerunner who has entered the heavenly sanctuary for us.

Worship in the new covenant is even more awesome than the terrifying meeting with God at Horeb (Heb. 12:18-24), and we have no confidence outside of Jesus. God's requirements for true worship have not essentially changed since the Old Covenant; our God is no less meticulous.

Fulfilling the Commandment.

Hebrews is also the only New Testament book that (to the delight of preachers) admonishes us to attend church services (10:25). We offer God true worship in the assembly of his people. Here the second commandment is fulfilled. And those who fail to do it pay the price to the third and fourth generation.

People have said too often that one can be a Christian without participating in the worship of God's people. At best such neglect might make a disobedient Christian.

Family instruction (Deut. 6:4-8, Eph. 6:4) and personal prayer (Matt. 6:6) are indispensable parts of our religion. But the people of God have no family altars, as the Buddhists do and the Mesopotamians did (the household gods of Gen. 31:34). Instead, the people of the Lord follow the trumpet call to the assembly (Old Testament), or they begin to worship together on Sunday morning. (The spontaneous institution of Sunday as the New Testament day of assembly has puzzled historians until today.)

In keeping with the nature of the new covenant, God has not given us detailed rules on liturgy. But taking care about proper worship is one of our most important assignments. For it is in the assembly that we learn *how* to worship Almighty God; that will have consequences for the third and fourth generations.

Lord's Days 36 and 37

OUR USE OF HIS NAME

***Q** What is God's will for us in the third commandment?*

***A** That we neither blaspheme nor misuse the name of God by cursing, perjury, or unnecessary oaths, nor share in such horrible sins by being silent bystanders. In a word, it requires that we use the holy name of God only with reverence and awe, so that we may properly confess him, pray to him, and praise him in everything we do and say.*

—Q & A 99

Translation.

The usual translation of the third commandment reads, "You shall not take the name of the Lord your God in vain" (RSV). But newer translations have "You shall not misuse the name of the Lord your God" (NIV). Or, as in Today's English Version, "Do not use my name for evil purposes, for I, the Lord your God, will punish anyone who misuses my name."

Which Name?

The name that may not be misused is translated as LORD (capital letters) in all the Bible versions quoted above. This is the mysterious name that God revealed to Moses, a name that Jewish scribes and rabbis refused to pronounce. We know this name as *Jehovah.* Thirty to forty years ago the Christian Reformed Church promoted the use of the American Standard Version (1901), which translates the name as *Jehovah* instead of LORD. The Jerusalem Bible, a Roman Catholic translation completed in 1966, uses the name *Yahweh.*

The Jehovah's Witnesses Association claims special knowledge of the secret name. The Jehovah's Witnesses' main distinctive teaching is that Jehovah is God and that Jesus is *a* god but not Jehovah.

In Hebrew the secret name has two forms: *JaH*—a form well known to us who sing hallelu-JaH ("praise JaH")—and a longer form spelled with four consonants—*JHVH.* When Jewish scribes and rabbis added vowels to the script of the Jewish Bible (which originally had none), they shied away from pronouncing the great name. They left the name JHVH in the Bible, of course, but they gave it the vowels of another name for God, *EdOnAj*—the name our Bibles translate as (my) *Lord,* with one capital letter. So they spelled the great name *JeHoVaH,* thereby telling the synagogue readers that they should say "EdOnAj" whenever they met the name. Thus the spelling *Jehovah* is actually a mixture of two names for God. That's why the Jerusalem Bible tries to correct the name to *Yahweh.* But we aren't quite sure how to say the name—in Hebrew or in English.

What's in the Name?

When God makes his name known to Moses and to the people, Moses and the people can "call" him. I heard the other day one little boy calling the name of his big brother, who was playing basketball with many other tall boys—and then the tall boy came to the little boy who had called his name. So those who know his name can call on the LORD, and he comes to their side. He becomes *present* to those who call on his name. Blessed are they who know his name.

Israel is the bearer of the great name. When the priests lift up their hands in blessing ("The LORD bless you and keep you . . . be gracious to you . . . give you peace."), the people are sure of God's favorable presence: "So [the sons of Aaron] will put my name on the Israelites, and I will bless them," says the LORD (Num. 6:27).

When the time had fully come, God sent the Son, who revealed the Father: "I have manifested thy name to the men whom thou gavest me out of the world," says Jesus (John 17:6, RSV), or, "I have revealed you to those whom you gave me out of the world" (NIV). The "name of God" *is* God as he has revealed himself. And Jesus prays, "Holy Father, protect them by the power of your name" (John 17:11). (Incidentally, this particular and great name, *holy Father*, occurs only here in the Bible. It is the name used by Jesus in addressing his Father. Yet this title is used constantly by Roman Catholic Christians when they address their earthly "papa," or pope. I cannot imagine that God is pleased by this name calling.)

Jesus Is Jehovah.

Only Israel knew the glorious name in Old Testament times. But the prophets said that the future would bring a vast difference: prior to the great and terrible day of the LORD, the Spirit of God would be poured out on all flesh, and in this new situation "everyone who calls on the name of the LORD [JeHoVaH] will be saved" (Joel 2:32). Peter (Acts 2:21) and Paul (Rom. 10:13) announce that this time has arrived: everyone who calls on the name of the Lord will be saved. But by the name *Lord*, they mean Jesus. Yet the Bible knows no contrast between the Old Testament JeHoVaH and the New Testament Jesus. The whole church is baptized in only one name (but of three persons, Matt. 28:19). In the New Testament the powerful name of Jesus heals the lame (Acts 4:10); everybody should know that "salvation is found in no one else, for there is no other name under heaven given to men by which we must be saved" (v. 12).

The prophets said that someday human rebellion will cease. The "ends of the earth" will flee to the true God. For JeHoVaH himself has made an oath: "Before me every knee will bow; by me every tongue will swear" (Isa. 45:22-23). Yes, says Paul in Philippians 2:10-11 (also Rom. 14:11), "At the name of Jesus every knee" will bow and every tongue will confess "that Jesus Christ is Lord."

The name of Jesus and the name of JHVH are now interchangeable. Jesus has revealed the God of Israel, whose name is holy. Jesus is still to be distinguished from his Father, but never to be separated from him, for he is God. The true bearers of the name of Jehovah-LORD are those who bow the knee before Jesus. Only they who have learned who Jesus is can properly confess (which is the opposite of "misuse") the name that is above every name.

Abuse of the Name.

What does God mean when he tells us that we may not "misuse" his name or "take his name in vain" or, literally, "lift up the name unto a vain thing"?

First (and obviously), God does not want us to use his name without reverence and without thought. Meaningless ritual is an insult to God. "Sitting through a church service" is much less innocent than most of us are inclined to think. "Stop bringing meaningless offerings!" says Isaiah (1:13). The word for "meaningless" here is the same as "vain thing" in the third commandment. Whoever calls on the name of the Lord must do so with reverence and fear. Do not call on the Lord or lift up hands (i.e., pray) when they are "full of blood," Isaiah says (1:15), and Paul says the same thing to the church of the New Covenant: "I want men everywhere to lift up holy hands in prayer, without anger or disputing" (1 Tim. 2:8).

A meeting with God must be a meeting in one spirit, his Spirit. So, says the preacher, "Guard your steps when you go to the house of God. Go near to listen rather than to offer the sacrifice of fools, who do not know that they do wrong" (Eccl. 5:1).

Second, we abuse God's name when we intend to do something with it that goes against his will—such as drawing the holy name into magic and enchantment. Magic is the art of controlling supernatural forces. In magic and enchantment, knowledge of the name plays a big role. Israel thought it could make God fight its battles by bringing the ark into the army's camp, but God was not present (1 Sam. 4). And the seven sons of Sceva, who thought that they could master evil spirits simply by "using" the name of Jesus, lost the battle—and their clothes (Acts 19:13-16). *We* may be used by *God*, but nobody should try to use the Lord for his or her own purposes.

Nations, heads of state, political leaders, and speechmakers are always tempted on memorial days to abuse the name of the Lord for national and party interests. People love it, but God hates it, and he "will not hold anyone guiltless who misuses his name" in the interest of a political career.

***Q** Is blasphemy of God's name by swearing and cursing really such serious sin that God is angry also with those who do not do all they can to help prevent it and to forbid it?*

***A** Yes, indeed. No sin is greater, no sin makes God more angry than blaspheming his name. That is why he commanded the death penalty for it.*

—Q & A 100

Solemn Abuse.

Preachers can be glib talkers about God. They can keep going on any text or Bible topic for an hour. They use the name a thousand times. Hymn sings may "raise the roof" but still not magnify the name. Worldly people who do not care about God or Christ will hire a clergyman or woman to recite some God-talk at their weddings and funerals. Theologians argue about God as if he himself were not present. And some elders and evangelists can find the right phrase at the right time so that they can appear to be pious. A wise man warned, "Do not be quick with your mouth, do not be hasty in your heart to utter anything before God. God is in heaven and you are on earth, so let your words be few" (Eccl. 5:2).

Misunderstanding.

This question and answer has produced some mistaken notions among us. We have understood *cursing* as the thoughtless or malicious profanity of the average citizen. We thought the confession that "no sin is greater" and that "he commanded the death penalty" were to apply to people who used such expletives. As a result, Christians influenced by the Heidelberg Catechism have organized campaigns and established organizations to oppose the abuse of God's name in society. (In 1960 such an attempt was made in Canada. I do not know of a similar effort in the United States, but thirty years ago I heard a sermon in Grand Rapids, Michigan, in which the uses of *gosh* and *gee* were condemned with all the vehemence of Answer 100.)

Answer 100's sole Scripture reference regarding the death penalty is to Leviticus 24:10-17, which is about the man who "blasphemed the name" and was put to death by stoning. He cursed the Name (JHVH) of the covenant God—which involves more than the mere use of profane speech. The catechism also gives the impression that cursing is the only sin for which God required the death penalty. God actually demanded the same punishment for particular sins against the first commandment (Deut. 13:5), the fourth (Ex. 35:2), the fifth (Deut. 22:21), the sixth (Lev. 24:17), and the seventh (Deut. 22:22).

Ignorant and Profane.

To people in contemporary society the names of God and of Jesus Christ are as light as breath. People use the name when they talk about the ball game, when they express surprise, pain, anger, indignation—whatever, whenever. It is a sinful outrage.

This kind of "cussing" and swearing arises mostly from ignorance. If people knew him whose name they abuse, they would stop swearing and start praying. Their cussing offends us, but it also accuses us. We bear the name of him who alone has the power to curse and to bless. And they still don't know him. Can we keep silent any longer?

Old but Relevant Question.

This separate treatment of the question whether a Christian may ever swear an oath comes from the Reformed tradition's historical controversy with the Anabaptists (Mennonites). They had read Jesus' saying that our "Yes" should be yes (Matt. 5:33-39) and the emphatic repetition of these words by James (5:12). Therefore they refused to swear oaths, even when the government required it.

Though Menno Simons, the founder of the Mennonites, died in Friesland, he arose in North America and his anti-oath and antiwar teachings are popular today. Hence Lord's Day 37 offers a relevant supplement to our thinking on the third commandment.

***Q** But may we swear an oath in God's name if we do it reverently?*

***A** Yes, when the government demands it, or when necessity requires it, in order to maintain and promote truth and trustworthiness for God's glory and our neighbor's good. Such oaths are approved in God's Word and were rightly used by Old and New Testament believers.*

—Q & A 101

***Q** May we swear by saints or other creatures?*

***A** No. A legitimate oath means calling upon God as the one who knows my heart to witness to my truthfulness and to punish me if I swear falsely. No creature is worthy of such honor.*

—Q & A 102

The basic error of the Anabaptists is their idea that once we belong to Christ, we are cut loose from the created, or natural, world. Anabaptists oppose not only Christians' participation in military and government services but also the swearing of oaths in courts of law. They have denied that childbirth is a vehicle of God's grace and—every now and then—have rebelled against the natural, or created, marriage institute. Calvinists, who wrongly opposed certain teachings of the Anabaptists about the relationship of the church of Christ to worldly society, rightly saw that the redemptive Word of the Son does not separate us from the world of God the Father.

A Confession in Court.

Sin has affected everything and everybody in the present world. It has poisoned the way human beings communicate. Our verbal statements are no longer reliable. When someone says something, we may have to ask if he knows what he is saying, if she realizes the implications, if he says what he means, or if she means what she says. Most communication through words and other symbols that hit our senses every day we do not, cannot, must not take seriously. Constantly we remind ourselves that the words, the pictures, and the prints are political or part of an advertising campaign or propaganda and that all talk is slanted toward specific goals. This makes living dangerous and difficult. Trust, the beautiful basis of human society, is ruined by distrust—but this is a distrust without which we would be victims of deceit at nearly every moment.

In the midst of all this confusion the oath is a light of God's grace. For what happens when we swear an oath? We make a confession, first, of our own unreliability: I cannot trust you, and you doubt my truthfulness. Second, we place ourselves before the face of Truth. Here and now we are in God's presence. The God who cannot lie will banish untruth or punish perjury. So help me God!

When trust, as the foundation of human life, is destroyed, our only hope for a solid foothold is God and his Word: "Let God be true and every man a liar" (Rom. 3:4).

Thus, with the oath, courts of law and government agencies give our words worth and dignity. In these oaths Christians see underlined what they believe every day: the continued existence of human society depends on the faithfulness of God.

Swearing: Right and Wrong.

God did not forbid his people to swear an oath. He commanded them to "swear by his name" (Deut. 6:13, 10:20, RSV). The Bible records the oaths of Abraham (Gen. 21:24), Jacob (Gen. 31:53), Joshua (Josh. 9:15), David (1 Sam. 24:22, 2 Sam. 3:35), and Paul (Rom. 1:9, 9:1, 2 Cor. 1:23). The high priest of Israel placed Jesus under oath, and Jesus testified (Matt. 26:63-64). Even God swore an oath (Gen. 22:16), which is totally unnecessary, because God is utterly reliable; but God did it, says the writer of Hebrews, "so that, by two unchangeable things [his word and his oath] in which it is impossible for God to lie, we . . . may be greatly encouraged" (6:18).

When oaths promote God's glory and our neighbor's good or when the government requires them, Christians may use them, says the catechism. But an oath is abused in the service of self. We must be used by God, but we may never use God (by taking his name in vain).

Neither may we swear by the saints, by the bank, by the beard of the prophet, by "all that is sacred," by the memory of mother, or by the virtue of Mary. All of this is idle talk and improper for Christians.

Redeemed Communication.

Although the oath is a light of grace in a dark world, it is, nevertheless, a temporary help, an emergency bridge from our present reality to the everlasting God. For Christians, truth speaking is not dependent on oath swearing. The children of God live in the presence of God at all times and at all places. Their thinking is obedient to the Word, and their homes are the territory of the Lord Jesus. Their lives have been redeemed from destruction. Their tongues have been tamed by the Holy Spirit. When they say "Yes," it simply means yes. And "No" means no. Anyone who has a need to constantly reinforce speech with strong and emphatic words shows that, in general, his or her tongue is still ruled by the devil.

Lord's Day 38

CELEBRATING SABBATH

***Q** What is God's will for you in the fourth commandment?*

***A** First, that the gospel ministry and education for it be maintained, and that, especially on the festive day of rest, I regularly attend the assembly of God's people to learn what God's Word teaches, to participate in the sacraments, to pray to God publicly, and to bring Christian offerings for the poor. Second, that every day of my life I rest from my evil ways, let the Lord work in me through his Spirit, and so begin already in this life the eternal Sabbath.*

—Q & A 103

No Reformed Consensus.

In the fourth commandment God said, "Remember the Sabbath day by keeping it holy" (Ex. 20:8). Christians in general and Calvinists in particular disagree, though, on the meaning of the fourth commandment for New Testament times.

The "Heidelberger" is remarkably sober: people usually discuss what God *forbids* in the fourth commandment, but our catechism asks what God *requires*. The catechism does not even mention the Sabbath day by name; that Sunday is our day of worship is assumed but not mentioned. In the Dutch translation of the catechism Peter Dathenus slipped in the words "*on the Sabbath, that is* the day of rest, and the English translation that we used until 1975 retained these words. The 1963 translation used by the Reformed Church in America reads "especially on the Lord's Day" for "especially on the festive day of rest." But the original mentions no specific day, no specific prohibitions. It requires only that we worship God, promote such worship, and have done with evil and enjoy the spiritual Sabbath.

In sharp contrast to the Heidelberger's restraint is the Shorter Westminster Catechism's *New Testament law*. Both the Westminster Confession and the two Westminster catechisms, which come from the Presbyterian tradition, state that God has set apart one day out of every seven for rest and worship and that this day was the seventh of the week in the Old Covenant and the first in the New. The Shorter Westminster Catechism's questions and answers about the Sabbath follow:

Q. 58 What is required in the fourth commandment? The fourth commandment requireth the keeping holy to God such set times as he hath appointed in his Word; expressly one whole day in seven, to be a holy Sabbath to himself.

Q. 59 Which day of the seven hath God appointed to be the weekly Sabbath? From the beginning of the world to the resurrection of Christ, God appointed the seventh day of the week to be the weekly Sabbath; and the first day of the week ever since, to continue to the end of the world, which is the Christian Sabbath.

Q. 60 How is the Sabbath to be sanctified? The Sabbath is to be sanctified by a holy resting all that day, even from such worldly employments and recreations as are lawful on other days; and spending the whole time in the public and private exercises of God's worship, except so much as is to be taken up in the works of necessity and mercy.

Q. 61 What is forbidden in the fourth commandment? The fourth commandment forbiddeth the omission or careless performance of the duties required, and the profaning the day by idleness, or doing that which is in itself sinful, or by unnecessary thoughts, words, or works, about our worldly employments or recreations.

Q. 62 What are the reasons annexed to the fourth commandment? The reasons annexed to the fourth commandment are God's allowing us six days of the week for our own employments, his challenging a special propriety in the seventh, his own example, and his blessing the Sabbath day.

Although many of us may never have seen a copy of the Shorter Westminster Catechism, the above teaching is familiar to most Reformed Calvinists because they, as well as their Presbyterian kin, were reared according to its understanding of God's will for "Sabbath observance." But the confessions of the Reformed churches do not officially teach that God has ordained Sunday as the Christian Sabbath. And we should not lay that doctrine upon the church, because the New Testament does not teach it either. Besides, the practice of godliness that has surrounded the observance of the Christian Sabbath (both in the British and Scottish Presbyterian tradition and in the continental Reformed branch of Calvinism) shows numerous lapses into legalism and Old-Covenant slavery. Westminster's prescriptions and prohibitions did help make the life-style of previous generations well regimented, but they did not promote growth to maturity in Christ.

Reformed Synods.

On May 17, 1619, during the Synod of Dort, the delegates from Zeeland raised a question about Sabbath keeping. The matter was referred to the theological professors. They had a conference with the Zeeland delegates in the morning and in the afternoon presented a statement with which the synod agreed. The statement was not supposed to be a doctrinal pronouncement, but it was never replaced. The Christian Reformed synods of 1881 and 1926 reiterated this statement from Dort as their understanding of our confession. The statement claims that the fourth commandment contains ceremonial elements—the Levitical Sabbath laws—which are no longer valid since Christ died and rose but that the moral teaching—that one out of seven days should be devoted to worship—is valid for all time.

This distinction between ceremonial (and civil) and moral laws goes back to Thomas Aquinas. It is often helpful. But we must remember that theologians, not the Bible, have thus divided the Old Testament laws. Ursinus, one of the authors of the Heidelberg Catechism, also believed that the fourth commandment had a ceremonial and a moral element. But John Calvin did not believe that this theological trick should be used to move the Sabbath to the first day of the week (*Institutes,* II, viii, 34).

Creation Ordinance?

Some of us think that God ordained a seventh day of rest as a pattern for humanity because of the Bible's explicit reference to creation: "God blessed the seventh day and made it holy, because on it he rested" (Gen. 2:3, Ex.

20:11). Many others would say that the creation "week" is not of the same order as our weeks: it wasn't simply the first week of calendar time.

Moreover, there's much evidence that seems to argue that a seventh-day Sabbath is not a creation ordinance: (1) We see no sign of a "Sabbath" outside of Israel. (2) God's creation pattern is only one among many reasons the Old Testament gives for enforcing Sabbath rest; other reasons are social (Ex. 23:12), cultic (Lev. 19:30), and for the remembrance of redemption (Deut. 5:15). (3) A strong biblical tradition indicates that the Sabbath laws were not instituted until the Sinai covenant (Deut. 5:15, Neh. 9:6-14, Ezek. 20:10-12). (4) The church does not observe the seventh day as a day of rest. This is the most difficult objection to the idea that the order of creation demands a seventh-day Sabbath. The early Christians did not merely replace the Old Testament Sabbath with Sunday—they did not think of making Sunday a day of rest until long after the apostles had died, and nobody mentioned that Sunday might replace the Jewish Sabbath until the time of Chrysostom, at the end of the fourth century. Christians who believe that the Bible reveals a creation order for a day of rest, instituted at creation and re-enforced at Sinai, have a hard time opposing "Seventh-Day" Christians. If the Sabbath law is forever, it is a stronger argument for seventh-day than first-day observance.

Unimportant to Paul.

Paul's letters contain only three sentences that may have a bearing on the Sabbath issue: Rom. 14:5 ("One man considers one day more sacred than another . . ."), Gal. 4:10 ("You are observing special days" as a sign of backsliding), and Col. 2:16 ("Do not let anyone judge you . . . with regard to . . . a Sabbath day"). If we believe that a weekly day of rest is ordained by God for all time, we can argue that Paul wasn't admonishing the early church about observing the Sabbath but only about certain ceremonial feast days. (See John Murray's commentary on Romans.) But this does not sound very convincing. It is hard to believe that Paul deemed one day more sacred than the others; it is more consistent to assume that he did not wish to recognize a holy day any more than he recognized holy places or holy foods.

One of the Ten Commandments.

The argument that carries special weight within the Presbyterian and Reformed traditions is that all of the Ten Commandments are lasting as the "moral" law of God and that not one of them can be annulled. But this argument appeals more to our familiarity with the Ten than to our rules of biblical interpretation. The New Testament does not quote the fourth commandment with approval. As a matter of fact, in the New Covenant, the first four commandments must be reinterpreted by God's revelation in Christ.

Then What?

I have spent much time over the years studying the relevant Bible texts and the many books written on the Sunday-Sabbath issue. It was for me no joy to discover that the Sabbath theology with which I had grown up was wrong—the most striking feature of the Christian life in the church of my youth was the way we observed the Lord's day. Today I am not sure that our conscientious care pleased the Lord. I *am* sure he did not require it.

I am more thankful today than ever that the Heidelberg Catechism answers the question on the fourth commandment so wisely and carefully. Frequently we find that one of these "Lord's Days," as formulated in the

1560s, needs updating. But in Lord's Day 38 the Heidelberg Catechism is ahead of most of us.

The catechism says that keeping Sabbath in the New-Covenant dispensation means that we support gospel ministry, identify with God's people in their assemblies, have done with evil, and begin the Sabbath life. This is a bold statement that goes to the heart of the matter, as I should now explain.

The Meaning of Sabbath.

God did not "rest" on the seventh day because he was tired. He desisted from work and entered into the enjoyment of what he had made. His rest means enjoying creation. When we share in that rest, we enter into the enjoyment of God and his creation. The Sabbath—that's paradise. And to rest means to live in paradise, with the Creator in his creation.

When a person works from May to August constructing a swimming pool in his backyard, "Sabbath" arrives on the day he and his friends swim in the pool. The work is finished, and, behold, it is very good. And when God's work was finished, he rested.

However, when a flaming sword barred the way to the garden and when sin stood between God and his people, there was no more "rest." Adam sweated between thorns and thistles as if he were a slave of the land. Eve moaned in pain because from then on life was produced only amid tears. And one boy was killed and the other was his killer.

The only hope for humanity at this point was God's promise that someday the poison would be removed and the Sabbath reinstated.

The Seventh Is the Sabbath.

When sin had alienated people from God and when the curse on the earth was tending to make us slaves rather than stewards, God found for himself a people—with whom he made a covenant. He taught them to count their days. "There are seven," God said, "and the seventh is holy and blessed. For six days you may, you must, you have to do your work. But then you must stop: drop everything, and I will teach you the meaning of your days."

God was strict and insistent that the Sabbath be kept holy and inviolate: it's a holy day of rest, and "whoever does any work on it must be put to death" (Ex. 35:2). The Sabbath was the Hebrews' sign of health and wholeness, and Israel proved that it wanted to keep covenant with the Lord by observing the seventh day. Whoever broke the Sabbath broke the covenant. God's wisdom surrounded Sabbath observance with threats and penalties, just as one surrounds a precious possession with a dragon-toothed fence.

You must rest, he told them. Those who work for you must rest; your animals must rest. In the seventh year the land must rest, and those who live on the land, Israelites and sojourners, people and animals, may eat whatever the land yields (Lev. 25:1-7).

God taught the people to count their days in order to give them a heart of wisdom (Ps. 90:12): Just rest! Don't be greedy, don't be worried; let me feed you, says the Lord. I am the Lord your God. And after seven times seven years, I want all your chains broken, and I want you to "proclaim liberty throughout the land" (Lev. 25:10). Consecrate the whole year as the Year of Jubilee. Then I will teach you the meaning of life: the goal of all living is in the Sabbath and the shalom (peace) that I give.

That was the lesson God wanted to drill into his people. But they disobeyed and kept carrying their loads through the gates of Jerusalem on the

Sabbath day. Therefore these gates were destroyed by God's fires (Jer. 17:21-27).

Jesus and the Sabbath.

Jesus was "born under law, to redeem those under law" (Gal. 4:4-5). Therefore he kept the laws on the Sabbath day, he taught their true meaning, and he fulfilled the Sabbath.

"On the Sabbath day he went into the synagogue, as was his custom" (Luke 4:16). Thus Jesus observed the Sabbath.

In numerous conflicts with the Jewish religious leaders, Jesus taught, first, that the Sabbath laws can never be quoted against the true well-being of human beings: "The Sabbath was made for man, not man for the Sabbath" (Mark 2:27). Therefore the Sabbath is a day *par excellence* to set free "a daughter of Abraham" who was "bent over and could not straighten up at all" for eighteen years (Luke 13:10-16) and to proclaim liberty to a man in Bethesda who had been a paralytic for thirty-eight years (John 5:1-10).

Second, Jesus taught that the Sabbath laws fall to his Messianic claims: if the laws of the Sabbath may not be quoted against the well-being of man, far less may they be used against the Son of Man, for "the Son of Man is Lord even of the Sabbath" (Mark 2:28; cf. Matt. 12:8, Luke 6:5). With this statement Jesus places himself on the side of the Lawgiver.

The Shalom of the Sabbath.

In the gospel of John, Jesus makes even stronger claims: "My Father is always at his work to this very day, and I, too, am working" (5:17). By saying this, he not only defies the notion of rest held by his opponents but also says that he and the Father are at work here (in the miracle of the healing of the paralytic). The work of the Father and the Son aims at the healing of humanity. And the Sabbath is only a shadow of the day of healing.

All the miracles of Jesus proclaim that the King, the Anointed, the Ambassador of God, has come to heal what was broken and make right what was wrong. Miracles are signs of the kingdom. That is why they fit the Sabbath so well: the Sabbath itself was supposed to be a sign of Paradise and of the shalom of God.

Jesus himself stated his mission to fulfill the Sabbath in his first message, in the synagogue of Nazareth: "The Spirit of the Lord is on me, because he has anointed me . . . to proclaim the year of the Lord's favor" (Luke 4:18-19; cf. Isa. 61:1-2, Lev. 25:8-55). It is never fully spelled out in the New Testament, but it is very clear to those who believe that Jesus is the Christ: he has inaugurated the Year of Jubilee, in which every day is holy, all things are possible, and there is no sorrow that heaven cannot heal.

Jesus has fulfilled the Sabbath. "It is finished" (John 19:30) marks the end of an era, and "the Lord has risen" (Luke 24:34) opens the gate to a new age.

From Sabbath to Sunday.

No, it is never fully spelled out in the Bible. But for those who believe that the death and resurrection of Jesus Christ decisively altered the course of the universe, it was the most natural thing to assemble for worship on the first day of the week. That was not prescribed by the law. But it was and is the believers' response to the gospel.

Sunday Is the Lord's Day.

In the New Testament we see the first indications of our tradition of assembling on the first day of the week (Acts 20:7, 1 Cor. 16:2, Rev. 1:10). It is very well possible that Jewish Christians who lived among their kin continued for a while to observe the Old Testament Sabbath. But within a generation they were outwardly isolated from their fellow Jews (by persecution) and inwardly estranged because for them the great Jewish institutions of Temple and Sabbath had lost meaning.

Christians gathered on the first day of the week, the day after the Sabbath. They did not call the Lord's day a day of rest, and they did not think of this day as their Sabbath. They came together because on the first day after the Sabbath the Lord had risen (Matt. 28:1, Mark 16:1, Luke 24:1, John 20:1). In that resurrection all of us were corporately born to new hope and new life (1 Pet. 1:3): Sunday is our birthday. It was on the day of the resurrection and in the light of the resurrection that the disciples learned the meaning of the cross from the Scriptures (Luke 24:25-27), and it was on that day that they ate with Jesus and recognized him (vv. 30-31). Jesus' second appearance to his disciples (this time with Thomas) took place again on a Sunday (John 20:26). And on a Sunday, or "Lord's day," John saw the worship of earth and heaven (Rev. 1:10).

The Need for Assembly.

Christ gathers and preserves his church as a community. He gathers, and we must congregate, or assemble. Since the first Sunday after Easter the assembling of the followers of Jesus has been not only an accepted pattern but a life condition (John 20:19, 26; Acts 1:15, 2:1, 2:44-46, etc.). The phrase used to describe the gathering of the church at Troas (Acts 20:7, "On the first day of the week we came together to break bread") became the standard expression for the coming together of the congregation not only in the New Testament (1 Cor. 11:20, 14:23) but also throughout the literature of the church fathers.

The survival of the church does not depend on a day (one in seven) or a place (the building). But the church cannot exist without assembly. Sometimes the church's enemies understand this better than its members do. Anti-Christian governments have never bothered much with Christians' "private" religious devotions, but they prohibited assemblies. Every Bible book mentions or implies the value of the assembly. Hebrews emphasizes faithful attendance at assemblies (10:25) as well as daily exhortation of each other (3:13), with a concern about the danger of backsliding as well as the certainty of the approaching Day. And in Matthew, where the church (*ekklesia*) is first mentioned, the secret power of its assembly is stated: where you come together, "there am I" (18:20).

No child of God lives apart from the people of God. No member of Christ lives apart from the body of Christ. No one who is indwelt by God's Spirit lives apart from God's temple (1 Cor. 3:16). The meeting, the mutual exhortation, and the communion table are essentials of Christian faith and practice. To forsake the assemblies is to forsake Christ. For it is in our assemblies that the living Christ himself makes us share in what he has accomplished, while, as the better Joshua, he leads us to the promised rest (Heb. 4:8-11).

From Sunday to Sabbath.

As New Testament Christians, we hear God say in the fourth commandment that we must promote and maintain the gospel ministry and be wholeheartedly engaged in the work of Christ's church. For the hope of the world is the Christ of the church. Through the gospel the eternal Sabbath and ultimate peace come to the world.

Our Sunday is not a modern-day Sabbath, and it is not yet the eternal Sabbath. We live between the times. We are freed by the gospel from the death penalty of the law. We have begun (and must enter) the eternal Sabbath.

We value the day of rest called Sunday. We cannot say that God prescribed one particular day. But God's wisdom given in the Old Testament law (the rhythm of one in seven) is a paradigm for today. We fight the tyranny of materialism, of work, of the dollar, of any other god; we strive to have our legislators make one day free for everyone. Yet the church has no right to teach that on Sunday God forbids what he allows on other days.

On Sundays we come close to the eternal Sabbath. On that day, in our assemblies and in works of mercy and mutual exhortation, we share "in the Holy Spirit," and we taste "the goodness of the word of God and the powers of the coming age" (Heb. 6:4-5). And we learn ever better, says the catechism, to "rest from [our] evil ways" on "every day" of our lives.

Sunday observance belongs to the realm of Christian freedom and discipleship. It requires discipline. A covenant community must adhere to its priorities with the devotion of love, which may be more strict than the demands of the law. For the young and immature, Sunday observance and worship attendance may be a matter of mere obedience. We apply temporary pressure so that no one will fail to enter the Sabbath rest (Heb. 4:11).

Lord's Day 39

AUTHORITY AND OBEDIENCE

Q ***What is God's will for you in the fifth commandment?***

A ***That I honor, love, and be loyal to my father and mother and all those in authority over me; that I obey and submit to them, as is proper, when they correct and punish me; and also that I be patient with their failings—for through them God chooses to rule us.***

—Q & A 104

The Place of the Fifth.

The Ten Commandments are divided into two tablets: the first four regulate our relationship to God (the vertical relationship), and the sixth through the tenth teach how we should love our neighbors (the horizontal relationships). The fifth, however, is clearly in between. We must treat parents and governors with respect, it says, because "through them God chooses to rule us." They are not entitled to the honor that we owe to God alone, yet they rule over us with an authority entrusted to them by God, and we honor them with a religious respect.

In the fifth commandment, the Ten Commandments make a transition from setting forth our obligations to the One above us to spelling out our duties to those who are next to us.

We can compare the Ten Commandments to a ten-story building (as we have done here before): the sixth through the tenth floors rest on the fifth. All the interpersonal relationships regulated in the sixth through the tenth commandments rest on God's rule about obedience and authority. When we disregard divine rules about authority and obedience, human society cannot exist. Obedience and authority form the beams and rafters of a solid society.

God teaches and the church preaches that the relationship between neighbor and neighbor cannot be right unless authority is properly used and obedience is rendered to those who have authority.

The Command in the Bible.

"Honor your father and your mother" (Ex. 20:12, Deut. 5:16) is again stated in Leviticus 19:3, but the parental order is reversed: "Each of you must respect his mother and father." The Jewish rabbis used to teach that God had the mother mentioned first in Leviticus and the father first in the other passages so that we might give equal honor to fathers and mothers.

The punishment for not honoring but cursing one's father or mother is as severe as the penalty for blasphemy: "If anyone curses his father or mother, he must be put to death" (Lev. 20:9, Ex. 20:12). In the book of Proverbs the father teaches wisdom, but sometimes so does the mother: "The sayings of king Lemuel—an oracle his mother taught him" (31:1). Proverbs also warns, "If a man curses his father or mother, his lamp will be snuffed out in pitch darkness" (20:20).

Jesus quotes the fifth commandment (Matt. 15:4-6, Mark 7:9-13) and disapproves of children who claim that their goods are *korban,* devoted to God, so that they cannot help their aged parents. Jesus "was obedient" to his parents as a boy (Luke 2:51). From the accounts in the gospels it appears that Jesus lived most of his life in Nazareth as the eldest son of a widowed mother. Evidently he took care of her. And even while he was suffering the pain of the crucifixion, he entrusted his mother to the care of his friend (John 19:26-27).

In quoting the fifth commandment (Eph. 6:1-4, Col. 3:20-21), Paul addresses children and parents separately, reminding the children of the promise attached to the commandment and warning the fathers not to irritate their children but to teach them about the Lord of parents and children.

The Bible's view of the family and the relationship between parents and children is vastly different from that of contemporary society. "No one owes more to Christianity than does the child," said William Barclay. And the duty of parents to both train and love their children has nowhere been taught more clearly or practiced with greater benefits than among people who have received God's special revelation.

A Religious Relationship.

All people are created as equals before God, and if one has say-so over another, it's only because God has given authority as a sacred trust. What Jesus said to Pilate everyone might say to anyone endowed with authority: "You would have no power over me if it were not given to you from above" (John 19:11).

Authority is exercised by representatives of God, and obedience is motivated by religious fear.

To honor is therefore more than to obey—although honor usually includes obedience. Shem and Japheth honored their father, Noah, even when he was in a shameful state: they walked backwards into the tent and covered his nakedness. But Ham, the father of Canaan, incurred God's wrath on that day (Gen. 9:20-27). We don't honor a father merely because he is honorable but because he is a father. Nor do we respect the government only when it governs rightly: when David gets his chance to kill Saul (who was trying to kill David), he shudders with religious fear at the thought: "The Lord forbid that I should do such a thing to my master, the Lord's anointed, or lift my hand against him, for he is the anointed of the Lord" (1 Sam. 24:6).

The honor that the fifth commandment requires is religious. We obey for God's sake. "Obey your parents in the Lord" (Eph. 6:1). "Children, obey your parents in everything, for this pleases the Lord" (Col. 3:20). "The authorities that exist have been established by God" (Rom. 13:1). Thus, we obey our parents not because they are the wisest and fairest, but because they are the parents God has given us. And we pay our taxes and honor presidents and prime ministers not because they are of our political party but because God demands it.

Power Has Purpose.

God gives authority to people not to lift them above others but to enable them to fulfill a mandate from him. He gives the power required to carry out a particular task.

Thus, the government of a country receives authority from God to maintain justice in the land. The government must exercise its power to restrain evil and to promote what is good and right. "For he is God's servant to do you good," says Romans 13:4 of the government official. Therefore the church must loyally and prayerfully support the government when the government fulfills God's assignment but must loudly protest a government that does not use its power for the citizens' good.

Judicial powers exist to mete out just punishments for the protection of society. So local governments have the power to place stoplights and regulate orderly life in the sphere that's entrusted to them. With the trust comes authority, and the authority is limited by the extent of the mandate. Teachers cannot fulfill their commission if they have no authority in the classroom. And church officers have authority from God to do a work for God. But in every one of these cases the authority is limited to the sphere of responsibility.

To parents God gave the most far-reaching authority, because they have the biggest task any human being can have with respect to other human beings: to "bring them up in the training and instruction of the Lord" (Eph. 6:4). Therefore parents, especially, must remember that their power has been given for a purpose. Unless they use their authority to fulfill God's assignment, they are abusing their power.

Disuse and Abuse of Power.

Once God has entrusted us with a task and the power to perform it, we are not free to be parents or not to be parents; governments may not renege on their responsibility to govern even when the measures required are unpopular. As parents, we may not shirk our parental duties when the son or daughter is not sympathetic to the measures that need to be taken. We are not parents because we like the job but because God has entrusted other human beings to our care.

Authority is always a borrowed good, a holding, a temporary trust. Not using it, as well as abusing it, renders us guilty before God, who entrusted this power to us for a purpose. And those who have authority are worthy of honor not because of any personal excellence they might have but because God "chooses to rule" through them, as the catechism says in Answer 104.

When cowardly parents and governments refuse to exercise authority at critical times, they are accountable to God for deserting their posts—like the captain who does not want the job when the weather gets rough. Those who do not use God-given authority at critical times commit treason. But those who use power in a way that's contrary to the purpose for which God gave it are tyrants.

The Need for Philosophy.

It is not the duty of the catechist and the gospel preacher to describe in detail this beautiful and intricate system of authority and obedience that upholds human society. But other Christians, especially those who teach philosophy, sociology, and political science, should enter deeply into describing and defining creation's various God-ordained spheres of authority-for-a-purpose as well as the role of authority in voluntary associations. The extent of institutional authority is an ever-urgent topic because power and money can do terrible things to people. In the interest of freedom and order, human society needs a Bible-directed theory and Bible-believing practitioners.

A biblically informed theory would not only take into account God's creational patterns and explicit legislation; it should also ponder the kingship of Christ. We are now living in an era in which the Father rules over all through the Son. That means that might and mercy are combined in the highest Authority.

Parental Discipline.

The first need of a child is for love from parents. This love is expressed in hugging, holding, kissing, talking, singing, and so on. The baby finds security and happiness in this love. It is an irreplaceable attention that every child should have. We have always known it, and modern research has confirmed it.

Parents' love seeks the well-being of the child. Therefore the child must be disciplined by the parent. The child does not know its own needs; parents do. All children will manipulate their parents and care givers if they have a chance. Thus the loving discipline of a child starts soon after it is born. Parents must say yes and no—consistently, lovingly, firmly.

Parents who refuse to train and discipline their children do not love them. Parental neglect is not only un-Christian; it is unnatural. It happens when parents regard their children as pets when they are very young and as financial liabilities when they get older. Hundreds of thousands of parents in North America have no time for their children. For some reason they are too busy. Such a sin of omission has the most serious consequences, even if it is forgivable by our Father God.

A child is still the greatest trust God can give to any human being. No parent may use less important things as an excuse for neglecting his or her greatest task.

Authority Is Goal-oriented.

The purpose of authority, which God entrusts to his servants, is cultivating the maturity of those who are placed under authority. Parents bring up their children in order to let them go as mature human beings. And church officers have a similar obligation: Christ gives the gift of authority to his church "so that the body of Christ may be built up until we all reach unity in the faith and in the knowledge of the Son of God and become mature, attaining to the whole measure of the fullness of Christ" (Eph. 4:12-13). One could argue that the kind of maturity envisioned in Ephesians 4:13 cannot be attained in the present life and that therefore the church can never exist without officebearers. It is true that the church needs special gifts and officers as long as this age lasts. But the ongoing need for leadership and help is no excuse for officers and church leaders to continue indefinitely their present assignments. They must try to work themselves out of a job. Those who have received instruction and guidance must themselves learn to give instruction and guidance, or we are merely busy preserving the system and the relationship between teachers and learners, leaders and followers. And that's not what God intends. The Lord wants the authority figure to be a servant, a helper. Education and authority are goal-oriented.

Parents Letting Go.

The danger is not great today that parents or grandparents refuse to let go of their authority. Patriarchs (in some cases matriarchs) have at times exercised authority long after their offspring should have been mature and independent. And this kind of clan hierarchy still does occur. Such situations are socially and culturally understandable, but they are never beyond the rule of the Bible: authority exists for service and never for self-aggrandizement. People hold authority in order to help others become what they are meant to be.

Parents need wisdom to know when to shift their responsibility to those for whom they are responsible. If they do it too soon or too late, they may cause much damage. And one rule does not fit all children, because they differ so much.

A pastor or parent cannot make decisions for another person. But we do need each other. Increasingly the Christian community is teaching its members about leadership and parenting so that each of us may know and do the will of God.

The Duty to Honor Endures.

When the child is very young, all the laws for its life can be summarized in one command: obey your parents. Later the parents make fewer rules for the child, and finally the grown person must make his or her own rules under God. But God's commandment that we *honor* our parents endures as long as we have parents (see 1 Tim. 5:1-8). We no longer express that respect by asking them what time we should be home and in bed, but we must honor them until the day we bury them. Even in cases of deep and painful disagreement we owe them respect.

One of our church's missionaries to Japan tells the story of a young man who was converted to Christ. On the day of his baptism, his mother attended the church service. She had done everything to discourage her son from becoming a Christian. Just before the man knelt to receive the water of baptism, he walked to the rear of the church building and bowed low before his mother. Then he came forward and received the mark of a Christian. And everyone understood and valued the son's obeisance to his mother and to God.

Threats and Promises.

The fifth commandment precedes the commands that regulate our behavior to our neighbors because authority-obedience relationships are fundamental to interpersonal relationships. If a society has a crisis in authority and obedience, it experiences troubles in all other relationships between people. Because thousands of parents don't love and discipline their children, hundreds of thousands of children live antisocial and rebellious lives.

We must honor authorities God has instituted, or human society cannot continue to exist. God's threats are real.

But God also attaches a promise to his command to honor parents: "so that you may live long in the land the Lord your God is giving you" (Ex. 20:12). Originally this promise referred to Israel's life in Canaan or Palestine. But God also holds out a similar promise to Gentile Christians: "that it may go well with you and that you may enjoy long life on the earth" (Eph. 6:3). I once heard a woman pleading on this text when her husband was dying: since he had always been such a loving son to his parents, she said God should remember his promise and give her husband a "long life on earth." We would give ourselves many problems, however, if we took this promise so individualistically. The truth of the promise is confirmed in the lives of families, clans, generations, and societies. Where children have the habits of obedience, family bonds are strong, and the elders are respected. Such communities have a solid and lasting way of life. But where family bonds are broken, communities disintegrate. These are the God-ordained consequences of our reactions to his commands.

Lord's Day 40

LOVE YOUR NEIGHBOR

***Q** What is God's will for you in the sixth commandment?*

***A** I am not to belittle, insult, hate, or kill my neighbor—not by my thoughts, my words, my look or gesture, and certainly not by actual deeds—and I am not to be party to this in others; rather, I am to put away all desire for revenge. I am not to harm or recklessly endanger myself either. Prevention of murder is also why government is armed with the sword.*

—Q & A 105

***Q** Does this commandment refer only to killing?*

***A** By forbidding murder God teaches us that he hates the root of murder: envy, hatred, vindictiveness. In God's sight all such are murder.*

—Q & A 106

The Text of the Commandment.

Exodus 20:13 does *not* say "You shall not kill"; it says, "You shall not murder" or "unlawfully put to death." The Old Testament words used for killing in war or in carrying out a judicial sentence are different from the word for murder (*ratzach*) used in the sixth commandment.

Thus it makes no sense to use the sixth commandment to say that one may not go to war or that the government may not enforce capital punishment, as even some educated people have said. The sixth commandment is not speaking of killing but of the unlawful putting to death called *ratzach*. Neither may one conclude that the Scriptures approve every other form of putting to death. The Bible distinguishes between authorized and unauthorized killing, and the latter, called murder, is forbidden in the sixth commandment.

The Second Five.

In the commandments of the second table God protects us members of the human race against each other in our present sinful environment. These commandments protect life (the sixth), marriage (the seventh), and property (the eighth). But God also forbids—in the ninth and tenth commandments—people to attack each other by means of words and desires. One might say (with Martin Luther) that God proceeds in the second table of the law from the major to the minor (from the deed of murder to covetousness). But the Lord's wise ordering of the statutes also teaches us that the law is fulfilled not when we are merely freed from murder but only when our hearts are sanctified.

What God Forbids.

God forbids murder—the unlawful killing of a person. But by mentioning the worst kind of attack on a person, he implies condemnation of all other sins against people, such as "to belittle, insult, [or] hate" them, even by "my thoughts, my words, my look or gesture." I may not even hate or kill myself, says the catechism.

Every attack on someone's life, through hatred or carelessness, in thought or word or deed, is condemned by God, the Maker and Protector of human life. The Old Testament contains many examples of God's protection of people's lives from other people. We may not pose a threat to anyone's life: "Do not do anything that endangers your neighbor's life" (Lev. 19:16). But we must also actively care for his or her safety: "When you build a new house, make a parapet around your roof so that you may not bring the guilt of bloodshed on your house if someone falls from the roof" (Deut. 22:8). The Old Testament sums up the laws of the second table in general and covers the basic commandment—the sixth—by saying, "Love your neighbor as yourself" (Lev. 19:18).

***Q** Is it enough then that we do not kill our neighbor in any such way?*

***A** No. By condemning envy, hatred, and anger God tells us to love our neighbors as ourselves, to be patient, peace-loving, gentle, merciful, and friendly to them, to protect them from harm as much as we can, and to do good even to our enemies.*

—Q & A 107

In the New Testament Jesus brings all of the Jews' teachings on the sixth commandment to a climax: "You have heard that it was said to the people long ago, 'Do not murder, and anyone who murders will be subject to judgment'" (Matt. 5:21). His hearers are familiar with the teaching of the rabbis that murderers must appear before the Jewish courts. Then Christ says, "But I tell you that anyone who is angry with his brother,will be subject to judgment." Here Rabbi Jesus declares that not merely the murderer but also the one who is angry at his neighbor is already a criminal, to be judged by the courts. "Again, anyone who says to his brother, 'Raca,' is answerable to the Sanhedrin." Stop making distinctions between minor and major sinners, he says: name-calling is a crime to be adjudicated by the highest earthly court. "But anyone who says, 'You fool!' will be in danger of the fire of hell" (v. 22): anyone who transgresses the commandment to love the neighbor, no matter how insignificant the transgression may appear in the eyes of human judges, is still guilty before God and liable to be thrown into hell.

In this way Jesus places us before the heart of the matter: the commandments do not consist of so many laws or rules that can be distinguished as major or minor; our crimes cannot be divided into the serious and not-so-serious. The law of God, rather, places us before God himself. We are either in the love and righteousness of our heavenly Father (Matt. 5:43-48), or we sin against him. We either love or hate.

Therefore God does not merely address murderers in the sixth commandment—those who should be doing time in prison or who are already waiting on death row. God is speaking to church members and catechism teachers. He is teaching the church that without his forgiveness and his Holy Spirit none of us can keep from murder or avoid the ultimate danger of hell.

Rationale for the Commandment.

Why must we respect and even love all other human beings? Because God made them in his image. Each human being has a likeness to God.

There's something sacred about the life of *all* living beings, according to the Bible. Originally, God did not give us the right to use animals for food; he made that concession after the flood (Gen. 9:3). Even then, the blood of an animal is not for human consumption (Gen. 9:4) because a creature's life is in its blood (Lev. 17: 11, 14). The killing of an animal is always somewhat unnatural in the Bible. And today a slaughterhouse is still a cultic place for orthodox Jews—and Muslims.

While in the Bible life itself is sacred, human life has unique value and unique protection. When someone murders a human being, that person has destroyed a likeness of God. Therefore God demands that the life of a murderer be taken (Gen. 9:6). The unassailability of human life does not rest on the general sanctity of life or on particular qualities of the murdered person. People may not kill people, because human beings are accountable and answerable to God! God created people in his image, and all people live to praise him.

Capital Punishment.

The question whether the death penalty may or must be inflicted on those who have committed intentional homicide divides the citizens of many countries and the members of most churches. Among good Christians we find those who believe that the Bible forbids capital punishment, that it permits the practice, or that the Bible requires it.

Those who say that the Bible *forbids* the death penalty usually cite the powerful Scripture motifs of love, forgiveness, and restoration; but these cannot be used to eliminate the equally central biblical concern for justice. Those who quote the sixth commandment—"You shall not murder"—as a prohibition against the state administering the death penalty do not understand the text, as I said earlier. In the Bible the infliction of the death penalty by the state is not called "murder."

Other Christians say that the Bible requires capital punishment for murder. This argument is based on the demands for the death penalty in the Mosaic laws (e.g., Ex. 21:12-17, Deut. 19:1-13) and on the statement in the New Testament that the government is entrusted with the sword (Rom. 13:3-5). Those who say that the Bible mandates capital punishment for homicides rely especially on the general rule in the covenant with Noah and creation: "Whoever sheds the blood of man, by man shall his blood be shed; for in the image of God has God made man" (Gen. 9:6).

In this interpretation, the question is whether the rule in Genesis 9 must be read as a law for all times and cultures. Its place in the covenant with creation favors this understanding. But the lack of detail (what about due process, witnesses, intentional and unintentional homicide, and the like?) and the proverb-like style warn us that it's not a simple law that can be applied to every murder throughout biblical history.

The Heidelberg Catechism takes no position on capital punishment: it says that God armed the state with a sword to *prevent* murder; it does not say anything about the retribution for such sin.

In 1981 the Christian Reformed Church recorded the following as its conviction: the state has the right to inflict, but is not obligated to practice, capital punishment; if capital punishment is exercised, it should be done with utmost restraint (*Acts of the Synod of the Christian Reformed Church, 1981*, p. 72).

Medical Services.

The success of medical science has given us the tools to sometimes prolong life longer than is desirable, and the same science can make murder seem clean. Thus ninety-year-olds who desire to depart are kept functioning in hospital beds. When may we "let them die"? And some babies that are prematurely delivered—or that are born with weaknesses that would have killed them had they been born a few years ago—can, amazingly, be sustained in the neonatal departments of our hospitals—because these babies are wanted. (Should we keep them at any price?) Yet in the same wing of the hospital, well-formed preborn children are clinically killed because they are not wanted.

Here lies a host of questions Christians must address and answer before the face of God in obedience to God's Word and law, with compassion for fellow human beings.

And we have not even mentioned nuclear war—the ultimate murder machine. Would such killing be morally defensible as a "just war"?

Love Them!

God not only created people (which is why we must respect each other), but he also loves people—and therefore *we* must love each other. God loved us so much that he permitted his Son to be killed in order to save his enemies. And now he says that the redeemed must also love—even their enemies (Matt. 5:44, Rom. 12:21).

The revelation of God's love in Jesus may be called the appearance of his people-love, *philanthropia* (Titus 3:4). God is a people-lover. God is a philanthropist, but the devil is a misanthropist—a people-hater. Anyone who does not love is not a child of God (1 John 3:10). Cain and those who are like him belong to the evil one. Cain murdered his brother. "Anyone who hates his brother is a murderer" (see 1 John 3:12-15). It is not only notorious murderers like Cain who have transgressed the sixth commandment. Christ said to seemingly respectable religious leaders that their father was the devil—"a murderer from the beginning" (John 8:44). Either we belong to the Creator-Lover and love our neighbors, or we are the children of the murderer. That's how Jesus sees us.

Some of us have trouble saying "God loves people," because we have heard that God throws people into a place of everlasting suffering—hell. But, first, love does not erase God's righteous judgment, and, second, God does not bring death and hatred. According to the Bible, God brings light and love into a world of death and hatred. All people are perishing, and that is no wonder, says the Bible. The miracle is that believers in Christ do not perish but are saved by his eternal, loving embrace (John 3:16-18).

God is love. God loves us. The children of God have love. And we love people not because we have discovered that some are lovable but because the Spirit of Christ is in us (Rom. 5:5).

The Unity of the Law.

The first and great commandment is that we love God with our heart and soul and all our being. But the second commandment, that we love our neighbor as ourselves, is like the first (Matt. 22:39). If we want to honor God, we must love our neighbor, for God's law is one, and his will is that we love.

Genesis 3 describes the first sin of our parents Adam and Eve. They did not love God above all but listened to the deceiver. Then, with inescapable logic, Genesis 4 tells us that Cain killed Abel. For when the first tablet of the law is broken, the second will be smashed.

Without God, we have no brothers and sisters. And unless people are our brothers and sisters, God cannot be our Father.

The Fulfillment of This Command.

God intended all people to be our neighbors—that is to be "neigh" or "nigh" or "next to" each other. We were not meant to be *over against* but *next to* each other, like the strings on the violin, the black and white keys on the console of the organ, or the colors of the rainbow. Together we were to blend and to be God's concert and God's painting.

Although that sounds poetic, maybe even romantic, it is a very practical matter. The expert in the law mentioned in Luke 10:25 wants Jesus to give a definition of *neighbor*. But Jesus tells a story in which a heathen, a "bad" Samaritan, is the good example. Then Jesus asks, "Which of these . . . do you think was a neighbor to the man who fell into the hands of robbers?" And the learned Jew correctly said, "The one who had mercy on him." He did not get a dogmatic conclusion but a practical commission: "Go and do likewise" (v. 37). Do what that Samaritan did. Then you *are* a "neighbor."

Jesus' choice of a Gentile as an example took the pride out of his contemporaries as well as his followers. The parable also implies that people have a natural love that is enormously valuable for natural life. We still have, here and there, good neighborhoods. But natural love has a hard time surviving the breath of the dragon. The human scene displays mainly hatred, lust, and greed. Every day thousands of people are stabbed, mugged, shot, choked, and annihilated by their fellow human beings. Natural love cannot save. God's love must do it. His love is community creating. We cannot produce this kind of love. It is *agape* (selfless love). It came from God and entered into our world through Christ, who died for the ungodly (Rom. 5:6-8)—for people who shoot, choke, and annihilate each other. We receive this gift of a new life by faith and pass it on as love (Gal. 5:6). We had better be very clear about it: "If anyone says, 'I love God,' yet hates his brother, he is a liar" (1 John 4:20).

Lord's Day 41

GOD, SEX, MARRIAGE

***Q** What is God's will for us in the seventh commandment?*

***A** God condemns all unchastity. We should therefore thoroughly detest it and, married or single, live decent and chaste lives.*

—Q & A 108

***Q** Does God, in this commandment, forbid only such scandalous sins as adultery?*

***A** We are temples of the Holy Spirit, body and soul, and God wants both to be kept clean and holy. That is why he forbids everything which incites unchastity, whether it be actions, looks, talk, thoughts, or desires.*

—Q & A 109

In the Beginning.

"God created man in his own image, in the image of God he created him; male and female he created them" (Gen. 1:27). Human beings are either male or female. The distinction was created (a word that occurs three times in Gen. 1:27), and therefore it is good.

The second creation account gives a fuller description of the creation of male and female. Here Adam is made first, and God observes: "It is not good for the man to be alone. I will make a helper suitable for him" (Gen. 2:18). The "fitting" or "suitable" helper does not indicate someone who can do little and big jobs for the male but one who can help or complement him in his very being as a man—a person distinct from all other creatures who were not human (2:19-20). So God "made a woman from the rib he had taken out of the man" (2:22). Why was she made from his rib? Obviously, the point is that she is not a new and different creation. And as for the rib (not a hand or a tongue), an ancient commentator says, "Therefore she shall cling forever to his heart."

Then Adam sings his wedding song: "This is now bone of my bones and flesh of my flesh" (2:23). And, therefore, the writer adds, "a man will leave his father and mother and be united to his wife, and they will become one flesh" (2:24), a new family unit, and a separate two-in-oneness.

Thus the Bible presents marriage as an institution of God at the dawn of history. And Christ reaffirmed God's intention when he said of this union: "What God has joined together, let man not separate" (Matt. 19:6).

Contrary to the notion that's fostered by popular pictures of cave dwellers who steal females and swap them again, the Bible tells the story of one man and one woman who were made for each other. God officiated at their wedding, and the setting was in Paradise.

Creation Ordinance.

Our sexuality, that is, our being male or female, belongs to the good creation. Therefore no one should be ashamed or feel guilty for the feelings and attractions that God himself created. But God created them for a purpose. Our sexuality and all his gifts must be used responsibly and obediently.

Marriage, as a lasting bond between one man and one woman, belongs to the good creation. Therefore it will survive even the worst of times. People will always be inclined to break it, because they are sinful; yet they will always return to it, because it is a wholesome institution that's indispensable to human society.

Marriage is a covenant that requires a complete commitment from the partners: "I am yours, and you are mine. You may always depend on me, and I will always love you, so help me God." The very character of marriage excludes such a thing as a trial marriage.

Many people disagree with this Christian teaching and claim that consenting adults may choose a different arrangement for their sexual relationship. But if sex and marriage have been given by God, we will have to live by the rules he established, or we will deeply hurt ourselves and each other. And God will punish us for breaking his laws.

The Law from Sinai.

Although monogamous marriage (having one mate for life) is the biblical ideal, polygamy (having more than one wife) entered history with Lamech, the seventh generation after Adam (Gen. 4:19), and was also practiced by the patriarchs Abraham and Jacob. The motivation was certainly not always lust. Abraham's union with Hagar, Sarai's maid, was a contemporary method of adoption (Gen. 16:1-4). Later, the kings in Israel had many wives. Solomon's wives (seven hundred of royal birth and three hundred concubines, 1 Kings 11:3) gave splendor to this Near Eastern king as a fleet of expensive cars does to today's moguls.

God, in the law he gave from Sinai, protects marriage against the intruder. Strictly speaking, adultery is the illegitimate relationship between a man (married or single) and a married woman. "If a man is found sleeping with another man's wife, both the man who slept with her and the woman must die" (Deut. 22:22, cf. Lev. 20:10).

The Old Testament laws against adultery protect the honor of the husband. His wife is his crown (cf. 1 Cor. 11:7). When his wife has given herself to another man, nothing but the death penalty can pay for the shameful deed ("A man who commits adultery lacks judgment. . . Jealousy arouses a husband's fury. . . . He will not accept any compensation; he will refuse the bribe, however great it is" [Prov. 6:32-35]). But if a man, married or single, has intercourse with a non-married and not-pledged woman, a penalty may be required, or he may have to take her as a second wife, but the immoral act is not considered adultery (Ex. 22:16-17, Deut. 22:28). A (married) man's going to a prostitute is improper and may make him a "laughing-stock" (Gen. 38:23), but his act is not adultery to be punished by death. In the New Testament, however, husband and wife have equal rights to each other's bodies (1 Cor. 7:4), and *adultery* gets a new meaning.

Marriage in the Old and New Covenants.

In the New Testament God does not replace his law, but he deepens the commandments of the Sinai covenant. He still protects human life against human attack ("You shall not murder"), but the emphasis shifts to the love we owe our neighbors. And he still protects the marriage of one couple against the attack of an outsider ("You shall not commit adultery"). Now God not only protects the honor of the husband but also demands that the covenant between two people not be violated. Under the Old Covenant adultery was punishable mainly because it was an intolerable offense against the honor of the husband whose wife was involved in the adultery. The act of taking someone else's wife was regarded as a theft of the husband's possession rather than as improper behavior toward a female person. Nathan's denunciation of David's sin with Bathsheba—very significant in that it shows that even a Near Eastern king was subject to the Word of God—emphasizes the shameful robbery of a poor man by a rich man. And the punishment includes this humiliation of David: "I will take your wives and give them to one who is close to you, and he will lie with your wives." "You did it in secret, but I will do this thing in broad daylight before all Israel" (2 Sam. 12:11-12). That's divine retribution: an eye for an eye and a wife for a wife, as Lewis B. Smedes said (*Mere Morality,* p. 159). But in the New Testament Paul writes, "The wife's body does not belong to her alone but also to her husband. In the same way, the husband's body does not belong to him alone but also to his wife" (1 Cor. 7:4). Now they have equal rights to each other. God's original intention for marriage must be realized in the Christian community. Marriage becomes again an exclusive partnership of one man and one woman, as it was "at the beginning" (Matt. 19:4-6).

In the early church, people who had more than one wife apparently did not dissolve their bigamous relationships when they became Christians. But by insisting that church officers should have only one wife (1 Tim. 3:2,12), the apostles did set the trend for the Christian community. And the most engaging model of tender and sacrificial love held up as the example of marital union in the teaching of the Christian church was the two-in-oneness of Christ and his church. Not only did Christ give his life to make the church his own, but all that he acquired is hers, and she herself is his body (1 Cor. 12, Eph. 5).

The Marital Covenant.

In marriage two lives are joined on the basis of vows, mutual promises, freely accepted obligations, and unique privileges. This is the marriage covenant, instituted by God and modeled in his own covenant of grace with us through Jesus Christ.

Marriage partners attempt to live out their oneness on all the levels of human existence: heart and mind and soul. Since the unity is concerned with all levels of living, the marriage can also break down in different spots: in faith, intellect, or emotion. As soon as one partner shuts the other one out of a particular compartment of his or her life, the marriage relation is damaged. Unfaithfulness is much more than having sexual intercourse with another person.

But the basic bond of a marriage is the marital covenant. In our culture it is usually mutual attraction that leads to marriage. And, of course, mutual attraction remains a great support throughout the years. Yet the continuation of the marriage is not dependent on the attraction— erotic or otherwise. The enduring strength of the marriage bond is covenantal loyalty. Basic to the whole intricate range of husband-wife relations is a steady commitment, a fidelity that is rooted in God's own covenant faithfulness.

The Sexual Side.

Sexual union of marriage partners expresses and strengthens the total commitment they have for each other. God has assigned a place to our sexuality in his creation order. We must accept and use this gift—and all of God's gifts—as he intended. Abuse of his gifts constitutes a sin and is a derailment of human life.

If there is a fire in your house, you don't have to worry as long as the fire is burning in the furnace or in the fireplace. There the fire fulfills its function and warms the house. But if the fire runs through the living room, it destroys your house. When sexual desires fulfill the God-assigned role within the marriage, lives are warmed and blessed. The flames are beneficial. But if sexual desires run wild, people are ruined.

Our contemporary culture tends to regard sexual union as a casual encounter or a payment for services—and most desirable when illegitimate. Apart from despising God's gift and provoking his displeasure, we are also cheapening our own lives to the point where the nobler traits that distinguish human life from other forms of living are sometimes hard to find.

Christians must be very alert to withstand the call for "sexual freedom" because it will lead us into terrible bondage. In our behavior we should be faithful to God and to each other.

"Not All Were Made in Heaven."

Marriage is a sacred and enduring covenant between one woman and one man. But not all marriages, apparently, were made in heaven. Many of them are broken because the partners see no way of reconciling their deep differences. Some say that they were unwise and impulsive when they married. Others say that they lost what once they held in common. They want to escape, finally, from an impossible, unlivable situation. They break their legal covenant. Such separations and divorces occur also among Christians.

Divorce and Remarriage.

Although the church always accepts forgiven sinners as regular members, it has problems accepting divorced people, especially when they have remarried. Forgiven sinners have repented of their sins. But in the case of persons who have divorced (and remarried), the church is unsure what it ought to accept as proof of repentance: should the church require someone who broke with one partner and married another to show genuine repentance by returning to the first? That does not seem right. That would compound the problem.

No Biblical Ground for Divorce.

During years of debate over the questions about divorce and remarriage, churches developed the custom of judging some couples to have and others not to have "biblical grounds for divorce." On the basis of Matthew 5:32 and 19:9 some have taught that adultery by one spouse gives the other one a "biblical ground for divorce." The Westminster Confession of Faith (1645), Chapter 24, cites two grounds that "warrant dissolving the bond of marriage," namely adultery and deliberate desertion—the latter based on 1 Corinthians 7:15.

Elders and pastors in the Reformed and Presbyterian traditions have spent much painful energy trying to identify the "innocent party" in divorces and in attempting to decide whether a spouse had "biblical ground for divorce."

Synods of the Christian Reformed Church, throughout the 1970s, appointed committees and read reports dealing with questions of divorce and remarriage. In 1980 the church reached some conclusions. We are now less inclined to speak of "biblical grounds" for divorce.

The Exceptive Clause in Matthew.

In Mark 10:10-11 and Luke 16:18 Christ taught that a husband or wife who divorces his or her partner and marries another one commits adultery. One who marries a divorced person also commits adultery, he says. In this saying Jesus speaks against the easy divorce that was often an excuse for getting another partner, and he calls it adultery. But in Matthew 19:9, while the same saying calls such divorce adultery, it adds an exception—"except for marital unfaithfulness." Although Jesus did not intend to give a justification for divorce, he acknowledged that sometimes his condemnation does not apply because of grave sins in the situation.

A similar statement would be "All killing, except in the case of provocation, is murder." Such a statement does not approve killing just because provocation has occurred. It does say that a further assessment of the whole situation is required before the murder charge applies. And in the same way, apparently, all divorce cannot be called adultery.

Scripture also considers divorce a possibility in 1 Corinthians 7:12-16. Thus, while the church cannot leave any doubt concerning God's will for marriage, it must also take into account actions and circumstances that happen in a sinful world and that are opposed to God's will for marriage.

The Good Pastor.

The pastoring role of the church is not easy in a permissive age. Society has become tolerant of divorce. The church is sometimes absolute, sometimes legalistic, and often unsure about the will of the Good Shepherd.

We must adhere to the biblical principles concerning marriage, and the church must teach them diligently. But we may not be absolutists, for the Bible itself takes into consideration the reality of our sinful situation when it instructs us on divorce and remarriage. We cannot ignore the human imperfections, transgressions, and limitations in our present sinful world. Nor should we attempt to write a list of permissible and nonpermissible causes for divorce. Rather, the will of God and the grace of our Savior must be found and applied in each case. Pastors and consistories may call on God's Spirit for wisdom when they apply the teaching of God's Word to concrete cases of marital difficulty (see "Marriage Guidelines," *Acts of the Synod of the Christian Reformed Church, 1980,* pp. 467-85).

The gospel always brings hope. And the good news is intended for people who have failed. While strongly opposing our society's present sexual immorality and marital infidelity, the Christian community must offer its own medicine for healing broken lives and marriages.

Lord's Day 42

GOD AND GOODS

Q *What does God forbid in the eighth commandment?*

A *He forbids not only outright theft and robbery, punishable by law. But in God's sight theft also includes cheating and swindling our neighbor by schemes made to appear legitimate, such as: inaccurate measurements of weight, size, or volume; fraudulent merchandising; counterfeit money; excessive interest; or any other means forbidden by God. In addition he forbids all greed and pointless squandering of his gifts.*

—Q & A 110

Q *What does God require of you in this commandment?*

A *That I do whatever I can for my neighbor's good, that I treat others as I would like them to treat me, and that I work faithfully so that I may share with those in need.*

—Q & A 111

The Eighth of Ten and Third of Five.

The Ten Words broadly cover our duties in all relationships, vertical and horizontal, to God and neighbor. In the second tablet we meet our neighbors as persons whose lives God protects ("you shall not murder," the sixth commandment), as male or female and as husbands or wives ("you shall not commit adultery," the seventh); and in trafficking in goods and paid services: "You shall not steal." This, the eighth commandment, demands that we know and do God's will in commerce and banking, property and possessing, buying and selling, saving and investing.

Theft of People.

Some Old Testament scholars say that originally the eighth commandment referred to kidnapping—the theft of *people*—and that the tenth commandment, "you shall not covet . . . [what] belongs to your neighbor," refers to the neighbor's *goods*. Kidnapping a person to use or to sell him or her as a slave was indeed a capital crime under the Sinai covenant: "Anyone who kidnaps another and either sells him or still has him when he is caught must be put to death" (Ex. 21:16). "If a man is caught kidnapping one of his brother Israelites and treats him as a slave or sells him, the kidnapper must die" (Deut. 24:7).

I will follow the traditional understanding of the commandment as taught by the catechism, however. (But I agree that the tenth commandment, which forbids coveting someone else's possessions, is very relevant to thievery. Covetousness is the mother of theft. Greed for goods makes us blind to other people's interests.)

Mutual Dependence.

God intends people to depend on each other in general and to depend on each other economically. He wants human beings to form a society held together by the cement of mutual trust. Each must contribute according to her or his ability and opportunity. The one is a hunter; the other grows grain. One bakes bread, and the next one makes clothes. Historically, people swapped things—until money became the value indicator. Then a chair was no longer sold for three bushels of potatoes but for $69.95.

Money is a tremendous timesaver, and experience shows that it works well until there is too much or too little of it, in which case we face inflation or deflation. Then, sometimes, a chair sells again for some measure of potatoes or rice.

What's Wrong with That?

Today our system of transferring goods has become so complex that it takes an enlightened insider to explain the difference between dealing and stealing in such areas as the car market and the stock market. And which Christians will help us determine what's fair and what's crooked on the government-subsidies gravy train?

Two factors blur our sense of fairness and our definition of a thief: first, our contemporaries make most of their money not by producing goods and services and selling these to others; the big money is in the shuffling of valuable papers from one to another. It's the buying and selling of money itself that constitutes the major occupation of our economies. In the society of a generation ago, life and the economy turned around the marketplace and the railroad station. In fact, most town centers consisted of a station, a market, a hotel, a bank, and a church. Today the core of every major city in the world has mammoth buildings owned by various financial institutions. Basically, they don't produce any goods. They deal in money.

The second factor that makes clarity about the demands of the eighth commandment difficult today is our impersonal society. Only seldom do we do business with ordinary people. Most of the time we deal with bloodless corporations. And the three or four levels of government under which most North Americans live are our biggest employers. "They" handle most of the money. Loving the neighbor is the fulfillment of the eighth commandment. But our neighbors are the bank and the company, and tomorrow the one may buy the other.

These are some of the reasons why, when it comes to making money, too many Christians are not acting according to Christian principles. They defend what they do by saying they "cannot see anything wrong with it." But that reason for action just isn't good enough.

People and Things.

The complexity of our culture makes it imperative that Christian economists, sociologists, and businesspeople enlighten the whole Christian community about right and wrong in today's marketplace; they must also teach us to discover the evils of certain *systems*. But none of us may attempt to escape the force of God's Word with an appeal to the complexity of our times.

God's overriding concern in the eighth commandment is for people. His law requires that we love people and use things. Those who love things and use people are opposing the Spirit of God.

Honesty as a Policy.

Theft is a sin "punishable by law," as the catechism says, in nearly all countries. Morally sensitive people also frown on any dishonest practice calculated to bring gain by deceit. The Old Testament mentions some deceitful practices by name and tells us that God detests the crooks who use such tricks to enrich themselves: "Do not have two different weights in your bag—one heavy, one light. Do not have two differing measures in your house—one large, one small. You must have accurate and honest weights and measures, so that you may live long in the land the Lord your God is giving you. For the Lord your God detests anyone who does these things, anyone who deals dishonestly" (Deut. 25:13-16).

Bible passages such as this one must have given rise to the popular saying that "honesty is the best policy" (compare this to "that you may live long in the land"). Society used to agree that crooks would be losers but that honest people's businesses would be established by their good reputation. Even those who did not take the Bible seriously still believed that "honesty is the best policy." But this is no longer the case. In current idiom, an "honest guy" tends to be one who is naive and of modest means. But calling someone "smart" suggests that the person "knows how to get away with it." He "knows the system"; she "has been around." And, we say, "If you are smart, you ought to be rich." There aren't many people, not even among Christians, who would rather be honest and poor than smart and rich. Therefore the church must remind us regularly that God detests crooks.

Love of Money.

The insatiable desire for money causes endless misery. It disturbs harmony among even friends and relatives. It is one of our most powerful drives for performance, but it brings no peace. Love of money has caused people to sell their honor, their friends, their country, their own bodies. Our culture constantly stimulates this love for money and always teaches that happiness is having a bank account.

We tend to forget how critical Jesus was of this yen for goods and money. Not only have some American preachers forgotten Jesus' warning about gathering treasures on earth, but also certain "evangelists" have developed religious schemes to make a bundle.

"What good will it be for a man if he gains the whole world, yet forfeits his soul?" (Matt. 16:26). In the teaching of Christ the riches of the inner person and the gathering of treasures in heaven—not earthly possessions—are the important things. The person who adds barns to barns and investments to investments might say to himself, "You have plenty of good things laid up for many years. Take life easy; eat, drink, and be merry." Countless people follow that pattern for their so-called golden years. But in the parable that Jesus told, the rich man heard this voice: "You fool! This very night your life will be demanded from you." And by this story Christ revealed what will happen to someone who "stores up things for himself but is not rich toward God" (Luke 12:16-21).

Honest to God.

Honesty toward neighbors and a weakening of greed (and greed is the fuel of theft) occurs in those who have learned to live *coram Deo* ("before the face of God"). When we are open before him, always aware of his majesty and grace, we worship God, love people, and use things. Our lives gravitate to a different goal than do those of worldly people. We find that "godliness with contentment is great gain. For we brought nothing into the world, and we can take nothing out of it." Opposing the pressure of our age, we confess that getting rich is far from comfortable; it is dangerous. "People who want to get rich fall into temptation and a trap and into many foolish and harmful desires that plunge men into ruin and destruction. For the love of money is a root of all kinds of evil. Some people, eager for money, have wandered from the faith and pierced themselves with many griefs" (1 Tim. 6:6-7, 9-10).

Going Straight.

Thieves must be arrested by law-enforcement agencies. And all citizens ought to support every legal effort to curb crime, theft, deceit in advertising, and bad business manners. We Christians must not be lukewarm about these matters. Far from being shy about opposing theft and dirty tricks, we must be involved in the promotion of righteousness. Let's help clean up corruption in high places. And wherever we work or do business, we ought not only refuse to comply with the practice of pilfering but should also call a thief a thief, even if he or she is our buddy.

With diligence, law-abiding people can curb sins against the eighth commandment. But the law of God will not be fulfilled through a campaign for civic excellence. The kind of attitude that the Lord requires in this commandment is taught by the Spirit to God's stewards.

Handle with Care.

The love of money is a form of idolatry that must never be underestimated. Being rich makes entrance into the heavenly kingdom very difficult (Matt. 19:23). The desire to be rich makes us wander from the truth and gets us caught in Satan's web (1 Tim. 6:10).

The people of God have suffered defeats at crucial moments in history because of someone's love of money: when, after forty years of wandering, the conquest of the promised land was finally on God's agenda, Israel received a stunning blow because Achan had stolen and hidden a beautiful robe, two hundred shekels of silver, and a wedge of gold (Josh. 7:21). When Jesus had finished his mission on earth, had returned to the Father, and had sent the power from heaven—when the conquest of the world was finally on God's redemption agenda—the Christian community also received a hard blow: Ananias and Sapphira lied because they were covering up their love of money (Acts 5).

The mystery of Judas Iscariot, who was in the Master's company for three years, day and night, is as deep as the riddle of evil itself. How could he do what he did? Scripture suggests that Judas's love for money was the reason why the devil could invade his soul: "he was a thief" (John 12:6).

We should never regard ourselves beyond the lure of money. Judas was not the only gospel preacher whose heart was in his wallet. All of us must guard our minds and hearts against this insidious killer. And we should instruct our children much more diligently than we do about the power of goods and money, a power for good or for evil.

May he who died between two thieves have mercy on all of us who have stolen. And those who have stolen "must steal no longer, but must work, doing something useful with [their] own hands, that [they] may have something to share with those in need" (Eph. 4:28).

Stewardship.

As Ephesians 4 says and the catechism teaches, to refrain from stealing is not enough; we must also use our possessions to honor God and serve our neighbor—"that I do whatever I can for my neighbor's good." This is the positive side of the eighth commandment.

If we wrote a catechism today, we would probably make the idea of stewardship central to the discussion of this commandment. And, in keeping with the Bible, we would now expand the idea of stewardship to include humanity's corporate, stewardly responsibility for earth and sky and sea.

Stewards take care of property that's not their own. Stewardship applies to our spiritual as well as our physical possessions. The New Testament stresses the church's corporate stewardship of what the Master entrusted to us (the parable of the talents, Matt. 25:14-30) and also teaches individual stewardship of the gifts of the Spirit (1 Pet. 4:10). Our stewardship of other possessions is implied in the basic teaching that "the earth is the Lord's, and everything in it" (Ps. 24:1). Therefore nobody can ever have absolute ownership of anything. It is obvious that "we brought nothing into the world, and we can take nothing out of it" (1 Tim. 6:7).

Temporary Trust.

We should not belittle the temporary possession of money and goods by saying that they are less profitable for Christians than spiritual gifts. By faithful stewardship of goods and money, we can further the growth of the church and influence our future with the Lord. The brokerage firms and investment corporations of this world do not teach this kind of investment. But the Bible teaches that we can use our present possessions to lay a foundation for the future (1 Tim. 6:18-19). Scripture teaches that even money, placed in the service of the Lord, gives dividends in the world to come.

Jesus told a parable about a smart but worldly steward. This shrewd fellow used goods and money—although the goods were merely temporarily entrusted to his care—to buy security for a rainy day. How much more, says the Lord, should the children of the kingdom use "worldly wealth" to gain friends; then, when this life and these goods are gone, those whom we have helped will welcome us into eternal dwellings (Luke 16:1-9).

Kingdom Investments.

We witness to our faith by the way in which we handle our temporary property. We acknowledge God as the ultimate Owner of ourselves and of all things. We participate in buying and selling, investing and saving, but people are more important to us than things. Things are means to worship God and care for people. Neither the miser's greed nor the prodigal's squandering fits the faith understanding of stewardship. We may not hoard money and things, and we may not waste them. We must serve God with our possessions. We must critically examine the life-style of our culture and not thoughtlessly copy it. Our attitude toward things must be shaped by knowledge of God and love for neighbor.

Lord's Day 43

TAMING THE TONGUE

***Q** What is God's will for you in the ninth commandment?*

***A** God's will is that I never give false testimony against anyone, twist no one's words, not gossip or slander, nor join in condemning anyone without a hearing or without a just cause. Rather, in court and everywhere else, I should avoid lying and deceit of every kind; these are devices the devil himself uses, and they would call down on me God's intense anger. I should love the truth, speak it candidly, and openly acknowledge it. And I should do what I can to guard and advance my neighbor's good name.*

—Q & A 112

"You Shall Not Give False Testimony Against Your Neighbor."

The commandments of the second table zero in on the fruit of the kinds of sin they forbid: *murder* is the bitter fruit of hatred, envy, and the like. *Adultery* is the end result of impurity and lust. *Theft* results from desire, greed, dishonesty. And *bearing false witness* is the sin that can do the most damage of all the sins in this category.

The Hebrew word for *witness* includes what we call the *plaintiff*—the one who accuses another in court. The commandment forbids the lie in court "against your neighbor," just as the third commandment forbids the false oath against the Lord. (This is the first time that the neighbor, the fellow Israelite, is mentioned in the commandments.)

"On the testimony of two or three witnesses a man shall be put to death, but no one shall be put to death on the testimony of only one witness" (Deut. 17:6). That does not mean that the judge need only count noses: "If a malicious witness takes the stand to accuse a man of a crime . . . the judges must make a thorough investigation, and if the witness proves to be a liar, giving false testimony against his brother, then do to him as he intended to do to his brother" (Deut. 19:16-19).

Nevertheless, innocent people can be killed because of lying witnesses. It happened to Naboth, when the immoral Jezebel set up two "scoundrels" to charge Naboth "before the people, saying, 'Naboth has cursed both God and the king'" (1 Kings 21:8-14). At the trial of Jesus, many false witnesses came forward, but they only agreed that Jesus had claimed he could destroy the temple of God and rebuild it in three days (Matt. 26:59-61).

The crucial role of the witnesses was also underlined at the execution of the condemned: "the hands of the witnesses must be first in putting him to death" (Deut. 17:7).

Judges must use their discernment, but they can act only on the evidence presented by the witnesses. In court two people's lies might ruin a person. So the ninth commandment forbids lying where it hurts most.

Truth and Falsehood.

A lie is a statement that is intentionally false. A lie is different from an unintentional error. Lies aim to deceive the hearers and to gain advantage for or protect the liars.

All human beings are inclined to lie. But God hates deceit and falsehood. His truthfulness distinguishes him from us sinners: "God is not a man, that he should lie" (Num. 23:19). Among the "six things the Lord hates" and the "seven that are detestable to him" are "a lying tongue," "a heart that devises wicked schemes," and a "false witness who pours out lies" (Prov. 6:16-19).

In biblical language truth means reliability. (Nearly all languages use *Amen,* a Hebrew word for truth.) God and God's Word are reliable, and on his promises we depend. But people's words are deceptive, unreliable, light, and vain. "Everyone lies to his neighbor; their flattering lips speak with deception." But "the words of the Lord are flawless . . ." (Ps. 12:2, 6).

Devices of the Devil.

Lying and deceit "are devices the devil himself uses," says the catechism. They are tools from his workshop. Speaking of the devil, Jesus said, "There is no truth in him. When he lies, he speaks his native language" (John 8:44).

In the Apocalypse (Revelation) the devil, as the dragon, has two beasts working for him—one beast from the sea and one from the earth. The first one is political, brutal, and blasphemous. The second one is religious, cultural, and acts like a prophet. Both of them do the most harm with their mouths. The beast from the sea "was given a mouth to utter proud words and blasphemies and to exercise his authority for forty-two months" (Rev. 13:5). The beast from the earth is deception personified: he looks "like a lamb," but he speaks "like a dragon" and he deceives the inhabitants of the earth (Rev. 13:11, 14).

The beastly deception is very real today. Our whole culture is interested not in truth but in perception, not in substance but in appearance, not in character but in image. We are totally occupied with fads and fake values. Words are not simple servants of communication but tools of manipulation. And the seemingly miraculous technical power for transmitting messages is (mostly) at the service of the beast, just as it is in Revelation 13.

"The Truth Will Set You Free."

(John 8:32). Truth, like the light of day, frees us from the distortion of the night. As long as we linger in the domain of the dragon and the beast, we are either cynical or credulous; we do not know the truth. But when Jesus opens our eyes, we see the truth, we know the way, and we have the life. Suddenly we see things as they really are and for what they are really worth. We know God as our Father, Christ as our Liberator, and the Spirit as the One who leads us into the truth. And gradually he teaches us to love the truth and to speak the truth in love.

Children of the Truth.

God's people know the truth. God showed it to them; it was like a light that chased away all the apparitions that plague people who live in darkness.

Once we know the truth, we must remain "in the truth." We must be truthful and reliable, not devious or deceitful. Under the Old Covenant, God said to his people, "These are the things you are to do: Speak the truth to each other, and render true and sound judgment in your courts" (Zech. 8:16).

In the New Testament the apostle Paul writes, "Each of you must put off falsehood and speak truthfully to his neighbor, for we are all members of one body" (Eph. 4:25).

In both these instances the Bible is concerned to have us behave truthfully to other members of the people of God. The ninth commandment itself says, "You shall not give false testimony against your neighbor" (Ex. 20:16, Deut. 5:20), and in the Old Testament "your neighbor" and "your brother" are usually the same person (cf. Lev. 19:16-18 where "your neighbor" is "one of your people"). The question might therefore be asked, Who else is my neighbor? But that question was raised by an expert in the law of Moses, and Jesus told him to learn from a "bad" Samaritan how to *be* a neighbor (Luke 10:25-37).

Tricks or Truth?

The catechism does not restrict our obligation to be truthful: "God's will is that I never give false testimony against anyone, twist no one's words . . . nor join in condemning anyone."

Yet saints have stretched the truth or tricked their opponents: the Hebrew pro-lifers, Shiphrah and Puah, told Pharaoh a story about the vigor of Jewish women in delivering babies, but God was kind to these women (Ex. 1:15-20). Other women who lied to their enemies and were loved by the Lord were Rahab—who said the spies weren't with her, though she had hidden them under the stalks of flax (Josh. 2)—and the wife of Bahurim—who hid David's servants in the well and told Absalom's men, "They crossed over the brook" (2 Sam. 17:20). These stories, together with David's fib, retold by his friend Jonathan to an unreliable Saul (1 Sam. 20:6, 29-30), could be interpreted as stratagems or ruses permissible in the holy war. (J. L. Koole suggests this in *De Tien Geboden.*) And the apostle Paul, who could be real tricky in a debate, set up the Sadducees against the Pharisees when he cried, "I am a Pharisee, the son of a Pharisee. I stand on trial because of my hope in the resurrection of the dead" (Acts 23:6). That may have been true, but it was less than the whole truth.

Law and Love.

We fulfill the law by loving God and our neighbor (Rom. 13:10). One may not use love to relativize the law, but one must use love as the key to understanding God's will. Thus, my relatives hid those who fled from the Nazis, and they misled the German soldiers with the words of Rahab and the ploys of the wife of Bahurim. And so they obeyed their Lord.

Love is also the key to the many questions we raise in jest and sometimes in earnest when we contemplate what absolute truthfulness would do to our relationships when answering "How do you like the painting?" or "How do you like the food?" Writes Lewis B. Smedes (in *Mere Morality,* p. 216), "The moral law does not rule out a good joke, the high art of fantasy or the low art of the tall tale. Does it rule out the acting profession? What about bargaining at a bazaar, where the rules of the game call for suspension of truthfulness? Could poker survive if truthfulness were an absolute moral law? Must every wife tell a boring husband that he is a clod? Ought a parishioner, on leaving the Sunday service, tell the pastor his sermon was a tedious blend of trivia and platitude?"

Since human relationships are complicated and because love is the fulfillment of the law, all of us must, from time to time, tell a "tender lie."

Love is also the fulfillment of the ninth commandment. Love cannot be untruthful; it "rejoices with the truth" (1 Cor. 13:6). But rejoicing with truth may also mean forgetfulness about the "record of wrongs" because "love does not delight in evil" (vv. 5-6). Being inventive, love knows how to avoid the lie and the painful truth at the same time. A good example is supplied by the sculptor who was known for his realistic and artistic statues. He was ordered to do a bust of the emperor, who had an ugly scar on his forehead. People wondered how the sculptor would live up to his reputation for truthfulness yet avoid the embarrassment of showing the emperor's scar. When the sculpture was finished, the admirers saw the emperor with his head cupped in his hand and his index finger covering the scar.

"Sanctify Them by the Truth"

(John 17:17). In Jesus Christ, who is the full revelation of God, believers are dedicated to truthfulness. The "truth" is a whole-life concept in the Bible. If we "belong to the truth" (1 John 3:19), we also walk "in the truth" (2 John 4). Christ *is* the truth (John 14:6), and therefore "belonging to the truth" is no different from being in Christ and living under the domination of his Spirit. This life began when "he chose to give us birth through the word of truth" (James 1:18). But even the regenerate must fight the lie as long as they are in the body.

Controlled by the Spirit.

The reborn person "belongs to the truth" and "walks in the truth." Those who do not belong to the truth are still the servants of the lie and walk in darkness (cf. 1 John 1:6; 2:21).The contrast (the antithesis) between those of the truth and those of the lie is absolute, because we are either inside or outside of Christ and his grace.

Yet in our daily lives we don't appear as brilliant light or utter darkness. The Christian life is a struggle to bring all thoughts, words, and actions under the control of the Spirit. What God reveals to us as the new situation in Christ is also a command, a law we are called and empowered to obey (see Rom. 6:11-14).

The Tongue Teaches.

In our ongoing struggle to express the new person, the taming of the tongue may be the most difficult part: "If anyone is never at fault in what he says, he is a perfect man, able to keep his whole body in check" (James 3:2). Therefore teachers, who do much talking and who have wide influence by what they say and how they say it, "will be judged more strictly" (v. 1).

James is speaking of religious teachers. Many young Christians would do much better to keep their mouths shut for five years instead of starting to teach so soon with so little. Liberal teachers will be judged for denying the basic truths of the Scriptures. But some orthodox teachers are so afraid of the truth that they are inclined to view the fossils in the rock of the world as divine deceptions. These teachers act as if they must protect God and the doctrine of creation.

All of us must "love the truth [and] speak it candidly," as the catechism says. "For we cannot do anything against the truth, but only for the truth" (2 Cor. 13:8). Religious teachers (and authors) must be especially careful that in their descriptions of other (competing) religious groups and churches they know the truth and "speak it candidly." Christians must be distinguished by their deep respect for truth. Our use of the tongue (and the word processor) denies or demonstrates the cultivation of our Christian character.

The Tongue Leads.

"We put bits into the mouths of horses" (James 3:3). These big animals can be led only when they are bridled. People, too, can go where God wants them to go only when their tongues are bridled. The tongue is only a little member, much smaller than the fist. But just as rudders steer big ships and just as small sparks make big fires, so the deeds of the tongue have great consequences (vv. 4-5). The tongue can sting with the fire of hell (v. 6) or drip with the poison of the old serpent (vv. 7-8). It is the tongue that can decide a person's destiny: "For by your words you will be acquitted, and by your words you will be condemned" (Matt. 12:37).

The tongue has the power of fire. The fire originates in hell or in heaven. If someone's tongue is fired from below, a world of restless evil will result (James 3:6). Gossip, slander, and lying are devilish sins not only because they originate with the liar but because they multiply evil like vermin. A gossip session is a murderous game. And when the session is over, nobody can put the broken pieces together again.

In an African village the tale-bearer was punished by the elder of the town: she had to scatter the feathers of a chicken along the way to her house. But after the wind had blown, she had to regather the feathers—all of them. And when she could not get them together again, she learned her lesson: evil words cannot be recalled; they go their way to wreak havoc.

The Holy Spirit is the fire from heaven. He not only appeared as "tongues of fire" (Acts 2:3) when he descended on the followers of Jesus, but he uses the tongues of people to make them declare the "wonders of God" (v. 11). As a matter of fact, the fire from heaven is the only cure for the evil that, through the human tongue, "corrupts the whole person, sets the whole course of his life on fire, and is itself set on fire by hell" (James 3:6).

"Set a Guard over My Mouth"

(Ps. 141:3). People who "would love life and see good days" get varied advice. The Bible's advice is surprising: a person who seeks a happy future "must keep his tongue from evil and his lips from deceitful speech" (1 Pet. 3:10; Ps. 34:12).

We must resolve, with God's grace, to respect truth, to love the truth, and to speak it lovingly. We shall speak only if it is true, we will say it in God's hearing, and we will love our neighbor while we speak.

We may not "witness against our neighbor unto falsehood," says the ninth commandment. That means, positively, that "I should do what I can to guard and advance my neighbor's good name." Thus when I hear my neighbor's name and reputation dishonored, I will follow the prompting of the Spirit and speak in his or her favor. For just as the Spirit pleads our cause, as our Advocate, or Paraclete, so he teaches us to speak in favor of others. The Spirit of God not only guards our lips so that we keep inside what should not be said, but he also shapes the words that bring healing and peace. Only God's Spirit can teach us to love God above all and our neighbors as ourselves—not merely in deeds but also with words.

Lord's Day 44

MY HEART'S DESIRE

***Q** What is God's will for you in the tenth commandment?*

***A** That not even the slightest thought or desire contrary to any one of God's commandments should ever arise in my heart. Rather, with all my heart I should always hate sin and take pleasure in whatever is right.*

—Q & A 113

Two Versions of the Tenth.

The tenth commandment, according to Exodus 20:17, reads, "You shall not covet your neighbor's house. You shall not covet your neighbor's wife, or his manservant or maidservant, his ox or donkey, or anything that belongs to your neighbor." But the reading in Deuteronomy 5:21 is slightly different: "You shall not covet your neighbor's wife. You shall not set your desire on your neighbor's house or land, his manservant or maidservant, his ox or donkey, or anything that belongs to your neighbor."

Three differences between the two texts deserve our attention: (1) The neighbor's wife is part of his household in Exodus, but she is mentioned separately in Deuteronomy. (2) A piece of real estate—"land" (or "field" or "acreage")—is inserted in the Deuteronomy version. (3) Exodus has "you shall not covet" twice, but Deuteronomy uses *covet* once and says the second time, "you shall not set your desire on"—a more inward and not-yet-malicious kind of wishing.

We should also observe that the Roman Catholic and Lutheran traditions make two commandments out of the tenth, while they combine what we call the first and the second. The only reason for splitting the tenth was, apparently, to reach the number ten.

The Original Reading.

It is not possible to answer the inevitable question How did the original tenth commandment read on the tablet of stone as "inscribed by the finger of God"? (Ex. 31:18).

Bible scholars suggest that the original and shortest form of the tenth commandment might have consisted of the words that the Exodus and Deuteronomy versions have in common: *You shall not covet anything that belongs to your neighbor.*

The Original Meaning.

Even more difficult is the question whether the original meaning of the tenth commandment had anything to do with *sinful intentions* or if it is consistent with the other nine and deals with *observable acts*. The commandments formed the constitution of a covenanted society of God's people. As such they regulated behavior with respect to God and neighbors. But did the tenth commandment alone address sinful desires *inside* the person?

Sometimes the word *covet* stands for more than a hidden intention in a person's heart: in Exodus 34:23-24 God says that the men of Israel must appear before him at a central place three times a year. And God promises, "No one will covet your land when you go up three times each year to appear before the Lord your God." The word *covet* should probably be translated here as "lay a hand on" or "stretch out the hand to (acquire)." Perhaps that should be the translation of the tenth commandment (J.L. Koole, *De Tien Geboden*). If so, this commandment actually addressed a visible threat against the safety of a neighbor's property.

From Sinai to Heidelberg.

When one tries to imagine the setting of the tenth commandment in the Sinai covenant, a big gulf seems to appear between, on the one hand, the commandment as it was (probably) first understood by Israel at Sinai and, on the other, the catechism's interpretation—that God here forbids every desire that is contrary to his law.

Yet other considerations would make the catechism's interpretation a proper approach to the tenth commandment.

First, it is obvious that, besides outer behavior, the Old Covenant also addresses the inner world of desires and longings that have not become deeds. For one poignant and profound example, one ought to read once again the description of the first sin. Eve went from observation to temptation to attraction and desire to the psychologically inevitable deed: "She took some and ate it," (Gen. 3:4-7). Second, the New Testament understands God, in the tenth commandment, to forbid sinful desire: "I would not have known what sin was except through the law. For I would not have known what coveting really was if the law had not said 'Do not covet'" (Rom. 7:7). The word *covet* here means "having sinful desires."

Give Him Your Heart.

Throughout the Bible God teaches us that righteousness is much more than outward behavior and that sin has its seat in our hearts.

Jesus taught that ceremonial cleanliness and outward correctness could not make us pure: "For out of the heart come evil thoughts, murder, adultery, sexual immorality, theft, false testimony, slander" (Matt. 15:19). Therefore we need a new heart. James says that sins are born from evil desires that drag us down (1:14-15). And the sinful cravings of which John speaks (1 John 2:15-17) are exactly those desires that are against the commandments of God and that the catechism links to the tenth commandment. These lusts constitute a below-the-surface layer of humanity's sinful rebellion against the holy will of the holy God: "For everything in the world—the cravings of sinful man, the lust of his eyes and the boasting of what he has and does—comes not from the Father but from the world." In 1 John this "lust" is contrasted with "love." The former is a quality of the world, the latter the supreme attribute and gift of God. Lust is selfish and endlessly hungry. Love is self-giving and born from God's generosity.

In the tenth commandment God demands the transformation of our deeply human and deeply sinful desires. And he alone can give what he demands.

Heart Transplant.

God condemns our evil desires. He himself wants to be the desire of our hearts, and he wants to teach us to love our neighbors as naturally as we love ourselves.

Buddhism says that the source of all human sorrow is in our desires. If our existence could be disengaged from these suctions and attachments, says the Buddhist, we would float into blessed nothingness. But Christianity considers desire to be evidence of life; Christians maintain that created life is good. Eternal life is not a "blessed nothingness" but an intensified kind of living. The Bible honors life, work, and ambition, and God expects all people to fulfill a cultural mandate in his world. Law and gospel do not aim at stifling but at developing human life.

It's not desires but evil that the Bible opposes. Evil desires are the hidden seeds and buds of evil actions. And we all have evil desires: God condemns sin not only as an act but also as a human condition. Therefore we, the children of Adam and Eve, are under the curse for being what we are.

Our sinfulness is total. For us, it is possible to desire the body of a person without regard for that person. We, who are sinners, can desire the goods and resources of people without caring for the people themselves. We, who are sinners, can desire God's world and even God's heaven without God. Our total sinfulness and our need for total deliverance are nowhere clearer than when we face God in the tenth commandment. And here, as nowhere else, we learn to beg for a new heart and a new desire.

Hidden Persuaders.

Especially since the 1920s and the beginnings of psychoanalysis, Western countries have given much attention to the desires, fears, and cravings in our subconscious life. Human beings are now regarded as pots full of unruly longings and appetites. We now believe that our desires tend to govern us, instead of reason ruling them, as the classics taught. The question is now whether we make *any* rational decisions. Who can analyze human motivations?

Those who are most eager to discover people's motivators are the ones who have a product to sell or a service to render. They do not do their jobs because they have humanity's true interests at heart. (See *Hidden Persuaders* by Vance Packard.) Such people are leading us by forces that are skillfully maneuvered. They have refined advertising to effectively pour fuel on the flames that burn high or low in every heart. We are being used without knowing it. Our "needs" are first created and next "fulfilled." In fact, all the existential concepts of need, satisfaction, and happiness are being spelled out for us by our culture's mass message, which is devoted to make-believe (says Malcolm Muggeridge). Without any concern or courtesy our advertisers play on our hidden weaknesses and secret desires to make us fall. And our governments are deeply involved in the gambling business to promote, they say, the "happiness" of the citizens of the land.

The Discipline of Desire.

More than ever, the covenant community must set priorities to ward off deception. "Martha, Martha . . . you are worried and upset about many things, but only one thing is needed" (Luke 10:41-42). We have only one really existential need, namely, that we be taught by Jesus. If we heartily believe that, life immediately becomes simpler and happier.

"Seek first [the Father's] kingdom and his righteousness, and all these things [other things we 'need'] will be given to you as well" (Matt. 6:33). If we order our lives by this rule, it will not be so hard to know where the limits and the boundaries are.

Whatever the age of depth psychology and hidden persuasion has done and undone, it has confirmed the biblical teaching that evil is inside us. Ever since Pelagius a broad stream of Christian teaching has optimistically denied our bondage to sin and declared our freedom to do good. But today "free will" sounds less convincing to everybody. And the Christians in the Pauline and Augustinian traditions are reconfirmed in their conviction that a new heart, a new desire, and a new power are the only hope for change.

If anybody expects to sit under the teaching of God's law without being condemned, the tenth commandment will change his or her mind. "You have set our iniquities before you, our secret sins in the light of your presence" (Ps. 90:8).

But the teaching of the law not only convinces us of sin; it spells out the rule of gratitude. "Thanks-living" involves our wills, but only after they have been set free to want what God wants. The new life grows out of the new principle implanted by the Spirit of God. It consists of a conscious refusal to be conformed "to the pattern of this world" and a deliberate effort to be "transformed by the renewing of" our minds (Rom. 12:2).

Even in our culture, in which our selfish and sinful desires are constantly tickled, it is possible "to work out your salvation with fear and trembling" precisely because "it is God who works in you to will and to act according to his good purpose" (Phil. 2:12-13). Not only actions but also desires and thoughts are now under the Redeemer's control: "whatever is true, whatever is noble, whatever is right . . . pure . . . lovely . . . admirable . . . excellent or praiseworthy"—we learn to "think about such things" (Phil. 4:8). We "take pleasure in whatever is right" (says the catechism).

Evaluation.

Having thought deeply about the will of God as expressed in the Ten Commandments, we ask ourselves if a converted person can keep the law. A converted person is a changed person; we are not asking if "anybody" can keep the law. So the catechism asks if converted people, whose desire is to please God, can "obey these commandments perfectly."

And the answer is no. If the question had been "Can converted people obey God?" the answer should have been yes. But their obedience is not going to be *perfect*. So in this answer we do not deny that the children of God love and obey the Lord, but we oppose the idea that they do so "perfectly."

***Q** But can those converted to God obey these commandments perfectly?*

***A** No. In this life even the holiest have only a small beginning of this obedience. Nevertheless, with all seriousness of purpose, they do begin to live according to all, not only some, of God's commandments.*

—Q & A 114

Imperfection.

Roman Catholics used to ascribe perfection to some of their "saints." But to us the idea that certain believers have been or will be perfect is even better known through the holiness movement. Some saints (speaking now in the biblical sense—people who are washed by the blood, sealed by the Spirit, and devoted to the Father) claim powerful enough "anointing by the Spirit" to finally get beyond the power of sin and the habit of sinning.

Belief in such perfectionism is related to our concept of sin. If we have a shallow idea of sin, we will have an optimistic view of people's ability to reach perfection. If we define sin exclusively as immorality and breaking God's rules, some spiritual athletes will reach the point where they are "sinless." But if we understand sin not only as a moral failure but also as spiritual bondage, alienation from God, and the reason for our transitoriness, people will believe that perfection is possible only after this life—as the Reformed tradition has stressed.

A most dangerous tendency in the Pentecostal holiness movement is that people begin to regard Jesus merely as a stepping stone to a higher life: "the life in the Spirit." And they imagine that once they have reached that mode of living, they need neither the teaching of the law nor the forgiveness of the gospel. We therefore ought to remind each other that anyone who thinks he or she can live without the cleansing blood of the Savior, for a day or for an hour, is lost.

The Sins in Our House.

I agree with the teaching of Q & A 114, but I am also very unhappy with the popular results that this no to perfectionism has had for the practice of Christian piety in Reformed churches. Popular practice has said, Since the *holiest* of Christian people have only a small beginning of obedience, what can you expect of poor me? People have been quick to take comfort from this catechism answer. And they know the text on which this answer is based. They use it as the supreme excuse for our failures: "What I want to do I do not do, but what I hate I do" (Rom. 7:15).

Undoubtedly, the thrust of Q & A 114 reflects the catechism authors' understanding of Romans 7. It seems likely to me that the expression "the holiest [of persons]" (a strange phrase for a document that is not inclined to talk in terms of people being holy, holier, and holiest) comes from a reading of Romans 7. To the Reformers, Paul was the holiest of persons. Yet, to the Reformers, Paul seemed to be excusing himself; he still did what he did not want to do and was still doing what he hated to do. But was their interpretation of Romans 7:14-24 correct? When Paul talks of the "I" in this passage, does he mean that he, the Christian, Spirit-possessed Paul, still does, willy-nilly, what the "flesh" wants? According to a growing number of Reformed scholars, this "excuse" interpretation of Romans 7 misunderstands Paul's teaching. And I am convinced that it makes no sense—in view of the great context of these verses—to say that the "I" of the Christian Paul was still impotent to do good. That would be the opposite of what he himself taught (Rom. 6-8) and contrary also to his personal testimony (Gal. 2:19-20).

Yet some teachers and preachers in the Reformed tradition appear to have taken this alleged teaching of spiritual impotence as their point of departure: they teach forgiveness upon confession of sins; then the law to show what is right; then our failure to do what is right, followed by the confession of failure; forgiveness of sins by the blood of the cross; and so on and so on. The whole cycle has an appearance of truth, but it is a gospel without liberation and a forgiveness without renewal. It's not according to Jesus, Paul, or the catechism.

Better Formulation Needed.

The catechism does teach that Christians can do good: by his Holy Spirit, Christ has made me "wholeheartedly ready and willing . . . to live for him" (Q & A 1). "It is impossible for those grafted into Christ by true faith not to produce fruits of gratitude" (Q & A 64). *Not* doing good is impossible for a believer!

We need a new formulation of Q & A 114 that says very clearly that, yes, converted people love God and their neighbors and that, no, their obedience is not perfect.

Preaching Law.

The catechism's assumption that God wants the Ten Commandments preached and that preachers have to do it "pointedly" (in a way that hits home) is not shared by all Christian traditions. The catechism reflects a typical Calvinistic emphasis. We believe that God wants the law preached because faith is not true without obedience. Calling Jesus Lord but failing to obey the will of the Father excludes people from the kingdom (Matt. 7:21). The best way to prove our love for God is by obeying his commands (John 14:15).

The Ten Commandments are often called the moral law, in distinction from the ceremonial and the civil laws that God gave under the Old Covenant. Sometimes we, our theologians, or our confessions put too much stock in this threefold division—which is not used in the Bible. It is enough to say that law, as an expression of God's will for his creatures, will never be abolished or altered but must be fulfilled. The high goal of the saving work of Jesus and the descent of the Spirit is to mold a holy people that meets the righteous requirements of the law (Rom. 8:4)! And therefore instruction in the law is an integral part of the education program of God's people.

Q No one in this life can obey the Ten Commandments perfectly: why then does God want them preached so pointedly?

A First, so that the longer we live the more we may come to know our sinfulness and the more eagerly look to Christ for forgiveness of sins and righteousness. Second, so that, while praying to God for the grace of the Holy Spirit, we may never stop striving to be renewed more and more after God's image, until after this life we reach our goal: perfection.

—Q & A 115

The First Benefit.

The first benefit Christians derive from the preaching of the law, according to the catechism, is an increased awareness of their own shortcomings and a renewed eagerness for the forgiveness and righteousness of Christ.

This benefit was often mentioned by Augustine (A.D. 354-430) and quoted by Calvin (see *Institutes,* II, vii, 9).

It is very necessary, however, that in sermons or instructional materials the church understand and teach the law as the law of love and the rule of the family of God. We do not learn to obey the law outside of Christ and then, overwhelmed by our inabilities, flee for Christ's merits as murderers flee to a city of refuge. Rather, as our Father's adopted sons and daughters, we have the Spirit in us and our Savior and Teacher for us.

We may not make the commandments less demanding than they are. Nothing less than holiness is required of us, for God is holy. And unless our righteousness exceeds that of the Pharisees (that means, unless we have learned to love better than they did), we have no part in the kingdom (Matt. 5:20). At the same time, the disciples of Jesus should be able to understand why their master's yoke is easy and his burden light (Matt. 11:30). The labor of love is never hard, even if it demands our all.

Nevertheless, the catechism is right: continued instruction in the perfect will of God for our holiness and perfection keeps us humble before God and totally dependent on Christ.

Never Stop Striving to Be Renewed.

The second benefit of law study and law preaching, says the catechism, is progress toward our goal, which is perfection.

Spiritual laziness is a more common sin among God's people than immorality. Most of us hate immoral behavior and try to live decent lives. But though most of us do little evil, we don't do much good. We believe in Jesus and the Bible, but too many of us have stopped "striving to be renewed more and more after God's image." Yet it is *good desire,* such as hungering and thirsting after righteousness (Matt. 5:6) and *craving for pure spiritual milk* (1 Pet. 2:2), that is the evidence of being spiritually alive.

John Calvin recommends the study of the law to get the "listless flesh" into action: "The law is to the flesh like the whip to the idle and balky ass, to arouse it to work. Even for a spiritual man, not yet free of the weight of the flesh, the law remains a constant sting that will not let him stand still" (*Institutes* II, vii, 12).

The only way we can overcome the bad desires condemned in the tenth commandment is by a flame of good desires, lit in us by the Spirit of God. It's exactly at this point, while speaking of ongoing renewal, that the catechism mentions "praying to God for the grace of the Holy Spirit." Thereby we are being prepared for the final section of the catechism, which explains prayer (Lord's Days 45-52).

Until We Reach Our Goal.

Our goal is to become like Jesus. To be like Jesus is to have "true righteousness and holiness" (Eph. 4:24), a spirit of obedience to God and service to humanity (Phil. 2:5-11), and mature knowledge of Christ (Eph. 4:14-15). It also means that we "are being transformed into his likeness with ever-increasing glory, which comes from the Lord, who is the Spirit" (2 Cor. 3:18). At the moment, we carry this divine glory in "jars of clay" (4:7), but we nevertheless possess it in "ever-increasing" measure. We get more from God and less out of ourselves. Finally we will reach the resurrection, and "when [Jesus] appears, we shall be like him" (1 John 3:2): completely converted!

So keep the goal in mind: "I press on toward the goal to win the prize for which God has called me" (Phil. 3:14). It was by grace that he called us. But we must "win" the prize.

Lord's Day 45

TEACH US TO PRAY

Q ***Why do Christians need to pray?***

A ***Because prayer is the most important part of the thankfulness God requires of us. And also because God gives his grace and Holy Spirit only to those who pray continually and groan inwardly, asking God for these gifts and thanking him for them.***

—Q & A 116

Sermons on Prayer?

Prayer is something that must be done, not talked about. Religious people are in danger of talking about prayer more than they pray. The church even sings about prayer: "Sweet hour of prayer." God forbid that we should spend more time singing and writing about prayer than we spend in actual prayer to God.

Yet prayer must be taught. One of the main tasks of a rabbi is to teach his followers how to pray. John the Baptizer taught his disciples how to pray (Luke 11:1). And Jesus taught his followers the "path of prayer" by word and deed. Therefore the church teaches us through the catechism *why, how,* and *what* we should pray.

When to Pray.

Lord's Day 45 of the catechism does not, however, discuss *when* we should pray. Some Christian traditions maintain rigorous schedules of prayer (as do the Jews and Muslims). Christians in the Reformed tradition have long-established customs of personal and family prayer at mealtimes and when retiring for the night. But outside of the official services for prayer and worship on the Lord's day, Reformed and Presbyterian churches have no prescribed prayer times.

Prayer can be done at any place and at any time, we say. But experience teaches that things that can be done at any time tend to be done at no time.

Therefore the church would do well to revive the ancient traditions of prayer at mornings ("matins") and evenings ("vespers") of stated days, in addition to Sundays. The tradition of liturgical prayers in branches of the Christian church other than the Reformed contains riches that we should covet.

As for personal prayer times, the people of God under the Old Covenant would pray three times a day (Ps. 55:17; Dan. 6:10). And we, "on whom the fulfillment of the ages has come" (1 Cor. 10:11), can do no less.

Continual Prayer.

Our Reformed ancestors omitted special calls to prayer meetings not because they wanted to pray less but because they wanted to pray more. In the New Testament we are called to "pray without ceasing" or to "pray continually" (1 Thess. 5:17) and to "give thanks in all circumstances" (v. 18). Paul speaks about his own practice of constant prayer and thanksgiving (1

Thess. 1:2; 2:13; Rom. 1:9-10). He expects other Christians to be "faithful in prayer" (Rom. 12:12) and to "always keep on praying for all the saints" (Eph. 6:18), and he gives this counsel: "devote yourselves to prayer" (Col. 4:2).

By "continual prayer" the Bible means that we should live in such communion with God that prayer, spoken or unspoken, is always easy and natural. But such a life of prayer, which is commanded throughout the New Testament and is not unknown in the Old (Neh. 2:4), does not imply that the Christian community should not have set times for prayer. Every person and the church, as a whole, need the discipline of set times in order to guard the lifeline.

Why We Pray.

Christians need to pray for three reasons, says the catechism: because God wants it, because prayer is the best of our good works, and because God's gifts can be had only by way of prayer. In other words, prayer is a required response, a love response, and an essential response to our heavenly Father.

A Required Response.

Every cry is not yet a prayer. The sailor who fell overboard hollered, "God, help!" but his hand found a rope while he was falling. So he added, "No, it's all right; I got the rope." Every human being, at one time or another, hurls a "Help!" to the skies. But that is not necessarily a Christian prayer.

Neither is meditation or stillness a Christian prayer. Recently a Western unbeliever pleaded for the reinstatement of "prayer" as a way to health. In our society a person is surrounded by noisy demands to listen, to do, to buy, to attend, to join. Our senses are bombarded by hundreds of sensations. Therefore, said this non-Christian, each of us needs a closet or inner chamber for wholesome self-protection. This teacher made it clear that in such solitude we would not be talking to Someone Else in the beyond, that we have no such bridge. But he recommended "prayer" as a turning inward, which, he said, is wholesome, nonsuperstitious, and necessary.

Although such semi-religious writing tends to irritate us, we must read it with compassion. This author represents an age of scientifically trained children who have lost their Father.

Christians do not deny the need for silence and sanity. But when we speak about prayer, our thinking is exactly opposite this "listening to the true self" kind of thing. Christian prayer is first of all an answer. We don't hurl words to the vault of heaven; we give a humble and expected reply to the Voice that has addressed us first. In our prayers we resemble Samuel: first the Word said, "Samuel! Samuel!" Then Samuel said, "Speak, for your servant is listening" (1 Sam. 3:10). For us, too, prayer is answering, "Here am I, your servant; I answer to your Word." Prayer, therefore, is also thanksgiving. For in our black night in which millions are estranged from God and one another, the Word has become flesh and found us. And we respond, "Abba, I was lost, but I am found."

The Best of Good Works.

Prayer is *required* of us, says the catechism. We don't pray when we feel like it; we pray, first of all, because God expects us to do so. Prayer is obedience, and through prayer we learn to obey.

Prayer is also the *best* fruit of an obedient life—"the most important part of the thankfulness God requires of us." This is not easy to show from the Scriptures. Indeed, prayer rises to God like an offering of incense that pleases him (Ps. 141:1-2), and in seeking the Lord's face we follow God's own prodding in our hearts (Ps. 27:8). In Revelation 8:1-4 the prayers of the saints are presented to God as an offering to which incense is added, signifying the Spirit's purification. These prayers rise to God during the awesome silence of "about half an hour." Thus Revelation 8 underlines the importance of the prayers of God's servants—not exactly as a show of gratitude, but as fulfilling their role in God's coming to judge and to save.

Yet I would agree that prayer is "the most important part of gratitude" because it is the most direct way in which we pour out our love and adoration for the God who redeemed us. Offering him our love is the fulfillment of all that God requires of us. It's worth more to him than any amount of money or service. He wants *us* as living sacrifices (Rom. 12:1). Don't just give him some thing; give him your self.

But then prayer passes from petition to praise, from the stage where we stand before God as beggars to the point where we become givers. Even then, though, we give what we first received. In that sense we can say that prayer is the most important part of the thankfulness God requires of us.

Ask, Seek, Knock.

Finally, we must pray, says the catechism, because we will receive only when we ask.

God is sovereign. He is "free." No power outside of him can force him to do or to refrain. Nobody, therefore, can "make him" give anything. Yet he has ordained that we pray before we can receive. When we ask in faith, he will give, when we seek, we shall find, and when we knock, he will open the door (Matt. 7:7-8). When we lack, the most logical explanation is that we did not ask. "If any of you lacks wisdom, he should ask God" (James 1:5). Far too often the simple truth is that "you do not have, because you do not ask God" (James 4:2). Many people are pleading their inability to resist temptation, but they have never asked for the power to resist. They don't have a steady faith and the ability to cheer people, but they have never asked for these gifts. They cannot speak of Christ, they say, and they cannot serve in a church office, but they have not asked. We do not have unless we ask.

We must unceasingly beg for the favor and the grace of God, even for the Holy Spirit himself, because none of us is *entitled* to any of God's gifts. But God *is* gracious. Our prayers don't collect earnings, yet prayer is the avenue through which we go to receive what he promised.

God's Word and the experience of Christians show that unless we ask continually, we no longer receive. Unless we groan inwardly (because all that is in us is craving for God), we no longer find him. When we knock, he opens, but when we get too tired or too lazy to keep knocking on heaven's gates, we no longer have access to his treasures.

How to Pray.

Having taught us *why* we should pray, the catechism instructs us in the "how"—the way by which we should approach the throne of God. Three things are necessary: (1) we must pray to the God of the Bible, (2) we must do so with honesty and humility, and (3) we must do so in Jesus' name. In other words, when we pray to God, we should have knowledge of God, of self, and of the Mediator.

The God of the Bible.

Prayer and Bible reading must be connected. When, during our "devotions," we read a Bible passage that speaks of God's holiness and then pray for sunshine at the picnic and happiness for our niece who is getting married, our prayers have not responded to the message. Happy are those who are trained in their youth to connect Bible reading and prayer. And none are too old to learn how to respond in prayer and thanksgiving to the reading of the Word.

Apart from a particular response to a particular Scripture reading, all praying must reflect the knowledge of the God revealed in the Scriptures. Asking for his help in committing a felony makes no sense. Neither will God bless us while we live in defiance of his will. When praying, our words and lives must show that we know to whom we are speaking.

***Q** How does God want us to pray so that he will listen to us?*

***A** First, we must pray from the heart to no other than the one true God, who has revealed himself in his Word, asking for everything he has commanded us to ask for. Second, we must acknowledge our need and misery, hiding nothing, and humble ourselves in his majestic presence. Third, we must rest on this unshakable foundation: even though we do not deserve it, God will surely listen to our prayer because of Christ our Lord. That is what he promised us in his Word.*

—Q & A 117

Know Your God.

Those who rob and murder their neighbors should not appear before God and lift up bloody hands in prayer, for God will hide his face (Isa. 1:15). And we should not expect forgiveness from God while we ourselves refuse to forgive others (Matt. 18:23-35). Neither does it make sense to ask riches of the God who tells us that "it is easier for a camel to go through the eye of a needle" than for a rich man to enter God's kingdom (Matt. 19:24). Even children know of certain things their parents will not give them. "No use asking him," they say of their dad, because they know that in their dad's opinion the thing they want is no good for them. And in the same way we ought to know our heavenly Father. "Do not be foolish, but understand what the Lord's will is" (Eph. 5:17).

We should know not only what he will not give but also what he longs to give. "If we ask anything according to his will, he hears us" (1 John 5:14). His will is to make us like Jesus and to give us the Spirit. Sooner would an earthly father give his child a snake for a fish or a scorpion for an egg than would our heavenly Father withhold the Holy Spirit from those who ask (Luke 11:11-13).

Although to pray is to ask, prayer is not a means of *getting* what we want; it is a means of *becoming* what God wants us to be.

And Know Yourself.

"Do not be quick with your mouth, do not be hasty in your heart to utter anything before God. God is in heaven and you are on earth, so let your words be few" (Eccles. 5:2). This Old Testament sense of reverence for the Holy One and our awareness of our own puniness may not evaporate when the Spirit testifies with our spirit that we are children of God (Rom. 8:16). What it means to be children of God we must not learn by looking around at average North American daddies and their sassy broods but by looking at the Son, whose Spirit we have received. Jesus also is the One who teaches us how to pray not so that we can turn stones into bread (Matt. 4:3) or avoid the cup that must be drunk (Matt. 26:42) but so that we may glorify the Father's name (John 12:27-28).

Know the Mediator.

When we pray, we must not only know who God is and who we are, but we must also know Jesus, in whose name we pray.

Some people have complained that our church and our catechism make Christian living too complicated. Even when we talk about prayer, they say, we must "know" one and two and three things before we can pray rightly. But praying is like what some people say about looking for a job: "It does not matter *what* you know; it all depends on *whom* you know." So it is with access to the Father who is in heaven. All depends on knowing Jesus: "You may ask me for anything in my name, and I will do it" (John 14:14).

***Q** What did God command us to pray for?*

***A** Everything we need, spiritually and physically, as embraced in the prayer Christ our Lord himself taught us.*

—Q & A 118

Needs and Wants.

Worldly-minded people and success-and-sensation-oriented preachers have done much damage with these words of Jesus: "Ask me for anything in my name, and I will do it." The catechism is wiser. Having said *how* we should pray (with true knowledge of God, of self, of Jesus), it asks, For *what* are we going to pray? And its answer speaks of needs for which God will provide. All of us must distinguish between our needs and our wants. The Lord teaches us to pray for all our *needs*, not *wants*.

Our society has reduced us to "consumers." By fulfilling our consumer wishes, they who manipulate us create new "needs" and higher demands. It is a vicious circle of never-ending greed. And we must not tie prayer into that process somewhere, or we might get prayer meetings to ask for the prize in the tournament and the jackpot in the sweepstakes.

Knowing One's Needs.

Having distinguished between needs and wants, we must learn one more important thing: most of us don't know what we need. Unless we are trained in God's school, we have very little insight into our own basic needs. But there is One who knows exactly what we need: "Your Father knows what you need before you ask him" (Matt. 6:8). This does not mean that you don't have to tell him, but it does mean that you cannot lead him astray. God knows our needs before we ask and in spite of what we ask. He keeps his eye on my sore spot, and he is not going to be confused by whatever I tell him. He knows! There is great comfort in that knowledge.

Once some people brought to Jesus a paralytic: a person who could not get up for his most natural needs and wants. When he was lying there, at the feet of Jesus, his real needs were evident to everyone, we would think. That man needed healing! Then Jesus said, "Son, your sins are forgiven" (Mark 2:5). And thereby Christ identified and provided for the man's deepest need.

Learning to live is learning our needs. When we ask, as that disciple did,

"Lord, teach us to pray" (Luke 11:1), we are also saying, "Lord, teach us our needs."

Father Knows Our Needs.

We do not tell God our needs in order to inform him of something he does not know. Our heavenly Father knows, and he cares. But he wants us to tell him. He also wants to hear if we perceive our real needs. For God is more interested in our salvation than we are.

When the Lord does not seem to answer, we should not conclude that God has turned against us. He knows our needs more thoroughly than we do.

The church in Laodicea, to whom Christ writes a letter through John the seer on Patmos, does not perceive its needs. The Lord says, "You say, 'I am rich. . . .' But you do not realize that you are wretched, pitiful, poor, blind and naked." Then the Lord tells them that they should buy eye salve from him (Rev. 3:14-22). In other words, he is saying, "You need me!" Our need is God, and it is not for anything that comes from him but for him himself.

Ultimately, prayer is not a search for things but for communion. Closer to God we cannot come than when, in our sighing for him, we taste his sorrow for us. And, in our seeking for him, we meet God seeking us.

Answered prayer is established communion. We are led to that communion by means of the Lord's Prayer, which asks for the fulfillment of "everything we need, spiritually and physically."

Luke 11:2-4.

The Lord's Prayer, as we call it because the Lord taught it to us, is also recorded by Luke, but in briefer form: "Father, hallowed be your name, your kingdom come. Give us each day our daily bread. Forgive us our sins, for we also forgive everyone who sins against us. And lead us not into temptation" (Luke 11:2-4).

Q *What is this prayer?*

A ***Our Father in heaven, hallowed be your name, your kingdom come, your will be done on earth as it is in heaven. Give us today our daily bread. Forgive us our debts, as we also have forgiven our debtors. And lead us not into temptation, but deliver us from the evil one [for yours is the kingdom and the power and the glory forever. Amen.]—taken from Matthew 6:9-13.***

—Q & A 119

The Text of the Lord's Prayer.

Everyone knows Matthew's version of this prayer. It is instructive, however, to compare these lines with the version in Luke. Matthew's version seems more Jewish: it uses "who lives in heaven" as a further (Jewish) designation of God. The petitions "hallowed be your name, your kingdom come," which ask for the inauguration of God's kingdom on earth, are made explicit and contemporary by Matthew's addition: "your will be done on earth as it is in heaven." "Debts" in Matthew is a somewhat different image than "sins" in Luke. Luke does not have "but deliver us from evil," which is an ambiguous phrase that might also mean "the evil one."

The differences between the two versions of the Lord's Prayer are doctored up in all later manuscripts. The doxology (for yours is the kingdom . . .) is not original but was a congregational response to the prayer, written into the text later by someone who copied Matthew's manuscript.

This textual variation has a warning for us: many Christians have an almost magical idea about the words and letters of the Bible. The Bible itself is much less slavish. Bible stories differ when they are told by different evangelists. And we cannot even say what the precise words of Jesus are in such "formularies" as the Lord's Prayer and the institution of the Lord's Supper. The content is more important than the form. The message is more important than the words. Of course, words and content cannot be separated. But God has left us no doubt about the content, while he gave enough variety in the words to warn us against the superstitious adoration of the form.

No Incantation but Model Prayer.

"This . . . is how you should pray," said the Master (Matt. 6:9). Notice that he said "this is how," not "this is what." He taught us the manner in which our prayer lives should be shaped. He did not teach us an incantation (*Paternoster*) to be repeated for sound effect.

Christ gave his disciples a model, or example, to be followed. An architect shows us a model house not so that we may live in it; he or she is telling us, rather, that this is the kind of house to be constructed.

Thus our prayers should show confidence ("Our Father") and should be concerned with the rule of God over the whole world. If we can pray this way with our hearts and lives, we are followers of Jesus. When our concerns are God's name, rule, and will, we may, as kingdom soldiers, also ask for daily supplies ("bread"), forgiveness, and help in temptation.

The construction of the prayer, especially in Matthew, is beautiful and meaningful. The first three petitions concern the rule of God, and they are climactically arranged: the Father's name will be adored when the kingdom has come, and the kingdom has come when God's will is done on earth as it is already done in heaven. And in the last three petitions we, Christ's followers, trust that God will supply our needs, physical and spiritual, and uphold us in the hour of trial with his strength, which is greater than that of the evil one.

Lord's Day 46

THE ADDRESS OF OUR PRAYERS

***Q** Why did Christ command us to call God "our Father"?*

***A** At the very beginning of our prayer Christ wants to kindle in us what is basic to our prayer—the childlike awe and trust that God through Christ has become our Father. Our fathers do not refuse us the things of this life; God our Father will even less refuse to give us what we ask in faith.*

—Q & A 120

***Q** Why the words "in heaven"?*

***A** These words teach us not to think of God's heavenly majesty as something earthly, and to expect everything for body and soul from his almighty power.*

—Q & A 121

Lines to the Beyond.

Christians believe that prayer makes sense. We are convinced that men and women and girls and boys can talk to "Someone 'way beyond the blue" in a simple activity called prayer. We believe that our words go beyond the ceiling and reach the One to whom they are addressed: our Father in heaven.

There was a time when practically everyone on the globe believed that people could communicate with a deity, as long as one knew that god's address. And nearly all members of the human family were convinced that all of us were always being watched by Someone in the sky. But today, on our continent at least, millions believe only in what has been checked and double-checked by the scientific method. We have found no scientific evidence that lines of communication run from here to the beyond. Recently we have erected towers from which we send exploratory messages into space, hoping that, if there is life out there, we may someday get reply signals. But while this exploration intensifies and while rumors of unidentified flying objects are eagerly retold, people show ever-lessening confidence in the possibility of prayer.

Revealed.

Christians do not speculate about what the sounds of their prayers bounce against. But they do begin with the certainty that they have been addressed by the Other One, by God.

We agree that "no one has ever seen God" (John 1:18). As a matter of fact, no one can see him and live (Ex. 33:20). He himself lives "in unapproachable light" (1 Tim. 6:16). But Christ, the Son, who is himself God, "who is at the Father's side, has made him known" (John 1:18). And this eternal Word, in human flesh and blood, gathered a number of Jewish people as his disciples and taught them, "This . . . is how you should pray: 'Our Father in heaven . . .'" (Matt. 6:9). Or maybe he said, "When you pray, say: 'Father . . .'" (Luke 11:2). In the two thousand years since that time, millions have prayed as he taught, and they have had communion with God.

Only once do we read in Scripture that Jesus rejoiced. It happened when he saw people battling spiritually to subdue Satan's forces and to establish the lordship of our Father: "At that time Jesus, full of joy through the Holy Spirit, said, 'I praise you, Father, Lord of heaven and earth, because you have hidden these things from the wise and learned, and revealed them to little children. Yes, Father, for this was your good pleasure'" (Luke 10:21). Notice that in this joyful saying Jesus ascribes two activities to his Father: "you have hidden" and "revealed." It is because of God's action that some cannot know, and it is because of the Father's action that others do know. Prayer is the prerogative of those who know God and his kingdom. This kingdom is a great reality that remains hidden for others. Only God's children may have access to the Other World. And they, only they, may speak to the Father.

God's Children.

In one sense, Jesus alone is a child of God, because he is the "only [begotten] of the Father." In another sense, all human beings are God's children, because they are all "his offspring" (Acts 17:28). But in the most common biblical sense, only those who are "born again," or "born from above," are God's children (John 3:3). "Those who are led by the Spirit of God are sons of God" (Rom. 8:14). Having God's Spirit is crucial: "The Spirit himself testifies with our spirit that we are God's children" (Rom. 8:16).

We should not be quick to judge, however, who is and who is not a child of God. It takes Jesus to see that some religious leaders are really children of the devil (John 8:44), but that insight is seldom given to us.

And let's not forget that to know God as Father means that we know him as a forgiving Father. Those who (re)turn to him and cry, "Father, I have sinned. . . . I am [not] worthy to be called your son," are embraced as is the young man in the parable of the lost son (Luke 15:11-31). In the parable, the father says, "Quick! Bring the best robe and put it on him. Put a ring on his finger and sandals on his feet. . . . For this son of mine was dead and he is alive again; he was lost and is found." In other words, God keeps no slaves, and he has no stepchildren. The new robe and the ring and the sandals say, "you are my son, with all the happy privileges of sonship."

The right to enter God's throne room by prayer belongs to the children of the King. But these privileged ones don't form an elite group. We did not make God our Father; he made us his children. And to those who don't know the way we should give God's address without hesitation. We know that only those whom the Father has chosen will come to Jesus, but we also know that the Lord "will never drive away" (John 6:37) anyone who comes to him.

Christians don't have all the answers for the ills of human society. But they know the address of God. And they ask the world to kneel with them and say, "Our Father in heaven. . . ."

Childlike Trust.

Christ taught us to address God as our Father, says the catechism, because we should approach God with childlike confidence. We must trust that

"God our Father will even less refuse to give us what we ask in faith" than would earthly fathers.

The catechism's reasoning is taken from Luke 11, where Jesus says that earthly fathers, although they are "evil," give "good gifts" to their children. "How much more will your Father in heaven give the Holy Spirit to those who ask him!" (v. 13; Matt. 7:11). This "how much more" of the heavenly Father occurs also in Hebrews 12:7-11. Here the writer encourages us to submit to the discipline of God. Our "human fathers" disciplined us for a little while, he says, and "we respected them for it. How much more should we submit to the Father of our spirits and live!" The implications of the Hebrews passage are even wider than those of the Luke passage, because in Hebrews we are called to trust God when we are hurting: "No discipline seems pleasant at the time, but painful" (v. 11). If earthly fathers did their best and we did not lose trust, "how much more" should we trust the perfect Father, who "disciplines us for our good, that we may share in his holiness" (v. 10).

Lack of trust in our relationship to God insults our Father. And it causes ineffectual prayer: "He who doubts is like a wave of the sea, blown and tossed by the wind. That man should not think he will receive anything from the Lord" (James 1:6-7).

Respect for Father.

In its origin, *father* is a title used more widely than just for biological fatherhood. It is still used in a broad sense for spiritual leaders in certain religious traditions. A father deserves honor and respect. "If I am a father, where is the honor due me?" said the Lord when people gave him blemished sacrifices (Mal. 1:6).

"Childlike awe and trust" should go together, the catechism teaches. And when Christ taught us to say, "Our Father *in heaven,"* he taught us "not to think of God's heavenly majesty as something earthly," says the catechism.

Right Relationship.

Thus the term *Father* combines respect and intimacy. This is the relationship God desires to have with us. We may not approach him on other terms. He is not our employer or policeman or enemy or evil conscience but our Father.

In the story of the prodigal (Luke 15:11-31), the lost son comes home feeling unworthy, but the father insists on having a father-son relationship and no other. And the elder son, though he never ran away from home, is actually lost. He lives as a hireling and looks for his pay. He has stayed with his father day in, day out, but he is a stranger to his father's heart. He thinks that he is entitled to wages, and he destroys the father-son relationship. That's why the parable ends with the hint that the older son is lost.

Love and Power.

Confidence—faith, trust—and not merely respect, is the main idea conveyed by the words "in heaven." God is not only a loving Father but also a heavenly Father. We may "expect everything for body and soul from his almighty power." All earthly parents know the pain and frustration of being unable to do what they in their loving hearts would like to do for their children. But God combines a loving heart and almighty power. He is able to do what his love wants to do.

God is in heaven, and we are on the earth. We look like ants in God's sight. This perspective makes human arrogance laughable. As a matter of fact, "the One enthroned in heaven laughs" at the rebellion of the ants (Ps. 2:4). But having a *Father* in heaven is better than having an uncle in the White House or your mother as a governor. In God love and power are combined. Therefore we should pray and not doubt.

Earthly Children of the Heavenly Father.

Meanwhile, anyone who addresses the heavenly Father has to be concerned with her or his earthly family: "Anyone who does not love his brother, whom he has seen, cannot love God, whom he has not seen" (1 John 4:20). Since love must express itself in action, we can show it most easily and tangibly to those we meet. But if we refuse to make use of the obvious opportunities to express love to the visible children of the heavenly Father, we don't love the Father himself. "Whoever loves God must also love his brother" (v. 21).

Although the Father knows every one of his children personally, none of us has a personal or private Savior or Lord. God is the Father of his worldwide family, and Jesus is the head of the body. Anyone who approaches heaven has to acknowledge his or her ties on earth. They who come to the invisible God are members of the visible church of the redeemed. Nobody who wants to pray can bypass the family, because Jesus has taught us to say, "Our Father in heaven."

Lord's Day 47

PRAYING FOR GOD'S GLORY

Q *What does the first request mean?*

A **Hallowed be your name** *means, Help us to really know you, to bless, worship, and praise you for all your works and for all that shines forth from them: your almighty power, wisdom, kindness, justice, mercy, and truth. And it means, Help us to direct all our living—what we think, say, and do—so that your name will never be blasphemed because of us but always honored and praised.*

—Q & A 122

Priorities in Prayer.

If we learn to pray rightly, we will live fully. When we train in the art of prayer, we become better at the art of living.

Happy are those who had or have a mom or dad teaching them how to say their prayers. "Now I lay me down to sleep; I pray the Lord my soul to keep." Or "Jesus, tender Shepherd, hear me; bless thy little lamb tonight; through the darkness stay thou near me; keep me safe till morning light." Learning to say our prayers is an essential part of a Christian upbringing. But hundreds of thousands of our contemporaries never get beyond "saying the prayers" they learned from their parents. They and we need to be confronted by the Master, who teaches us not how to say our prayers but *how to pray.* We must learn to construct our prayers—all our prayers—after the model that Jesus taught. And his paradigm says that the first concern of the followers of Jesus is the glory of our Father's name. "What would you like best?" asks the Lord. "What shall I give you first? What would give you the greatest joy?" And we are supposed to answer, "Help us to really know you, to bless, worship, and praise you. . . . Help us to direct all our living . . . so that your name will never be blasphemed because of us but always honored and praised." We say, in other words, "Hallowed be your name."

In Our Own Words.

The Lord does not mean, of course, that we must begin all of our prayers by repeating the words he taught us. Of course not. But he says that we must learn to make his honor the first concern in our lives: when we want to thank for health or pray in sickness, the big thing is that credit and glory go to our heavenly Father. When we're looking for a job or considering an appointment, accepting a call or taking an assignment—the big thing is the glory of God's name. When there's a death in the family or a newborn baby, Jesus says, then you must be anxious that the Father's name be hallowed. For selfish and sinful people this new desire and prayer is an unnatural, even painful thing. But conversion never comes without pain. And the best evidence of conversion is a rearranged life in which God has the first place.

Meaning.

To hallow a name is to make it holy. The name we make holy is the Father name, for that is the name God used to reveal himself through Jesus. And that's how we should address him in prayer.

When we ask that his name be made holy, we don't mean that his name is not holy yet (for threefold holy is the Lord); we pray, rather, that his holiness receive recognition. We are working for name recognition. We want God to be known, honored, and praised for what he is.

This is a prayer for missions and evangelism, a petition "that all nations might believe and obey him," thus rendering honor to "the only wise God" (Rom. 16:26-27).

The prayer does not name those who should sanctify or glorify the name. The first three petitions read, literally translated, "Let be sanctified your name, let come your kingdom, let be done your will." The prayer assumes that God the Father will cause this to happen in the world and through us, without being dependent on us. When God answers this prayer, people who now dishonor and ignore the name are going to get hurt.

"I Will Glorify My Name."

About seven hundred years before the birth of Jesus the army of the king of Assyria laid siege to Jerusalem. Commander Sennacherib, the king who had subdued many nations (he brags about it in writings on a clay prism, now in the British Museum), scoffed at Hezekiah (the king of Judah) and his God. Sennacherib had a letter delivered to Hezekiah in which he said, "Do not let the god you depend on deceive you when he says, 'Jerusalem will not be handed over to the king of Assyria.'" Other gods, he said, were not able to stand against him either! Hezekiah took that letter to the temple "and spread it out before the Lord." Then he prayed, "Deliver us from his hand, so that all kingdoms on earth may know that you alone, O Lord, are God." In other words, "Hallowed be your name."

Through the prophet Isaiah, God answered Sennacherib: "Against whom have you raised your voice and lifted your eyes in pride? Against the Holy One of Israel!" And then the Lord took action: "That night the angel of the Lord went out and put to death a hundred and eighty-five thousand men in the Assyrian camp"—all because someone taunted God and another began to pray "Hallowed be your name" (the account is in 2 Kings 18-19 and Isaiah 36-37).

Who Is Boss?

When in a family a father has been disobeyed and sassed by the children, he must eventually rise and show that he is the father. And someone will get a spanking. When in this world people act impudently, sassing the God and Father of us all, the time will come that God will hit the table with his fist, so to speak. To that end we pray not only "Please, God, show who is Boss" ("Let the nations know they are but men," Ps. 9:20) but also, in New Testament language, "Make your Father name great!" We pray that we may see the conversion of a hundred and eighty-five thousand people to the glory of God, the Father of Jesus Christ.

Central Issue.

It should not surprise us that the glory of God has priority in the Lord's model prayer. God's honor is the beginning and the end, the goal of creation and salvation. His name is majestic in all the earth (Ps. 8:1, 9). Like a shepherd, he guides his people beside quiet waters and in paths of righteousness "for his name's sake" (Ps. 23:3). All things are "from him and through him and to him," and "to him be the glory forever" (Rom. 11:36). In the end, when the redemptive work of the Messiah is finished, the Son will give his mandate back to the Father "so that God may be all in all" (1 Cor. 15:28). Therefore, "whatever you do [including your prayers], do it all for the glory of God" (1 Cor. 10:31).

The first of the Ten Commandments requires that we worship God the Redeemer exclusively. And the first of the six requests in the Lord's Prayer asks that the Father's name be hallowed. Biblical religion is entirely God centered. Jesus' mission was to do the will of his Father (John 4:34), and he surrendered to death, praying "Father, glorify your name!" (John 12:28). Christ taught us the same God-directed life-style: "Seek first his kingdom" (Matt. 6:33).

Praying Thoughtfully.

Jesus taught his disciples this model prayer after he had warned them not to imitate the show of piety of the hypocrites or the mindless babblings of the pagans (Matt. 6:3-7). So it's a bitter irony that the Lord's own prayer has been used for centuries as a sort of magic incantation by the faithful who, by moving beads on a string, count the number of times they pray. Even some evangelical Christians insist that the Lord's Prayer be said in public schools and at civic events, where few have a mind to honor the name of God the Father. The Heidelberg Catechism thoughtfully analyzes what it means for us to ask that our Father's name be "hallowed." We might fault the catechism for not mentioning the worldwide missionary implications of this prayer (but it does so when it explains the next petition, "your kingdom come"). The catechism does say very clearly what we ask for our own lives when we pray this first request of the Lord's Prayer.

A Prayer Against Ignorance.

We cannot glorify God when we don't know him. People are busy with many—too many—names of stars, heroes, companies, countries, even churches. And they work hard for the glory of those names. But millions don't know the name that needs to be honored by all. When we say this first request of the Lord's Prayer, we pray against the prevailing ignorance of God's name. And if we pray with integrity, we ourselves will attempt to know God better and more intimately than before.

People who have no time for or interest in Bible study are not honest when they pray that God's name be honored. For the prayer means, "Help us to really know you."

Those who pray this with heart and mind stand committed to work for name recognition. They counteract the ignorance of God in heart and home and school and church and state and society.

Knowing God in All His Works.

We know God by two means, creation and Scripture. And the catechism wants us to learn to praise God for all his works. In all God's works his "almighty power, wisdom, kindness, justice, mercy, and truth" are visible to those who know his signature.

We glorify God's name when we praise his *power* in the vastness of the ocean and in the beauty of a crystal dewdrop.

Praying "hallowed be thy name" means learning to "bless, worship, and praise" the Father for his *wisdom* in the design of mountains and prairies and of the fingers of a child and even in the gift of the computer (which is exceeded only by the human brain).

We bless, worship, and praise our Father for his *kindness,* for it still exists in our sinful environment. We praise the Source of kindness every time we find some of his love in those around us.

For *justice and mercy and truth* we praise him! Not only do we see some traces of his virtues in the world, but also we have seen the place where justice and mercy embraced: our Savior's cross. We praise him for the truth of the gospel and for the unwavering fidelity of his covenant.

Open Eyes.

When we say, "Let your name be hallowed," we pray that all people's eyes (including our own) may be opened. God is everywhere, and his works praise him. But by nature people are blind to God's signs, handcraft, painting, sculpture, and writing. We are mute when it comes to praising him. And when we say, "Hallowed be your name," we ask, "Father, let the eyes be opened, let everyone now see what you have shown to us." "Help [me and all people] to really know you, to bless, worship, and praise you for all your works and for all that shines from them." The ignorance and the blindness must cease.

People are spiritually handicapped. That's why they cannot see and sing as they were intended to. But we have begun to pray for them. And when our prayers are answered, those people will bless the name of our God, which is written in the Book and in creation.

Those Who Bear the Name.

When Joshua had led Israel across the Jordan and the mighty walls of Jericho had fallen, the armies of Israel were stopped by the people of a small town named Ai. Israel was shamefully defeated, and thirty-six Israelites were killed. Then Joshua and the elders of Israel lay in the dust; they cried to God, and Joshua prayed, "O Lord, what can I say, now that Israel has been routed by its enemies? The Canaanites and the other people of the country will hear about this and they will surround us and wipe out our name from the earth. What then will you do for your own great name?" (Josh. 7:8-9).

Had Joshua lost his sense of proportion? He asked, "If the nations of Canaan succeed in wiping us out, what then, God, are you going to do for your name?"

No, Joshua was not confusing God's cause and Israel's cause, but he did know that God had tied his name to Israel. The glory of God was definitely connected with the glory of Israel. (As you know, the defeat at Ai occurred because Achan had stolen. First the sin had to be removed from the camp of Israel; then God could bless and use his people again.)

It has pleased God to choose a people to be his own. The behavior of this people can either bring glory or dishonor, praise or blasphemy, to the name of God. His chosen people was Israel under the Old Covenant; it was Jesus, as one person, in the fullness of time; and today his one holy catholic church is the people with whom he identifies. The church bears the Father's name. Christians can give God a good name or a bad name in the world. Just as a country's name is affected by the behavior of its citizens, just as a husband's name is honored or dishonored by the behavior of his wife, and just as a couple's name and honor are affected by the behavior of their children, so—and even more so—is God's Father name glorified or vilified by the behavior of *his* children.

The Tarnished Name.

Many times during Israel's existence as a covenant nation its people caused shame to God's name. Israel was the reason that "God's name [was] blasphemed among the Gentiles" or nations (Rom. 2:24; cf. Isa. 52:5, Ezek. 36:22).

The same thing may happen and does happen today through the lives and behavior of God's children who are named after Christ and who pray to their Father in heaven. Our divisions (a broken church in a broken world) do not give credit to the biblical teaching that there is one body and one Lord. By our behavior we seem to say that there are many different lords. When we fall into sin—sometimes an immorality "that does not occur even among pagans" (1 Cor. 5:1)—something about which even pagans would shake their heads, then the name is not hallowed but blasphemed. When well-known evangelists or lesser-known ministers show that they are slaves of the same old sins of greed and sexual pleasure to which our culture is in bondage, the great name is not honored but is blasphemed on our account.

Organized for God's Honor.

"Help us to direct all our living . . . so that your name will never be blasphemed because of us but always honored and praised," says the catechism.

The worst thing my life can be is an obstacle between anybody and God. And the best thing I can be is a stepping stone by which someone reaches the Father's house.

The catechism teaches that when we pray for God's honor, we must organize our lives (and that includes our thoughts and words) in such a way that the picture of the whole—like a vase of flowers— makes observers anxious to know him from whom we derive virtue and beauty, graciousness and courage.

Aimless or Directed.

The majority of people we know are not very goal oriented, unless their goal is to get rich or to pursue some other idolatry. Most people live from day to day, enjoying a diversity of opportunities, filling in time, knowing but never admitting that the end is in sight.

Christians are supposed to be quite different. They must have one overarching goal that influences the way they think, talk, and act. They want their lives to bring credit to the gospel, glory to their Father, credibility to Jesus. That's why every day they pray, Father, let your name be hallowed through me. Paul said it once as a personal testimony—"To live is Christ and to die is gain" (Phil. 1:21)—and once as advice to the church—"Whatever you do, do it all for the glory of God" (1 Cor. 10:31).

Soli Deo Gloria.

God's glory is the real goal of every day and every life. Being goal oriented requires discipline of thoughts, words, and actions, says the catechism. Nobody can serve God acceptably without this kind of God-glorifying self-discipline. And nobody can do what is required without the powerful Spirit of God: "Help us to direct our living—what we think, say, and do—so that your name will never be blasphemed because of us [because that would be the worst thing I could do] but always honored and praised."

In other words, write your name legibly in my life, Father, so that others can read and heed. May this day, this hour, my writing, my sermon, my sickness, my health, my going out and staying home, my money spending and money saving, everything and all of me, bring glory, Father, to your name.

Lord's Day 48

YOUR KINGDOM COME!

Q What does the second request mean?

A **Your kingdom come** *means, Rule us by your Word and Spirit in such a way that more and more we submit to you. Keep your church strong, and add to it. Destroy the devil's work; destroy every force which revolts against you and every conspiracy against your Word. Do this until your kingdom is so complete and perfect that in it you are all in all.*

—Q & A 123

The Kingdom.

The word *kingdom* must make us think of kingship or rule rather than of a territory. The prayer asks, Let your royal rule be real, here and now!

God's kingship must "come." We can ask for it to *come* only because it is not yet here. But is not God King? Certainly. God did not allow the devil to take over rulership of the cosmos when people sinned. "God is the Ruler yet," we sing. Psalm 97 begins with these words: "The Lord reigns"; it exhorts, "Let the earth be glad." Psalm 99 starts the same way: "The Lord reigns." Then it adds, "Let the nations tremble." We rejoice or tremble at his rule according to whose side we are on. But both sides must confess or admit that God is the sovereign: "The Lord has established his throne in heaven, and his kingdom rules over all" (Ps. 103:19).

When we speak in the Lord's Prayer of the Father's kingship, or rule, we are not talking about the Creator's sovereignty, which has existed from the beginning and will never cease. We *are* speaking of a heavenly rule of grace and fairness that is promised in the Old Testament and that John the Baptizer said was "near."

God's King, the Messiah.

In the Old Testament God ties the promise of his reign of peace to David's house and David's Son. The covenant with David ("Your house and your kingdom will endure forever," 2 Sam. 7:16) became the topic of prophecy, expectation, hope, and song. The kingship of David's Son would bring prosperity to the land, peace to the afflicted, and defeat for the oppressor; he would rule from sea to sea, and his reign would endure forever—as long as the sun (Ps. 72). God himself would say to David's Son, "Sit at my right hand until I make your enemies a footstool for your feet" (Ps. 110:1, which is more frequently quoted in the New Testament than any other psalm).

The good news of the New Testament is that the Messiah has come. This gospel, as told by Matthew, says, Here is Jesus, the Son of David (1:1), who had to suffer and die before he could enter his glory. But now he is on the throne: "All authority in heaven and on earth" has now been given to him. And he will subdue "all nations" by making them his disciples through the church (28:18-20).

The book of Acts is the story of what Messiah Jesus does from the throne. He sends divine power to the earth. He rules over his people by Word and Spirit. He extends his kingship from Jerusalem to Rome, the capital of the world. The unfinished story of the coming kingdom ends with these words: "Boldly and without hindrance [Paul] preached the kingdom of God and taught about the Lord Jesus Christ" (28:31).

Already and Not Yet.

Since Jesus has ascended to the throne, he holds kingship and power. "The kingdom of the world has become the kingdom of our Lord and of his Christ" (Rev. 11:15). The battle has been won. The devil's stranglehold has been broken. "The accuser of our brothers . . . has been hurled down" (Rev. 12:10). "The seventy-two returned with joy [from a preliminary operation by the members of the church, who are the children of the kingdom] and said, 'Lord, even the demons submit to us in your name.' [Jesus] replied, 'I saw Satan fall like lightning from heaven'" (Luke 10:17-18).

Christ's victory is complete, as the resurrection shows. The sacrifice was perfect, never to be repeated (Heb. 10:18). We may still be sinners, but we aren't slaves any longer (Rom. 6:10-14). Even if we look like sheep taken to the slaughterhouse, we identify with Jesus, and therefore we are "more than conquerors" (Rom. 8:36-37).

The battle has been won, but the war is not over yet. The new order has come, and the new values are becoming real for us here and now, but the old order still lingers. The church experiences the tension. We experience the new order when we gather around the communion table. But the next day we may meet around a grave. It has not yet been revealed that we are "more than conquerors." Our Lord is on the throne, but all his enemies are not yet "under his feet." The "last enemy to be destroyed," according to God's agenda, is death (1 Cor. 15:26).This tension of "already and not yet" presses us to pray, "Establish your royal rule, O Father! Your kingdom come!"

Between D-Day and V-Day.

I lived in German-occupied territory during World War II. In June 1944, the Allied armies broke through the Atlantic Wall's fortresses. They paid a costly price, but they established a beachhead in Europe that they never surrendered again. That was D-Day, the time of the successful invasion. Then we knew that the battle was won. And Hitler knew it too. Yet the war was not finished until May 1945, and never did we suffer so much pain and hunger as we did between D-Day, the day of the invasion, and V-Day, the day of victory.

The church is praying between the D-Day of God's invasion and the V-Day of his total victory. The liberation has begun; please complete it, Lord. Make us completely free. Your kingdom come!

Soldiers of the King.

After Christ's ascension and before his return, we live as disciples of Jesus the Servant, who is now the Ruler. In this time, we must pray the kingdom prayer he taught.

How must we pray it? With our mouths, of course, but also with our lives. If our lives go in one direction and our prayers in another, we are split personalities—unhealthy human beings. If our words say one thing and our lives the opposite thing, we are hypocrites—we are spiritually very sick.

Prayer is, indeed, the most important part of our Christian endeavors. But works show the sincerity of our prayers. Works show that we really want what our words say. Those who pray with their lips alone pray judgment upon themselves.

Among church members are people who are not interested in the work of evangelism—that's for pious ones, they say. They don't want to come to Bible study—because people might think they have become fanatics. They don't read a church paper or much of anything else except the comic strips in the local newspaper. But if you ask them if they ever pray "Your kingdom come," they'll tell you that they say this prayer every day.

Such people are actually lying. Or they simply don't know what they are saying.

All of us should be forced to put in our own words what this prayer means: Father, be king! Rule over me, rule over the world! Come, Lord Jesus!

The Lord's Prayer has been "used" too often. People don't hear what they are saying, and that can be very painful. For how can we ask for the full revelation of the kingdom without being willing to sacrifice and suffer for that kingdom? In theory, all Christians agree that we should put God, his kingdom, and his righteousness first in our lives. But those who do it—in education, labor, industry, and politics—are considered funny fanatics by mainline Christians.

If we share in the death and resurrection of Christ and if we pray daily for the completion of his work, our whole style of living must adopt the color, the shape, the music of that new realm—the new order of his kingdom. We must make a radical decision, a clear choice between *Playboy* philosophy and God-ordered living, between the greed of the present economic system and the stewardship of God's creation, between the arrogance of humanism and the righteousness of God.

The Catechetical Form of the Prayer.

The catechism explains the six requests of the Lord's Prayer in six answers that are really prayers themselves. We should pray these prayers more often.

Rule us by your Word and Spirit in such a way that more and more we submit to you. In the present dispensation, Christ rules over us from his throne. He uses two tools: his Word (the Bible) and the Spirit. He uses *both.* Those who rely only on the whisperings of the Spirit tend to get puffed up. Those who, like scribes, do nothing but go through the pages and the words tend to get dried up. But those who depend on the Word and the Spirit get built up.

The purpose of Word and Spirit is to teach us complete obedience—not that of slaves but of children.

Keep your church strong, and add to it. The church is not the kingdom, although church members have citizenship in the kingdom; as a community, they have signs and foretastes of the kingdom to come. The strength of the church is spiritual, and its growth is related to its faithful use of the treasures of which it is steward (Matt. 25:14-30).

Destroy the devil's work; destroy every force which revolts against you and every conspiracy against your Word. In many ways—with subtle charm or brute force—the great opponent of Jesus will try to make us disloyal to our Lord and will attempt to cause people to hate Christ's rule. But through our prayers, Christ will slay him. So we ask that God will destroy "every force which revolts against [him]." For there are powers that aren't so devilish yet are anti-Christian. Neutrality, for instance, can be an anti-Christian power. It does not deny the Lord, but it will not confess him!

And destroy "every conspiracy against your Word," the catechism asks. Since the Bible as the once-for-all-delivered Word of God is the foundation of the church, an attack on the Bible is an effort to make the whole church collapse. We pray that God will neutralize such attacks, and we promise to watch out.

Do this until your kingdom is so complete and perfect that in it you are all in all. Do it, Lord—preserve, keep, and arm us, until. . . .

That word *until* is a big one in the Christian vocabulary. We remember and proclaim the Lord's death *until* he comes (1 Cor. 11:26). And we have the Spirit as a guarantee *until* we are completely redeemed (Eph. 1:14). Our times will have a conclusion.

We must pray "Your kingdom come" with our lives. And we must make the prayer completely our own: "Lord, Father, make me faithful; let everything I say and do serve in a natural way the coming of your kingdom."

God's Answer.

With our lives and our lips we pray for the final and perfect appearance of the kingship of Jesus Christ. But we cannot program Christ's coming. The way in which the kingdom comes remains God's secret. Here is an illustration of that truth:

"This is what the kingdom of God is like. A man scatters seed on the ground. Night and day, whether he sleeps or gets up, the seed sprouts and grows, though he does not know how. All by itself the soil produces grain—first the stalk, then the head, then the full kernel in the head. As soon as the grain is ripe, he puts the sickle to it, because the harvest has come" (Mark 4:26-29).

Growth does not depend on the farmer: "Whether he sleeps or gets up, the seed sprouts and grows." The kingdom comes as a result of an energy that isn't ours and that we cannot quite understand: "he does not know how."

For us the coming of the kingdom is above all a matter of prayer and thanksgiving. The prayer must be steady and must involve more than our lips, as we have said. And God's surprises will be causes for thanksgiving all along the way, until our eyes see the last surprise unveiled.

Vertical and Horizontal.

To Pilate Jesus said, "My kingdom is not of this world" (John 18:36). Jesus did not deny, as many people do, that his kingdom takes shape in the present, temporary world. It was precisely because his kingdom exists in the here-and-now that Jesus did come into the world. But in his words to Pilate, Jesus was saying that his kingdom's origin lies in heaven and that his kingdom does not depend on worldly measures to survive and succeed. ("If it were, my servants would fight".)

The kingdom of God breaks into our present reality wherever people believe the gospel and acknowledge Jesus as Lord. From this moment of recognition on, we not only have worship services to "him who sits on the throne and to the Lamb" (Rev. 5:13), but also all of life becomes service and all our work worship. The power that comes from God works through us. Jesus extends his kingdom of grace and peace from prayer room to living room to bedroom to classroom and conference room. His kingship is very much a part of our earthly, everyday existence. In this time and age we are permitted to see individuals and tribes change from not knowing the Lord to loving him. We can see and experience a community life marked by the peace and power of Christ. All of us ought to pray and work for these experiences here and now; they are not only possible but are also likely to occur, because the Spirit and the gospel are here.

Thus the coming of the kingdom may be experienced both as it spreads to all parts of a person's and a community's life (intensively) and as it spreads to all nations on the globe (extensively). In these victories God is at work through his servants to "demolish strongholds" and make rebellious thoughts and people the captives of Christ (see 2 Cor. 10:4-6). When that happens, one may say, God is answering our prayers for the coming of the kingdom.

At the same time, we must always resist the temptation to think of the coming of the kingdom as the ever widening circle of our church or Christian organization. The coming of God's kingdom has something to do with church growth. But the kingship remains with the Lord, and none of us can serve as his counselor (Rom. 11:34).

Still Unfulfilled.

If we are Christians at all, all of us long for the perfection of the kingdom of Christ. Anyone who has a taste of the world to come craves the whole package (Rom. 8:23).

Pentecostalists and other Full Gospel Christians, who insist on a radical experience of the transforming power of the Holy Spirit, tend to become too optimistic about kingdom results in this present life. Some of them think that they can get beyond sin and illness. To them Paul's words are applicable: "Already you have all you want!" and "Some of you have become arrogant" (1 Cor. 4:8, 18).

Calvinists have never shared such optimism about individuals. None of us has ever taught the possibility of perfection in this life. Some of us do not even believe in the possibility of doing good. But since the days of Abraham Kuyper and separate Christian organizations, we have often suffered from an inordinate optimism for corporate perfection. And it is not only tough on our pride but sometimes hard on our faith that Christian political clubs cannot come up with the solution for which society is waiting.

The Lord has come, Jesus is on the throne, and his Spirit is here. But the sons and daughters of the kingdom are still subject to all sorts of weaknesses. Therefore they pray daily, "Let the kingdom come" and "Come, Lord Jesus!"

Today's Issue.

The greatest thing that's now happening in the world is the coming of the kingdom of heaven. No matter what issue is "in the news" or is directly affecting our lives, the coming of Christ's kingdom is *the* issue.

Sometimes the Lord works in a spectacular way so that all must take notice: he may heal suddenly or convert a noted enemy of his. In our times God is moving into the Asian continent in a way nobody foresaw. The

Chinese, whom Western Christians could not reach and God seemed to have forgotten, are embracing the gospel by the millions.

Most of the time God does not work spectacularly; the kingdom comes, rather, like growing wheat. And one has to be born from above to "see" this kingdom (John 3:3). Just as it took a heavenly revelation to know that the Carpenter of Nazareth was the Son of God (Matt. 16:17), so it takes the discernment that the Spirit gives to know that through the little deeds of ordinary people, through love and sacrifice and the blood of martyrs, God's kingdom marches on.

Nothing should engage our attention more than the coming of the kingdom. All competing interests should be subject to this, which is God's agenda and the church's overriding interest.

Today Jesus is the Lord of the universe. Those who do not obey him rebel against him. As yet, he rules by the gospel, and he comes to people with a call—a gospel call. There's a life-or-death earnestness about this call. It's made not only "softly and tenderly" but also insistently and urgently. Obey now or regret it forever. Bow low and "kiss the Son, lest he be angry and you be destroyed in your way, for his wrath can flare up in a moment. Blessed are all who take refuge in him" (Ps. 2:12).

The Shalom of God.

Between Christ's coming in grace and his coming in glory, the Lord uses our prayers and our works to establish his kingship in this present world. He can and will use anybody, especially the weak, the lowly, and those the world despises.

Between the first and second coming of the Lord is the time of the church's testing. We must now show endurance, believing that the end is near: "The God of peace [shalom] will soon crush Satan under your feet" (Rom. 16:20). God does the crushing, yet it happens under our feet.

But in the end God will not work or rule through people, not even through the Mediator: "The Son himself will be made subject to him [the Father] . . . so that God may be all in all" (1 Cor 15:28). Then, when everything and everybody is subject to God, the whole universe will have found its destiny. The kingdom will have come, and God's shalom will last forever.

Lord's Day 49

PRAYER AND OBEDIENCE

Q *What does the third request mean?*

A **Your will be done on earth as it is in heaven** *means, Help us and all people to reject our own wills and to obey your will without any back talk. Your will alone is good. Help us one and all to carry out the work we are called to, as willingly and faithfully as the angels in heaven.*

—Q & A 124

The Last of Three.

The first three petitions in the Lord's Prayer explain each other: God's name will receive due honor and recognition when the kingdom has fully come, and God's kingdom will be fully established when all that lives obeys our Father's will.

In the version of the Lord's Prayer preserved in Luke 11:2-4, the third petition, printed above, is absent. Strictly speaking, we don't need it. If we have prayed for the establishment of God's one kingdom, we have already asked that all subjects obey one *will.*

But the catechism follows the version of the Lord's Prayer in Matthew 6:9-11, with its symmetry of two sets of three petitions. Basically, the first three petitions make but one request: heavenly Father, finish your gracious work of redemption! This prayer is uttered with climactic urgency in three petitions. Here we are thinking about the third one—the prayer for obedience.

Not a Prayer of Resignation.

"Your will be done" must not be prayed with a sigh of resignation but as a prayer for personal and universal obedience.

It's a classic misunderstanding that by saying "Your will be done," Christians bow, passively and reverently, to the will of God.

We don't deny that we ought to bow before God. We should acknowledge his sovereignty. And we ought to admit that the Father is wiser than we are and that he knows our needs better than we do. These are important components of our relationship to God. But these are not the reasons why Christ taught us to say, "Your will be done." He wanted us, rather, to *do* that will in our homes and towns and churches. This is a prayer for obedience, not of resignation.

Gethsemane.

Those who teach that "Your will be done" is a prayer of resignation tend to appeal to Jesus' prayer struggle in the Garden of Gethsemane. Here Jesus himself prayed what he had taught his disciples to say: Father, your will be done.

Bowed to the ground underneath the olive trees in the garden, he cried,

"Father, if you are willing, take this cup from me; yet not my will, but yours be done" (Luke 22:42).

It would be wrong, however, to say that in this intense struggle Jesus was merely bowing to the inevitable. He was at the door of the final stage of his suffering. The cross and death and hell were agonizing prospects to his heart and mind. He grasped for his Father, whose will alone is good, as the catechism says.

Yes, Jesus rejected his own desires (to speak once again with the catechism), and when he arose from prayer to face the crowd and the traitor, his heart was united with the Father's will.

He did not *submit* to the inevitable; he *carried out* the will of the Father. The will of the Father was *done* by the Son. And the Son teaches us how we, too, must be obedient until death.

Paul's Obedience.

There's one occurrence in the Bible of the phrase "The Lord's will be done" that is indeed a kind of resignation (Acts 21:14). The apostle Paul was on his way to Jerusalem. In his farewell address to the elders of Ephesus he had said, "I am going to Jerusalem, not knowing what will happen to me there. I only know that in every city the Holy Spirit warns me that prison and hardships are facing me" (Acts 20:22-23). Paul's friends did their utmost to keep him from going to Jerusalem, because of the dangers. At Caesarea, Paul's last stop before reaching Jerusalem, they pleaded with him intensely to stay back. But Paul said, "Why are you weeping and breaking my heart? I am ready not only to be bound, but also to die in Jerusalem for the name of the Lord Jesus." And then Luke, the writer, adds, "When he would not be dissuaded, we gave up and said, 'The Lord's will be done'" (Acts 21:13-14).

But was that really "resignation"? Was that "saying yes with a sigh"? Perhaps it was that for Paul's friends. They did not argue any longer, and they gave up when Paul's trip appeared unavoidable. But for Paul this incident was clearly an active commitment to *do* the will of God. He had learned obedience from his Master, and, like a good disciple, he followed in his Teacher's footsteps. He denied his own desires, and he did the perfect will of God.

The Hidden and the Revealed Will.

This third petition of the Lord's Prayer has nothing to do with how we pray for health and for recovery from illness. Yet generations of Christians have said "Your will be done" when praying for healing.

Everyone wants his or her loved ones to recover from illness. At our child's sickbed, we wrestle with God. Millions have done it. And by adding, "Not my will, but yours be done," sensitive Christians bow in advance to a decision that might run counter to their own desire.

I do not wish to chide godly people for praying in this way. But the Christian church should make clear to everyone that "Your will be done" in the context of the Lord's Prayer refers not to what God has decided to do (his *hidden will*) but to what he has told *us* to do (his *revealed command*). We are not saying in the Lord's Prayer that we will bow to God's decision, but we are pledging that we will do what he wants us to do.

Of course, we must accept God's decisions with reverence. While his child was ill, King David fasted and prayed for seven days and seven nights. But when the child died, David bathed and dressed and went to God's house to worship (2 Sam. 12:15-23). When we know God's decision with certainty, we must continue to trust him, because he is our Father.

However—if I may repeat it once more—in the Lord's Prayer we are asking that the revolution against God on this planet may cease and that all God's children may be united in doing the will of their Father as obediently as do the angels in heaven.

A Disciple's Prayer.

When they pray at all, people naturally tend to pray for happy living. Even Christians pray more for happy living than for obedient living. We offer many petitions for wholesome food and healthy digestion, prosperous journeys, tranquil environments, painless aging, and peaceful dying. But the Master wants his followers to pray that their obedience will be as complete on earth as it is in heaven.

The disciples of Jesus say this prayer in a divided world and, too often, with a divided heart. We pray it against the devil, the world, and our own flesh: "Father, your will be done."

In the present world many people do not live according to God's will, and many conditions are not as he wants them to be. Christians refuse to accept the present world, as they find it, with its customs, traditions, and values. Christians are willing to pay the price of obedience in a lifetime of reshaping their environment to conform to the will of God. We don't accept even ourselves—we don't excuse our lapses and frailties by saying "That's who we happen to be." Rather, we are committed to change, and we are confident that our Lord has the power to effect it through our works and prayers.

That's what it means to pray "Your will be done."

Three Assumptions.

When disciples of Jesus pray for universal obedience— "your will be done on earth as it is in heaven"—they are expected to (a) know God's will in all ordinary matters, (b) search for God's will in other things, and (c) learn God's will in union with other Christians.

We Know What God Wants.

The revealed will of God is clear. It is the a-b-c of the church's teaching: love God above all, and love your neighbor as yourselves. God has made this central command specific in many separate commandments in the Scriptures. So we must know the Scriptures; it is the duty of disciples to know and to obey all that the Master has commanded (Matt. 28:20).

Sometimes Christians fall into the temptation of debating the will of God rather than doing it. To have discussions about the will of God as if it were a secret yet to be discovered is a subtle form of disobedience. God's revealed law must not be disputed but learned and obeyed. As the catechism says, "Help us and all people . . . to obey your will *without any back talk.*"

We know God's will with respect to the mission of the church and the purpose of our lives. God has taught us what we owe to authorities, parents, spouses, children, to all people and things. And to God himself we owe our lives.

The Weight of Obedience.

In the Scriptures we find that the main difficulty of God's people is not knowing God's will, but doing it. The wise man who builds his house on the rock is the one who not only hears but also *does* the word of his Lord. The fool is the one who only hears it (Matt. 7:24-27). The Scriptures never imply that doing God's will comes easily or that his command coincides with our wishes (except when the Spirit makes God's law our desire by writing it in our hearts [Jer. 31:33, 2 Cor. 3:3]).

Saying yes to God usually means saying no to our own desires. Therefore our "discussions" of his will are often smokescreens to hide our reluctance or unwillingness. Following Jesus means self-denial (Matt. 16:24), and that does not come easily to anyone.

"Help us and all men to reject our own wills and to obey your will. . . . Your will alone is good." We pray and confess these words with the catechism. We want to obey God even when doing so goes against our own desires or our advantage as we see it. We cannot pray "Your will be done" unless we ourselves are steadfastly obedient.

Obedience is better than worship—services and sacrifices (cf. 1 Sam. 15:22). As a matter of fact, obedient lives are the only living sacrifices the Lord is looking for (Rom. 12:1).

Searching for God's Will.

We cannot know God's will without the Bible. But it takes more than quoting Bible texts to answer our questions. Finding God's will demands a certain activity from us, as Romans 12:2 makes clear: "Do not conform any longer to the pattern of this world but be transformed by the renewing of your mind. Then you will be able to test and approve what God's will is—his good, pleasing, and perfect will."

The first sentence in this passage says that Christians, who do not really belong to the present age although we live in it, must be alert not to conform to worldly patterns. Rather, we must increasingly be transformed by the new power of the Holy Spirit—in the "mind," that is, in the center of our conscious lives. The transformation of our behavior proceeds from this new principle. And this new life-style is not a matter of our own fancy but of obedience to the will of God: "Then you will be able to test and approve [or "by searching find out" or "by testing establish"] what the will of God is."

Here we learn that the purpose of salvation is that we obey the will of God. And that knowing the will of God in a particular situation takes more than a simple reference to a Bible text. By Bible study, prayer, and the hard work of the regenerate mind, we have to find what is good and God pleasing and perfect in his sight.

Today the Christian church must restudy this text (Romans 12:1-2). We have to reevaluate our life-style to see if it is consistent with surrender to God, which is the only proper response to the gospel. For we cannot pray that God's will be done on earth as it is in heaven unless our whole lives show how serious we are about this prayer.

Fellowship of Obedience.

Once, while Jesus was teaching in a house crowded with people, someone told him that his mother and brothers were outside, looking for him. "Then he looked at those seated in a circle around him and said, 'Here are my mother and my brothers! Whoever does God's will is my brother and sister and mother'" (Mark 3:34-35).

Obedience to God creates the brother-and-sister-hood of the church. When the church has become a company of those who find their unity in similarities of race, color, or social status, the church has degenerated. It is and must be, rather, a fellowship of the obedient. And the work and prayer of this community aims to bring the whole earth into obedience to the God of heaven and earth.

Our primary goal is doing God's will. And our greatest temptation is not doing his will. These were also the goal and temptation of Jesus. Jesus came to do the will of him who sent him (Heb. 10:7, John 4:34, etc.). And when he was tempted by the devil, first in the desert and later in Gethsemane, obedience to God's will was the issue. It was not a power struggle; the question was whether or not he would be obedient. And Christ did God's will on earth as faithfully as it is done in heaven.

The New Obedience.

Through the disobedience of one we were lost. Through the obedience of the Other One we were "made righteous" (Rom. 5:19).

We are saved not by our obedience but by Christ's. Once we are redeemed, however, *we obey* the will of God. As a matter of fact, the whole purpose of redemption is "that the righteous requirements of the law might be fully met in us, who do not live according to the sinful nature ['flesh'] but according to the Spirit" (Rom. 8:4). God's will is now done by a people whose debts are paid and whose wills are set free to obey their heavenly Father. God "broke the power of canceled sin." A free people obeys on earth as God's angels do in heaven. This reborn people produces the fruit of a new creation (James 1:18).

A Covenant People.

The big requirement that God made of people in the Old Testament was obedience. And the great failure of Israel was disobedience. But God promised a better time and a New Covenant. In this New Covenant God would write the law in the minds and on the hearts of his people. They would be a mature people, no longer dependent on the mediation of priests. And God would blot out their sins forever (Jer. 31:31-34). This covenant has now come—through the blood and the Spirit of Jesus Christ. We who follow him are the people of God's New Covenant (Matt. 26:28; 2 Cor. 3:3, 6; Heb. 9:15, 18).

We must now make the proper, obedient, covenantal response to God in everyday living. Whatever we do—digging, building, governing, teaching, driving, learning, writing, cooking—we do it as part of God's covenant people. We must do it faithfully, correctly, to the glory of God, and to our neighbor's benefit. The catechism teaches us to pray, "Help everyone carry out the work he is called to as willingly and faithfully as the angels in heaven." Doing God's will covers the whole of human activity, without distinction between "sacred" and "secular." We do everything knowing that we have a Master in heaven (Col. 3:1) whom we obey on earth. We have a covenantal relationship with him. He has shown us what is good: "To act justly and to love mercy and to walk humbly with [our] God" (Mic. 6:8).

Living is learning to love and to obey. To love *is* to obey. We learn by doing. Christ himself "learned obedience from what he suffered" (Heb. 5:8). That is to say, on the road of suffering he learned the full weight of obedience. And thus "he became the source of eternal salvation for all who obey him" (5:9). Our obedience to the Son as our covenant head corresponds to the Son's obedience to the Father. We follow and obey Christ, even if we must suffer with him.

As Faithfully As the Angels.

Angels are more excellent than we are, because they do God's will perfectly. We pray that we may do it as they do.

When we have been redeemed, we can obey, but we cannot yet obey perfectly. We still have some distrust in our behavior, some holding back in our giving, some reservation in our love.

The angels' first assignment is to praise God: "Praise the Lord, you his angels, you mighty ones who do his bidding, who obey his word" (Ps. 103:20). This first assignment they have in common with everything and everybody. Further, the angels assist God in his work of revelation (*angel* means "messenger") and of salvation. At God's command they serve by helping us reach full and final salvation (Heb. 1:14).

When we do God's will on earth, we will be opposed by many people, but we will be served by angels. That's what happened to the obedient Son (Matt. 4:11); it will also happen to all God's children (18:10).

Although angels are more obedient than human beings, we know God in a way that they will never know him. They will never fathom the mystery of salvation (1 Pet. 1:12), because they have never been lost. A child who has been ill for many years knows a tenderness in the hearts of parents that another child who was always healthy might not know. In the same way we have experienced the Father's love as has no other creature.

We don't know whether angels pray for our salvation, but they certainly rejoice when sinners return to God (Luke 15:10). They and we know that the creation will only reach its destiny through universal obedience.

In the last chapter of the Bible John lost his sense of proportion and knelt before an angel. Right away the angel said, "Don't do that. If you are going to kneel, I will kneel next to you" (see Rev. 22:8-9). People and angels have been created for the worship of God. And we who do God's will on earth, who now obey "the words of this book," kneel as the equals of the angels before the throne of God.

Lord's Day 50

OUR DAILY BREAD

***Q** What does the fourth request mean?*

A** Give us this day our daily bread* ***means, Do take care of all our physical needs so that we come to know that you are the only source of everything good, and that neither our work and worry nor your gifts can do us any good without your blessing. And so help us to give up our trust in creatures and to put trust in you alone.

—Q & A 125

Context.

In the first three petitions of the Lord's Prayer we said "your" three times: *"your* name," *"your* kingdom," *"your* will." In the second set of three requests we speak of "our" and "us": *"our* bread," *"our* debts," and "lead *us* not into temptation." Just as the first tablet of the law deals with our vertical relationship to God and the second with our relationships to our neighbors, so the Lord's Prayer speaks first of God's kingdom and then of our world. But we should not think that in the first three petitions God gets his due, after which we turn to our concerns. Rather, we learn to pray as Christ's followers and as children of the heavenly Father. The focus of our prayer and the thrust of our lives is the new world of the coming kingdom. And the prayers about bread, sins, and temptations beg for the Father's provisions, grace, and support as long as we are between the world from which he has called us and the new one to which we are going.

The Text.

The fourth petition of the Lord's Prayer reads, "Give us today our daily bread" (Matt. 6:11), or "Give us each day our daily bread" (Luke 11:3). But for centuries Western Christians prayed, "Give us today our supernatural bread." They did so because their authoritative Latin version of the Bible (the Vulgate) said *panis supersubstantialis* ("supernatural bread"). The faithful probably understood this prayer as a request for the benefits of the Eucharist, the bread from heaven, Christ himself, sacramentally received in the Lord's Supper.

The Greek word *epiousios,* translated as "daily," is rare. We have no clearcut evidence of the occurrence of this word anywhere outside of the Lord's Prayer. *Epiousios* appears to be a Greek word coined specifically to translate whatever Aramaic word Jesus used for "daily."

While scholarly search and study continue, two things are sure and widely acknowledged by Christians of all traditions: first, the prayer Jesus taught us asks for ordinary bread not for spiritual bread. Second, by saying "Give us today our daily bread," we ask our Father to provide our ration for today. This petition is in substantial agreement with Agur's prayer: "Give me neither poverty nor riches, but give me only my daily bread" (Prov. 30:8).

Outline.

Jesus teaches us three things when we pray to God for our daily needs: he teaches us *modesty* as we ask not for a year's supply but for our daily portion. He teaches us to have *concern for others* as we ask *our* Father for *our* bread. And he teaches us to pray with *confidence* as we address our requests to our Father in heaven.

Not by Bread Alone.

The petition for bread follows the petition for obedience. We don't want bread if it will cost us our obedience to God. We know what life, real life, is like. Living is not having something to put into our mouths, as worldly people think. We don't have life if we don't hear and obey what God says. "Man does not live on bread alone but on every word that comes from the mouth of God." Israel failed to learn this truth during forty years in the wilderness (Deut. 8:3). The Israelites put food before trust. But Jesus went hungry for forty days in the desert, refusing to eat the food of disobedience. He determined to place God first: "Man does not live on bread alone" (Matt. 4:4), he said to the tempter, and he remained obedient to the Word of his Father until his death on the cross.

We, too, face the temptation of thinking that daily food has top priority. But God did not place food at the top of the list of necessities for humanity. He put himself and his Word first. If we could eat only if we disobeyed our heavenly Father, it would be better to go hungry. Loyalty to God, listening to what comes out of his mouth—*that* has top priority.

We Need Food.

No food at the expense of obedience. But food and drink are essential for living. Unless we eat and drink, we die. And God knows it, because he made us.

Bernard of Clairvaux (1090-1153), the most famous monk of the Middle Ages, advised those who entered his monastery to leave their bodies outside. He meant they should give up the desires of the body. Spiritualism and mysticism and asceticism tend to despise food and the body. The Latin version of the Lord's Prayer fit well the mood of the monks: "Give us today our supernatural bread."

But Jesus taught us to pray for ordinary bread, because he knows that we need it.

Elijah was as fiery a lover of God as Bernard, and when his desperate love for God found no echo in Israel, he ran off to Mount Horeb, begging for death. But God sent him an angel, who offered him a meal: "Get up and eat, for the journey is too much for you" (1 Kings 19:7).

Even in our greatest ecstasy on earth, we are still on earth. When that astonishing miracle had happened in the house of Jairus—when people fell over each other in amazement and that mother embraced her twelve-year-old daughter in utter joy—Jesus "told them to give her something to eat" (Mark 5:43).

The early Christians were so much governed by the Spirit that they could be accused of being drunk. Yet "they broke bread in their homes and ate together with glad and sincere hearts" (Acts 2:46).

Let's be careful, however, when we speak of Bernard of Clairveaux. Maybe he did not eat well, but he loved his Master. Most of us eat well, but it is not so clear that we love God deeply. We'd rather skip a church service than a meal.

Needs, Not Wants.

Jesus taught us to ask our heavenly Father for our daily portion of "bread." He does not want us to ask for a barn full or a freezer full but for only the bread we need.

The catechism says that "bread" stands for "all our physical needs." And that seems a fair assumption. No doubt Paul spoke in the spirit of this prayer when he said, "If we have food and clothing, we will be content with that" (1 Tim. 6:8). Evidently "food and clothing" are the sum total of our "physical needs," as far as Paul is concerned. The rest would be extra luggage, unnecessarily weighing down the pilgrim. "For we brought nothing into the world, and we can take nothing out of it" (v. 7). Anything we pick up along the way may hinder our movements, and, finally, we will have to leave it anyway. Possessions are no real "gain." "But godliness with contentment is great gain" (v. 6).

Our Uneasy Conscience.

The Lord's Prayer dates from a time when most people spent most of their days in activities that were directly related to obtaining and maintaining sufficient clothes, adequate shelter, and a daily supply of food. In that setting the prayer asks no more than most people could reasonably expect or hope for. In numerous countries, even today, most people's worries concern their "daily bread" or rice.

But in North America, Western Europe, and a few more areas, the provisions that are the daily worries of the rest of the world are matters of course that are taken for granted. Nearly all readers of this page have items in their monthly budgets that are much more substantial than the cost of the food and clothes that they *need.* Many of us have seen in our own lifetimes how yesterday's luxury becomes today's necessity. And whatever is now considered a luxury may tomorrow be claimed as a "right" that everyone ought to enjoy.

Actually, many costly things simply are not luxuries to people who have to live and work in our society. In most of our towns, ordinary lower and middle-class housing is expensive. For a family to pay for a house, more than one member of the household must bring home a paycheck. And very few people can function in our society without an automobile.

Many Christians do not consider a Christian day-school education for their children a luxury; to them it's a necessity. And it is a big item in their budget.

The prayer for daily bread makes us uneasy because of our confusion about needs and wants. And perhaps it should make us uneasy. But we do need to translate the "physical needs" of the catechism into today's terms.

God Is Not Skimpy.

In the same chapter in which Paul reminds us that we came naked into the world and that we can take nothing out of it and that we ought to be content with food and clothing, he also addresses "those who are rich in this present world" (vv. 17-19).

Evidently rich people were members of Timothy's congregation. Paul tells Timothy that he should warn the rich. (The Bible hardly ever speaks of riches without a word of warning.) But Paul goes on to describe God as the One who "richly provides us with everything for our enjoyment" (v. 17). Note two things: God is generous, and what he gives is to be enjoyed!

The picture of a God who begrudges us anything more than a bare minimum is as unbiblical as the message that God wants us all to be rich.

Trust Our Father.

Why, then, if God is generous and we should feel free to enjoy the material things he provides, is the Bible generally critical of riches, and why is it always warning us of the dangers of wealth? Why has God told us explicitly not to seek riches but to seek "godliness with contentment" instead? If God makes a choice between the rich and the poor, the Bible shows him on the side of the poor. Some Christians have so over-emphasized this theme in the Bible that they believe that poverty is next to piety and that wealth is inherently wicked.

The real reason why God always warns the rich and why Jesus teaches us to pray only for necessities is that we should trust in God as our Father and not in the false security of our possessions. We cannot be Christians if we lose our sense of childlike dependence on God. Money tends to rob us of that essential ingredient. The Bible does not teach that a poor person is better than a rich one. But the poor are sooner inclined to trust in God, and the rich will naturally rely on their own resources. Having money gives us a sense of independence. And no one can be a Christian unless he or she signs a declaration of dependence: "I am not my own. . . ."

Since we are not our own, we must not live as if we can or must take care of our own lives. The catechism wants us to pray, "Father, 'you are the only source of everything good, and . . . neither our work and worry [no, not even] your gifts can do us any good without your blessing. And so help us to give up our trust in creatures [and things] and to put trust in you alone.'"

Day by Day.

God's insistence that we live day by day in complete dependence on him, even for snacks and sandwiches, has a further implication for our life-style. We must avoid wastefulness and regard even ordinary food as a gift of God. This demands a certain thoughtfulness about God's daily gifts—a virtue that's not easy to cultivate in our culture. We tend to "grab a bite" on the go, make use of fast-food services, and have a TV dinner. The development of a Christian life-style, on the other hand, requires discipline.

Communal Thinking.

The Christian religion is intensely personal but never individualistic. Each Christian must pray personally, but all must pray to "our" Father and ask for "our" bread. (Luke's version of the Lord's Prayer does not say "our Father" but "Father." It does say "Give *us* each day *our* daily bread" [11:2-3].)

The employer as well as the employee must ask "our" Father for "our" bread. No one is allowed to isolate his or her needs and forget about others. Egotism is out because we belong to a family in which One has given himself for all, and now all live for the One in serving each other. When we have asked, "Give us our daily portion" and some of us receive more than we need, we are obliged to share.

The Bible views the sharing of food and clothing as evidence of faith. It sees the refusal to share these gifts as a clear sign that a person's faith is dead: "Suppose a brother or sister is without clothes and daily food. If one of you says to him, 'Go, I wish you well; keep warm and well fed,' but does nothing about his physical needs, what good is it? In the same way, faith by itself, if it is not accompanied by action, is dead" (James 2:15-17).

Global Thinking.

Jesus Christ laid down his life for us. The same kind of self-giving love makes his followers willing to give up not only what they have but life itself. Those who are unwilling to give away material things to people in need present evidence that they are strangers to the love of God, no matter what they *say*. "If anyone has material possessions and sees his brother in need but has no pity on him, how can the love of God be in him?" (1 John 3:17).

Some Christians are still trying to escape this biblical reasoning by pointing out that the text says "*brother* in need." They argue that a "brother" is a person who is a fellow believer in Christ. However, the passage is not placing any emphasis on "brother" but on the impossibility of at the same time having Christian love and lacking compassion.

Even in Old Testament times "love" was not reserved for fellow Israelites but was extended to "strangers and sojourners." In the New Testament, Christian love as revealed in Christ is indiscriminate; it extends "to the evil and the good." We don't love people and give away material possessions because we have found someone who is worthy of our love but because *God's* love is in us.

And to defend limiting charitable giving (personally and as a church) to believers within the Christian community is to place far too much weight on the "brother or sister" texts. In the parable of the sheep and the goats, for instance, Jesus identifies himself with the hungry, the thirsty, the stranger, the prisoner, and the one in need of clothing. It is not so clear that he is talking about *believers only* (see Matt. 25:31-46).

Love does not try to find a loophole to justify keeping food and clothing. We who have eaten the living bread pray the Lord's Prayer with all its social and global implications. Just as one cannot keep aloof from the mission of the church when one prays for the glory of God's name and for the coming of God's kingdom, so one has to share food and clothing when one asks our Father for our daily bread.

Work Without Worry.

If we pray sincerely for the honor of God's name and the coming of his kingdom, we also work to bring glory to God in our daily living. Similarly, we may not ask for bread with words only: we must also ask with works.

God is very much opposed to laziness. "A sluggard does not plow in season; so at harvest time he looks but finds nothing" (Prov. 20:4). "Lazy hands make a man poor, but diligent hands bring wealth" (10:4). Paul told the converted thief in the Ephesian congregation that he should "steal no longer." He was directed to "work, doing something useful with his own hands, that he may have something to share with those in need" (Eph. 4:28).

Prayer for bread does not eliminate work for bread but demands it. And if, in spite of our work, we have no bread, God may choose to feed us with the gifts of others, just as he may feed others with our gifts when he has blessed us. It is, of course, "more blessed to give than to receive" (Acts 20:35). But we who live by grace must not be too proud to receive when

God has withheld from us what he gave to others. This may be the way in which God chooses to answer our prayer for our daily needs.

Although this prayer does not take the place of work, it does take the worry out of our daily labors. Our prayers and our life-styles show modesty and confidence: we are merely asking for our daily portion as soldiers in God's army, as children in God's house, as people who have been enlisted in Christ's service. And just as earthly fathers don't give stones to children when they ask for bread, so our heavenly Father will see to it that our needs are satisfied.

We work—like everybody else. But we work without the fear that haunts those who always worry about tomorrow and without the greed that often makes workers dishonest. We work without worry because we know that it is "neither our work and worry" nor bread itself that can do us any good. But his favor we seek, and for his blessing we beg when we say, "Our Father, give us today what we need."

Lord's Day 51

FORGIVENESS: PRAYER AND PRACTICE

***Q** What does the fifth request mean?*

A** Forgive us our debts, as we also have forgiven our debtors **means, Because of Christ's blood, do not hold against us, poor sinners that we are, any of the sins we do or the evil that constantly clings to us. Forgive us just as we are fully determined, as evidence of your grace in us, to forgive our neighbors.

—Q & A 126

A Christian's Request.

A Christian is someone whose sins have been forgiven because of the merits of Jesus Christ. But if Christians, by definition, are *forgiven* and *cleansed*, is it really the Lord's will that they should daily pray, "Father, forgive, as we have forgiven"?

Some Christian groups and churches in Methodist/Pentecostal or "holiness" tradition teach that born-again believers should not continue to pray for forgiveness. This seems to be a strange teaching, because our Lord himself gave us this model prayer, in which we ask for daily bread, daily forgiveness, and daily protection in temptation.

They answer, though, that Christ gave the prayer before he had made complete atonement for all our sins by dying on the cross. Christians are increasingly transformed by the power of the Spirit, they argue. Christians do not stay in the pit of sin but walk on ever higher ground, tracing the road to perfection.

These Christians' favorite text for bolstering their doctrine of perfectionism is 1 John 5:18. In the King James Version this text reads, "We know that whosoever is born of God sinneth not; but he that is begotten of God keepeth himself, and that wicked one toucheth him not." But no other translation (except the New King James Version) gives this sense.

A better translation (the New International Version) reads, "We know that anyone born of God does not continue to sin; the one who was born of God [*that is, Jesus*] keeps him safe, and the evil one cannot harm him."

Dusty Feet of Pilgrims.

Christians are definitely not "dead in [their] transgressions and sins" (Eph. 2:1). We were "raised from the dead, in order that we might bear fruit to God" (Rom. 7:4). Worse than perfectionists are preachers who want us to think of ourselves as captives of the devil. "For [the Father] has rescued us from the dominion of darkness and brought us into the kingdom of the Son he loves" (Col. 1:13). We may not and *cannot* continue to sin; yet neither can we live without sinning.

The atoning sacrifice of Christ is an accomplished fact, and its merits are enough for all people of all times. But the grace of forgiveness must be asked for, received, and passed on, day by day. Forgiveness is not automatically settled as if it's a kind of paid-up life insurance. Let nobody imagine that he or she can live one day or one hour beyond the shelter of the forgiveness provided by the blood of Christ.

At the Last Supper, Jesus acted out his mission on earth by assuming the role of a slave and washing the feet of his disciples. When he came to Peter, this temperamental disciple first objected, "you shall never wash my feet." Then, after Jesus said, "Unless I wash you, you have no part with me," Peter blurted, "Not just my feet but my hands and my head as well!"

But Jesus washed only the disciple's feet, having explained, "A person who has had a bath needs only to wash his feet; his whole body is clean. And you are clean . . ." (John 13:8-10).

When we have a part in Christ and his work, we are clean. But we need Christ and his forgiveness every hour. And we pray, every day, "Father, forgive. . . ." For as long as we have to walk this earth, the dust will cling to our feet.

Debts/Transgressions/Sins.

Since the Lord's Prayer is one of the few prayers all Christians have memorized and can pray together, most of us have experienced discord in the chorus during the fifth petition: some have said "trespasses," and others have said "debts." Strictly speaking, the Lord's Prayer in Matthew 6:12 reads, "Forgive us our *debts*, as we also have forgiven our *debtors*." Yet after Jesus has given the prayer, he goes on to teach, "For if you forgive men when they *sin* against you [now the word is the usual one for *transgression* or *trespass*], your heavenly Father will also forgive you. But if you do not forgive men their *sins* [same word], your Father will not forgive your *sins* [same]" (v. 14).

"Debts" are what we owe to God and to others but have not paid. A debt is more than a "trespass" or a "transgression," which are sins of commission; *transgression* means going against the law, stepping over the line.

However, since in verse 14 the Lord speaks of "transgressions" and clearly means nothing else than what he calls "debts" in verse 12, one should not make too much of the difference.

Luke 11:4 says, "Forgive us our *sins* [a different word than the ones Matthew used], for we also forgive everyone who *sins* against us" (but here it really says "every *debtor*").

Conclusions.

If we pray the Lord's Prayer according to Matthew 6:9-13, as Christians usually do, we will say "debts" and not "trespasses." But the context in Matthew and the version of Luke show clearly that the Lord did not mean to distinguish sharply between sin as *good we did not do* (debt) or sin as *law breaking* (trespass) or sin as *missing the mark*. We must ask forgiveness and give forgiveness for every kind of sin.

"Poor Sinners That We Are."

We must, says the catechism, pray as "poor sinners" when we ask for forgiveness.

But in some pietistic Christian circles a poverty of righteousness becomes a sort of riches. Calling oneself a "poor sinner" gains one the esteem of fellow believers.

The story is told of a woman who, in order to demonstrate her piety, told Charles Spurgeon that she was a very bad sinner. With deep sighs she insisted she was the greatest of all sinners, worse than Paul and not worthy to be called a Christian.

Quite bored with her whining, Spurgeon said, "You did not need to tell me all of that, Madam, because I knew it already. Other people have told me what a sinner you are." Then the penitent sinner flared up, "How does anybody dare say such a thing about me! Who said it?"

Sinning and Confessing.

That woman was not the only insincere person in Christ's church. Many of us have no trouble making an orthodox, general statement about sin and human corruption without having any personal conviction that we ourselves are "poor sinners." But in Christian circles it is customary to confess that we are sinners. Even Christians who feel like the Pharisee will often pray like the publican because, among us, it's more acceptable.

Confessions of sinfulness are dangerous, and I am not sure under what circumstances the church should hear them. A "sinners' bench" is something the self-righteous love to see. A public confession of sin, which some churches still require, is not helpful. It unnecessarily humiliates one in the presence of many who either are squirming because they, too, are guilty or are feeling good when they shouldn't.

Knowledge of Sin Necessary.

But without a deep awareness of sin, one cannot have part in the blood of Jesus. Christ said that he did not come to heal the healthy or to save the righteous (Mark 2:17). Obviously, he was using irony. He did not mean to pronounce the religious leaders of the people spiritually healthy or morally righteous. But, said Jesus, these people don't *see* that they are poor and needy and therefore they *cannot* be helped.

Like the members of the church at Laodicea, all the self-righteous think that they are healthy and wealthy and wise, but they don't know they are "wretched, pitiful, poor, blind and naked" (Rev. 3:17) until they confront him who stands at the door and knocks (v. 20).

Holy Versus Sinful.

Our sense of being sinners must come from a realization of the holiness of God. For the deepest contrast between God and human beings is not that he is eternal and we are temporal or that he is all-powerful and we are but limited. No, the deepest contrast between God and us is between his holiness and our sinfulness. And when we grow up as Christians, our sense of sin and unworthiness does not diminish. Instead, we gain a more profound knowledge of his glory and our own imperfection. That's part of growing up in Christ.

A meaningful, God-pleasing prayer for forgiveness requires that we confess our sin to God and to those against whom we have sinned.

Without knowing God's holiness, we cannot possibly see, either, that it is the *blood of Christ* that must cover our sin, as the catechism says. Only Christ's atoning death enables us to confidently pray for forgiveness. And it is because the writers of the catechism know the holiness of God that they teach us to ask forgiveness for the "sins we do" and for the *sinful ones we are*: we ask forgiveness for "the evil that constantly clings to us."

The Knowledge of Grace.

Our first answer to the question, How must we pray for forgiveness? was, As "poor sinners." Our second answer is that we pray as those who have learned the miracle of God's forgiveness and who are now practicing forgiveness as "evidence" of God's grace.

The saying of the Lord in Isaiah 55:8 is often misunderstood: "My thoughts are not your thoughts, neither are your ways my ways." People usually mention these words when they speak of the mysterious and wholly-other ways of God. He has reasons beyond our understanding for what he does and what he allows: his thoughts are not our thoughts.

But the context of these words actually deals with forgiveness: "Let the wicked forsake his way and the evil man his thoughts. Let him turn to the Lord, and he will have mercy on him, and to our God, for he will freely pardon" (v. 7). This generous and forgiving attitude of God toward rebels is then explained in the following lines: "'For my thoughts are not your thoughts, neither are your ways my ways,' declares the Lord."

The contrast between our thoughts and God's thoughts, between divine ways and human ways, in Isaiah 55 does not hint at mysterious connections between sin and pain. Those who visit the suffering have been inclined to say so ever since the three friends of Job went to call on the sick. But this text in Isaiah speaks of the generosity of the mercies of the Lord. "Your thoughts" in this comparison are like the ideas of the prodigal's older brother, who became furious at forgiveness: "When this son of yours who has squandered your property with prostitutes comes home, you kill the fattened calf for him!" It's unfair!

But God says, Those are *your* thoughts and *your* ways. My thoughts and my ways are "Let's have a feast and celebrate" because "this brother of yours was dead and is alive again; he was lost and is found" (see Luke 15:11-32).

Grace Is Extraordinary.

Forgiveness belongs among the deeds that are typically divine.

Sometimes we have difficulty believing and accepting certain Christian doctrines, such as providence (that God rules in even the minutest details of our present lives) or the resurrection of the body on the last day. But though we frown when we think about activities of God that are far beyond human resources, we readily accept the teaching that God forgives our sins for Jesus' sake. Creation and the final judgment are mind-boggling, we say, but "of course" our sins are forgiven.

Actually, the forgiveness of sins by grace through faith is an astonishingly novel and happy announcement of the New Covenant. It tests our imagination and is beyond our understanding. We should at least wonder at the news that we have been forgiven, if we do not find it hard to believe.

The Lord wants to make sure that we know what we are talking about when we say we have been forgiven. That's why in our prayer for forgiveness we must say something about our own readiness to forgive. A forgiving spirit is the evidence of being forgiven.

The Miser with a Million.

In answer to Simon Peter's question "How many times shall I forgive my brother when he sins against me?" Jesus said, "Seventy-seven times" (Matt. 18:22). This is the evangelical counterpoint to Lamech's ancient song of revenge: "If Cain is avenged seven times, then Lamech seventy-seven times" (Gen. 4:24).

Jesus followed through on this question by telling a pointed parable to show that they who receive grace must be gracious (Matt. 18:23-35). A man who lived at the court, he said, found it very easy, apparently, to borrow money. This man had taken out millions of dollars when, suddenly, the day of reckoning came. He begged his master for mercy, and, to his immense relief, his lord forgave him the huge debt. But when this happy man saw a fellow servant who owed him a hundred dollars, he showed no mercy. He had the fellow put into prison until such time as someone would pay the fellow servant's debt.

When the king discovered the first servant's deed, he became very angry: "Throw him in jail," he cried. For there is no forgiveness for the unforgiving! Those who have received a million forfeit their fortune when they live like misers.

Conditional Forgiveness?

Throughout the gospels we find this teaching about the relatedness of God's forgiveness and our willingness to show his grace. Sometimes it sounds as if our forgiving our debtors is the condition for having our debts forgiven: "If you forgive men when they sin against you, your heavenly Father will also forgive you. But if you do not forgive men their sins, your Father will not forgive your sins" (Matt. 6:14-15).

We should not underestimate or play down this dependence of forgiveness upon forgiving. But it would not be helpful to say that God's forgiveness is conditioned by ours, because forgiveness is by grace and does not arise from any work of ours.

Paul's formulation of the same teaching goes like this: "Forgive whatever grievances you may have against one another. Forgive as the Lord forgave you" (Col. 3:13).

Our forgiving of our debtors is not a legal condition for receiving God's forgiveness. But we do well to remember that we cannot have one without the other.

(Incidentally, the catechism's use of the word *neighbors* in the last line of the answer is not correct. It should be *debtors* or *those who sin against us*. *Neighbors* is also used in the German and Dutch texts. But that does not make it any better.)

Is It Hard to Forgive?

The "debtors" we forgive are people who "owe" us, who don't acknowledge us, who slight us, hurt us, offend us, speak evil of us, steal from us, crucify us (Luke 23:34), or stone us to death (Acts 7:60).

We do not need to tell each other how difficult it is to forgive frequently insensitive people and repeat-offenders. At times it seems that God has put certain people in our environment for the sole purpose of testing our discipleship and loyalty to him. Sometimes we are inclined to say, "Now let her or him come to me first." The question "Who should go to whom first?" is often debated among Christians. But those who are eternally grateful that God came to us "first" will go an extra mile or two.

By saying that we forgive those who have sinned against us, we do not intend to gloss over sin in any form. Love cannot rejoice in evil (1 Cor. 13:6). And those who love the Lord also see clearly the difference between right and wrong. We do not say of wrongful deeds and words, "It's okay," and, "It does not matter." It *does* matter. Through God's Spirit we receive not only the capacity to forgive but also a passion for justice and righteousness.

We have acquired a tender conscience that is informed by the law of love. But we have lost a tender ego that seeks personal satisfaction or vengeance, because we live in the blazing generosity of a forgiving Father. And we seek the glory of his name, not ours.

If it has ever happened to you, as it has to me a few times, that someone actually asked for your forgiveness, you know the embarrassment of that moment. For suddenly you realize that this is not a matter of the guilty party coming to the righteous one. Here are two who need forgiveness. Together you must kneel.

Lord's Day 52

FAITH UNDER FIRE

Q *What does the sixth request mean?*

A **And lead us not into temptation, but deliver us from the evil one** *means, By ourselves we are too weak to hold our own even for a moment. And our sworn enemies—the devil, the world, and our own flesh—never stop attacking us. And so, Lord, uphold us and make us strong with the strength of your Holy Spirit, so that we may not go down to defeat in this spiritual struggle, but may firmly resist our enemies until we finally win the complete victory.*

—Q & A 127

What Do We Ask?

In the sixth petition of the Lord's Prayer, we ask our heavenly Father not to lead us into temptation. That seems to imply that he might do so: God could "lead us into temptation," but we pray to him *not* to do it.

We don't believe, however, that God leads us to *sin.* He never does and never will; to suggest that God makes us sin is itself a sin.

Saying that God leads us into temptation without tempting us seems to be doubletalk to many interpreters. Harry Emerson Fosdick (who had contact with many thousands of people through his nationwide program) said, "No verse in the Bible puzzles more people than the petition on the Lord's Prayer 'Lead us not into temptation.' 'Is it not a shocking idea,' many say, 'that God leads men into temptation and that we must beg him to stop doing it?'"

Temptation.

I do not believe we may alter the reading of the text in order to make the matter more simple, as some interpreters have attempted to do. But we must make some distinctions: in biblical language, it is possible for a human being to tempt God, for God to tempt us, and for Satan to tempt human beings, but these are three different kinds of temptations.

When people tempt or test God, they dare him to show his power; they taunt him to interfere. That's what the Israelites did in the wilderness (Ex. 17:2), it's what we would do if we should willfully sin (1 Cor. 10:9), and it's what Jesus refused to do when Satan suggested that Jesus throw himself from the pinnacle of the temple. Said Satan, God's angels would have to catch you anyway (Matt. 4:5-7).

God Tests People.

People's loyalty to God must be shown in situations in which they face the possibility of disobedience. Adam and Eve faced the possibilities of obeying or of disobeying the original command in the garden (Gen. 2:16-17). Their obedience was tested.

We prefer not to use the word *temptation* for this activity of God. But we do say that God "tests" us to see if we love him above everything else. That's what he did when he ordered Abraham to sacrifice Isaac (Gen. 22:2). And Abraham passed that test. Moses said God tested Israel during the wilderness journey. God led them through the wilderness for forty years "to humble [them] and to test [them] in order to know what was in [their] heart, whether or not [they] would keep his commands" (Deut. 8:2). And Jesus, who taught us to say "Lead us not into temptation," was himself "led by the Spirit into the desert to be tempted by the devil" (Matt. 4:1).

God "tests" or "disciplines" us as a father disciplines his children (Deut. 8:5). And although no discipline and no test (in high school or in life's academy) "seems pleasant at the time," later on it "produces a harvest of righteousness and peace for those who have been trained by it" (Heb. 12:11).

James's Distinctions.

James uses the words *to tempt* and *temptation* half a dozen times in the first chapter of his letter. The word is the same as in the phrase "lead us not into temptation" used in the Lord's Prayer. Our translations, however, use *tests* or *trials* for the temptations that are good for us (v. 2: "consider it pure joy . . . whenever you face trials"; compare v. 12).

Many trials or tests are necessary to train us in God's service. But nobody may say that God is tempting us. "God cannot be tempted by evil, nor does he tempt anyone" (v. 13). Tempting someone in order to make him or her unfaithful is Satan's work. The very thought that God wants us to sin must be rejected.

Why Pray This?

If, then, on the one hand, the various trials and tests of this life are a necessary part of our earthly training and if, on the other hand, God himself places his children (Abraham, the people of Israel, Jesus, and everyone God loves) in a position where Satan may attack them, why should we even ask *not* to be led into temptation?

Because only fools would rush in where even Jesus feared to tread. Sometimes the commander has to send his troops into battle. When he does so, the soldiers know that there is no other way to peace than through this war. But only those who do not know the perils of war desire the battle.

"Lead us not into temptation, Father, because we are weak," we pray. Only the immature trifle with temptations. This prayer, as the catechism rightly says, is prompted by the knowledge of our own weakness and of the opponent's strength. We know that without the Spirit we "go down to defeat in this spiritual struggle."

Jesus Under Fire.

It was Jesus' calling to overcome the evil one by perfect obedience. God led him to face the devil during the temptations in the wilderness. There he resisted the devil's suggestions that he take a shortcut to glory. He persisted in his Father's way, even though it was a road of suffering. And during the last violent battle in Gethsemane, he faced the same temptation again.

He asked if God would, please, take away this cup (of suffering). He asked to be led *out* of temptation. He cried that the battle was fierce and the flesh weak. But in his all-absorbing struggle he still found time to think of his sleepy followers. He warned, "Get up and pray so that you will not fall into temptation" (Luke 22:46). Watch, pray, and avoid temptation, because you are weak, Jesus said to us.

Deliver Us from the Evil One.

The prayer has two parts that belong together: first, *Our Father, let us not enter into the battle,* and, second, *protect us from the power of the evil one.*

Deciding whether the text says deliver us *from the evil one* or *from evil* is impossible. History has eminent defenders of both sides. John Calvin says that arguing this point is useless because the meaning remains the same in either case. Yet, it seems to me, those who use "the evil one" are closer to the thought-world of Jesus and of Matthew. Behind all the evils we face in this life lurks the evil one. And in this petition the disciples of Jesus call on the Father of Jesus, asking that when they meet the *tempter* (cf. Matt. 4:1) in their hour of temptation (cf. Matt. 26:41; Luke 22:31-32), they may be rescued by a power stronger than their own.

Having prayed for the forgiveness of our sins ("Forgive us our debts"), we now ask to be kept from sin ("Deliver us from the evil one").

Christian Vigilance.

The sincerity of our prayers is always evident in our style of living. That holds when we pray for the glory of God's name, the coming of his kingdom, or the doing of his will. To pray for bread without sowing is insincere, and to ask forgiveness without being gracious does not make sense. Neither does it make sense to pray that we be kept from temptations while we flirt with the devil.

Children play with fire—and infants do not fear danger—simply because they don't know enough to be afraid. Mature people know their humanness—that is, their weakness. They "flee" temptations. They never try to see how close they can get to a fire without getting burned. They get away as far as possible.

Flee from Evil.

Members of the Corinthian church tended to be super-spiritual (1 Cor. 4:8), but they deserved warnings: "flee from sexual immorality" (6:18); "flee from idolatry." And the apostle adds, "I speak to sensible people" (10:14-15).

It is utterly sensible to avoid reading pornography and seeing dirty movies, and it is wise to handle alcohol and money with great care, knowing that many have perished by these means. We know that having much leisure time and "having nothing to do" are open invitations for a visit from the tempter.

On the other hand, any healthful and worthy interest helps us to overcome temptation to sin. When people who are always busy tell you, "It keeps me out of mischief," they have a point.

Communal.

We should also remember that we say this prayer as a community. Just as we ask *our* Father for *our* bread, so we ask *our* Father not to lead *us* into temptation. Our behavior must never cause the fall of one of Christ's little ones. Because that would meet with God's terrible wrath (Matt. 18:6).

Christ not only told us, "Pray that you will not fall into temptation" (Luke 22:40). More often we read that he said, "Watch and pray" (Mark 13:33, Luke 21:36; Eph.6:18; etc.). This wakefulness or watchfulness is required of the Christian community. We must be on the alert for present dangers as well as for the Master's sudden return. Only then can we pray with a good conscience, "Lead us not into temptation, but deliver us from the evil one."

Enemies.

The catechism names three forces in our hostile environment that should be branded "our sworn enemies": "the devil, the world, and our own flesh."

The *devil* is our great opponent: he is powerful though not almighty and is equipped with many tricks, wiles, or schemes (Eph. 6:11). He aims to kill us in a sometimes violent, sometimes subtle, but always incessant battle. His main approach is to convince us that there is no God. He also slanders God, or he gives us a wrong picture of God and a deceptive picture of life without God. He is the total liar.

The *world* as our enemy is not the "world" of John 3:16: "For God so loved the world. . . ." We, as well, must love that world. But the "world" is the *saeculum* (from which we get the word *secular*), or the *age* to which we do not belong but which has not yet passed away. It is the whole mass of people, ideas, attitudes, expressions (mirrored in contemporary culture) to which we may not conform (Rom. 12:2).

The devil is an opponent who attempts to murder us. The world is the hostile environment in which we live. And *our own flesh* is the enemy inside. It's what makes a temptation so hazardous.

The word *flesh* makes most people think of bodily sins, especially sexual sins. And these sins certainly belong to what is "of the flesh." But *flesh* does not mean material as opposed to those things that one cannot touch. In the Bible, lacking unity, having a party spirit, and being jealous are also called "carnal" or "fleshly" or "worldly" (1 Cor. 3:1-4). Our flesh is allied with the devil and the world, and it can be overcome only by the Spirit, the Holy Spirit of God, who comes to dwell in us when we believe in Christ (see Gal. 5:16-26). The Spirit is our friend, but our own flesh is a nest for our enemy.

"And so, Lord, uphold us and make us strong with the strength of your Holy Spirit, so that we may not go down to defeat in this spiritual struggle . . . ."

Trained for Battle.

If we pray, "Lead us not into temptation, but deliver us from the evil one," we must have the wisdom to flee temptations, as we have said. We must also know our enemies and their tricks. But we have our best chance of survival if we do what the apostle says: "Put on the full armor of God." Then we will stand and not fall in the evil day (Eph. 6:10-18).

It's good to warn a Christian community against the enemies of the Christian faith, especially the three sworn enemies that are always close: "the devil, the world, and our own flesh." It is necessary to know the enemy. But it is better to train a Christian community in wearing the armor of God. It is better to live close to our Lord and be filled with his Spirit. He will enable us to "firmly resist our enemies until we finally win the complete victory."

Since we are weak, we pray, "Lead us not into temptation." Since we know the designs of our enemies, we avoid their seducing powers, and we live disciplined lives. And if it pleases God to lead us into battle, we will enter the fight as Jesus did—armed with the Word and the Spirit (Matt. 4:1-11).

The Real Test.

Christians tend to have a narrow view of temptation. We do hear the tempter's voice when we get an invitation or an opportunity to steal, to cheat, or to do something else that's indecent. And, no doubt, on these occasions God tests our loyalty. But if we look back once again at the so-called temptations of Jesus, we note that in *his* tests the stakes were higher and the issue was different. During the temptations in the wilderness as well as in the Garden of Gethsemane, the big issue was Jesus' willingness to obey his Father at any cost. Would he or would he not be obedient unto death? Would he do the Father's will at the price of pain and shame and blood?

The real test of the church of Christ in the present age is whether it is willing to pay the high price of obedience.

The temptation to be indecent is more obvious than the temptation to love less than we should.

We live under enormous pressure to be less than fully obedient. More than likely our church and even our own parents have settled for a kind of middle-of-the-road Christianity. Instead of pursuing consistent discipleship and listening afresh to the Scriptures, most Christians fall in line with a tradition in which the voice of God is both echoed and muted. This is a typically "Christian" temptation: even our expressions of godliness become pleasing to the flesh. But it's not so clear that they are pleasing to God.

If we would learn once again to pray the prayer Jesus taught us at a stone's throw from where he writhed in agony under the olive trees, we would more keenly know what it means to obey and what it costs to be obedient.

FROM PRAYER TO PRAISE

Q *What does your conclusion to this prayer mean?*

A **For yours is the kingdom and the power and the glory forever** ***means, We have made all these requests of you because, as our all-powerful king, you not only want to, but are able to give us all that is good; and because your holy name, and not we ourselves, should receive all the praise, forever.***

—Q & A 128

Not in the Text.

The doxology ("For yours is the kingdom . . .") that concludes the Lord's Prayer in some translations of the Bible was not in the original Greek text of Matthew. This is the conclusion of most scholars, including Benjamin B. Warfield and William Hendriksen.

If the church ever has the opportunity (or courage or freedom) to restate the catechism, we should deal differently with the doxology at the end of the Lord's Prayer. As it is, the Heidelberg Catechism regards these lines as an integral part of the prayer. And the catechism places too much emphasis on the word *For.* The catechism deals with the doxology as if it were the *ground* on which we plead, the *reason* why we dare ask.

The doxology as we have it in the King James Version does not appear in Greek texts of the gospel until the sixth century. But the remarkable thing is that some form of a doxological (praise) statement occurs at the end of the Lord's Prayer in translations since the second century. The *Didache* (Teaching of the Apostles), one of the very oldest Christian writings (after the New Testament), includes "for thine is the power and the glory forever" at the close of the Lord's Prayer.

This means that in the liturgies of the Christian church a doxology was usually said at the close of the prayer. And Jewish worship before the Christian era was no different. The words of the doxology as we have learned them in the Lord's Prayer are a shorter version of David's words of praise in 1 Chronicles 29:11:

"Yours, O LORD, is the greatness and the *power*
and the *glory* and the majesty and the splendor. . . .
Yours, O LORD, is the *kingdom;*
you are exalted as head over all."

Doxology.

Although Jesus did not teach these last words as a part of the Lord's Prayer, he may have used these or similar words himself to praise his Father. And, certainly, the church has from the beginning used doxologies to conclude its prayers. (*Doxology* is the name for any liturgical form of praise to God.)

We should continue to use words of praise not only at the conclusion of the "Lord's Prayer" but at the end of all our prayers. All prayers must end in praise.

When we at last have forgotten our petitions because God has satisfied all our needs, we will still sing the doxology.

Praise Creates Unity.

Christians are intimately tied together by common prayers. These prayers may be jointly spoken, or they may be so-called sentence prayers, in which Christians take turns voicing the needs of the group. When they are not together, Christians still meet before God's throne in intercessory prayers. Prayer thus strengthens our unity. But praise unites us even more closely.

In our prayers we still seek the fulfillment of personal needs. In praise we *adore* our common Lord and Savior. Adoration is self-forgetting. Together we go out not to get our share but to meet God. Each contributes his or her share of thanksgiving as one flower in a huge bouquet. In discovering the greatness and goodness of God, we forget our needs, and we find our unity.

Praise Excels over Prayer.

What we seek in our prayers, ultimately, is not merely the gift but the Giver. Yes, of course, we depend on God to give us every little thing. Therefore most of the time we appear before him as begging children. Yet prayer must be more than asking for things; it is also seeking communion. At the end of our quest we do not expect the answer to all of our questions. We expect that we shall find *him*, God himself.

At the end of our praying—or at the end of our earthly life—we will not be able to say that we got all we asked for, but we will come to *God* and desire no more.

A wife who does not love her husband will constantly ask him for things. A husband who does not love his wife will use her to get what he wants. But a couple of lovers want each other.

Unbelievers can understand our need to ask. But the doxology we cannot explain to cynics—only to those who love the Lord.

Ascribe to Him Glory.

The doxology that traditionally goes with the Lord's Prayer says, "Yours is the kingdom and the power and the glory forever." In this sentence, *kingdom* equals kingship or dominion, as it does very often in the Bible. We acknowledge that our Father, to whom we have addressed this prayer, rules over everything and everybody. We also express our faith that he can and will establish his new world and powerfully guard us as his children.

The Lord's Prayer is only a *model* for our prayer life and for the prayer life of the whole church, as we have stated repeatedly. That holds for its six petitions and for its doxology. We must exalt our God, we must ascribe glory to him, but the Lord did not give us a formula to repeat forever. We must give shape to our adoration personally and corporately.

Expressions of Praise.

Under the influence, especially, of the late-twentieth-century charismatic movement, nearly all churches have become more free in voicing praise to

God. In some gatherings an unrestrained and uncoordinated *hallel* is still encouraged. But usually Christian communities eventually agree on fitting forms of praise. (Until the rules become too oppressive. Then the next generation finds its own way again; praise always wants liberty).

Praise can be read and said together, but more commonly it is sung.

Congregational singing is most desirable. Music making and singing by gifted individuals and groups can be inspiring. The music of one can lift all.

Professionalism and "performer-ism," however, endanger the holy congregation. God loves beauty, as we know, but in his eyes and ears there is no beauty without authenticity. Whenever praise is genuine, God is pleased. So God tolerates professionals in his church only as long as they use their skills to increase the faith, knowledge, and praise of all.

The Singing Church.

Much of the strength, joy, and health of the church is in her singing, because in our song of praise, we come closest to our reason for existence. Most of us are better when we sing than when we argue. According to a German proverb, evil people have no songs.

Yet Christian singers are also prone to evil. Not only does the church have acid debates about what to sing and not to sing, but also, historically, choirs, choir conductors, organs, and organists constitute battlegrounds. Satan probably attacks the church's musical efforts so much because he knows that our songs are our strength.

As long as self-interest and self-concern rule us, we cannot praise. But selfishness is overcome when we are absorbed in something or somebody that's too big for words. And if singers know God, they let go of sin and self and pettiness and make music for the ears of the Lord God almighty.

***Q** What does that little word "Amen" express?*

***A** **Amen** means, This is sure to be! It is even more sure that God listens to my prayer, than that I really desire what I pray for.*

—Q & A 129

The Meaning.

Amen is a Hebrew word that has been taken over into Greek, Latin, and all modern languages. There's probably no other word as universally used as "that little word 'Amen.'"

The original word indicates something that's *reliable, firm, true,* and *sure*.

Personally I understand the word best from something that people used to say when I was a child: certain people would speak of an "immes cup of coffee." *Immes* is a Yiddish word that comes from *Amen*. And an "immes cup of coffee" was the genuine stuff, the real McCoy!

Unfortunately, in a large part of the church *Amen* is merely a signing-off word in worship and liturgy. Changing such church habits is extremely hard.

Usage: Affirmation.

The Bible shows different ways in which *Amen* may be meaningfully used. One important use of the word is as an *affirmation to a declaration*.

For instance, in Deuteronomy 27 Moses describes how the Levites should read the law and how the people should respond:

"'Cursed is the man who carves an image or casts an idol. . . .' Then all the people shall say, 'Amen!'. . .

"'Cursed is the man who leads the blind astray on the road.' Then all the people shall say 'Amen!'"

And so on. The Word of God is spoken, and the people affirm their assent and obedience by their "Amen."

The Israelites give the same kind of response to Ezra's reading of the law: "and all the people lifted their hands and responded, 'Amen! Amen!'" (Neh. 8:6).

"Amen" is not only the people's believing and obedient answer to the law. It's also and especially their *believing and affirming response to prayers and praise.*

In 1 Corinthians 14 the apostle Paul emphasizes the importance of the "Amen" when he writes that enthusiasm in worship is not enough. The mind, he says, should also be in gear when one prays. The other worshipers should understand what's being said. For "how can one who finds himself among those who do not understand say 'Amen' to your thanksgiving?" (v. 16).

The most impressive worship scene recorded in the Bible, chapters 4 and 5 of the Apocalypse, concludes with creation's "Amen" and with adoration by the church: "the four living creatures said 'Amen,' and the elders fell down and worshiped" (Rev. 5:14).

God Says "Amen."

When Jesus made a solemn statement, he would often introduce it with "Amen, Amen," translated as "Verily, verily" or (in the NIV) "I tell you the truth . . ." (see John 3:3, 5; etc.).

In such sentences *Amen* serves almost as an oath to assure the listener and affirm the truth.

All God's promises are utterly reliable, and in Jesus Christ he has "said yes" to us in a way that may not be doubted. In 2 Cor. 1:20 we have a beautiful interplay of God's affirmation and his people's affirmation of faith: "No matter how many promises God has made, they are 'Yes' in Christ. And so through him the 'Amen' is spoken by us to the glory of God."

Jesus himself is called "the Amen" in Revelation 3:14. Because he is the truth, he is reliable; he is "the faithful and true witness, the ruler of God's creation."

Affirming Praise.

And, finally, *Amen* is used very frequently as the climax and closing of a statement of praise (Rom. 11:36; Gal. 1:5, and others) or at the close of a benediction (Rom. 15:33, 16:27, etc.).

This usage comes closest to the somewhat stereotyped way in which we use *Amen.* Frequently these doxological sayings end with ". . . for ever and ever. Amen" (Heb. 13:21; 1 Pet. 4:11, 5:11; 2 Pet. 3:18; Jude 25; Rev. 1:6, 7:12).

A Faith Response.

The catechism rightly considers *Amen* an expression of faith in the reliability of the God who promises. Closing with "that little word 'Amen,'" says the catechism, means that we don't send our prayers off with a "maybe" or a "let's hope so." But we say them with a certainty that exceeds our desires.

Yes, we must pray in faith, or we insult the God whose promises are made "Yes" in Jesus.

Who Says "Amen"?

In the Bible and in early church history, believers said "Amen" to the proclamation of God's revealed will and to prayers offered by members of the congregation. It makes no sense for a minister to say "Amen" to his own sermon. Neither is it fitting that the one who leads in prayer is the only one who says "Amen."

It is hard, though, to have both order and enthusiasm in worship. In some churches this "saying Amen" became confused and confusing—like a chorus of religious cheers. In other churches the congregation became muzzled; they forgot how to say "Amen" "to the glory of God" (2 Cor. 1:20).

As an expression of its faith in the certainties of God, the congregation should say "Amen" to the proclamation of the Word.

If the minister or whoever leads in prayer closes by saying "Amen," he or she ought to be joined by the congregation. Each member of the congregation should make the prayer and praise his or her own. We do that with a personal "Amen" expressing our confidence in Christ. This should be (or become) our custom at home, in church gatherings, or wherever we pray in groups.

When they express our trust in him who spoke his reliable word in Jesus Christ, our "Amens" will edify people and please God.